Economic Growth and Developme

Also by Matthew McCartney

Pakistan: The Political Economy of Growth, Stagnation and the State, 1951–2008
Political Economy, Growth and Liberalisation in India, 1991–2008
India: The Political Economy of Growth, Stagnation and the State, 1951–2007

Economic Growth and Development

A Comparative Introduction

Matthew McCartney

macmillan education   palgrave

First published 2015 by
PALGRAVE

Palgrave in the UK is an imprint of Macmillan Publishers Limited, registered in England, company number 785998, of 4 Crinan Street, London N1 9XW

Palgrave Macmillan in the US is a division of St Martin's Press LLC, 175 Fifth Avenue, New York, NY 10010.

Palgrave is the global imprint of the above companies and is represented throughout the world.

Palgrave® and Macmillan® are registered trademarks in the United States, the United Kingdom, Europe and other countries

ISBN 978-1-137-29029-8   ISBN 978-1-137-29031-1 (eBook)

DOI 10.1007/978-1-137-29031-1

A catalogue record for this book is available from the British Library.

A catalog record for this book is available from the Library of Congress.

Typeset by Cambrian Typesetters, Camberley, Surrey, England, UK

To Imdad and his refreshing lemonade

Contents

List of Illustrative Material

Tables

Figures

Boxes

List of Abbreviations

ANC	African National Congress
BMI	Body mass index
CMH	Commission on Macroeconomics and Health
EFA	Education for All
EIU	Economist Intelligence Unit
ELF	Ethnolinguistic fractionalization
FDI	Foreign direct investment
GDI	Gender-related development index
GDP	Gross domestic product
GEM	Gender empowerment measure
GNP	Gross national product
HDI	Human Development Index
HDR	Human Development Report
HIPC	Highly indebted poor country
HYV	High-yield variety
ILO	International Labour Organization
IMR	Infant mortality rate
IPR	Intellectual property rights
ITT	International technology transfer
LDC	Less developed country
LIC	Low-income country
LMC	Lower-middle-income country
MDGs	Millennium Development Goals
MFA	Multi-Fibre Agreement
MNC	Multinational corporation
NGO	Non-governmental organization
OECD	Organisation for Economic Co-operation and Development
OOP	Out of pocket payment
PPP	Purchasing Power Parity
R&D	Research and development
RBM	Roll Back Malaria
RTA	Regional Trade Agreements
SEZ	Special Economic Zone
TFP	Total factor productivity
TFR	Total fertility rate
TRIPs	Trade-Related Intellectual Property Rights
TVE	Township and Village Enterprise
UMC	Upper-middle-income country

UN	United Nations
UNDP	United Nations Development Programme
UPE	Universal primary education
WHO	World Health Organization
WTO	World Trade Organization

Acknowledgements

A big thanks for those long years at SOAS teaching Comparative Economic Growth and to all my wonderful teaching assistants (Giovanni *et al.*). It was there the ideas and organization of this book were slowly developed. Likewise a big thanks to Oxford where Africa, Asia and history provided a stimulating break from an otherwise exclusive India focus. To the usual crowd, especially Daryl who enjoyed parts of the start of the Introduction; Marko who corrected one equation; Bhargavi who was distracted by absent African data but nodded knowingly and Ashwin whose epic feedback notes are eagerly awaited. To Imdad and Azam who refreshed long hot South Asian evenings with glasses of lemonade. To Mueen and the Malangs, about whom I am yet to hear an Oxford anecdote involving learning, libraries or lectures. To the Changals for the bookshop-free tours of Bangalore. And of course to Ranjana without whose love and support this book probably would still have been written but more grumpily and more slowly without the sausage-mash and reviving chai fuel. Thanks to Steven Kennedy at Palgrave for his editing and endless patience, to one anonymous reviewer in particular for fantastic comments and support, and to Keith Povey and Nancy Richardson for some terrific editing.

MATTHEW MCCARTNEY

The author and publishers would like to thank the following who have kindly given permission for the use of copyright material: OECD Publishing for Tables 1.3 and 13.1, reproduced from A. Maddison (2006) *The World Economy: Volume 1: A Millennial Perspective* and *Volume 2: Historical Statistics*, Development Centre Studies, http://dx.doi.org/10.1787/9789264022621-en; Oxford University Press for Tables 2.5 and 2.6, reproduced from N. Crafts (1999) 'Economic Growth in the Twentieth Century', in the *Oxford Review of Economic Policy*, vol. 15, issue 4, pp. 25 and 26 respectively; and the American Economic Association for Table 2.7.

Introduction

On my first visit to India as an economics undergraduate in the 1990s, I had £900 to last for three months – a budget of £10 a day. I travelled in unreserved second-class trains which involved an often brutal scramble merely to board the train; actually finding a seat was at best an occasional and unexpected pleasure. I stayed in some fairly seedy hotels, some of which cost not much more than the price of a newspaper at home. But I always treated myself to a good dinner, and in small towns this was often at the best restaurant in town. My fellow diners were the prosperous families of the town with often a driver sleeping in the car waiting for them to finish. If the restaurant was a bit quiet I would often chat with the waiter. Where was I from? What job did my father do? Why was I not married? A common lament I often heard was that the waiter had graduated from university, sometimes having an MBA degree and so was working in a restaurant until finding a job in a 'respectable profession'. It was odd. Why was a poor student able to eat in a good restaurant among the prosperous and be served his food and drink by a waiter with much better academic credentials?

The central fact in our economic world: global inequality

That this incongruous situation could easily still occur in the 2010s reflects the central fact of global economic life: the massive inequalities prevailing in the world economy. In 2012, according to World Bank figures, Norway had an average income per person ($66,657) that was 436 times greater than Burundi ($153), or average incomes in Burundi were only 0.23 per cent of those in Norway. I certainly didn't work harder than Indian waiters, I hadn't been more innovative, I hadn't saved for longer. I was eating in a good restaurant and he was serving a poor student because he had been born in India and I in England. In the mid-1990s the £900 I had saved for the trip was equivalent to four or five times the average annual income of an Indian person.

To put this massive disparity – which only rarely finds its way into the media – into perspective, the much-reported global financial crisis saw average incomes in Britain *drop* by 2 per cent in 2008, the worst year. Greece saw incomes fall from US$28,640 in 2008 to US$25,460 in 2012, a drop of around 10 per cent. Income levels in the other European countries that generated the most doom-laden discussion – Ireland, Italy and Portugal – are now more or less back to where they were in 2008.

Similarly European news reporting has been full of dramatic talk of a crisis in education, social services and health care. Per capita expenditure on health

1

has fallen in many European countries: according to World Bank data from US$3,760 in 2008 to US$3,609 in 2011 in the UK, US$3,314 to US$2,864 in Greece and US$5,241 to US$4,542 in Ireland (World Development Indicators, 2014). Wider comparative perspectives are lost amid the heated debate and discussion. If there is a crisis it is only in relation to the recent history of developed countries and the expectation that incomes and social spending would rise rapidly, year after year.

Stepping back from a narrow domestic debate confined to the wealthiest countries in the world and thinking in global and comparative terms can help put this 'crisis' into perspective. In China, for example, spending per person on health between 2008 and 2012 increased from $157 to $278, in India from $43 to $59, and in the South Sudan declined slightly, from $34 to $32.

It is not just in spending but also in terms of access that there are glaring global inequalities in health provision. The UK National Health Service may be squeezed but it remains free at the point of use. In India recent estimates show that more than 30 million people drop into absolute poverty every year (not earning enough income to eat enough to properly exist as a human being) as a result of having to divert household income to emergency health care. In Ethiopia 30 per cent of children under five are malnourished and in Sweden virtually 0 per cent. Healthy nourishment in children is associated with better school performance, being healthier later in life and earning higher lifetime incomes.

In Somalia only 7 per cent of the population have access to improved water supplies and in Austria virtually 100 per cent. Poor water quality is linked to the deaths of three million children per year. In Niger only 50 per cent of the relevant age group complete primary school and in Hungary nearly 100 per cent. Primary education is associated with better health care, more employment and higher incomes later in life.

The world's media may headline growth rates but it is often forgotten just how large are global inequalities and how long they will take to close. Were Burundi to experience 10 per cent annual GDP (gross domestic product) growth for the next decade (an economic boom equivalent to the best ever recorded in any country) its per capita incomes would rise to about $400 and its living standards to 0.60 per cent of those in contemporary Norway. Or alternatively, per capita growth of only 1 per cent in Norway would raise incomes there by $666 per person, more than four times the 2012 level of GDP in Burundi. This crude calculation shows that even if health expenditure in India continues to increase by $5 per person per year, it will take over 700 years to reach current UK levels and over 1,700 years to reach current US levels.

The vast inequalities in global incomes generate a massive discrepancy in the availability of resources. A small proportion of the world's population, whether in their own countries they count as rich or poor, students or employed, young or old, will be able to consume, travel and get better health care than the vast majority of the world's population, regardless of how rich-country governments prioritize their budgets or how long the current global financial crisis lasts. That is the central fact of our economic world and it will remain so for a very long time.

Two questions arise from these comparisons. When did this global inequality originate, and how have a relatively small number of countries managed to achieve such high levels of income and welfare?

Chapter 7 of this book shows that it was only quite recently that significant gaps in income levels between countries began to emerge. Depending on which historian one reads or what evidence one uses, in ca.1800, ca. 1600 or ca.1500 average incomes in the richest and poorest countries in the world were quite similar. Chapter 1 shows that disparities between many other measures of well-being, such as life expectancy, were also much smaller in these years than today. In his 2012 BBC Reith Lectures, Niall Ferguson asked:

> Why, after around 1500, did Western civilization – as found in the quarrelsome petty states of Western Eurasia and their colonies of settlement in the New World – fare so much better than other civilizations? From the 1500s until the late 1970s, there was an astonishing divergence in global living standards, as Westerners became far richer than, well, Resterners. (Ferguson 2012:21)

What distinguishes those earlier years (some time between ca.1500 and ca.1800) when average incomes were quite similar from the contemporary world marked by massive inequality is economic growth. Lots of economic growth. Economic growth over many decades in some parts of the world, and intermittent bursts of economic growth dragged down by long decades of stagnation and economic decline in other parts. Economic growth is discussed in more detail in Chapter 2, but for the purposes of this Introduction a couple of quick clarifications may be useful at this stage. First, economic growth can be defined as the increase in the amount of goods and services produced in an economy over a period of time, usually one year. Second, economic growth is usually expressed in 'real terms' to account for population growth. So if an economy has expanded by 5 per cent and population by 2 per cent over the course of one year, real growth, or income per capita (they mean the same) has gone up by 3 per cent. The maths is straightforward: economic growth (5 per cent) minus population (2 per cent) equals increase in real average incomes (3 per cent).

The first countries to surge ahead in this Great Divergence were mainly located in Western and Central Europe, North America, and Australasia. In the last 150 years they have been joined by a small number of catch-up countries, including Japan after the 1870s and especially after the 1950s, and South Korea, Hong Kong, Singapore and Taiwan after the 1960s. Though they remain further behind, many would add Malaysia and Thailand after the 1970s. China and Vietnam have enjoyed rapid economic growth since the 1980s but remain so far behind that it will be many decades before incomes and well-being have caught up with the global leaders.

The big problem is that so many countries have consciously tried and failed to catch up, often making a successful beginning, experiencing rapid economic growth for a decade or more but then falling back into slow growth or stagnation without making any substantial impact on the enormous gap in incomes. We may associate Sub-Saharan Africa with relative economic failure in the decades since independence, but between 1967 and 1980 ten countries experienced annual economic growth of more than 6 per cent, including Gabon, Botswana, Congo, Nigeria, Kenya and Côte d'Ivoire. Much of Africa then lurched into two decades of economic stagnation after the 1980s. Pakistan is not associated with economic success but was one of the fastest growing economies in the world in the 1960s. Argentina has spent much of the twentieth century as a developing country plagued by stagnation, hyperinflation and political violence but in ca.1900 its GDP per capita was double that of Italy and probably slightly higher than Germany's.

The five key concerns of this book

The importance of sustained economic growth

There are important debates about the impact of inequality and what, if anything, should be done about it. The 2009 book by Richard Wilkinson and Kate Pickett, *The Spirit Level: Why Equality is Better for Everyone*, contributed to a very lively debate about the negative social and economic consequences of inequality within countries. Debates about the morality and efficacy of foreign aid, particularly the rather passionate disagreements between economists William Easterly and Jeffrey Sachs, have focused attention on global efforts to reduce inequality between countries. This book is concerned with the origins rather than the impact of inequality and so its first concern is with the 'Great Divergence': those long years after 1500 or 1800 when steady economic growth of no more than 2 or 3 per cent per year in Western Europe created those massive inequalities we see today. As the example of Norway and Burundi showed it is not a decade of rapid growth that makes the big difference; it is, rather, long years of sustained economic growth.

Sustained economic growth has a remarkable impact on average incomes. An economy that began with an average income of $100 per person would have seen average incomes rise to $1,200 after 250 years of annual growth of 1.0 per cent, $4,100 with annual growth of 1.5 per cent and $14,100 with annual growth of 2.0 per cent. With growth of 2.5 per cent that economy would have become one of the richest in the world with average incomes of almost $50,000 per person.

The emphasis on sustained economic growth reminds us not to pay too much attention to growth rates in a single year or differences in growth rates over several years or indeed to the recent global slowdown. What is more important is that growth rates over the last two centuries in India and China have been slower than in Western Europe, not that they have slowed to 5 per cent in India in the last couple of years or been maintained at 7 per cent+ in China.

A combination of economic theory and history

Economists are generally good at measuring and comparing the impact of various policies, such as considering the relative impacts of education and infrastructure on economic growth, and hence which a growth-enthusiast policy-maker should prioritize for reform. Historians have had more success in uncovering those long-run forces that lead to higher education or more infrastructure. For example, several hundred years ago, various, then developing, countries were dominated by large landowners. Landowners like cheap and pliable labour that can work on their land for low wages and long hours, and dislike the education that may enable their labourers to leave them for employment in a distant town. Landowners are generally not very keen on democracy, when one landlord would be at great risk of losing political power in an election against more numerous of his labourers. There is some historical-statistical evidence to support the argument that patterns of land ownership, even centuries ago, can help explain contemporary progress in education and democracy and so, in turn, economic growth (Sokoloff and Engerman, 2000).

This book attempts to integrate the economic and historical approaches into a framework for thinking about growth, or in the terminology of economists, an economic model. Economic modelling in pages of the leading economic journals such as the *American Economic Review* or the *Quarterly Journal of Economics* is typically dense with mathematics, economic theory and statistics and so is inaccessible to all but graduate economists. This book does engage with such scholarship but attempts to make the effort readable and accessible. Economists and historians may never end up best friends, but they have a lot to learn from each other's efforts to understand growth.

The distinction between 'proximate determinants' and 'deeper determinants' of growth

The proximate determinants of economic growth are the efforts households, firms or governments make to create new factors of production (land, labour and capital) or to combine existing factors of production in more efficient/productive ways to produce more output. These two processes are influenced by the deeper determinants of economic growth: culture, openness, geography, institutions and colonialism.

The basic model used in this book first relates growth to factors of production and efficiency which are the proximate determinants of growth. The factors of production are labour, capital and land (some economists also include natural resources or energy). These are combined in various ways by households and public or private sector enterprises to produce output.

Subsistence agriculture in developing countries, for example, may utilize a lot of (family) labour on a small plot of land with only simple farming equipment (little capital) to produce food for their own consumption. Large-scale commercial agriculture in developed countries may use little labour, lots of land and large amounts of capital (such as fertiliser and tractors) to produce crops for export. A given stock of factors of production can produce more output if they are used more efficiently or if technical change permits more output to be produced. A given quantity of land may produce more output (a higher yield) by using modern fertilisers. A given stock of labour may become more productive if people are better educated. A computer today produces more output than one eighteen months old. Total output (called gross domestic product or GDP) is equal to the total stock of land, labour and capital being used in production and a measure of the efficiency with which those factors of production are utilized. The measure of efficiency is called total factor productivity (TFP) and captures the combined impact on total output of changes in efficiency of all the factors. A measure of efficiency such as labour productivity only measures the efficiency of a single factor of production so is only a partial measure of productivity. Therefore:

> GDP level = total labour supply + amount of land + total capital stock + level of TFP
>
> GDP growth is then equal to the change in these components
>
> GDP growth = growth of labour supply + growth of land + growth of capital (investment) + change in TFP

The accumulation of land can and has been important. The opening of the trans-continental railroad in the 1860s and subsequent settlement of North America opened enormous new tracts of agricultural land. Cutting down the rainforest in Brazil has increased the supply of farmland in more recent decades. Over long periods of time land tends to make only a marginal contribution to economic growth. Growth rather comes from raising the yield of existing agricultural land through new seed types or fertiliser or converting land to more productive manufacturing industry. For this reason land will not be considered in great detail in this book.

Many economists stop here and derive some rather straightforward policy conclusions: that more growth requires some combination of more labour, more land, more investment and more efficiency. They also explain the higher growth rates in East Asia relative to Sub-Saharan Africa over the last fifty years by much higher investment rates (creating capacity to export and infrastructure to make those exports competitive) and by higher TFP (more technological change and a better educated workforce). Policy, they suggest, should focus on efforts to raise levels of investment, to motivate foreign firms to use Sub-Saharan Africa as an export base, or to improve education. Such 'analysis' risks becoming rather banal, based around mantras such as 'investment is good for growth, therefore we need more investment'. If growth is a good thing, all

Figure I.1 *The deeper and proximate determinants of growth*

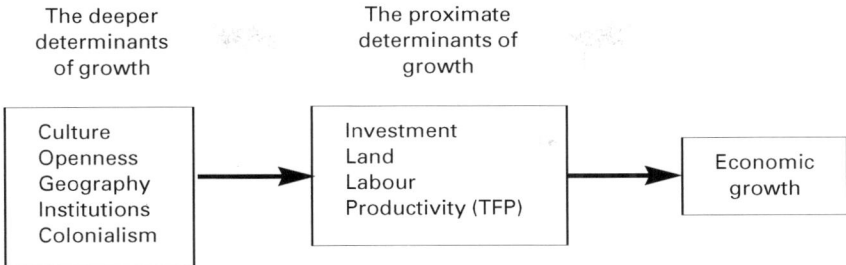

The deeper determinants of growth → The proximate determinants of growth

The deeper determinants of growth	The proximate determinants of growth	Economic growth
Culture Openness Geography Institutions Colonialism	Investment Land Labour Productivity (TFP)	Economic growth

governments seem to want more of it, and its causes are so evident, why does any country experience extended spells of slow economic growth? Remember how few countries have either originally or subsequently participated in the Great Divergence. We need to take a step back to a deeper level of analysis and explain what factors cause or influence the accumulation of factors of production or TFP. Figure I.1 illustrates the extended model used by this book.

The deeper determinants of economic growth – culture, openness, geography, institutions and colonialism – impact on economic growth indirectly through the proximate determinants. Culture, for example, can impact economic growth through its influence on whether countries are receptive to productivity-enhancing ideas and innovations. Openness can influence economic growth through its impact on the supply of labour (immigration or migration) or the supply of Foreign Direct Investment (FDI).

The importance of combining the proximate and deeper determinants of growth can be seen by reviewing two very influential studies: one by Robert Barro (an economist) seeking to understand the proximate determinants of growth, and another by William Darity (a historian) seeking to understand the deeper determinants of growth. The following discussion of these two approaches sets the scene for this book, which attempts to combine their advantages.

Robert Barro and the proximate determinants of growth
The aim of Robert Barro's 1991 paper, 'Economic Growth in a Cross-Section of Countries', was straightforward – to measure what factors promoted economic growth and so influence policy-making by comparing the relative influence of those factors. Barro's 'proximate determinants' method used cross-country growth regressions, paying due attention to issues of endogeneity, robustness and significance. Although these rather forbidding concepts have deterred non-economists from reading the paper, they *can* be explained in more accessible language.

Barro gathered data on growth rates and those factors considered by economic theory to be related to economic growth, such as education, investment, government spending and political stability. Barro used data from 98 different countries for the years 1960 to 1985 to run a cross-country growth regression. A growth regression can be thought of as a sequence of questions, about what factors influence growth. Barro asked: How strong and reliable is the influence of education on economic growth holding all other factors constant? The question was repeated for investment, then government spending and so on. Barro found that poorer countries (measured by average incomes in 1960) tended to grow faster than richer countries. This suggested that over time there would be a process of convergence (or narrowing of gaps) in the average standard of living between countries. This finding was surprising, given the facts of the Great Divergence which show that exactly the opposite has happened over a much longer period than covered by Barro's data. Barro found that investment (private, not government) had a strong positive impact on growth. Government consumption as a share of national income had a negative impact. These two findings supported one of the big economic ideas of the 1980s and 1990s: the relative role of the state, whether through government investment or more interventions, should be reduced (and that of the private sector increased). Barro's statistical results were weaker for Latin America and Sub-Saharan Africa, indicating that important aspects of the growth process in both regions remain unexplained. Case studies, such as those in this book, provide a more focused approach that tries to find out why the growth process may differ between regions or countries.

This type of statistical analysis has allowed researchers to compare the relative influence of all these various drivers of economic growth. A common finding in the many studies over the years since Barro's pioneering effort is that girls' education has a much stronger and more reliable impact on growth than does trade policy (such as reducing taxes on imported goods). This provides strong evidence in support of policy-makers spending less time taking part in international trade negotiations and more time trying to improve the education of girls. We can only speculate then why ministers have spent so much time in recent years travelling to World Trade Organization trade conferences in Bali (Indonesia), Geneva (Switzerland), Cancun (Mexico), and Hong Kong and not to the dusty and distant villages of their home countries to open schools for poor, rural girls.

Although research inspired by Barro identified more than ninety determinants of economic growth over the following decade, this research effort feels stale and confusing, and the inherent problems of the method are becoming increasingly evident now that twenty years have passed. These problems are discussed in more detail in Chapter 2 but a few are introduced here.

There is generally a significant problem in interpreting causation in such studies. Whilst education and growth are clearly related, does education cause economic growth by making workers more productive and better able to utilize new technologies or does economic growth cause education to expand by providing the government with tax revenue and parents with income to pay for education and by creating well-paid jobs that motivate people to acquire more education? Researchers have also questioned the value of the statistical results produced by Barro and others as guides for policy-makers. The original idea that policy-makers could compare the strength and reliability of the link between various policy factors and economic growth, was overly simplistic. For example, the finding that girls' education offers a high return offers no guidance as to how policy-makers can actually improve primary education. Should policy emphasize private or public education? Comprehensive or selective education? A centralized or community-based education system? Education in philosophy or engineering? How should teachers be trained or incentivized? Should schools receive fixed grants from the government or should pupils be given vouchers to spend in the school of their choice? A final question arising from such statistical work is: why, then, do so many countries suffer from extended spells of stagnation? Rather than suffer years of declining per capita GDP after the early 1980s countries in Sub-Saharan Africa should have conducted some statistical tests then promoted those policies offering the biggest impact on growth. There are more than fifty countries in Sub-Saharan Africa. We would have expected a few to measure and implement growth-promoting policies, and others to learn from and follow those pioneers.

William Darity and the deeper determinants of growth
The second approach to studying economic growth is the 'deeper determinants' method, which has mostly, though not entirely, exchanged the maths and statistics for detailed historical case studies, drawing on lessons and ideas from various academic disciplines. On my bookshelves I can see examples from nutrition, biology, sociology, geography, ecology, climatology and theology. One very influential example is Jared Diamond's (1998) *Guns, Germs and Steel: A Short History of Everybody for the last 13,000 Years*. So diverse were the ideas that Diamond drew upon to explain historical growth and contemporary inequality that one reviewer suspected the author's name of actually being 'the pseudonym for a committee of experts'.

In his 1992 article 'A Model of "Original Sin": Rise of the West and Lag of the Rest', William Darity discusses how enslaving Africans in the seventeenth and eighteenth centuries for transportation to the Americas had a negative long-term impact on growth (and development) in Africa and a long-term positive impact in the now developed world. Drivers of economic growth in Europe resulting from the slave trade included, according to Darity, the growth of ports in Liverpool, Nantes and Bordeaux; the acquisition of private fortunes that stimulated consumer demand; the growth of the textile industry to produce the goods necessary to exchange for slaves in Africa; shipbuilding in Bristol; firearms in Birmingham; and the raw sugarcane produced by slaves in the West Indies and processed into sugar by industry in England. Slavery, he argued, initiated a commercial and industrial dynamic that stimulated long-term economic growth in Europe. In Sub-Saharan Africa the most lucrative activity in the eighteenth century was 'for those with the power to enslave ... to procure human exports for the slave trade'. Profits were made in conquest and destruction, not in expanding production, acquiring new technologies or improving skills and education. This difference, argues Darity, began the process of 'uneven development' and was 'the "original sin" that began the partition between the rich and poor regions' (Darity, 1992:166).

An approach focused on these deep determinants of growth avoids some of the problems associated with the Barro approach. The method can help explain differences in long-term growth rates. The long-term effect of the slave trade, according to Darity, was to destroy emerging state structures; to create incentives for conquest and violence rather than production and growth; and to undermine notions of private property and the development of a formal legal system. These factors militated ever after against the ability of governments to pick and implement good policies. For example, the modern state structures emerging in various parts of the world during the eighteenth century were destroyed in Sub-Saharan Africa by the slave trade, and so after independence post-colonial governments there inherited none of the institutions of modern states so were unable to raise tax revenues to invest in primary education and infrastructure. The lack of good policy-making in Africa, according to Darity, was not a matter of incompetent or corrupt rulers; rather, it was a product of those deep historical determinants of growth.

The deeper determinants approach also has problems. Barro estimated the exact impact of the various proximate determinants of growth, finding for example that educational enrolment in 1960 had a stronger (and positive) impact on income growth after 1960 than any other proximate determinant. By contrast, Darity, focusing on a single historical case study, does not engage with comparative questions. Much of Central and Eastern Europe was subject to a slave trade organized by the Ottoman Empire until the nineteenth century, but such countries are today developed. Why the difference? Inhabitants of Britain were subject to slavery by the Romans until the fifth century and by the Vikings and Normans over the subsequent centuries but escaped the 'original sin' lock-in effect to later industrialize. Darity suggests such a lock-in effect has lasted several centuries for Africa, but how long will it last? Why was 500 years enough time to escape in Britain but 200 years not enough in Sub-Saharan Africa? Why hasn't the expansion of global trade in goods and services over recent decades strengthened the incentives in Sub-Saharan Africa to overcome those anti-production incentives left over from the slave trade? What explains the very different economic and social outcomes among ex-slave countries such as the rapid economic growth and flourishing democracy of Ghana and the failing dictatorship of Chad? How were Europeans able to enslave Africans? How did Europeans acquire the shipping technology, the guns and the political organization necessary to be the slavers? Darity has only pushed the question further back in time; the original sin cannot be the slave trade. The original sin was whatever created the power and willingness of one society to enslave another. Big-picture explanations offer plausible analytical narratives but lack the rigorous statistical method quantifying the impact of alternative explanations. Other big explanations offered by scholars for the Great Divergence include Christopher Wolmar's focus on the spread of railway transport; Jared Diamond's emphasis on geographical differences in

11,000BC; Max Weber's focus on the Protestant religion in Europe after ca.1520; Daren Acemoglu's and others stress on proximity to the Atlantic trade system; and Douglass North's focus on the protection of property rights.

This book begins with a comparative examination of the proximate determinants of economic growth (labour, capital and productivity), using the work of mainly economic theorists to compare and contrast their impact. I then take a step back to examine the deeper determinants of economic growth, critically examining the strengths and weaknesses of each determinant separately and eschewing a single favourite story in favour of a comparative perspective. We should recognize that good economic policy is not just about spotting a problem and proposing a remedy (the naive analysis of many economists) but also in examining the deep constraints on the choice and effectiveness of policy tools.

A comparative and historical focus

We can learn a lot about the contemporary world through a comparative and historical perspective. An example is the concern voiced by the media and politicians in much of the developed world in recent years about the rise of China and India. China and India both experienced a sudden sustained acceleration in economic growth from 1980 onwards and in view of their large physical size and populations many argue that the twenty-first century will be the 'Asian Century'. Commentators worry that Chinese and Indian firms are becoming a competitive threat to developed-country firms' exports by absorbing technology from developed countries and combining it with much cheaper labour. A comparative (and historical) perspective can place this debate in a more realistic context and raise an important question that is usually forgotten when the media or politicians focus only on recent economic change, as the following three examples illustrate.

First, China and India are returning to (though are still a long way from) the central place in the world economy that they held in the centuries leading up to the Great Divergence. The fall of Asia (not the rise) was the real historical aberration. In 1820 India and China accounted for around 50 per cent of world GDP and Western Europe 25 per cent. In 1973 the share of India and China had shrunk to less than 8 per cent and Western Europe's had surged to 51 per cent. By 2003 India and China were approaching again their historical norm with a share of 23 per cent and Western Europe had slowly declined to 40 per cent.

Second, the impact of China and India on the developed world in terms of changing patterns of trade, investment or economic growth is little different from the earlier impact associated with the rapid economic growth of Japan after the 1950s. Between 1987 and 2003 GDP growth averaged 7.85 per cent in China (7.86 per cent between 1952 and 1978 in Japan), export growth averaged 14.4 per cent a year (13.2 per cent per annum in Japan) and China increased its share of world GDP from 4.6 to 17 per cent (3 to 7.8 per cent in Japan) (Maddison, 2007:380–1).

Third, in the late 1950s there was deep unease in the developed world. Two of its leading military powers (Britain and France) had just been humiliated in a failed military intervention in Egypt, the 'Suez Crisis' (there are evident parallels with contemporary Iraq). The USSR had beaten the US in the race to launch a satellite into orbit and for many this symbolized an industrial and economic threat to the US. When the Soviet leader Nikita Khrushchev then proclaimed to the US 'We will bury you', many feared this could be true (for a parallel situation, see contemporary China, whose leaders are openly contemptuous of the Western democratic model).

Economic growth is not everything

There is economic growth – the main focus of this book – but there is also development, and the two need not coincide. It is true that whether an economy is growing and expanding is the most widely accepted and potent symbol of economic success. Economic growth and its accumulated impact on average income defines whether a country is eligible to join the club for the wealthy, the Organization for Economic Cooperation and Development (OECD), or is side-lined at international meetings and treated as an impoverished supplicant. How we think about the contemporary world is heavily conditioned by economic growth. The lack of economic growth is what most commonly is used to define and measure the 'failure' of Sub-Saharan Africa over the decades since independence. The growth rates of 8 per cent+ define the 'miracle economy' stories of Japan in the 1950s, South Korea in the 1970s, Thailand in the 1980s and China in the 1990s. Growth rates since 2008 have been used to judge the success or failure of countries across Europe in coping with the global financial crisis.

There are a number of well-known problems in using growth in average incomes as a measure of well-being. The benefits of economic growth may be monopolized by a small fraction of the population. Despite steady, if not spectacular growth in average incomes in the US between 1973 and 2010, the average incomes of the bottom 99 per cent of the population actually fell. All that growth and more went to benefit the top 1 per cent of the population. Income growth again says nothing about what is being produced, whether it is guns or medical treatments. Higher incomes may reflect longer and more intensive working hours, unsustainable exploitation of the environment or the accumulation of debt.

The concept of 'development' must incorporate some consideration or measure of 'better'. Better is ultimately a value judgment, comparing two states and judging that development has occurred if one is better than the other. Many measures of development have been used by scholars, including education, clean water, shelter, political freedoms and nutrition. If economic growth involves the poor experiencing income growth (not always true as the US example showed) and if poor people choose to spend increasing incomes on those measures then we can say that economic growth leads to development. The state may also siphon off resources created by economic growth through taxation and use them to provide free or subsidised developmentally nice things, such as free and compulsory vaccinations or mid-day meals at schools. In reality the relation between growth and development is more complex. First, people do not always spend extra disposable incomes on 'good' things; instead of being used to educate children and improve nutrition higher household income may be spent on alcohol or fast food. If a poor person freely chooses to spend higher income on foods high in saturated fats and develops health problems as a result, are they in poverty or are they exercising a free choice? If our measure of development is, say, nutrition we may judge development has not occurred, and if the measure is freedom to choose we may be more optimistic. Maybe our conclusions change if the decision was influenced by clever advertising or if an adult was choosing a non-nutritious meal on behalf of a child? Other commentators, often from outside the discipline of economics, are suspicious of 'more things is better' thinking. Current industrial-transport systems typical of developed countries are energy- (particularly carbon-) intensive so economic growth increases the emissions of greenhouse gases and contributes to global warming. In the longer term growth will threaten the depletion of non-renewable natural resources such as oil and gas and even renewable resources such as timber. These concerns lead some to call for the goals of growth and totems of 'faster' and 'more' to be replaced by 'sustainable'. Sustainable growth/development has been most influentially defined as 'development that meets the needs of the present generation without compromising the ability of future generations to meet their own needs'.

The two important concepts here are 'needs' – that the needs of the world's poor should have priority – and that sustainability should be considered in relation to 'generations' – that growth and development in this generation should not compromise the ability of future generations to meet their own needs. The definition is broad enough to encompass purely environmental constraints on sustainability and also the more narrowly economic: if the current generation is piling up debt, future generations will be squeezed when they receive the bill. On both counts the high-debt, carbon-intensive economic system prevailing before 2008 would have been found wanting. There is of course an obvious difficulty: in an uncertain world how can we know anything about the needs of future generations?

An example of a debate about growth: the British Industrial Revolution

Every aspect of the model of proximate and deeper determinants is subject to a lively academic debate. We know a lot more about growth than ever before; advances are being made all the time in data collection and data testing. Angus Maddison spent a lifetime constructing estimates of the levels and growth of GDP for much of the world economy running back hundreds of years. Nathan Nunn undertook a detailed and painstaking exercise to estimate the numbers and ascertain the place of origin of slaves from Africa to test whether there had been long-term effects on growth and development into the post-slavery era. Daren Acemoglu and others have collected historical evidence to estimate the health/disease environments of now developing countries in the seventeenth century to answer similar questions. These exercises have opened up new areas for research, posed new questions and broadened the debate. An introduction to one ongoing debate in economic history shows how the growth framework used in this book can help organize the question 'what determines growth?' The British Industrial Revolution was the first instance of modern economic growth, so to some extent all subsequent scholarly discussion of growth draws from its images of industrialization, exploitation, urbanization and demographic change. The great contemporary scholars of the era such as Adam Smith, Thomas Malthus and Karl Marx who placed the eighteenth- and nineteenth-century British economy at the centre of their work have continued to influence thinking about economic growth ever since.

By the mid-nineteenth century, England in particular had been substantially transformed from an rural-agricultural economy to an urban-industrial one. The effort to explain, measure and date this process has become an 'industry' in itself in the scholarship of economic history. The framework used in this book helps frame this discussion and brings clarity to an often confusing scholarly debate. It helps to draw together, for example, the work of Charles Feinstein on investment, Robert Brenner on labour and Douglass North on institutions. There are long-standing debates about important 'causes', the weak statistical base on which much of the discussion hinges and even a problem with conceptualising the meaning of 'industrial revolution'. Is an 'industrial revolution' something that can be defined and measured in terms of economic growth and productivity, or is an 'industrial revolution' something more qualitative, linked to changes in the way people view the world, how they live their daily lives and connected to the role of science versus religion in society, concepts that are much harder if not impossible to measure?

The British Industrial Revolution: proximate determinants

Each of the key proximate determinants of growth has been extensively debated and quantified in terms of its causal influence on the industrialization of Britain at the end of the eighteenth century. This part of the debate shows first, how measuring economic growth, employment, investment and productivity is very difficult, especially using eighteenth-century data, and second, how important aspects of the process of economic growth such as the organization of firms, the quality of the labour force and its working conditions, and the role of innovations and technology are even harder to measure.

Growth
Estimating aggregate growth requires accurate information on the growth of output of different goods and on the total output of each in relation to the whole

economy (what statisticians refer to as an appropriate weight). The big problem with eighteenth-century Britain is the spectacular rise of the cotton textile industry. Between 1770 and 1815 cotton output increased by 2,200 per cent, while output in other sectors at most doubled. This huge increase in output was combined with a very competitive market and so sharp falls in the relative price of cotton. To calculate 'correct' weights we need to account for these huge and simultaneous shifts in output and relative prices. There is no widespread agreement among statisticians on how to do this. There are also significant problems with data as the first occupation census (survey) in Britain did not take place until 1841 and the first census of industrial production not until 1907. There is also little price information for the cotton sector before the 1790s.

Overcoming these big problems to produce estimates of GDP growth for eighteenth-century Britain has become an academic specialization in its own right. From pioneering work in the 1960s through to more recent work there has been a gradual revision downwards of growth estimates as data and techniques have improved (Deane and Cole, 1962; Crafts and Harley, 1992). Early estimates showing GDP growth suddenly accelerating to over 3 per cent per annum after 1780 have been superseded by estimates showing a more gradual acceleration to around 1.3 per cent. John Nef (1934) argues that British industrialization was actually a long process dating back to the sixteenth century. Nef finds good evidence of an enormous expansion, beginning in the mid-sixteenth century, in the output of coal, salt, glass, ships, alum, soap, gunpowder and metal goods. The annual output of a coal mine before the middle of the sixteenth century rarely exceeded a few hundred tonnes; by the century end collieries producing between 10,000 and 25,000 tonnes of coal annually were 'common'.

The idea of 'revolutionary change' has been revived by some scholars who look beyond the cotton textile sector and argue that there was dramatic change in more traditional industries such as food and drink, shoemaking, tailoring and blacksmithing (Berg and Hudson, 1992). The wool textile sector, for example, developed new forms of wholesaling, retailing, credit and debt. They argue that there was no *British* Industrial Revolution but a regional story that has been missed by the use of national aggregate statistics. While the output of the British wool textile sector increased by (only) 150 per cent during the entire eighteenth century this period marked its dramatic concentration in Yorkshire, which accounted for about two-thirds of national output by 1800.

Labour
There is no agreement among scholars on whether there was any significant acceleration of population growth that contributed to economic growth (Wrigley and Schofield, 1981; Pomeranz, 2000). What is more widely agreed upon is that there were dramatic changes in patterns of labour mobility and the composition of the labour force. In 1500 18.5 per cent of the English labour force worked outside agriculture in either rural or urban areas and by 1800 this had increased to 64 per cent (Brenner and Isset, 2002).

Some argue that this 'mobility' was driven by the 'enclosure movement', the forcible eviction of people from the land by landlords to facilitate a shift from cultivating land with crops to sheep grazing (which required fewer workers) to take advantage of expanding international markets for woollen ware. Much of this land had previously been held under common ownership and was taken over by landlords and turned into private property. Others scholars emphasize technological change in the cotton textile industry which drew women and children in from the household and agriculture to make them part of the industrial labour force. The spinning jenny (a key textile technology, discussed later in this chapter), for example, had a horizontal wheel requiring a posture most comfortable for children aged between nine and twelve. By the 1830s about three-quarters of employees in English textile mills were women and children. There is little evidence of any 'quality' change in the labour force during these years; the new entrants were mainly illiterate. As late as 1801 to 1831 primary school enrolment was only 36 per cent, and even by the end of the nineteenth century secondary school enrolment was only 17 per cent (Crafts, 1995:754).

Investment
As part of the older 'revolutionary' school of thought, Charles Feinstein (1978) argued that there was a significant rise in investment in the late eighteenth century. Nick Crafts (1995) has used his new estimates of national income to show that investment increased from under 6 per cent of GDP in the mid-to-late eighteenth century to around 8 per cent by the end of the nineteenth century. Other scholars have argued instead that the level of investment was less important than the fact that changes in technology associated with the early Industrial Revolution in cotton mills, coal mines and iron furnaces were relatively simple and cheap, requiring little investment. Furnaces, buildings, hammers and boilers were not normally installed by outside firms but were built, maintained and altered by the firm's own workers at relatively low cost. Another change was again not about more investment, but the concentration of the existing capital stock in much larger factories (Nef, 1934, Pollard, 1964).

Productivity (TFP)
Early studies of productivity during the Industrial Revolution also tended to emphasize its 'revolutionary' aspects. This view argues that from the late eighteenth century a series of technological innovations often associated with a 'heroic entrepreneur' transformed the British cotton textile sector and gave rise to the modern factory system. These innovations included the spinning jenny 1766, Arkwright's water frame (1769), Crompton's mule (1779) and Cartwright's power loom (1787). Efforts to measure the impact of this technological change have never found more than a small impact. Estimates of productivity (TFP) growth for the late eighteenth century declined from early estimates of 1.3 per cent per annum to later estimates of only 0.1 per cent per annum (Feinstein, 1978; Crafts and Harley, 1992). Others have argued that

calculating productivity is inappropriate for a period of revolutionary industrial change that included changes in science, economic organization, new
products and processes, market creativity and skills (Berg and Hudson, 1992).

The British Industrial Revolution: deeper determinants

Each of the key deeper determinants of economic growth has found support
among scholars as being *the* key driver of the British Industrial Revolution,
although comparative assessment of these arguments is difficult. The impact of
deep determinants is rarely quantified and the explanations rely on different
evidence and different historical time frames.

Colonialism

According to some scholars, profits and plunder from the colonization of much
of the rest of the world by countries mainly in Western Europe provided the
source of savings that funded the investment that drove in turn the Industrial
Revolution. The perceived immorality of colonization often gives such arguments a fierce passion: 'from all these continents under whose eyes Europe
today raises up her tower of opulence, there has flowed out for centuries
towards that same Europe diamonds and oil, silk and cotton, wood and exotic
products. Europe is literally the creation of the Third World' (Fanon, 2001: 81).
Anecdotal evidence offers many examples. The combined profits for 1954 and
1955 of the Diamang Diamond Company in Angola (mainly Portuguese
investment) came to 40 per cent more than the total of invested capital
(Rodney, 1972: 212). David and Alexander Barclay engaged in slave trading
and in the 1730s used their profits to set up Barclays Bank in London. The
owners of West Indian slave plantations financed the English steam engine
developed by James Watt. The famous insurance firm Lloyds of London
started as a small London coffee house and expanded into banking and insurance through profits from the slave trade.

Moving beyond examples to the aggregate data leaves us with a 'small
numbers' problem. In 1800 commodity trade between Western Europe and the
whole developing world accounted for only 4 per cent of aggregate gross
national product (GNP) so it could not have generated sufficient profits for the
investment of the Industrial Revolution. The evidence of declining prices of
sugar, pepper, coffee, tobacco and tea on the London commodity market over
the second half of the seventeenth century does not suggest that abnormal profits were sustained in these colonial trades. Finally, the domestic savings rate in
Britain between 1760 and 1860 (about 12–14 per cent of GDP) was more than
enough to fund the modest capital requirements of the early industrialization.

Institutions

It has been suggested by Douglass North that the establishment of property
rights accounted for 'the rise of the West' and of England in particular. The
British monarchy, argues North, was defeated by Parliament (with its strong

representation of business and merchant interests) in the English Civil War of the 1640s and again in the Glorious Revolution of 1688. This gave Parliament the authority to curb the exercise of arbitrary and confiscatory power by the Crown through judicial independence and ultimately the supremacy of Parliament. The long-term consequences were the increased security of property rights, greater incentives to undertake long-term investments and so ultimately the onset of the Industrial Revolution. France and Spain had absolutist monarchies that took longer to create a system of law and property rights existing independently of the Crown. The historical failures were the Ottoman and Mughal empires where property was held at the discretion and whim of the Crown and Sub-Saharan Africa where property was held communally. Chapter 7 examines why well-established private property rights in fifteenth-century China failed to generate similar patterns of growth as in Western Europe.

More specific case-study evidence of the link between good institutions and innovation is hard to find in respect of Britain. Beginning in the 1760s, the stream of technological innovations in British textiles noted above transformed the industry. Yet, even during the height of the Industrial Revolution, England was not good at rewarding innovation and many of the innovators died in poverty as the secrets of their innovations quickly leaked to others (Clark, 2007:236). The story of coal was the same. Between the 1700s and 1860s coal output increased nearly 20 times but the leading pioneers Trevithick, Stephenson and Davy captured very few rewards. Innovation mainly benefited consumers in the form of lower prices rather than the innovators in the form of higher profits (Clark, 2007:237).

Geography

The growth of Western Europe from the sixteenth to nineteenth centuries was almost entirely accounted for by the growth of nations with easy geographical access to the Atlantic Ocean (Britain, France, the Netherlands, Portugal and Spain). The most rapid economic growth occurred in those countries which had freer political institutions where this growth in trade enriched and strengthened commercial interests outside the royal circle and so enabled them to demand the institutional changes (such as non-arbitrary taxes and well-protected property rights) necessary for long-term economic growth (Acemoglu *et al.*, 2005). Others have explained this growth pattern in terms of the availability of natural resources rather than political and institutional change. Trade and conquest in the Atlantic world made possible the importation of sugar and grain for food, cotton for manufacturing and timber for heating using slave labour. This enabled first England then later elsewhere in Europe to avoid diverting extra acres and labour that would otherwise have been required to produce them and to use them instead for working in industry. There is not much evidence for this second explanation. Until the early 1820s, long after the onset of industrialization, wheat imports into England were negligible and even by the 1840s wheat imports were only 12 per cent of consumption and mostly came from Russia and Prussia, not the Americas.

More generally right up until the 1930s the developed world as a whole was a net exporter of energy, which in the 1880s included 20 million tonnes of coal exported to developing countries from Britain (Bairoch, 1993).

The causal link here runs from a peculiar geographic location that enabled parts of Western Europe to participate in trade with and colonization of the New World and to benefit from the import of goods and energy necessary to expand output (investment) and to feed more people (labour).

Culture

The achievements of the 'heroic entrepreneur' in Britain reflect a distinct cultural difference separating Britain (and Western Europe) from the rest of the world (Landes, 1998). In medieval Europe the authority of the church was limited by competing secular authorities and by religious dissent from below. This created space for the rise of a rational science freed from the constraints of religious orthodoxy. The first European university was established in Bologna in 1080 and by 1500 there were 70 such centres of secular learning in Western Europe. Gutenberg produced his first book in Mainz in 1455 and by 1500 there were 220 printing presses and Western Europe had produced 8 million books. By the mid-seventeenth century the 'scientific revolution' had been firmly established in North-western Europe, culminating in the 1687 publication of Isaac Newton's *Principia Mathematica* which showed that the whole known universe was subject to the same laws of motion and gravitation. The British Royal Society and the French Académie des Sciences were founded in the early 1660s and the Paris Observatoire and Greenwich Observatory founded in the 1670s to disseminate this new knowledge (Landes, 1998; Maddison, 2007).

The Protestant religion in Europe was closely associated with this new learning and encouraged people to read and consider the Bible for themselves (rather than relying on a priest). This gave a big boost to literacy and so facilitated these wider scientific debates and thinking. Catholic countries responded to the challenge of Protestantism (the Reformation) with repression. Spain imposed the death penalty in 1558 for importing foreign books without permission. The impact was long-lasting. In 1900 3 per cent of the population of Britain were illiterate, compared with 48 per cent in Catholic Italy, 50 per cent in Spain and 78 per cent in Portugal (Becker and Woessmann, 2009).

The key causal links run from culture to education (labour) with an emphasis on savings (investment).

Openness

From the sixteenth century onwards the Spanish Inquisition was an attempt to assert the dominance of the Catholic Church throughout Europe and to repress free-thinking 'heresy' and foreign ideas. The works of Copernicus, Galileo and Newton were banned by the Spanish Jesuits (the enforcers of this religious orthodoxy) until 1746, and those printing presses that were permitted were monopolized by the church. After the defeat of the Spanish Armada in 1588

England was largely free from these threats. England has been portrayed as a country long very open to goods, ideas, migration and change. During the late sixteenth century France withdrew toleration of non-Catholic minorities (the 1685 Revocation of the Edict of Nantes). In the early seventeenth century Spain attempted to purge its colonies in the Spanish Netherlands (modern-day Belgium and the Netherlands) of non-Catholic groups. In both cases many of the persecuted minorities fled to England; prominent among them were skilled textile weavers who established production in many parts of the country. Even today in places like Colchester or Spitalfields, London it is possible to see the beautiful town houses of these migrants, testimony to the skills they translated into industrial wealth.

England and Western Europe more generally were fundamentally changed as a consequence of this openness. Goods, people and ideas were not merely imported and gazed at as exotic *curiosa* but had a fundamental impact on everyday life. Tea reached Europe from China in 1606 and by the 1650s reached England via Holland. During the eighteenth century English tea consumption increased dramatically and the spread of this hot, sweet, caffeinated drink transformed meals and forms of social interaction, provided bursts of energy and reduced hunger. Sweet tea was an ideal prop for the long hours and concentration required by the modern factory system. A detailed historical-statistical study shows that the welfare gains in England from imports of tropical-colonial goods (mainly tea, coffee, sugar and treacle) by 1850 were equivalent to about 15 per cent of national income (Hesh and Voth, 2009).

The key causal links ran from openness to goods (which enhanced real standards of living), to ideas (which enhanced productivity), migration (which supplied new, and skilled labour) and change (which speeded up the integration and diffusion of goods, ideas and people).

PART I

The Proximate Sources of Growth in the Modern World Economy since 1950

Economic growth – or the lack of it – happens as a result of the millions of day-to-day decisions made by individuals in households, firms and governments. Individuals decide whether to go to work, to take time off, to be a househus-band/wife, or to go travelling; when at work they decide how much effort to expend. Firms rake in profits and decide whether to utilize that surplus to boost executive pay, to return money to shareholders in the form of dividends or to invest in extra capacity to expand production in the future. 'Good' govern-ments may make decisions that directly promote economic growth, through investing in new transport links and agreeing international trade treaties to expand market access, or do so indirectly by re-training workers to use new technologies or reducing interest rates to make it cheaper for firms to borrow from banks to invest in new machinery. The decisions of 'bad' governments may undermine economic growth, encouraging a debt-fuelled boom in consumption at the expense of investment in the run-up to an election, appoint-ing teachers to reward political supporters rather than to provide pupils with motivated professionals, or squeezing resources from high taxation of the private sector so that the President can live in luxury.

Those millions of decisions can be grouped into those related to investment, to land, to labour and to productivity, each of which is a proximate determinant of economic growth. They have promoted sustained long-term growth in some parts of the world and not in others, and their impact can be measured in terms of economic growth, the focus of Part I of this book. Growth is about how aver-age incomes or material living standards change over time. The first and key conceptual chapter defines gross domestic and gross national product (GDP/GNP). Once we measure economic growth we can illuminate the nature and origin of global income inequalities. The chapter questions the assumption that economic growth can always be considered to represent progress: how, for example, do poverty, nutritional standards and environmental quality change with economic growth? Chapter 2 examines growth in the modern world econ-omy, looking at the patterns of convergence and divergence in global income distribution, and the growth miracles and failures that have characterized the world economy since 1950. Why, for example, was per capita GDP growth in Angola 11.4 per cent, New Zealand 1.1 per cent and Zimbabwe –5.4 per cent in 2005/06? Why was growth in South Korea sustained at levels of 7–8 per cent while growth in India was little more than 3.5 per cent in the three decades after 1950? What caused growth in India and China to accelerate rapidly in the early 1980s such that by the 2000s they were among the most rapidly growing economies in the world, while after decades of rapid growth in Japan, that country's economy has been stagnant since the 1990s?

These millions of decisions can be grouped into those decisions related to investment, to land, to labour and to productivity; each of these is a proximate determinant of economic growth.

Chapter 3 examines domestic and foreign investment and finds these to have (particularly the former) the most robust link with GDP growth of any of the proximate growth determinants. Chapter 4 examines demography, which impacts on growth through the supply of labour. Higher fertility can (with a lag) increase entrants to, and declining mortality reduce exits from, the labour force. Chapter 5 examines technology which impacts directly on labour productivity or land yield. Chapter 6 examines education and health, both important proximate determinants of growth and end goals of human development.

The chapters can be read alone or in sequence or the reader may follow through particular ideas across different chapters. Each one follows a similar pattern. A concept (such as education or investment) is defined, the economic theory and related empirical work showing how the concept is linked to economic growth is reviewed, and finally each chapter examines relevant policy conclusions.

Chapter 1

Thinking about Growth

When we have numbers we can quantify things and compare them. In the 1960s growth in South Korea was 7 per cent per annum and in India around 4 per cent. These numbers allow us to quantify that the Korean economy grew nearly twice as fast as that of India and would lead to the Korean economy doubling in size every decade. Sometimes it is relatively easy to attach numbers (such as numbers of teachers or output of steel) but very often far more difficult (such as the extent of liberalization or democracy or the quality of education). The most important numbers in economics are those for measuring the total size or growth of the economy: gross domestic product (GDP) and sometimes gross national product (GNP). This chapter first shows how economists have tried to measure total GDP and GNP and the problems they have encountered in doing so, then assesses the three main ways of thinking about growth: as a process of change, as progress towards an ideal end-state and as an assumption of progress. Growth gives us a sensation of relentless upward movement but this does not mean that all good things go together in a growing economy. The broader concepts of the good society or well-being require us to think about how economic growth interacts with, causes and in turn is influenced by phenomena such as poverty, inequality, nutritional status and environmental quality.

What is growth?

The starting point in thinking about growth is GDP, which is defined as the total value of all goods and services produced within a country in a single year. GDP is based on the geography of production. GNP is defined as the total value of goods and services produced by nationally owned factors of production in a single year. GNP is based on the ownership of production. The two may differ due to the activities of multinational corporations (MNCs). If a US-owned company invests in France and earns profits, those profits are part of US GNP because they are the income of a US-owned firm, so US GNP is higher than US GDP. For France, the profits of the US MNC are added to GDP, because they represent income earned within France but reduce French GNP because those profits are not earned by a French-owned firm. In general developing countries tend to host MNC investment and those MNCs remit profits back to shareholders in their home country so GDP for developing countries tends to be higher than GNP.

There are three ways of calculating GDP. First, the total value of output:

Value of ice creams + Value of computers + Value of aircraft + …

It is important that only the value of final goods is included. We include only the value of bread eaten by the consumer; if we also added in the various inputs used to produce bread, such as the flour sold to the bakery, we would be double counting.

Second, the total value of income:

Wages + Rents + Interest + Profit

Wages are earned by workers, rents from renting out land or property, interest from lending out money and profit by entrepreneurs/businesses from the difference between revenue and costs.

And third, total expenditure:

Consumption + Investment + Government spending + Net exports (exports − imports)

In principle these methods should yield the same result, but in practice they don't and statisticians have to undertake many revisions, estimates and best guesses to bring them into alignment. Total GDP gives a measure of the total size of an economy. Table 1.1 gives estimated total GDP for selected countries in 2012.

A country's total GDP is a useful estimate of its economic influence in global politics and is an indication of the size of its internal market, but it does not reflect standards of living. Dividing the size of the economy by the total population gives us average income or GDP per capita. Inflation will lead to

Table 1.1   *Total GDP in 2012 (current US$)*

Country	National income US$ billion
Japan	6,100
China	7,700
Vietnam	137
UK	2,400
South Korea	1,100
Saudi Arabia	589*
Cameroon	25
Ethiopia	34
Ghana	39

* 2011.

Source: Data compiled from *World Development Indicators* (2014).

Table 1.2   *GDP per capita and GDP adjusted for PPP*

Country	GDP per capita, 2011	GDP per capita, PPP-adjusted, 2011
Luxembourg	77,390	64,110
France	42,420	35,910
Ireland	39,150	33,520
Poland	12,380	20,260
Chile	12,280	16,300
Brazil	10,720	11,420
China	4,950	8,390
Senegal	1,070	1,940
Democratic Republic of Congo	190	340

Source: Data compiled from *World Development Indicators* (2013).

increases in the *nominal* value of output: higher prices of ice creams increase the value of output. Statisticians make adjustment to focus on the *real* value of output by stripping out the impact of inflation, for example using '2005 prices', so measuring output over an extended period of time at the market price prevailing in 2005.

Statisticians add together the monetary values of output such as the prices of ice creams and computers in the local currency. Once calculated, GDP is usually converted into a single currency (the dollar) to enable international comparisons. There is a significant problem with this process: the values of currencies fluctuate against each other over time on international financial markets. The value of the Indian rupee, for example, has fallen sharply against the dollar over the past few years. Sometimes statisticians use current market exchange rates, or to avoid short-term fluctuations they use an average of the market exchange rate over several years. A common if complicated adjustment is to use purchasing power parity (PPP) exchange rates. This allows for the fact that prices differ systematically between developed and developing countries. With labour much cheaper (wages are lower) in poor developing countries a dollar can buy a lot more of the goods and services produced by labour-intensive methods, such as haircuts. By contrast, refining petroleum is mainly done by computers and machinery so cheap labour will have little influence on the final costs which will differ little between developed and developing countries. Making adjustments for lower prices in developing countries means that actual living standards are often considerably higher than is suggested by straightforward measures of GDP per capita. Table 1.2 shows that incomes nearly double in China, Senegal and the Congo when adjusted for PPP. GDP per capita incomes in the Congo are 0.25 per cent of those in Luxembourg and when adjusted for PPP, 0.53 per cent – the income gap is halved but remains enormous.

Ways of thinking about growth

To an economist there are three main ways of thinking about growth: as a process of change; as progress towards an ideal end-state; and as an assumption of progress. In addition to incomes we may be concerned with wider measures of human well-being or 'development'. There are many ways to conceptualize development including GDP growth, capabilities, basic needs, the Millennium Development Goals, nutrition and happiness.

Growth as a process of change

Economic growth was the main policy goal of newly independent developing countries in the 1950s and 1960s; how to increase the growth rate was the central concern of the emerging school of Development Economics. Walt Rostow (1956) examined the pre-conditions for developing countries to experience a takeoff into *self-sustained growth*, while Ragnar Nurkse (1953) advocated *balanced growth* across economic sectors, and Albert Hirschman (1958) argued the government should promote those sectors of the economy whose expansion would *spill over* and promote growth in other sectors. Recent research has noted that developing countries seem to find it relatively easy to start growth but that sustaining it is much harder. For example Congo, Nigeria, and Côte d'Ivoire all experienced rapid (6 per cent+) growth in the 1960s, followed by economic stagnation.

Using GDP growth as a measure of change is problematic in a number of ways, however. GDP growth only measures market transactions so ignores the *subsistence/household production* common in developing countries and non-marketed household work (usually by women) common throughout the world. Measuring GDP only gives something a value if it has a price or wage. Non-marketed household labour plays a crucial role in sustaining the health and nutritional status of the current labour force and promotes the education levels of the future labour force so clearly has a crucial value even if it has no market price (there is a strong relationship between the literacy levels of a mother and her children). As an economy and incomes grow over time individuals tend to shift from household-based production (baking bread) to market transactions (buying bread in a supermarket). Making allowance for this change over time would tend to reduce GDP growth rates in developing countries because some of the measured increase in GDP represents, not higher output, but a shift from non-market to market-based transactions.

Corporate accounting has clear rules to distinguish total or gross from net investment. Net investment accounts for the depreciation of buildings, machinery and other assets. But oddly, GDP measures are not corrected for using up the *environmental stock*. Incomes earned from converting a tree into wood and furniture and selling it are included, but the loss of the tree that has been felled is not. Making these adjustments for Indonesia in the 1970s and 1980s when 40 per cent of its GDP and 80 per cent of its exports were dependent on the natural environment would have reduced the country's growth rate from an average of 7 per cent to only 4 per cent. However, there is no easy way of undertaking environmental accounting. How should we value the depletion of oil or fish stocks? How should we value the preservation of a beautiful view or the preservation of unspoilt wilderness? Using GDP growth as a measure of change also fails to consider the sustainability of that growth. Sustainability has been considered either in general environmental terms (such as energy-intensive growth closely linked to greenhouse gas emissions) or more narrowly economic terms (such as the debt-fuelled growth of Mexico in the 1970s that stalled in the 1980s when it became time to start repaying that debt). GDP accounting makes no distinction between $1 spent on a hamburger or $1 spent on medical care, environmental protection, education or investment in infrastructure.

GDP growth also tells us nothing about *distribution*: whether growth is enriching a broad cross-section of the population or is limited to certain classes, regions or urban areas. We noted in the Introduction that between 1973 and 2010 average incomes of 99 per cent of the US population actually fell; the steady growth in GDP over these decades went to enriching the top 1 per cent of the population. In the US the proportion of adult women in paid employment increased from 33 per cent in 1948 to 62 per cent in 1992. The average number of hours worked in the US increased from 859 per year in 1950 to 931 in 1996. This indicates that much of the GDP growth in the US over these years reflected more labour inputs (so less leisure) so we should be careful when drawing conclusions about the likely welfare implications of GDP growth and higher incomes. Measures of GDP growth do not distinguish between intensive growth (based on longer hours and more working people using a greater quantity of land and raw materials) and extensive growth (based on higher productivity per worker or using environmental resources more sustainably). It is difficult to estimate the size of the illegal or *black economy*, which has been estimated at 50–60 per cent of the total in India and even 15 per cent in developed Italy.

A more encompassing idea of change than GDP growth is suggested by Amartya Sen in *Development as Freedom* (1999); here development is defined as the 'process of expanding the real freedoms that people enjoy'. What is ultimately important, according to Sen, is that people have the freedoms or valuable opportunities (he calls them capabilities) to lead the kind of lives they want to, for example, being nourished, being able to travel, or taking part in political discussions. Sen states that there is only an indirect and uncertain link between GDP growth and freedom. For example, a woman in a patriarchal society may find it harder to convert income into the ability to travel outside the household or a sick person may require more income to live a normal life due to the extra need for medical services. Capabilities should not be measured by outcomes (number of apples consumed) but by the opportunity to choose (between apples and oranges). This makes the concept difficult to operationalize. How do we measure and aggregate the benefits of the choice actually made and also the possible choices not taken? In practice researchers have tended to measure factors associated with enhancing the ability and freedoms to choose, such as life expectancy, health and literacy, which can make the approach end up being rather similar to that of 'basic needs' (Laderchi *et al.*, 2003).

The focus on growth as a measure of change can also distort our understanding of crucial issues, making us, for example, value education as human capital because it contributes to growth by making workers more productive. For Sen this link is important but limited: education can also enhance the ability of human beings to lead lives they have reason to value and to enhance the substantive choices they have. Work by Craig Jeffrey (2012) on education in small towns in North India shows that parents often value education for their children in the belief it will give them the social awareness, confidence, and good manners to be more socially mobile. Female education helps reduce gender inequalities and fertility (Sen, 1997). Studies show that happiness is positively related to years of schooling and shows no relation with income growth (Kahneman and Krueger, 2006). Sen (1982) famously argued that no democracy with a free press has ever experienced a famine. He later summarized the argument:

> [F]amines are extremely easy to prevent if the government tries to prevent them...[through re-generating the lost purchasing power of hard hit groups]...and a government in a multi-party democracy with elections and free media has strong incentives to undertake famine prevention. (Sen, 1999:52)

The freedoms approach implies that people are not just a labour force that can be made more productive with better health and education. People are not just alternatives to machines in the process of production. People are more than the means of growth; their well-being is an end goal for a good society.

Most measures of development generate some political controversy. Does, for example, the ability of young people to choose a marriage partner represent freedom or does it undermine the social norms, traditions and family cohesion associated with arranged marriages? An exception is life expectancy. A long life is universally and strongly valued, is valued for its own sake and is also necessary to enable people to do those things they have a reason to value. So life expectancy is not a bad single measure and proxy for capabilities. Interestingly the two decades that showed the greatest improvement in UK life expectancy (1911–21 and 1941–51) were those that encompassed the First and Second World Wars. The explanation for this paradox is that although the total supply of food per head declined, under-nutrition also declined because of the more equal sharing of food through rationing systems (Sen, 1998). The use of capabilities as proxied by life expectancy gives us a very different picture about patterns of change. Life expectancy data since 1870 on nineteen countries including India, Brazil and Russia show a pattern of divergence during 1913 and 1950 and strong convergence thereafter. Life expectancy in India was

Table 1.3   *Life expectancy, 1000–1999 (years at birth for
both sexes combined)*

	World	West	Rest	Difference (West – rest)
1000	24	24	24	0
1820	26	36	24	12
1900	31	46	26	20
1950	49	66	44	22
1999	66	78	64	14

Source: Data compiled from Maddison (2006:33).

only 44 per cent of that in England in 1931 but increased steadily to 82 per cent in 1999 (Kenny, 2005:5). Table 1.3 shows that life expectancy in the West was the same as in 'the rest' in AD1000; the difference peaked at 22 years in 1950 and declined thereafter.

Between 1990 and 2001 high-income countries increased life expectancy by 1.8 years per decade, in South Asia by 4.5 years per decade, 3.6 in the Middle East and North Africa, and 2.7 in Latin America and the Caribbean. By contrast Sub-Saharan Africa lost 3.6 years of average life expectancy (due to the HIV/AIDs crisis) (Bloom *et al.*, 2004:10).

The Human Development Report (HDR) has been published annually by the United Nations Development Programme (UNDP) since 1990 and represents an 'extensive and sustained effort to translate some core ideas of the capability approach among other work into accessible language and operational policy prescriptions' (Alkire, 2005:126). Enlarging one's choices or capabilities, according to the report, is accomplished by living a long and healthy life, being educated, and having a decent standard of living. The report constructs a tool to measure capabilities – the Human Development Index (HDI). In the HDI longevity is approximated by life expectancy, knowledge by the literacy rate and the standard of living by real GDP per capita. According to the 1990 HDR report the lowest country on the HDI index was Niger and the highest Japan; by 2012 Japan had dropped to tenth and Norway topped the table while Niger remained firmly at the bottom (in 186th place).

There are notable data problems with the HDI. For the first half of the 1990s only 59 of 171 countries had estimates of extreme poverty (living on less than $1 per day) and only 30 had sufficient data to estimate life expectancy at birth (Harkness, 2004). Unlike the national income accounts (GDP) and external trade statistics there is no internationally agreed standard for presenting statistics on indicators of human development. Literacy, for example, is defined differently in different countries. School enrolment data are not comparable, since quality of schools, drop-out rates and the length of the school year vary substantially within and between countries. Despite these problems scholars

Box 1.1 Historical calculations of HDI

Historical calculation of HDIs by Nick Crafts reveals a distinct pattern of progress. By the late 1990s the HDI in most developing countries exceeded that of Western Europe in 1870. The gaps in HDI between Western Europe and each of Africa, China and India were smaller in 1999 than in 1950. These outcomes have been heavily influenced by widespread gains in life expectancy.

In 1870 the HDI was 0.516 in Australia, 0.515 in Switzerland and 0.506 in the US. By 1999 these had been surpassed by most developing countries, such as Egypt 0.635, Bolivia 0.648 and Sri Lanka 0.735, but were still above Malawi 0.397, Mozambique 0.323 and Nepal 0.480. Contemporary developing countries have also improved their HDIs at a much faster rate. The HDI in Australia increased by 0.264 (from 0.516 to 0.780) in the eighty years between 1870 and 1950. Sudan, despite enduring civil war and famine, increased its HDI by 0.236 (from 0.161 to 0.397) between 1950 and 1999 (Crafts, 1999:396–7).

have tried to calculate historical measures of HDI (see Box 1.1) enabling long-term comparisons of broader ideas of development. The HDRs have acknowledged and tried to engage with the poor data quality. In 1991 the index of educational attainment included both adult literacy rates and mean years of schooling. In 1995, owing to problems in measuring educational attainment, the variable was changed to a combination of adult literacy (two-thirds weight) and gross combined primary, secondary and tertiary enrolment (one-third weight) (Tisdell *et al.*, 2001). The very fact of the reports being published annually has provided a spur to the better collection and presentation of relevant data.

Some have argued that the HDI could be improved by including indicators of political freedom and human rights. The importance of political freedom is striking in the work of Amartya Sen. A Political Freedom Index was included in the HDR in 1992. This index had five components – personal security, rule of law, freedom of expression, political participation and equality of opportunity – and drew on data from 102 countries. It was dropped from the HDR the following year for political, not academic reasons. The ranking of countries according to these subjective criteria generated a lot of controversy (Fukuda-Parr and Kumar, 2003). In the 1995 Report two new indices were introduced: the Gender-related Development Index (GDI) and the Gender Empowerment Measure (GEM). The GDI uses the same variables as the HDI but makes an adjustment if life expectancy, educational attainment and income measures are unequal between men and women. The GEM is an indicator of the empowerment of women measured by their relative presence in national parliament and administrative, managerial, professional and technical positions. No country in the world has a GDI as high as its HDI, indicating that all countries in the world have some gender gaps. The gap is lowest in Sweden where the GDI is only 1 per cent smaller than the HDI. The largest gender inequality penalties are found in the Middle East and North Africa where the GDI is up to 33 per cent lower than the HDI. These gaps are not just a product of low incomes. South-east Asia and Sub-Saharan Africa impose very small penalties for gender inequalities comparable to those found in much richer OECD countries. The GDI has been criticized for its focus on gender gaps in earned income which downplays gender gaps in education and largely ignores those in mortality, which are the two most important problems facing women in many developing countries (Bardhan and Klasen, 1999). The abnormally high mortality of women in India and other developing countries is discussed in more detail in Chapter 4. The concept of earned income to construct the indices excludes un-paid labour which is substantial in many developing countries and so devalues its implicit worth. The GEM is criticized for being too heavily focused on representation at the national political level so misses the substantial representation of women in local governments in for example, India. The GEM makes no allowance for the lack of power of some parliaments. China and Cuba have high proportions of women in parliament, but parliaments have little influence so higher GEM rankings do not reflect the actual political power held by women (Bardhan and Klasen, 1999).

Growth as progress towards an ideal end-state

GDP growth can be understood as progress towards some ideal end-state or goal. The World Bank, by classifying countries according to income groups, has a clear notion of an ideal end-state. For 2006 these groups were low-income countries (LICs) with a GDP per capita of $905 or less, lower-middle-income countries (LMCs), $906–3,595, upper-middle-income countries (UMCs), $3,596–11,115 and high-income countries, $11,116 or more. The common usage of the term 'developing countries' then refers to countries with a GDP per capita less than $11,116. The ideal end-state is clear; it implies that developing countries should promote rapid economic growth until they have achieved income levels sufficient to give them high-income developed-country status. In 1991 the then Prime Minister of Malaysia, Dr Matahir Mohamad, launched 'Vision 2020', an ambitious thirty-year set of goals for the country:

> Hopefully the Malaysian who is born today and in the years to come will be the last generation of our citizens who will be living in a country that is called 'developing'. The ultimate objective that we should aim for is a Malaysia that is a fully developed country by the year 2020. (Vision 2020)

The plan aimed to double real GDP every ten years for three decades by targeting 7 per cent growth in real GDP per year. Growth alone was not considered enough:

> Malaysia should not be developed only in the economic sense. It must be a nation that is fully developed along all the dimensions: economically,

politically, socially, spiritually, psychologically and culturally. We must be fully developed in terms of national unity and social cohesion, in terms of our economy, in terms of social justice, political stability, system of government, quality of life, social and spiritual values, national pride and confidence. (Vision 2020)

This is quite typical. The ideal end-state is rarely seen in terms of higher incomes alone. Many scholars, visionaries and philosophers have defined their vision of an ideal society, so progress can be seen and measured as movement towards that end-state. Many have drawn from writings in the Bible, the Koran and other holy books and been inspired to create a religiously ordained ideal state on earth. Examples include the Christian Puritan communities in eighteenth-century America, contemporary arguments among some groups for an Islamic Caliphate, and Hindu Ram-Raja in India. It is not easy to distinguish between a genuine belief that a particular social order has divine sanction and the self-interested motives of rulers seeking to legitimize their own rule by appealing for divine support. Did seventeenth-century European kings really believe they were 'God's appointed rulers'? Karl Marx in the nineteenth century argued that the ideal end-state was communism, which he defined as a situation when resources were distributed 'from each according to his ability to each according to his need'. Marx saw development as proceeding through a series of stages of social organization (what he called 'modes of production') from hunter-gatherer, to slavery, feudalism, capitalism, socialism and finally communism. Each stage gave way to the next, usually after a revolution, and each was progressive in that it represented a higher standard of material and cultural life than the preceding stage, laying the foundations for progress to the next stage. Marxists have tried to measure progress through this series of end-states by documenting the emergence of social classes and divisions between classes, trade union organization and the growth of revolutionary political parties. The US government in more recent years has changed its perspective on 'development': whereas previously poverty was a central concern, the goal today is to create a liberal free-market democracy. This can help explain why the US has expended such vast resources promoting democracy in Iraq and Afghanistan.

One of the most practical and influential visions has been that of 'basic needs', associated with the work of Dudley Seers, Paul Streeten, Irma Adelman and Cynthia Morris in the 1970s. This approach argues that development should be less concerned with average incomes than with achieving universal access to a basket of goods and services including food, clothing, housing, education and public transportation.

There are conceptual problems with this approach. Who is to determine what constitutes those basic needs? Basic needs can be (and often are) measured as the income necessary for a household to purchase this basket of goods and services, and those with lower incomes than this cut-off counted as being in poverty. Should basic needs be considered as the actual consumption by households of the basket of goods and services needed for a healthy life or just the opportunity to acquire them regardless of whether individuals actually exercise that choice? Frequently people make choices to consume foodstuffs high in saturated fats and sugar or alcohol and so even with enough disposable income to purchase sufficient healthy and nutritious food, people do not fulfil their basic needs. Are then people exercising genuine choices or acting out of ignorance? We may tend towards 'choice' in the case of adults making a decision for themselves but perhaps not so in the case of a girl-child who is being deprived of nutrition and health care by a household who prefer to ensure the survival of her brother. What about the rational adult who is suffering malnutrition because he is 'choosing' to be an alcoholic or is heavily influenced by advertising, so consuming Coca-Cola rather than more nutritious food and drink? The 'basic' of basic needs may ensure a person survives but with a miserable and austere sense of existence. What about luxuries and pleasures? There is no indication of how or whether progress continues once basic needs have been fulfilled. Should basic needs include non-material aspects such as free speech, equality before the law and participation in democratic elections? Are basic needs universal or context specific? Differences in cultural norms are likely to imply the latter, for example the possession of chopsticks may be considered a basic need in China but not so in other countries where food is eaten by hand. If basic needs differ between countries/cultures, any sort of comparative work becomes much more difficult. Basic needs may also change over time with rising incomes, urbanization and industrialization. Literacy may not be necessary in a traditional rural economy but becomes increasingly essential to work and interact socially in an urban industrial setting. A recent initiative in the spirit of the basic needs approach are the Millennium Development Goals (MDGs) discussed in Box 1.2.

A second ideal end-state is the achievement of universal adequate nutrition. Nutrition is usually considered part of the basket of basic needs but is often focused on as a distinct issue. There is also a fascinating and somewhat perverse link between nutrition and economic growth.

Nutrition can be measured in terms of physical intake. Calorie availability is computed by converting food quantities (purchases and consumption from own production) into nutrient intakes, using special conversion tables. There are problems with this method. First, it assumes no food is wasted. Second, consumption and production surveys tend not to take into account meals that are given to guests or employees. A more direct method to estimate nutrient intake is to ask respondents to recall patterns of consumption over a defined prior time period. The shorter the recall period the more atypical consumption is likely to be, the longer the recall period the more problems there will be with errors in recall. Trying to relate nutritional intake to need is also difficult and has to consider the demands placed on nutrition through illness, pregnancy and labour. Dysentery, for example, can quickly counteract the effect of a diet with otherwise ample nutrition. A more accurate but time-consuming and expensive method is through anthropometric measurements, that is, measuring people's

Box 1.2 The Millennium Development Goals

The MDGs originated from a series of UN resolutions and agreements made at world conferences in 2000. The MDGs have provided a framework for the World Bank and other donors to target aid and technical assistance towards achieving them and for recipient countries to measure general progress and request aid according to whether they are being fulfilled. The MDGs are:

(a) Reducing the proportion of people living in extreme poverty by half between 1990 and 2015.
(b) Ensuring that all children are enrolled in primary school by 2015.
(c) Reducing gender inequality through eliminating the gender gap in enrolments in both primary and secondary school by 2005.
(d) Reducing infant and child mortality by two-thirds during 1990–2015.
(e) Reducing maternal mortality rates by three-quarters during 1990–2015.
(f) Ensuring that all women have access to reproductive health services by 2015.
(g) Reversing loss of environmental resources through implementing sustainable development strategies.

In the early 2000s progress towards achieving the MDGs was poor. Of 24 Sub-Saharan African countries only in Ghana and Madagascar were poverty rates declining at a pace sufficient to reach the relevant MDG. Only Kenya and Cameroon were likely to realize the goal of universal primary enrolment by 2015. In Zambia, Madagascar and Zimbabwe there were actually significant declines in primary enrolment. Only urban Burkina Faso, Tanzania and Zimbabwe and rural Madagascar and Tanzania were on target to meet the goal of gender equality in primary and secondary education. In only eleven of 24 countries was the improvement sufficient to realize the goal of reducing the infant mortality rate by two-thirds by 2015 (Sahn and Stifel, 2003).

physical attributes such as height, weight, or upper-arm circumference. These latter measures have highlighted a particular concern with nutrition driven by an apparent paradox in South Asia.

One of the MDGs is to halve the number of underweight children. A particular puzzle is that India has a high proportion of children with low weight for age and low height for age compared with other developing countries and relative to anthropometric ideals. Despite rapid economic growth and falling poverty these figures have changed little. Tables 1.4 and 1.5 use two measures of malnutrition, low height for age and low weight for age for a number of poor developing countries from Asia and Sub-Saharan Africa. On both indicators malnutrition in India remains high and stagnant between the mid-1990s and mid-2000s. Countries such as Bangladesh that experienced much higher levels of both in the 1990s showed sharp improvement in the 2000s to levels below India. Those countries that had comparable levels of malnutrition to India, measured by height for age, by the mid-2000s, such as Malawi, Zambia,

Table 1.4   *Malnutrition, low height for age*

Percentage of children under five malnourished			
India	48.5 (1997)	51.0 (1999)	47.9 (2006)
Bangladesh	59.7 (1997)	62.4 (1999)	47.0 (2006)
Sri Lanka		18.4 (2000)	19.2 (2009)
Malawi	63.6 (1998)	54.6 (2000)	53.2 (2006)
Zambia		57.9 (1999)	48.8 (2007)
Ethiopia		57.4 (2000)	44.2 (2011)
Tanzania	49.7 (1996)	44.4 (2004)	42.5 (2010)

Source: Data compiled from *World Development Indicators* (2013).

Table 1.5   *Malnutrition, low weight for age*

Percentage of children under five malnourished			
India	41.1 (1997)	44.4 (1999)	43.5 (2006)
Bangladesh	52.5 (1997)	52.0 (1999)	39.8 (2006)
Sri Lanka		22.8 (2000)	21.6 (2009)
Malawi	26.3 (1998)	21.5 (2000)	15.5 (2006)
Zambia		19.6 (1999)	14.9 (2007)
Ethiopia		42.0 (2000)	29.2 (2011)
Tanzania	26.9 (1996)	16.7 (2004)	16.2 (2010)

Source: Data compiled from *World Development Indicators* (2013).

Ethiopia and Tanzania have shown more improvement over time, seeing rates drop by ten percentage points. In most of these cases rates of malnutrition measured by low weight for age are less than half those in India. Despite similar low levels of income and a brutal civil war Sri Lanka has reduced levels of malnutrition, according to both measures, to consistently around half of those in India.

Malnutrition among adults is also widespread and higher in India and South Asia than elsewhere. Nutrition in adults is often measured by the Body Mass Index (BMI) which is defined as the ratio of weight (in kilos) to the square of height (in metres). The standard cut-off point associated with 'chronic energy deficiency' is a BMI of 18.5. The proportion of women aged 15 to 49 falling below this level in the mid-2000s was high across South Asia – India 35.6 per cent, Bangladesh 34.3 per cent and Nepal 24.4 per cent – and generally much lower in Sub-Saharan Africa – Burkina Faso 20.8 per cent, Nigeria 15.2 per cent, Ethiopia 26.5 per cent, Zimbabwe 9.3 per cent and Kenya 12.3 per cent (Deaton and Drèze, 2009:54).

A second puzzle is that the problem of malnutrition/under-nutrition in India is not just about poverty. Although underweight children are more prevalent among the poor (47 per cent of the poorest third of the population by income), the problem is still high among the richer (25 per cent among the highest third by income). Under-nutrition also varies strikingly even within single households. Mortality linked to inferior nutrition allocation by parents is higher among girl children in Indian households (Das Gupta, 1987). For a more extended discussion on the reasons for this last 'paradox' see the section on missing women in Chapter 4.

In India, 80 per cent of the population do not consume the daily 2,400 calories in rural and 2,100 calories in urban areas that have long been designated as the cut-off point for adult poverty. For all India per capita calories specifically from cereals declined from 1,600 in 1983 to 1,326 in 2004 (Deaton and Drèze, 2009:44). Some argue that calorie consumption is good proxy measure of poverty so these figures indicate poverty was much higher (80 per cent) in India by the late 2000s than suggested by the official statistics (20–25 per cent). The fall in per capita calorie consumption has been explained by the worsening income distribution and an absolute decline in incomes and purchasing power for a major part of the population, outweighing the minority with fast rising incomes; the malnutrition crisis is then a question of distribution (Patnaik, 2007, 2010). It is difficult to square these arguments with clear evidence from other sources, that per-capita consumption of other goods and services among all expenditure classes in India has been increasing and surveys showing self-reported 'hunger' declining (Deaton and Drèze, 2009, 2010). While Patnaik argues that declining calorie consumption indicates rising poverty it is difficult to reconcile this argument with evidence that the decline in per capita calorie consumption is more marked among high-income households and also that per capita calorie consumption tends to be higher in poorer states of India (Bihar and Orissa) than in richer states (Punjab and Haryana).

This debate is at the heart of the discussion about how to judge whether basic needs (such as nutrition) are being fulfilled. How do we make a value judgement when a household with sufficient disposable incomes does not consume a nutritious diet? There is good evidence from consumer surveys that Indian consumers have been shifting to higher-priced calories such as meat, sugar and milk and away from more nutritious grains. Are such households falling into poverty or exercising choice?

There is also good reason to suppose that the consequence of economic growth has changed nutritional basic needs in India, reducing the need for calories and making comparisons over time harder, this was a general problem we discussed with the Basic Needs approach. Improvements in vaccination, access to drinking water and sanitation have reduced the incidence of health conditions such as diarrhoea that drain away the nutritional value of calorie consumption. The total fertility rate in India has declined from 6.6 in the 1960s to 2.8 average births per woman in 2005, reducing the need for extra calories to support pregnancy. The shift from agriculture to urban industry has reduced the need for high calorie consumption by manual labourers. The calorie requirements of an 'average Indian man' weighing 60kg are almost 60 per cent higher if he is engaged in heavy rather than sedentary activity (3,800 and 2,425 calories respectively). There has also been a big increase in television ownership (indicating more sedentary leisure pursuits) and bicycle ownership (reducing the need for calories to sustain physical effort) (Deaton and Drèze, 2009).

Historical and contemporary case studies show the Indian paradox to be more typical than some commentators have considered. Estimates show that wages in Britain increased for most occupations between 1770 and 1850 but as with contemporary India, per capita food consumption declined. In 1863 the average English adult agricultural worker consumed 3,262 calories per day, a level far in excess of modern consumers. The decline of manual agricultural labour, falling fertility rates and improved health together reduced the demand for calories and rising real incomes were diverted into increased consumption of new and more expensive foodstuffs such as tea, sugar and fresh milk (Clark *et al.*, 1995). The case of historical Britain is remarkably similar to that of contemporary India. China offers a slightly different example. Despite rapid income growth between the 1980s and 2000s average nutrition availability in China declined after the mid-1990s. For the wealthier, we again see a familiar story of calories derived from cereals being (more than) compensated for by increased consumption of fruit, vegetables, meat, fish and eggs. For the poor, expenditure on calories was crowded out by increased food prices as a result of reduced government subsidies (particularly till 1993) on health care, education, housing, and other non-food necessities (Meng *et al.*, 2009). This story lacks the optimistic angle; here calorie consumption was not declining because the poorest were exercising choice.

Globally the transition to a diet characterized by high consumption of sugar, saturated fats and refined foods and reduced intake of fibre is happening at much lower income levels than in earlier history. There are various possible reasons: lower food prices (certainly between the 1970s and 1990s); global media images; technological change that increases sedentary work and leisure activity; and consumption of processed foods made easier by supermarkets and microwaves (Popkin, 2003). In consequence obesity and diabetes are now increasing globally. The concept of 'basic needs' based on what an expert chooses to be an ideal consumption basket is becoming increasingly difficult to sustain. This discussion leaves us facing some big questions. Is development fundamentally about paternalism and doing good, using persuasion, subsidies and even coercion (for example making vaccination compulsory) to push people into adopting lifestyles compatible with well-being? Or is development about empowering people to make choices, even if those choices involve using ample disposable income to choose a diet that undermines nutritional status? Just whose ideal end-state are we aiming to achieve?

The 1776 US Declaration of Independence takes it as self-evident that the 'pursuit of happiness' is an 'unalienable right' alongside life and liberty. The goal of happiness – as the ideal end-state of economic and social development is the third approach considered in this chapter. Happiness could provide a direct measure of human well-being. This may seem unlikely but recent research has shown an interesting and complex relation between economic growth and happiness. Oswald (1997:1818) used the General Social Surveys of the US (which since 1972 have been questioning people about their levels of happiness) and found that happiness between 1972 and 1990 was stable or increasing slightly. Old people systematically reported higher levels of happiness, and controlling for this demographic effect Oswald found a very slight but positive upward trend over time overall and that men tended to become happier while women experienced little change. For Europe the Euro-barometer Survey Series asks 'on the whole are you very satisfied, not very satisfied or not at all satisfied with the life you lead?' Answers are available for random samples from 1973 onwards for 12 European countries. Levels of life satisfaction show a slight increase since the early 1970s, though with large differences across nations. In Denmark more than half the population say they are 'very satisfied' while in Italy the figure is around ten per cent. Some of this difference is likely to reflect cultural and linguistic differences. There will be difficulties in translation because for words like happiness, contentment and satisfaction there are subtle differences between English and other languages.

The consistent finding from both the US and European data is that happiness has not increased in line with rising incomes. There are two explanations for this apparent paradox. The first is that individuals compare themselves with other individuals rather than to their own past levels of income so that it is not the absolute level of income that matters most but rather one's position relative to other individuals. Second, additional income and consumption initially provides only transitory happiness which soon wears off. This process is called adaptation and implies that wants are insatiable – the more one gets, the more one wants (Frey and Slutzer, 2002). There is supporting evidence showing that lottery winners do not experience long-term gains in happiness (Kahneman and Krueger, 2006).

The implications of happiness research for policy are striking. Much economic policy over recent decades has emphasized the importance of increasing labour market flexibility by reducing controls on hiring and firing to allow rapid adjustment to changing market conditions or technology and permit labour to be quickly re-allocated to sectors in which it can be used most productively. A robust finding from happiness research is that happiness is very negatively impacted by job insecurity or unemployment. In the early 1990s mental distress was twice as high among the unemployed as among those who had work (Kahneman and Krueger, 2006). This implies that what might be good for growth is not necessarily good for happiness.

Growth as an assumption of progress

How do we make value judgements about whether things have got better over time? In particular how do we make a judgement if some things have got better and some things have got worse? The most explicit notion of economic growth as progress comes from the modernization school of development. In economic terms modernization implies industrialization and urbanization and the technological transformation of agriculture. In social terms it involves the weakening of traditional ties and the rise of achievement (rather than factors based on birth such as caste or kin) as the basis for personal advancement. Culturally modernization is represented by the decline of religion and increased secularization of society arising from the spread of scientific knowledge. One of the most influential models of modernization came from Rostow (1960) who argued that there were five stages of economic growth. These were in turn the 'traditional society', 'preconditions for takeoff', 'takeoff', the 'drive to maturity', and the 'age of mass consumption'. Takeoff required that society be prepared to respond actively to new possibilities for productive enterprise, which argued Rostow was likely to require political, social and institutional changes in response to economic change and innovation. An example has been the cultural acceptance of young women working outside the household in response to increasing job opportunities in textile factories. The beginning of the takeoff could usually be traced to a sharp jolt such as a political or technological revolution. Karl Marx was also a modernist and argued that history progressed through stages from slavery to communism. Modernization has often been criticized as a historical description of economic and social change in North America and Western Europe in the eighteenth and nineteenth centuries, wrongly heralded as a universally applicable process (Ingham, 1993). Recent historical experience shows that it is wrong to assume modernization and education necessarily lead to secularism. In the Middle East urbanization and the growth of a literate middle class have accompanied the resurgent influence of Islam, not secularism. It is also naive to assume that local or indigenous alternatives must be good. Many such alternatives have simply reflected the interests of a brutal minority. The Khmer Rouge in Cambodia promised to build an agricultural paradise free of foreign influence in the early 1970s and murdered millions in the process. Opposition to modernization often comes from those who had benefited from the violence and repression and exploitative structures and institutions of traditional societies (Ingham, 1993).

Human history has not always been about a linear process of improvement or the decline of the traditional and rise of the modern. The collapse of the Roman Empire in the fifth century led to a collapse of long-distance trade and urbanization and resulted in a massive decline in income levels in Western and Southern Europe that were not achieved again for perhaps a thousand years. In the 1930s liberal, democratic and prosperous Germany lurched into the brutal and totalitarian Nazi dictatorship. There never have been unambiguous benefits from modernization and whether such change is progress depends upon how one weighs up its costs and benefits. There *have* been widespread gains associated with economic growth including material standards of living, consumption of food and clothing, and technological improvements (such as supermarkets and washing machines) that have freed millions from burdensome physical tasks (Goulet, 1992). There have *also* been costs of growth. Diseases of affluence (such as cancer, heart disease, and obesity) can kill just as can diseases of poverty (cholera, diarrhoea and malnutrition). Traditional cultures and their associated extended families and kinship groups have been undermined. The 'disease' of manic consumption and resulting social stresses in developed countries have been labelled by one writer as 'affluenza' (James, 2007). There are important questions about who makes these value judgements about progress. Experts? Aid agencies? Domestic or developed country governments? The poor themselves?

Economic growth and human development

GDP growth and improvements in human development are closely but not perfectly related; there is no consensus about whether the relation is causal and some countries have achieved much higher or lower levels of human development than we would guess given their levels of average income.

There is generally a close fit between levels and growth rates of GDP and human development. Measures of human development have also improved more rapidly in developing countries than in developed countries during their own history. For almost every potential quality of life variable there has been convergence, including life expectancy, infant survival per 1,000 live births, calorie intake, female literacy as a percentage of male literacy, political and civil rights, telephones per capita, and the percentage of population with access to clean water.

It is important to remember that a correlation between two variables (such as GDP and a measure of human development) says nothing about causation. It does not provide evidence that efforts to promote growth of either GDP or human development will automatically see the other variable rise as a consequence. Various studies have explored the nature of this link in more detail. Dasgupta and Weale (1992) examined data for 48 countries going back to the 1970s; they found a close relation between national income and measures of human development (including life expectancy at birth, the infant survival rate, adult literacy rate, and political and civil liberties). Anand and Ravallion (1993) returned to the question again found that average incomes in developing countries were correlated with the prevalence of absolute poverty, infant mortality and under-five mortality (negatively) and with public spending on social services (positively). Furthermore, they found that the positive relationship between life expectancy and income vanished entirely once the level of poverty and public health spending were accounted for. This implies that it is not economic growth in itself that is crucial but whether higher incomes are used to expand public health services. We can use these findings to explain why the US has one of the lowest life expectancies of any developed country. The reason is that the benefits of that economic growth over recent decades has been monopolized by the top echelons of the income distribution and not taxed by the government to provide public services.

An important caveat to this result is that despite the overall close relation there are many outliers. Sri Lanka in the early 1990s had an income per head of $500 and a life expectancy of 71 years while Oman with an income of $6,700 had a life expectancy of only 66 years (Streeten, 1994). The Sri Lankan achievement owes much to government provision of decent health and education and extensive subsidies on basic foods. An attention to social welfare predates independence but owes much to the granting of universal adult franchise in 1931. The first Health Unit in Sri Lanka was established in 1926, providing primary health care and control of infectious diseases. Similar interventions did not start in some other developing countries for another 50 years. After independence real public health spending per capita increased rapidly even though GDP growth rates were low. Ranking countries by GNP per capita and by HDI in the late 1980s showed that Sri Lanka had the largest difference (being 45 places higher on the HDI ranking), with China coming a close second (+44). Countries ranking higher on their GNP ranking included Oman (−56), UAE (−50), Gabon (−46) and all oil-producing states (Fukuda-Parr and Kumar, 2003). The existence of outliers illustrates that improved human welfare can be achieved even at low levels of income, or alternatively that even decades of economic growth may not enhance human welfare – what we could call 'development without growth'.

As noted above there are also numerous examples of countries that have achieved high rates of economic growth over several decades without this growth being translated into equivalent improvements in measures of human development. Ravallion (1996) argues that the presence of such outliers is interesting but distracts from the more general finding that the poor typically *do* share in the benefits of economic growth. To turn our attention back to this general finding the influential Indian economist Jagdish Bhagwati published a powerful book in 2013. It was suitably called: *Why Growth Matters: How Economic Growth in India Reduced Poverty and the Lessons for Other Developing Countries.* Where measures of human development remain low it is Ravallion suggests more often a case of low/no growth than low-quality growth. Rather than outliers the most important lesson according to Bhagwati and Ravallion is for researchers to focus on the regularity with which growth does promote human development.

Ranis *et al.* (2000) took the question to its final stage and explored the possibility of a two-way relationship between human development and economic growth. Economic growth provides resources to households and the government to invest in human development; more human development (a healthier and more educated labour force) promotes economic growth. Using data for

1960 to 1992 they showed that growth is good for human development and that GDP is positively affected by the initial level of life expectancy but less so by the rate of adult literacy. These results support the idea that a country could follow a virtuous circle with high levels of human development leading to high growth and high growth in turn further promoting human development (or spiral into an opposite and vicious circle). During these decades they found that eight developing countries had experienced virtuous growth: seven in East and South-East Asia, plus Botswana. Of the 37 countries experiencing a vicious circle 21 were from Sub-Saharan Africa and nine from Latin America.

Key points

- GDP growth can be defined as 'the increase in the total real value of all goods and services produced within a country in a single year'.
- There are huge inequalities in average living standards in the world economy today.
- There are three ways of thinking about growth discussed in this chapter: growth as a process of change, growth as progress towards an ideal end-state and growth as an assumption of progress.
- Growth as a process of change is discussed here in terms of GDP growth though there are distinct problems with the use of GDP.
- A more encompassing measure of change is that of freedoms/capabilities. There is only an indirect and uncertain link between incomes and freedoms/capabilities.
- Freedoms/capabilities are difficult to measure but have been proxied by life expectancy and the Human Development Index (HDI).
- Growth can be thought of as being progress towards an ideal end-state, that of a high-income 'developed' country.
- The idea of an ideal end-state is rarely so limited and many scholars have tried to define such an ideal; those discussed in detail here are basic needs, universal adequate nutrition and happiness. Each of them has only an uncertain link with economic growth.
- The notion of growth is one closely based on an assumption of progress.
- There are typically good and bad outcomes associated with economic growth.
- Though there is a close statistical relation between growth and measures of human development such as life expectancy and education the pattern of causation is not clear.
- There are many of examples of growth without development and development without growth.

Chapter 2

Growth in the Modern World Economy since 1950

In the period after 1950, most countries had largely recovered from the effects of the Second World War and were turning their attention to renewed growth rather than recovery. Accelerating economic growth became the key policy goal for many developed and developing countries. The newly formed United Nations (UN) made a substantial effort to develop improved and standardized GDP data presentation methods, which made economic data increasingly comparable across countries and made people increasingly aware of the gap between developed and developing countries. Newly emerging post-colonial countries focused on this gap and imbued it with various forms of nationalism to argue that without economic growth (and industrialization) they would remain vulnerable to exploitation and new forms of colonization. The emergence of Development Economics as a distinct discipline within Economics placed growth at the centre of its concerns and gave developing-country governments an array of policy tools to promote growth, including the 'big push' popularized by Paul Rosenstein-Rodan; 'balanced growth' from Ragnar Nurkse; and the 'take-off into self-sustained growth' from Walt Rostow. The politics of the Cold War gave the US government an incentive to promote poverty-reducing growth in its allies and client states, to ward off the temptations of communism. The apparent success of the USSR (the horrors of Stalinism were less well known in 1945) since 1917 gave many developing countries a role model of state intervention and rapid economic growth to aspire to.

This chapter looks at statistical methods of measuring the causal influences on growth, and at the economic drama and the many fascinating stories of growth since 1950. The stories, like all good drama, are often completely unpredictable. The USSR was in the 1950s seen as a serious rival to the US; by 1989 it was bankrupt and undergoing catastrophic economic collapse. Uganda and Ghana were among the most disastrous economic stories of post-independence Africa until the mid-1980s when both abruptly became celebrated success stories. The Nobel Prize-winning economist James Meade in his study of Mauritius in the 1960s forecasted doom. Mauritius was a tropical country, located far from large markets, it was dependent on exports of sugar which faced poor prospects in world markets and suffered from rapid population growth that looked set to overwhelm any increase in production. In terms of growth, exports and improvements in human welfare between the 1970s and

43

1990s Mauritius has been labelled a miracle. This chapter outlines some of those catastrophes, some of the miracles and many of those countries that muddled along somewhere in between.

Growth in the world economy since 1950

Growth statistics enable us to understand the big stories in the contemporary world economy: the 'golden age' of world economic growth after the 1950s; the decline of Britain and later the US; the rise of Japan, then South Korea, then China; the collapse of the USSR; and the (until very recently) ongoing stagnation in Sub-Saharan Africa.

The world in 1950 and sixty years later

Table 2.1 provides two snapshots of major economies, in 1950 and 2010. Japan's rapid growth enabled it to close the gap with the developed world and converge with Germany, France, the UK and the Netherlands by the early 1990s, before suffering twenty years of stagnant economic growth. In 1950 the UK was the second richest economy in the sample; by the 1990s it had fallen behind Italy, Germany, Japan and France before relatively rapid growth after the 1990s saw it overtake the latter three by the mid-2000s.

The UK's share of world industrial output fell from nearly a quarter in 1880 to only 3.5 per cent in 1998. The share of Western Europe was relatively stable between 1880 and 1913 at around 30 per cent, declined to 17.7 per cent in 1953 then recovered to 28 per cent in 1998. North America, which experienced rapid economic growth during both world wars, peaked in 1953 at 32 per cent, declining to 25 per cent in 1998. After 1953 Japan's share increased rapidly to

Table 2.1   *GDP in ten large economies, 1950 and 2010*

GDP per capita, 1990$	1950	2010
US	9,561	30,491
China	448	8,032
Japan	1,921	21,935
India	619	3,372
Germany	3,881	20,661
France	5,586	21,477
UK	6,939	23,727
Netherlands	5,996	24,303
Mexico	2,365	7,716
Former USSR	2,841	7,733

Source: Data from the Maddison Project (http://ggdc.net/maddison/maddison-project/home.htm).

15 per cent in 1998; China's somewhat less so to 6.3 per cent in 1998 (Crafts, 2004:52).

Much in line with our discussion in the Introduction, Lans Pritchett argues that 'Divergence in relative productivity levels and living standards is the dominant feature of modern economic history' (1997:3). He estimates that between 1870 and 1990 the ratio of per capita incomes between the richest and poorest countries increased by a factor of approximately five. There are exceptions to this trend, one of which is that among today's 24 developed (OECD) countries there has been strong convergence in per capita incomes. The poorest six (and richest five countries) in 1870 had the fastest (slowest) national growth rates until 1960. Such historical time series data has a built-in problem. Examining the growth story of the now high-income countries almost guarantees finding convergence. If they hadn't all had similar growth rates for an extended period they wouldn't be today clubbed together as high-income countries. The sample ignores countries that failed to converge, were rich and grew more slowly like Argentina, or were poor and continued to grow slowly.

The post-war boom and bust

The period 1950 to 1973 with its relatively rapid rates of growth encompassing both developed and developing countries has been labelled the 'golden age of capitalism'. This marked a sharp shift from the years of stagnation during the worldwide depression of the 1930s. The years after 1973 marked a significant slowdown in GDP growth rates across the developed world, most dramatically in Japan, and also a shift into stagnation in Africa. Two exceptions were China and India where growth rates accelerated (see Table 2.2).

The end of the 1980s saw the spectacular collapse of the USSR. Russian national income declined by 34 per cent in 1989–91, by a further 30 per cent in

Table 2.2 *Growth rates of real GDP per capita (average annual percentage changes)*

	1950–73	*1973–98*
UK	2.44	1.79
US	2.45	1.99
Germany	5.02	1.60
Brazil	3.73	1.37
China	2.86	5.39
India	1.40	2.91
Japan	8.05	2.34
Former USSR	3.36	−1.75
Africa	2.07	0.01

Source: Data compiled from Maddison (2006:186, 196, 216, 225).

1992, 10 per cent in 1993 and 25 per cent in 1994. In 1994 alone the output of the machine-building industry fell by more than 40 per cent. The fall in GDP was reflected in declining welfare. While luxury products made a sudden appearance in shops there were large falls in consumption of basic food and non-food items. The physical output of textiles and shoes fell by around half between 1991 and 1993 and cotton textile output fell by 38 per cent in 1992/93 alone. There was a sharp rise in morbidity and poverty. Between 1990 and 1993 the incidence of tuberculosis increased by 34 per cent, syphilis 300 per cent, whooping cough 72 per cent, and measles by 142 per cent. There was a large increase in crime with murders increasing by 42 per cent in 1992. Poverty (defined as insufficient food consumption to maintain a normal body weight at an average level of activity) increased to 37 per cent by the early 1990s. From having among the lowest death rates in the world in the early 1960s, the death rate in Russia by 1993 was on a par with those of Bangladesh and the Sudan (Nolan, 1995).

To put this in comparative perspective, during the Great Depression the US economy (after expanding by 5.02 per cent in 1929) contracted by about one-third between 1930 and 1933, or less than half that experienced in the USSR after 1989. The current global financial crisis that has caused such disquiet in the US led to a fall of 4 per cent in GDP in 2009 with positive growth in 2008 and 2010.

Episodes of growth and stagnation

Pritchett (2000) uses data on 111 countries beginning in 1960 and identifies six distinct patterns of sudden change in growth or as economists label it, 'structural break'. These included sudden accelerations (steep hills), accelerations followed by growth declines (mountains) and sudden collapses in growth (cliffs). Hausmann *et al.* (2004) find that growth accelerations are quite frequent and they identify more than 80 between 1957 and 1992. Apart from the number of accelerations the magnitude of acceleration is also striking. The average acceleration was 4.7 per cent per annum and there are many episodes of 7 per cent acceleration or more, such as Ghana in 1965 (8.4 per cent), Pakistan in 1962 (7.1 per cent) and Argentina in 1990 (9.2 per cent). Of the 110 countries studied, 54.5 per cent had at least one acceleration and 20.9 per cent two accelerations; Asia had 21, Africa 18, Latin America 17 and the Middle East and North Africa 10. Jones and Olken (2008) find that about 90 per cent of countries have converged with the US in this respect over some ten-year period.

The acceleration of growth in China after 1978 is striking, though (see Table 2.2) not much different from the earlier rise of Japan. Average GDP growth in China was around 10 per cent per annum between 1978 and 2005. In the late 1970s investment had reached 30 per cent of GDP, increasing further to 35 per cent in the 1990s and 40 per cent in 2004. This growth was reflected in improved welfare; housing space per person doubling between 1978 and

1992, and poverty (according to a World Bank estimated poverty line) fell from 270 million people in the late 1970s to 100 million in the late 1980s; and mortality rates improved for females and children of both sexes (Nolan, 1995; Naughton, 2007). Declining standards of nutrition (see Chapter 1) do not seem to have had an adverse impact on mortality rates in China.

In Sub-Saharan Africa, the long-term story since around 1960 is of slow or negative growth. The enduring problem in this region has not been starting but rather sustaining growth. Between 1965 and 1985 average GDP growth per capita was minus 1 per cent, meaning that countries with two-thirds of the population of Africa had lower per capita income in 1985 than in the mid-1970s. Between 1965 and 1980 agriculture in Sub-Saharan Africa grew by 2 per cent per annum, less than the rate of population growth. As well as long-term stagnation there are also interesting patterns of instability and volatility in growth. Ten African countries had growth of more than 6 per cent per annum between 1967 and 1980. These included some mineral-rich economies (Gabon, Botswana, Congo and Nigeria) and some without minerals (Kenya and Côte d'Ivoire) (Mkandawire, 2001). Many developing countries (in East Asia, Latin America, Sub-Saharan Africa and the Middle East) shared good growth performances in the 1960s and 1970s but only a small minority managed to sustain growth after the mid and late 1970s, and most of those were in East Asia (Rodrik, 1999). Economic performance in Sub-Saharan Africa has more recently improved markedly. Average GDP per capita growth (PPP) increased from –0.07 per cent between 1975 and 1994 to 1.88 per cent between 1995 and 2005. Africa's top performers are again comparing favourably with fast-growing countries in other regions. Arbache and Page (2009) ask how fragile this growth revival is. They find that resource-rich countries are more likely to experience growth accelerations than non-resource-rich countries, or as they put it, 'geology has trumped geography' (2009:3). Oil exporters have grown at 4.5 per cent per annum since 1995, double the region's growth rate. They find little evidence that better policies (changes in investment, trade, budget deficits, inflation or real exchange rates) or institutions (measures of institutions published by the World Bank) underpin the increased frequency of growth accelerations. Private investment, for example, only increased from 11.5 to 12.5 per cent of GDP in resource-rich countries. The dependence of this growth on raw material prices rather than policy change means that the growth revival remains 'fragile' to any future downturn in those prices (Arbache and Page, 2009). The case of Zambia, whose economic fortunes have long been tied to world copper prices, is discussed in Box 2.1.

The African equivalents of the 'Tiger Economies' of East Asia are those that show a sustained (six-year) increase in growth rates above the country's long-run (1975 to 2005) average (Arbache and Page, 2008). Eight countries, termed 'Leopards', fit this criterion (Angola, Botswana, Cape Verde, Chad, Mozambique, Sudan and Tanzania). Surprisingly, countries that have been widely praised as good performers, such as Ghana, Senegal, Rwanda and

Box 2.1   The revival of Zambia?

In Zambia copper and copper products account for almost 80 per cent of exports, though now only 6–9 per cent of Zambian GDP, and around 10 per cent of formal employment. After several decades of stagnation, encompassing years of rigorous state intervention and free trade and open markets, Zambia experienced average growth of nearly 5 per cent per annum in the 2000s. The cause of this growth is apparent – high copper prices. The price per tonne of copper increased from US$2,000 in 2002 to US$6,500 in 2007. This was led by demand from China, now the world's largest consumer of copper. Increased copper prices boosted the value of exports and (by Zambian standards) more mining-related foreign direct investment (FDI) to increase capacity in copper mines. By the mid-2000s Zambia was the third-largest host of Chinese FDI in Sub-Saharan Africa (and 19th in the world). Refurbishing mines and expanding capacity helped increase the aggregate investment rate to 27.1 per cent of GDP in 2003. Chinese FDI has included purchases of mines and the construction of a US$200 million copper smelter. Chambishi copper mine was bought and re-opened in 1998 and a new Chinese copper mine opened in Kitwe in late 2007, creating 1,500 jobs at a cost of $100 million. More FDI and expatriate mining engineers and investors brought with them new spending power. The South African-owned Shoprite supermarket chain expanded throughout Zambia in response. Initially Shoprite tended to import South African products, displacing local producers, but later they put an assistance programme in place to help small farmers and now source 90–95 per cent of their fresh produce from Zambia, although they still import most processed goods from South Africa. There is some evidence pointing to the fragility of this growth – specifically the failure of African economies generally to diversify the structure of their exports. In 2007 the Zambia–Chinese Mulungushi Textile Joint Venture with the Chinese government was closed down as it could not compete with cheap Chinese imports. This was the largest textile factory in Zambia, producing 17 million metres of fabric and 100,000 pieces of clothing a year, employing 1,000 people directly and around 5,000 cotton growers indirectly. The government budget has benefited little from the rapid growth of mining. In the early 2000s the mining sector enjoyed a marginal effective tax rate of approximately 0 per cent. Recall the work of Anand and Ravallion (1993) who found that two-thirds of the link between higher incomes and higher life expectancy runs through higher public spending. If mining profits are not taxed this mechanism is unlikely to operate in Zambia. More recently the government has started making some efforts to correct this and in the 2007 budget the mineral royalty tax was increased from 0.6 per cent to 3 per cent (Carmody, 2009).

Uganda, are not included. A concern about these potential Leopards is that five of them are resource-rich, and three (Angola, Chad and Sudan) have a long history of conflict. Mauritius, despite sustained growth, misses out (probably unfairly) because the definition is predicated on a recent acceleration in growth.

World inequality

A summary statistic that captures one aspect of all these growth stories is inequality between countries, and which indicates whether country income levels are tending to converge or diverge over time. A fuller measure of world inequality would also have to consider how the internal income distributions are changing over time but as most inequality in world income distribution reflects inequality between the country averages rather than inequality within countries (Wade, 2001) country-level growth rates are the crucial variable driving international patterns of inequality so are a good place to start. There is considerable debate as to how between-country inequality should be measured. First, how to measure income: whether GDP per capita should be converted to US dollars using market exchange rates or be adjusted for PPP across countries. Second, whether each country is weighted as one unit or by population (any results weighted by population tend to be dominated by what is happening in India and China), and third, which measure of inequality should be used. Some of the widely used measures of inequality include the Gini coefficient and the ratio of the income of the richest decile of world population to that of the poorest decile (Wade, 2002). The only method consistently showing declining between-country inequality uses population-weighted country per capita PPP-adjusted income (Jha, 2000; Dollar and Kraay, 2002). However, this method does not account for the rising inequality within many countries.

This focus on trends in inequality can distract our attention from the enormous scale of poverty and inequality. Roughly 85 per cent of world income (measured at market exchange rates) goes to 20 per cent of the world's population (Wade, 2002). More than a billion people live on incomes that are not sufficient to purchase the basic goods and services necessary to properly survive as human beings. The introduction to the book noted just how many decades it will take even those countries converging with developed-country living standards to close a significant portion of existing income gaps.

Introduction to the proximate causes of economic growth

The proximate causes of economic growth are the accumulation of factors of production (land, labour and capital) and the efficiency with which those factors are utilized – the total factor productivity (TFP). Methodologies used by scholars to explore their relationship with economic growth include cross-country regression analysis, growth accounting and case studies.

Cross-country growth regressions

Robert Barro's 1991 paper (see the Introduction) is a famous example of a cross-country growth regression. This method involves finding data on those factors economic theory considers important in influencing growth for as large a number of countries as possible over as long a time period as possible. Unfortunately the results from regressions remain very poor. Even those factors many would accept as self-evidently related to economic growth, such as investment, fiscal policy and education, have an ambiguous empirical relation to economic growth within cross-country regression analysis. These points are illustrated using regression results for Pakistan.

Investment can have either a direct link with growth (such as a new factory producing more output) or an indirect link (such as a new road increasing the incentives of farmers to expand production which can now be better marketed). Levine and Renelt (1992) took a number of variables commonly used in econometric growth analyses and ran them in thousands of regressions. They found that only investment was robustly related to economic growth. Evidence for Pakistan based on simple regression analysis supports this general finding. Khan *et al.* (2005) find a positive relation between investment and growth in Pakistan between 1971 and 2004. Khan (2005) finds a positive relation between investment and GDP growth between 1980 and 2002. Iqbal and Zahid (1998) find a positive relation between investment and growth between 1959/60 and 1996/97. This link is even stronger when looking at sub-components of overall investment. De Long and Summers (1991, 1992, 1993) and Jones (1994) found a positive correlation between investment in machinery and equipment and productivity growth. While transport investment reflects differences in needs caused by urbanization, geography and population density, equipment, they argue, is more directly linked to growth in the manufacturing sector.

There remains a problem with identifying causality in the investment–growth relation. Blomstrom *et al.* (1996) find an inverse causal relation between growth and investment. Growth induces subsequent capital formation (perhaps firms creating capacity to meet expected increases in market demand) for their sample of 101 countries between 1965 and 1985. A particular theoretical question relevant for empirical studies of the investment–growth relation is that of 'credibility'. Rodrik (1989) argues that only a 'credible' policy change will be likely to promote growth in the private sector. Credibility can be thought of as a policy change the private sector thinks the government are committed to and will sustain. If, for example, private entrepreneurs believe an investment tax incentive will be later rescinded they won't undertake any long-term investment in response. Credibility is a very difficult concept to test using cross-country regression techniques (and is discussed in more detail in Chapter 5).

Fiscal policy can affect the proximate determinants of growth by changing the incentives for investment (Rebelo, 1991). Barro (1991) found a significant negative association between the ratio of real government consumption (minus spending on education and defence) and economic growth. In Pakistan, Tahir (1995) found government defence expenditure had a positive, Iqbal and Zahid (1998) found the government budget deficit had a negative and Ghani and Ud-Din (2006) found government consumption had a positive relation with GDP growth. More generally Levine and Renelt (1992) found no robust relation between growth and the ratio of total government expenditure to GDP, government consumption expenditure, capital formation, or educational expenditure.

Education has been understood as 'human capital' in growth analysis. Human capital can directly raise the productivity of labour or facilitate the absorption of new technology and so raise TFP. The results from empirical testing remain poor and ambiguous. Pritchett (2001) finds a *negative* correlation between higher school enrolment and TFP growth in developing countries, a paradoxical finding due to an incentive structure commonly found in developing countries that diverts talented individuals to privately profitable (they offer high wages) but socially wasteful activities and to policies that reduce the demand for skilled labour (such as import tariffs that hinder the importation of advanced technology from abroad). As has been more memorably expressed, if it is more profitable to be a pirate than an engineer, people will be pirates and the economy will suffer. Bils and Klenow (2000) find evidence of reverse causation: economic growth increases the expected return from and so incentives to acquire education. These ambiguities are reflected in empirical studies of the education–growth link in Pakistan. Khan (2005) finds positive and significant results linking literacy rates, average years of schooling, and gross secondary school enrolment to GDP growth. Iqbal and Zahid (1998) find various measures of education including primary, secondary and high school enrolment, are either insignificantly or negatively related to GDP growth. Khan (2005) finds that education expenditures have no clear link with TFP growth.

A theme running throughout this literature is the problem of finding a measure of human capital (Mankiw *et al.*, 1992:418–19). Education investment includes direct spending (by the individual, family and state) and indirect cost (forgone earnings). Much schooling is provided free at the point of use and there is an inherent difficulty in measuring the output or productivity of teaching and hence in constructing any numerical measure of 'education investment'. A common measure used in much statistical work is the share of the working-age population in secondary school. This fails to measure the quality of education (influenced by teacher absenteeism), those instances where enrolment rates bear little resemblance to actual children in school being educated or the learning on the job that takes place in the workforce. Hanushek and Woessman (2009) in recent work have used internationally comparable test data to try and measure the *quality* of education. This data, though avoiding many of the problems with earlier data, is difficult and expensive to collect so is not yet available for a particularly broad cross-section of countries. Many of the benefits from education are non-material, such as female empowerment and reduced fertility (see Chapter 1 on Sen and 'capabilities'). Finally, not all expenditure on education is intended to generate productive human capital; much is about improving the ability of an individual to participate in wider social processes.

There are many more general reasons for these weak empirical results. The most obvious is the statistical problem of correctly measuring the variable of theoretical interest (for example using school enrolment to try and capture human capital). In regression analysis policy variables are typically added to regressions separately which allows for no interaction between and among them. Economic theory suggests complementarity is important. Education, for example, may only be related to growth if individuals earn higher wages as engineers rather than as pirates. Cross-country growth regressions often test the relationship between the rate of economic growth and the level of government expenditure. Any government using Keynesian-style demand management policies will be likely to boost government spending when GDP growth slows. This will generate a spurious negative relation between the 'size' of government and economic growth. Growth effects may be contemporaneous, some take several years (changed investment incentives), others even decades (incentives affecting the rate of technical change), which is difficult to capture in statistical testing. Some policy variables may have output/growth effects at all three horizons – cyclical, transitional and steady-state. There is no reason to assume these are of the same magnitude or even the same sign (Temple, 1999:124). Higher taxes, for example, may reduce growth in the short term by reducing demand in the economy but boost growth in the longer term by providing the government with a source of revenue to invest in education and infrastructure.

In order to run large cross-country regressions researchers are making the assumption of universalism: that the relation between a factor like education and growth is identical across countries so each individual country provides evidence that can be used to help measure this one underlying universal economic relationship. Many studies explain Africa's slower growth as a function of different levels of explanatory variables: that the population is less literate, or that Africa has a more unforgiving climate or a more adverse colonial history. This method seeks to explain African growth as the result of a common worldwide growth process that begins from different levels of the same explanatory variables. However significant regional effects remain common in much of the empirical literature. As we saw in the Introduction, Barro found the growth process worked differently in Sub-Saharan Africa and Latin America from the rest of the world. The usual reaction to this finding is that if the statistical effort is failing to explain growth in particular countries or regions there must be missing variables which then need to be discovered. This has led researchers to propose and test ever more variables in the hope that growth in Sub-Saharan Africa will finally be 'explained'. An alternative methodology is to drop the assumption that only the levels of explanatory variables are different and explore the idea that the growth process in Sub-Saharan Africa works differently (McCartney, 2011). There are a limited number of studies that suggest this latter idea may be true. Block (2001) finds that trade openness in Sub-Saharan Africa has a much stronger effect and fiscal policy a weaker effect on growth than in other regions. Brock and Durlauf find 'the operation of ethnic heterogeneity on growth is different in Africa' (2001:264). Mosley (2000) finds that inequality only has a negative impact on growth in regions other than Sub-Saharan Africa. The broader implication of this discussion is that growth is not a universal process, cross-country growth regressions are an intrinsically poor mechanism to analyze growth and each growth experience should be treated as potentially unique, that is, as a case study.

Case studies of boom and bust

The use of case-study research rather than statistical methods in economics has declined, as the former were increasingly regarded as subjective, non-rigorous and non-replicable (Gerring, 2007:5–6). Several scholars have more recently attempted to provide rigour for the case-study approach (Sambanis, 2003; Yin, 2003; George and Bennett, 2005; Gerring, 2007).

Barro-style cross-country growth regressions seek to measure the impact of a change in one variable (perhaps literacy rates) on the dependent variable (GDP growth). The statistical testing procedure then throws up various criteria by which a researcher can judge how reliable that estimate is, but the method does not examine the reasons for the relation. Does literacy have a positive impact on economic growth because it makes workers more productive or because it allows firms to use more complex technology? In the latter case education would not have a positive impact on economic growth unless it was also possible for firms to acquire that new technology. Case studies can examine any form of causal process in more detail. Econometrics typically focuses on a linear (straight-line) relation between a policy variable and economic growth: for example, an increase in investment will have the same impact on growth, whether investment is increasing from 2 to 3 per cent of GDP or 32 to 33 per cent of GDP. The 'big push' theory, for example, argues that self-sustaining growth will only occur once investment has reached a critical threshold and until that point investment is likely to have little impact on growth.

The use of case studies to examine the causal mechanism is called 'process tracing' (George and Bennett, 2005:205). This method involves the researcher putting together a detailed narrative inspired by economic theory and supported by rigorous empirical evidence to analyze a whole sequence of possible causal/historical processes. All intervening steps between cause and effect can be taken into account and each step be preceded by a consideration of relevant economic theory and evidence (Gerring, 2007:181). Comparative case-study analysis has been useful, for example, in distinguishing the paradox between deep reform and stagnation in post-Soviet Russia and moderate/heterodox/gradual reform and rapid growth in 1980s China (Nolan, 1995).

A common criticism of the case-study methodology is that there is no formal method of case-study selection, leading to a frequent suspicion that the analytical results will be pre-determined by the choice of the case study: for example, the case studies of growth among 'now-developed' countries pre-determined the finding of convergence discussed earlier in this chapter. A useful finding from this chapter is that growth and stagnation occur in distinct episodes. These episodes can be utilized as easily identifiable case studies and the economic, political, institutional and policy conditions that accompany these break points can then be examined as a case study.

For example, Hausman *et al.* (2004) find that the vast majority of growth accelerations are unrelated to standard determinants such as political change or economic reform. They find that only 14.5 per cent of growth accelerations are associated with liberalization and 85.5 per cent are not. Jong-a-Pin and De Haan (2011), using an index containing a number of features (presence of marketing boards, a socialist economic regime, a large black-market premium for foreign currency and tariff and non-tariff barriers to trade) to measure 'liberalization', find a significant link between changes in their index and subsequent accelerations in growth. Various scholars have found that trade has quite consistently expanded for African countries undergoing growth accelerations (Hausman *et al.*, 2004; Jones and Olken, 2008). However, this was caused not by greater trade liberalization increasing the volume of imports and exports, but by the expansion of trade (particularly through higher commodity prices) after 1995 among the resource-rich countries.

Evidence linking specific policies to growth acceleration is also mixed but does offer some clearer results. Exchange rate depreciations are commonly found in the general literature to have been associated with growth accelerations (Hausman *et al.*, 2004). There is clear evidence to show that the extent of exchange rate overvaluation declined sharply in Africa after the 1990s so the timing does seem to be closely linked to growth accelerations. The real effective exchange rate in Africa, for example, halved between 1975 and 1994, and from 1995 to 2005 (Arbache and Page, 2009:19).

Increased investment is also commonly associated with growth episodes in both developing and developed countries (Hausman *et al.*, 2004; Jones and Olken, 2008), with the exception of Africa. Here, increased growth after 2000 was accompanied by only marginally increased investment rates: from 15.25 per cent share of GDP between 1975 and 1994 to 16.69 per cent between 1995 and 2005 (Arbache and Page, 2009:19). This remains a long way below the 30 per cent+ shares of investment experienced by East Asian countries during their economic booms of the 1970s and 1980s, and by China after 1980 and India after 2003. Africa joined the wave of global democratization in the 1990s and beyond. Although political and popular sentiment has often linked this to improved macroeconomic outcomes after 2000, scholars have found find that autocracy has a strong and positive relation to growth episodes (Hausman *et al.*, 2004), that autocracies are 70 per cent more likely to experience growth accelerations (Jones and Olken, 2008) and even that democracy is a robust predictor of growth declines (Cuberes and Jerzmanowski, 2009). Jong-a-Pin and De Haan (2011) are unusual in finding that a move towards democratization is often associated with growth episodes but that this effect is only temporary and declines the longer the democracy has been in place.

Growth accounting

Growth accounting gives life to the formula for the proximate determinants of growth by calculating the impact of factor inputs and TFP but severe empirical problems are associated with this method. The measurement of TFP, for example, depends critically on assumptions about how the various factors of production are translated into output, and there are problems with accounting for the quality of inputs. A further problem is aggregating all the roads, computers, buildings and tractors in which individuals, households and firms have invested into one measure of the capital stock and then accounting for depreciation.

Growth accounting is not a formal test of any economic theory. This book makes the simplifying assumption that the accumulation of factors of production or productivity growth (TFP) causes economic growth, but there are other potential arguments. This chapter has discussed a number of studies that suggest economic growth stimulates the incentive to acquire greater levels of education (human capital), so that the causal relation can work the other way round.

The Solow Surprise
One of the earliest attempts at growth accounting was by Nobel Prize winner Robert Solow who argued in a 1957 paper that the key source of long-term growth is technological change. He found that TFP growth accounted for nearly 90 per cent of US growth per worker over the first half of the twentieth century. This finding undermined many early Development Economics theories that physical investment was the key to boosting economic growth. More recent work has tended to support this finding (Klenow and Rodriguez-Clare, 1997; Easterly and Levine, 2000). Mankiw *et al.* (1992), exceptionally, disagreed with the Solow Surprise. They argued that 80 per cent of the international variation in country per capita incomes could be explained using only population growth and investment in physical and human capital. This finding was based on two controversial assumptions: first, that investment rates are not related to the level of income; and second, the human capital variable only measures the variation in secondary schooling (and ignores primary schooling) so exaggerates the variation in human capital across countries. When correcting for these Klenow and Rodriguez-Clare find that the Mankiw *et al.* model only explains around half of the variation in incomes and does leave a central role for technology and productivity.

Growth accounting and developed countries
We can use growth accounting to draw some interesting comparative historical conclusions. The general story for the UK, US and Japan in the modern era is that growth has been based on productivity gains (improving factors of production rather than accumulating more of them). Growth has been based on a better educated workforce, using more and better capital equipment and

Table 2.3   *Hours worked in now-developed countries, 1870–1998*

	UK	US	Japan
	Hours worked per person employed		
1870	2,984	2,964	2,945
1913	2,624	2,605	2,588
1950	1,958	1,867	2,166
1973	1,688	1,594	2,042
1998	1,489	1,610	1,758

Source: Data compiled from Maddison (2006:347).

working for shorter hours, in contrast with much of the nineteenth century when growth was based on accumulating more factors of production. Recall from the Introduction the debates about the role of 'labour' in driving the Industrial Revolution in England. This story also agrees with the Solow theory that growth in high-income countries tends to be based on productivity increase rather than factor accumulation. Table 2.3 shows that in the UK, US and Japan hours worked per head of population increased significantly in the early nineteenth century but declined after 1870 and especially after 1913.

Falling working hours were accompanied by rising average years of education per person employed, though at a slower pace over time: in the UK from an average of 2 years of education per person employed in 1820 to 4.44 in 1870, 10.6 in 1950 and 15.79 in 2003; in the US from 1.75 to 3.92, to 11.27 and 20.77; and in Japan from 1.50 to 1.50, to 9.11 and 16.78 (Maddison, 2007:305). The quality of the labour force, as we saw in the Introduction, played but a small part in the early stages of the Industrial Revolution in England.

There were dramatic increases in the gross stock of machinery and equipment per capita, especially in Japan (a 25-fold expansion between 1950 and 2003). In the US (five-fold) and the UK (seven-fold) the growth of the capital stock was much slower, which in part reflected lower investment rates and an earlier shift than Japan away from an industrial to a service-based economy which is less dependent on investment in physical machinery and equipment to sustain output growth (Maddison, 2007:305).

Table 2.4 shows that shorter working hours, better education and more capital equipment contributed to a massive increase in labour productivity measured in terms of GDP per hours worked: between 1950 and 1973 a doubling in the US and UK and a six-fold increase in Japan; and in the thirty years to 2003 another doubling in all three.

Table 2.5 divides the world economy after 1945 into two spells, the 'golden age' prior to 1973 and the twenty years that followed. The contribution of labour inputs to growth was consistently higher in the US than other developed

Table 2.4   *Labour productivity in now-developed countries, 1870–1998*

	UK	US	Japan
		GDP per hour worked (1990 $)	
1870	2.55	2.25	0.46
1913	4.31	5.12	1.08
1950	7.93	12.65	2.08
1973	15.97	23.72	11.57
1998	27.45	34.55	22.54

Source: Data compiled from Maddison (2006:351).

Table 2.5   *Growth-accounting breakdown of sources of growth (average annual percentage changes)*

	Capital (%)	Labour (%)	TFP (%)	Output
1950–73				
Japan	3.1 (34%)	2.5 (27%)	3.6 (39%)	9.2
UK	1.6 (53%)	0.2 (7%)	1.2 (40%)	3.0
US	1.0 (26%)	1.3 (33%)	1.6 (41%)	3.9
West Germany	2.2 (37%)	0.5 (8%)	3.3 (55%)	6.0
1973–92				
Japan	2.0 (53%)	0.8 (21%)	1.0 (26%)	3.8
UK	0.9 (53%)	0.0 (0%)	0.7 (44%)	1.6
US	0.9 (38%)	1.3 (54%)	0.2 (8%)	2.4
West Germany	0.9 (39%)	–0.1 (–4%)	1.6 (65%)	2.3

Source: Data compiled from Crafts (1999:25).

countries owing to higher migration levels. In general the contribution of labour to growth has been promoted by higher levels of human capital (education) and undermined by declining hours and slowing population growth. There were across-the-board slowdowns in the growth rates of factors of production (labour and capital) and also in growth of TFP after 1973. In Japan, for example, TFP growth was 3.6 per cent between 1950 and 1973 and only 1.0 per cent between 1973 and 1992. Although we have characterized TFP as driving growth in developed countries it nevertheless slowed dramatically in absolute terms after 1973. Scholars are still not clear what explains this general effect across the developed world.

Growth accounting and developing countries
Table 2.6 shows that, contrary to the Solow hypothesis, capital made a larger contribution to growth than productivity (TFP) in developing countries. Population growth also tends to be higher in developing countries and this is

Table 2.6 *Sources of growth in developing countries, 1960–94 (average annual percentage changes)*

	Capital (%)	Labour (%)	TFP (%)	Output
East Asia	3.4 (50%)	2.3 (34%)	1.1 (16%)	6.8
South Asia	1.8 (43%)	1.6 (38%)	0.8 (19%)	4.2
Latin America	1.8 (43%)	2.2 (52%)	0.2 (5%)	4.2
Africa	1.7 (59%)	1.8 (62%)	−0.6 (−21%)	2.9
Middle East	2.5 (56%)	2.3 (51%)	−0.3 (−7%)	4.5

Source: Data compiled from Crafts (1999:26).

Table 2.7 *Sources of growth: China, India, and East Asia, 1978–2004 (percentage average annual GDP increase)*

Period/ country	Output	Employment	Output per worker	Contribution to output per worker of Physical capital	Education	TFP
1978–2004 China	9.3	2.0	7.3	3.2	0.3	3.6
1978–2004 India	5.4	2.0	3.3	1.3	4.0	1.6
1978–1993 China	8.9	2.5	6.4	2.4	0.4	3.5
1978–1993 India	4.5	2.1	2.4	0.9	0.3	1.1
1993–2004 China	9.7	1.2	8.5	4.2	0.3	3.9
1993–2004 India	6.5	1.9	4.6	1.8	0.4	2.3

Source: Data compiled from Bosworth and Collins (2008:49).

reflected in the consistently high contributions of labour. TFP growth has made a negligible contribution in all developing regions, even turning negative in both Africa and the Middle East. The contribution of capital being higher in poorer countries confirms another important idea, that of diminishing returns to investment (see Chapter 5).

Both China and India had very low per capita incomes in 1980; India's was roughly equal to the World Bank average for all low-income countries, and China's about two-thirds of that level. By 2004 GDP per capita had roughly doubled in India and risen seven-fold in China. Table 2.7 shows that average GDP growth in China and India averaged 9.3 and 5.4 per cent respectively between 1978 and 2004. Both countries experienced an acceleration of growth in output per worker after 1993. In both China and India the growth in output per worker is equally split between increases in physical and human capital per worker and gains in TFP (although absolute values for China are twice those for India). The contribution of physical capital to India's growth remained below those evident during the investment-led rapid growth experiences of East Asia. By contrast China achieved an investment rate comparable to that of East Asia between 1978 and 1993 and in more recent years has achieved an even higher rate.

Comparisons are not often made between the former Soviet Union and super-successful Singapore. Paul Krugman (1994), however, notes some striking similarities in their patterns of growth. Rapid Soviet growth was based on an immense state-led effort to mobilize factors of production: shifting labour and resources from agriculture to higher-productivity industry and women from the household to the factory; increasing hours of male employment; a massive expansion of education; and suppressing levels of consumption to raise the rate of saving. 'Communist growth rates were certainly impressive but not magical. The rapid growth in output could be fully explained by rapid growth in inputs' (1994:63). Krugman argued that 'Popular enthusiasm about Asia's boom deserves to have some cold water thrown on it' (1994:64). Growth rates of 8.5 per cent (6.6 per cent per capita) in Singapore between 1966 and 1990 were 'based on perspiration rather than inspiration' (1994:70). The perspiration consisted of raising the employed share of the population from 27 to 51 per cent, raising educational standards (in 1966 more than half had no formal education at all and by the 1990s two-thirds completed secondary education) and raising investment as a share of output from 11 to more than 40 per cent. The Singaporean economy, according to Krugman, had always been relatively efficient, but was previously starved of capital and educated workers: 'If there is a secret to Asian growth, it is simply deferred gratification, the willingness to sacrifice current satisfaction for future gain' (1994:78). Young (1995) accepts the thesis of negligible TFP growth in Singapore. He argues that the state-directed Singaporean economy had forced its citizens to save too much and pushed itself too fast up the technological ladder without fully realizing the benefits of learning and consequent productivity gains at each stage, but this is a pessimistic view. It is more likely that the rapid rate of TFP growth has been underestimated by such studies. Without TFP growth the very high rates of investment would have quickly run into diminishing returns. The rapid diversification of exports could not have happened without East Asian countries successfully mastering new technology and producing those new exports to a decent and competitive standard. In 1960, for example, Taiwan produced virtually no electronic goods and by 1990 these accounted for more than 20 per cent of all manufacturing exports.

Key points

- Since 1950 there have been huge improvements in the production of standardized national accounts, making GDP figures comparable across countries and over time.
- There are many interesting patterns in the growth story of the modern world economy.
- The rapid growth of Japan enabled it to close the gap with the developed world and overtake Germany, France, the UK and Italy by the early 1990s.
- The UK was the second richest economy in the world in 1950 and by the 1990s it had fallen behind Germany, Japan, Italy and France.
- The growth experience of China after 1978 is striking though not particularly different from the earlier rise of Japan.
- The general story in Sub-Saharan Africa since 1960 is of slow or negative growth, though there has been a revival of growth in the 2000s.
- The economy of Russia collapsed at the end of the 1980s.
- The world economy grew rapidly during the years 1950 to 1973, after which there was a generalized slowdown. Two exceptions were China and India where growth rates accelerated.
- The proximate causes of economic growth have been analyzed and measured in three principal ways: cross-country growth regressions, case studies of boom and bust, and growth accounting.
- Results from growth-accounting exercises show a general pattern of growth based on TFP in developed countries and growth based on factor accumulation (especially investment) in developing countries.
- The use of relatively long averages hides an important empirical regularity about growth in the modern world economy, its instability and volatility.
- Lans Pritchett argues that 'Divergence in relative productivity levels and living standards is the dominant feature of modern economic history'.

Chapter 3

Domestic and Foreign Direct Investment

We can all agree that investment is a good thing. Or can we? It is certainly true that exhaustive testing by Levine and Renelt (1992) showed that no other variable had such a close association with economic growth. Many commentators equate more investment with good economics. For them investment is the forgoing of present consumption in order to create an asset that will generate an expected future return. An important part of this definition is 'create'. Economists use the term 'investment' much more specifically than is commonly understood. Investment to an economist does not mean the buying of shares or other assets. This is more properly referred to as 'portfolio investment' and represents the transfer of ownership, or part ownership, of existing assets. Investment in this sense is not discussed here. Investment necessarily requires a reduction in resources available for current consumption, and the creation of productive assets to (hopefully) generate higher consumption in the future. So investment proper is all about being virtuous, reducing current consumption to create something for the future, about thinking long term and contributing to sustainable economic growth.

However, this is not always true. A household may cut down on frivolous consumption of alcohol in order to invest in a child's schooling. Or the choice could be made by a dictator. In the late 1920s and early 1930s Stalin, the Soviet dictator, forcibly requisitioned grain from peasants to facilitate the expansion of output and employment in urban heavy industry. Industrial growth was rapid but millions of peasants starved. Current consumption in North Korea over recent years has been reduced to the extent that many observers believe there has been a substantial famine. Investment was increased, not as under Stalin to boost industrialization but rather to build a nuclear bomb. A market or capitalist economy may stimulate investment as firms struggle to gain a competitive edge over their rivals, to reduce costs or introduce new products and processes. Investment by one firm may then drive others out of business. The history of capitalism is littered with examples of firms, industries or entire economies making huge investments that are simply mistaken. Not all investment projects will generate a future return. A firm may invest in expanding capacity, but find there is no market for the extra output and so realize no gain. Some projects labelled as 'investment' were never about creating future returns, but had a completely different motivation. In 1983 President

Houphouet-Boigny of the Côte d'Ivoire moved the capital from Abidjan to his home village Yamoussoukro, where he constructed a five-star hotel, motorway, conference centre and a cathedral. There was no economic rationale or prospect of any future return from this 'investment' which would probably be better labelled as grandiose consumption. This chapter explores when, where and how investment can be good for economic growth.

Investment and economic growth

Investment as a proximate determinant of growth influences both supply and demand conditions in an economy. Unless there is underutilized capacity, investment to increase the productive capacity of the economy is likely to be required for economic growth. This could be direct investment in new plant and equipment (including improved technology), or indirect investment in infrastructure – increased power supply for example – to enable an expansion of textile production. Keynes argued that investment also has an important influence on growth via demand (see Box 3.2 on p. 72). Investment typically accounts for some 10–30 per cent of aggregate spending and consequently increases consumer spending power and so the market for producers. Investment also influences growth through education and productivity. Investment in human capital may improve the productivity of the labour force. These linkages are shown in Figure 3.1.

Some advisers treat investment as a variable that can be chosen by governments. Calls to 'increase investment' typically occupy a central place in economic policy-making. To take one typical example; for the first South African multi-racial elections in 1994 the African National Congress (ANC) argued in their election manifesto:

> As a legitimate government, the ANC will be able to work with others to create an environment of peace and stability, boosting investor confidence.

Figure 3.1   *Investment and economic growth*

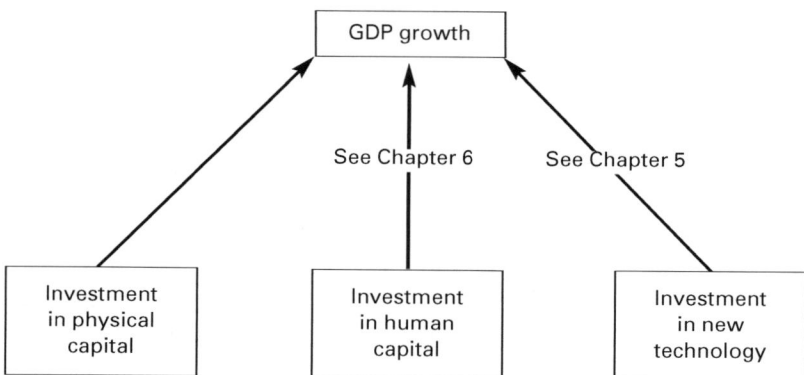

The international community is already responding positively to our call for massive investments.

In 1994 South Africa invested around 17 per cent of GDP. Over the following decade the ANC government adopted a very free-market economic policy, was open to international trade and investment, offered strong incentives to domestic and foreign investors, and maintained a stable democratic political system. This stance was both promoted by, and widely praised by, international organizations like the IMF and World Bank. After ten years there had been absolutely no change in the investment ratio, which still hovered around 17 per cent of GDP. Consequently growth rates were disappointingly slow and little dent was made in South Africa's very high levels of poverty.

Policy, expectations, and shocks (such as sudden increases in the price of oil) clearly influence investment. Investment rates often fluctuate dramatically, indicating that they are influenced over the short and medium term by more than a fixed deep determinant. In Zambia, for example, investment as a share of GDP dropped from 41 per cent in 1975 to 14 per cent in 1979. In China during the Great Leap Forward investment increased from 12 per cent of GDP in 1957 to 31 per cent in 1960. As discussed above the most important explanation for inequalities in the contemporary world economy is not fluctuations over a few years but instead relentless economic processes that persist through decades. Short-term factors like policy and shocks cannot explain why for decades investment rates were more than 30 per cent of GDP in much of East Asia and less than 10 per cent of GDP in Sub-Saharan Africa, or why

---

Box 3.1 Karl Marx and the crucial importance of investment

The ownership of capital was a crucial determinant of Karl Marx's theory of exploitation, social and economic change. It marked the division of capitalist society into two different classes. In a pre-industrial, pre-capitalist society most production is conducted on a small scale, by craftsmen who own their capital equipment and small farmers who own their land and implements. In an industrial-capitalist economy the scale of production increases enormously and tends to be organized into ever larger units. All the capital equipment (what Marx called the means of production) is owned by a small class of capitalists, whilst the bulk of the population, the workers, own only their labour. Capitalists own the capital equipment and control the human capital embodied in the labour they employ, from which they earn a profit. Workers perform labour services for the capitalists, from which they earn a wage. To undercut rivals capitalists are driven to invest and expand the scale of production, which boosts profits and provides the key dynamic driving the economy forward. Capitalists also boost their profits by squeezing workers' incomes below the value of their productivity (exploitation) which contributes to conflict between the two classes.

investment rates surged to over 40 per cent of GDP in response to generous tax incentives in Singapore in the 1980s and 1990s, yet similar incentives in Pakistan over the 1990s led to investment falling to below 20 per cent of GDP. Part II of this book analyses the deeper determinants of economic growth.

Some scholars (see Box 3.1) view investment as far more than just a driver of economic growth.

Investment: the basic concepts

Investment can be divided into physical and human capital. Physical capital investment includes expenditure on buildings, machines, and infrastructure by households, firms or the government. Human capital investment includes education and learning-by-doing. Learning for its own sake, perhaps philosophy rather than engineering, would not then count as investment. There is an obvious problem in measuring additions to the aggregate capital stock (investment). All of the existing machinery, roads, buildings and human capital must be measured, valued and summed. This is a large statistical exercise, which may not be possible at all in poor developing countries where much investment occurs at the level of small-scale production by the household and goes unrecorded.

There is an important distinction between gross and net investment. Gross investment is aggregate addition to the (physical and human) capital stock, usually measured over the course of twelve months. However the capital stock will deteriorate over time. Roads will break up, machines will become less reliable and cost more to maintain. Even human capital will atrophy as learned skills become obsolete.

A true measure of real investment is net investment, so:

Present capital stock = Prior capital stock + Net investment
where
Net investment = Gross investment – Depreciation

Again, this is very hard to estimate so company accountants and economists use rules of thumb. The British tax system, for example, assumes that the real value of buildings depreciates by 4 per cent per year, and plant and machinery by 20 per cent per year.

Robust empirical results and an elusive quest

The literature that explores the link between investment and GDP growth is both reassuring and confusing. It offers two widely accepted conclusions. First, that investment is robustly related to economic growth (reassuring), and second that investment fails to explain observed growth rates and differences in growth between countries (confusing). In other words, investment has a significant and positive relationship with economic growth but the causal relationship is weaker than other proximate causes of growth. One economist calls this 'an elusive quest for growth'. This section reviews these findings and argues that the small impact of investment is wrong for developing countries.

Robust empirical results

Many early models of economic growth dating from the 1940s and 1950s, developed by economists such as Roy Harrod, Evsey Domar and Arthur Lewis, placed investment at the centre of their analysis. As countries shook off colonial rule from the mid-1950s onwards, newly formed independent governments turned to such theories in their efforts to boost growth rates. These theories had clear, if simplistic, policy implications. Increasing growth required more investment which in turn required some combination of higher domestic savings and more foreign exchange (the latter if imported machinery was necessary). Government intervention was often seen as necessary to mobilize those extra savings, and to ensure that scarce foreign exchange was not frittered away on imported consumer goods. This thinking also influenced the international aid industry that grew up after the 1950s. Economists could calculate the GDP growth rate required in a developing country to promote industrialization and reduce poverty at a reasonable rate. The investment rate required for this growth could be compared with existing and future resources available from domestic savings, government tax revenue and foreign exchange (export revenue). Donors could then plug the gap with a mixture of loans and grants. William Easterly notes that between 1950 and 1995 Western countries gave $1trillion (measured in 1985 dollars) in aid mostly using this method or what he calls the 'financing gap approach'. This was, he suggests, 'one of the largest policy experiments based on a single economic theory' (Easterly, 2001b:33).

Both cross-country growth regressions and growth accounting (see Chapter 2) have found a positive relationship between investment and economic growth. Numerous cross-country growth regressions find investment to be positively linked with economic growth. Thus Islam (1995) finds that physical (and human capital) leads to more rapid economic growth, and Ojo and Oshikoya (1995) find that investment has a positive impact on growth among 17 African countries between 1970 and 1991. There are inevitable problems in demonstrating a causal link between investment and economic growth. The theory discussed above proposes that investment can drive economic growth through augmenting capacity. The inverse is also possible; economic growth can drive investment. According to the British economist John Maynard Keynes a growing economy with expanding markets and rising profits may motivate the 'animal spirits' of entrepreneurs to invest (see Box 3.2 on p. 72). So investment can be both a cause and effect of economic growth. One study using a sample of 101 countries between 1965 and 1988 confirms this point, finding that past growth has a significant effect on current investment (Blomstrom *et al.*, 1996).

Another problem is that the positive relation between investment and growth can be strongly influenced by the presence of a few outliers. For example a study of 29 African countries using data from 1970 to 1997 showed that private investment had a significant, positive and strong effect on growth, (even after attempting to control for its causality) (Devarajan *et al.*, 2003). However this study also found that private investment was only correlated with growth if Botswana (being the only high-growth, high-investment country in Africa) was included in the sample. While much of this book shows how particular case studies exhibit different patterns from the typical experience, this is an example of how one unusual case can drive an entire statistical relation. Such problems with outliers show how the statistical findings may not survive changes in the sample such as dropping some data points (here Botswana) or testing different regions of the world economy or using data drawn from different time periods. Statistical work on growth now checks the robustness of such findings. Using a much larger sample than Africa the positive relationship between investment and growth is not found to depend on a few outliers. Most countries in the world are high-investment/high-growth, low-investment/low-growth or reassuringly somewhere in the middle on both variables.

Despite these statistical problems the early development economists had hit upon an important truth. Investment does have a real causal relation with economic growth. In fact, no other variable has such a robust positive relation with economic growth as does investment. Levine and Renelt (1992) compared the impact of a number of variables that economists had suggested were important in explaining economic growth. These included fiscal policy indicators, international trade and price distortions, monetary policy and political indicators. They collected data for 119 countries for the years 1960 to 1989. They found that only the investment share of GDP showed a consistently positive and robust correlation with economic growth.

But still an elusive quest

Although investment has a robust and positive relation with economic growth it does not explain everything. Other factors are more important in explaining economic growth variations over time and between countries. For example, The Gambia and Japan both increased their capital stock per worker by over 500 per cent between 1960 and 1985. In the Gambia output per worker rose 2 per cent and in Japan it rose by 260 per cent (Easterly, 2001b:67). Easterly and Levine argue strongly that the attention given to investment is misplaced; it is the *productivity* of the investment which matters. They say that the 'central problem in understanding economic development and growth is *not* understanding the process by which an economy raises its savings rate and increases the rate of physical capital accumulation' (2001:177). Easterly (2001b) does not accept that the link between investment and growth is robust or strong enough, and argues that there is still an 'elusive quest for growth'.

Figure 3.2 *Diminishing returns to investment*

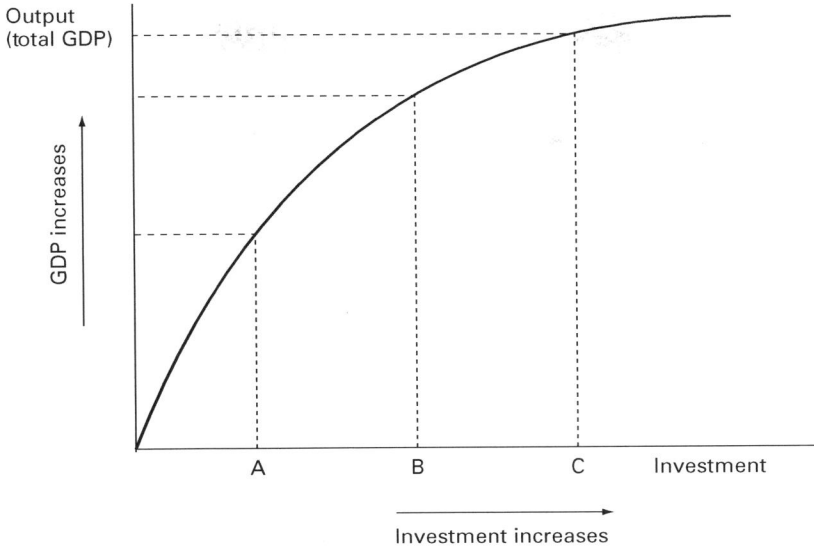

The attention Easterly and Levine give to productivity stems from the obser-vation by Robert Solow in his influential 1957 article, which stated that 'investment is not the key to growth'. Solow found that productivity increase had accounted for nearly 90 per cent of US growth in the first half of the twen-tieth century. Much subsequent empirical evidence supports the argument that differences in growth rates between countries are accounted for by differences in productivity rather than investment (Benhabib and Spiegel, 1994; Klenow and Rodriquez-Clare, 1997; Easterly and Levine, 2000).

The effect of diminishing returns to investment, illustrated in Figure 3.2, can partially reconcile the robust empirical results linking investment and growth with the elusive quest. An important concept in the relation between capital and output per worker is that of diminishing returns. Figure 3.2 shows that additions to the stock of physical or human capital (investment) increase output, but at a diminishing rate. The increase in output (GDP growth) as total investment increases from B to C is less than the increase from A to B. Each increment to the capital stock yields an ever smaller increase in output, so that eventually even substantial increases have only a minimal impact on output. The economic Law of Diminishing Returns states that incrementing one factor (here investment) while holding all others constant (here land and labour) will yield progressively smaller increments in output. Another example is in agri-culture. Investing in irrigation to reduce reliance on rainfall would generate a large increase in output, moving from canal to borehole irrigation would make that irrigation more reliable, moving from borehole to drip-feed irrigation (where the water is delivered directly to plants) will further boost output and save on water. Each step in this process will raise output but at a diminishing rate. Eventually increasing output further by changing the way water is delivered to the same seeds, soil, mechanical equipment and labour force will become nearly impossible. The importance of diminishing returns is that the relationship between investment and growth will be stronger in a developing country. Developing countries have a smaller capital stock (both in physical and human terms) so we can expect investment to yield a greater return. Chapter 2 provides supporting evidence for this proposition.

A second explanation for the puzzle is that the studies of investment we have referred to tend to use aggregate measures of investment (summing all investment in an economy over a period of time). De Long and Summers (1991, 1992, 1993) argue that it is not all forms of investment, but specifically investment in equipment that promotes economic growth. Jones (1994) confirms this by examining a sample of 65 countries between 1960 and 1985 and finds that the most crucial element is machinery (which includes capital ranging from tractors to computers). Thus aggregate measures of investment are likely to underestimate the impact of investment on growth. There is an intuitive rationale behind this finding. Investment in equipment such as machinery and computers, which are directly used in production, is more likely to promote economic growth than investment in water supply or housing which is more closely linked to the demands of urbanization. De Long and Summers argue that high rates of equipment investment accounted for nearly half of Japan's rapid growth after the 1950s. Their results suggest that the social returns to equipment investment are around 20–30 per cent per annum.

Policy and investment

Having established the causal relation between investment and economic growth, the next question is what factors or policies cause investment? A huge number of studies seek identify the policy factors related to investment and whether the free market or state intervention is the best means to promote high and efficient investment. From a bewildering array of results for cross-sections of countries and specific countries over various time periods, very few generalizations can be drawn or generally accepted findings stated:

- Barro (1991) finds that initial human capital has a positive impact, and government consumption a negative impact, on future physical investment for a sample of nearly 100 countries.
- Jenkins (1998) finds that investment in Zimbabwe is positively influenced by foreign direct investment (FDI), profits, the price of industrial output, and negatively by the debt-to-GDP ratio.
- Ndikumaru (2000) finds that indicators of financial development, the trade ratio, and GDP growth had a positive impact, and the black market premium on the exchange rate, inflation, external debt and public borrowing from the

financial system a negative impact on investment in 30 Sub-Saharan African countries between 1970 and 1995.
- Greene and Villanueva (1991) find a positive impact on investment from GDP growth, the level of per capita GDP, public sector investment, and a negative impact from the real interest rate, domestic inflation, debt-service ratio, and debt-to-GDP ratio on investment in developing countries between 1975 and 1987.
- King and Levine (1993) use an 80-country sample to find that between 1960 and 1989 financial development (size of liquid liabilities to GDP and volume of private sector credit) is significantly related to subsequent investment.

The statistical results offer no real guidance for policy. Barro's finding that human capital is related to growth offers no guidance to policy-makers on how to increase human capital. Private or public education? Comprehensive or selective education? Investing in primary or higher education? A centralized or community based education system? Education in philosophy or engineering? How should teachers be trained? Incentivized? Should schools get block grants or pupils be given vouchers to spend in the school of their choice?

This literature fails to examine the deeper determinants of growth. A policy such as subsidized credit is more likely to encourage investment in a country with well-protected property rights, a favourable geography and in which equipment can be readily imported from abroad. We see here an example of an important theme of this book: that the study of proximate determinants of economic growth is incomplete without any consideration of the deeper determinants.

Thus policy is likely to have better chance to promote investment, and so growth, in a developing country, but there are many cases where such efforts have failed. Little policy guidance can be drawn from empirical studies. We conclude that both market forces and government intervention can work to promote investment and growth, but each will succeed only under specific conditions.

Investment and the free market

It has been argued that the free market is the best way to promote efficient and productive investment. In a free market sensible and forward-looking (called by economists 'rational') individuals will make decisions about their savings. The 'life-cycle hypothesis', for example, suggests that people save during their mid-life high-earning years, but spend more than their income when young and old. Savings will form of pool of resources in banks that are then available for firms to borrow and invest. These firms are compelled by market competition to compete for the attention of profit-maximizing banks, by developing the most alluring and profitable business plans. As well as mobilizing savings and allocating resources to productive uses, freely operating financial markets provide other stimuli to growth and productivity. Stock markets can help investors to monitor managers. Investors can compare share prices of different firms in the same industry. Poorly performing firms can be taken over by more efficient managers, through buying sufficient shares to gain control. These arguments have been the central consideration of much IMF and World Bank lending to developing countries since the 1980s. The corresponding policy advice has focused on liberalizing the financial sector by privatizing state-owned banks, allowing the entry of foreign financial firms, removing restrictions on the free setting of interest rates, facilitating the growth of a stock market, and removing political interference in the lending and borrowing decisions of firms and banks.

There is a general, and after the recent global financial crisis growing, acceptance that the state must retain a role in monitoring and regulating the private financial sector. In any fractional-reserve banking system (whereby the banks lend out a multiple of the financial reserves they keep in their vaults) there is the possibility of a run on deposits which cannot be met by available reserves, leading to a collapse of the financial system. This creates needs for: regulation to ensure that banks control lending risks; deposit insurance; and a Central Bank to act as a lender of last resort if banks get into financial difficulties.

The problem with these 'liberalize, invest and grow' arguments is that, after the early 1980s, developing countries did much liberalizing but experienced little evident boost to investment and economic growth. All countries in Latin America significantly liberalized international trade, external capital flows and the domestic financial sector. The results were disappointing. While GDP per capita increased by 2.7 per cent annually between 1950 and 1980 it declined by 0.9 per cent in the 1980s. A key reason for the stagnation after 1980 was the failure of investment (and savings) to increase in response to liberalization (Ocampo, 2004). Broader data from developing countries across all continents shows that average per capita income growth fell from 2.5 per cent between 1960 and 1979 to 0.0 per cent between 1980 and 1998. This reduction in growth occurred despite 'improved' liberalization across developing countries, as measured by financial depth, trade liberalization, price and exchange rate liberalization and removal of controls on the setting of interest rates (Easterly, 2001b). The two key reasons why liberalization failed to generate higher investment and growth are credibility and expectations.

How the free market can fail

Policy reforms intended to boost investment, such as devaluation or reduced profit tax will only work to the extent that private entrepreneurs consider them 'credible'. Trade liberalization, including currency devaluation, will make exports more competitive, but this will only work in the longer term if it stimulates private sector investment in new capacity to produce goods and services for export. Entrepreneurs will not invest in new capacity if there is a likelihood that the liberalization-devaluation could be reversed and exporting ceases to be profitable. Such capacity would probably be scrapped, rather than converted for other purposes. Private entrepreneurs might not believe in the lasting power of a liberalization-devaluation strategy for many reasons. Trade liberalization might not be credible if accompanied by an import surge and a resulting large balance of payments deficit, if the tariff cuts generate an unsustainable government budget deficit, if liberalization causes redistribution of income in the domestic economy (see below) that is not politically sustainable, or if government is not truly committed to the liberalization (perhaps because it has been imposed by foreign donors in return for aid). Rational entrepreneurs would then withhold investment until any uncertainty regarding the success/sustainability of reforms is eliminated (Rodrik, 1990). Yet without that investment reforms will fail to generate exports and economic growth. The failure of reforms will become a self-fulfilling vicious circle.

It is almost impossible to quantify the credibility beliefs of private investors, but there are good reasons to consider that much of the 1980s liberalization in developing countries was not 'credible'. Because liberalization was often imposed by the IMF at moments of crisis, investors doubted that the domestic government had any real commitment to it. Liberalization (particularly cuts in subsidies and import tariffs) generated enormous political opposition; from farmers who benefited from fertilizer subsidies, from manufacturing firms that depended on protection from imports and from urban workers who enjoyed the cheap imported consumer goods provided by an overvalued exchange rate. Investors rightly concluded that this would pressurize governments into reversing many aspects of liberalization.

Liberalization was in many cases accompanied by stabilization. Through unsustainable budget and trade deficits in the 1970s, countries had run into debt crises in the 1980s. Higher world interest rates in the early 1980s added to their burden of debt and higher oil prices after 1979 added to import costs. Governments in developing countries responded by strenuous efforts to reduce budget deficits, by cutting spending and raising tax revenue. Much of the world lurched into recession in the early 1980s, and across the developing world real wages fell sharply. The 1980s were thus not conducive to private sector industry investment, even though savings were becoming more easily available through liberalized and privatized financial systems. The work of Keynes dating back to the global depression of the 1930s, discussed in Box 3.2 explains why.

Regarding the work of Keynes it is evident that the animal spirits of entrepreneurs in the 1980s were depressed by stagnant global markets and falling profit expectations. The liberal model wrongly assumed that private firms would compete to borrow all available resources to invest. The Keynesian model rightly assumed that banks would be left with surplus liquidity if private firms lacked the motivation to borrow and invest. The contemporary world economy offers another such example. The top one hundred firms, as listed on the UK Stock Market, were by 2013 sitting on a cash pile (surplus cash holdings in banks) of almost $270 billion, up by $70 billion since 2008. Firms had the resources but were simply not investing.

Box 3.2 John Maynard Keynes, growth and investment

John Maynard Keynes, the British economist, studied the economics of depression in the 1930s. His insights have achieved new relevance in the current global financial crisis. Keynes wrote his seminal work *The General Theory of Employment, Interest and Money* in 1936 at the height of the world depression. Incomes in many developed countries had dropped by up to one-third and unemployment had risen to a quarter of the labour force. Keynes asked what had caused the depression and placed investment at the centre of his analysis. Keynes argued that investment was dependent on the expectations of entrepreneurs about future market size and profitability. He argued that such expectations were subject to waves of optimism or pessimism or what he called the 'animal spirits' of investors. This effect Keynes argued is exaggerated by what he called the 'accelerator effect'. An investment of $400 million in new machinery might be necessary to produce an extra $100 million in output (in economics this is known as having a capital-output ratio of 4:1). The prospect of an expanding market will therefore call forth a much greater increase in investment to supply it. The Accelerator Effect will impact on demand in the economy and so amplify both booms and busts. What Joseph Stiglitz called the Roaring Nineties in his 2003 book about the US boom in the 1990s (and subsequent bust) was driven by over-optimistic expectations about the future profitability and market growth in telecommunications and the internet. No government, Keynesians argue, can hope to stabilize the economy at a high level of employment and output without understanding and accounting for these 'animal spirits'.

Sri Lanka, after 1977, provides a good example of a reform effort that *was* considered credible by private investors . The private sector had no doubt that the government was committed to sustained liberalization. It was widely perceived that the state-led, interventionist, alternative had been discredited by very poor economic performance between 1970 and 1977, and that a fresh start was needed. The reforms were implemented by the newly elected United National Party (UNP) government, which won 140 of 168 seats. It was strongly committed to liberalization and had campaigned on that agenda. For the first time in Sri Lanka since independence, the anti-market Marxist parties failed to win a single seat. Trade and payments were liberalized, import controls largely abolished and tariffs rationalized, export licensing phased out, and the currency devalued. Public sector monopolies were ended, opening up new swathes of the economy to private sector participation. Price controls were replaced with a greater reliance on market signals to determine resource allocation. Unlike many other reform efforts during this era there was no contractionary stabilization; instead there was expansion. There was large-scale government investment in transportation, telecommunications and energy. This was backed by a surge in foreign aid, which financed 20 per cent of total investment between 1971 and 1977 and 40 per cent of a much higher total after 1978. Growth doubled from an average of 3 per cent between 1970 and 1977 to nearly 6 per cent between 1977 and 1985. This was led by a huge surge in investment, from 14–16 per cent of GDP before 1978 to 33.7 per cent in 1980 (Bruton, 1992).

From the free market to the state–business alliance

Although Keynes doubted the ability of the market to ensure a stable level of investment, he did argue that the market was good at allocating investment between different sectors. Entrepreneurs, he considered, would be adept at investing in growing more oranges if selling them was more profitable than selling apples. Keynes was writing about developed countries. An alternative and more realistic view for developing countries is that state intervention is needed not only to stabilize investment, but also to ensure that it is directed towards those sectors crucial to long-run growth and development. One interpretation of this role is a state–business alliance, whereby the state promotes investment through policies that enhance the profitability of existing businesses. There is a clear difference between such a strategy and free-market liberalization. Pro-market reforms aim to ease the entry of new businesses and encourage competition between existing businesses, new entrants and foreign imports. As a result, they are likely to reduce the profitability of the former.

Governments have acted to increase profitability in various ways. The increase in growth in India around 1980 has been ascribed by some to the state adopting a pro-business strategy that resulted in higher profits and investment. The pro-business policies included withdrawing constraints on existing businesses to expand or enter new areas of production, liberalizing access to credit, tax relief for big business, undermining the strength of trade unions, and maintaining an expansionary fiscal policy (Rodrik and Subramanian, 2004; Kohli, 2006). In South Korea and Taiwan during the 1960s and 1970s the state brutally suppressed trade union organization, to prevent profits being diverted to higher wages. In South Korea (Amsden, 1989:152) and Taiwan (Wade, 1990:185) in industry generally, and in Malaysian banks (Koy-Fay and Jomo, 2000), price controls prevented firms competing with one another on the basis of price, thus undermining profitability. In Singapore the government used its monopoly control over public utilities to raise the prices of water, energy and telephones to boost the profitability of public enterprises and so raise resources for public investment (Huff, 1999).

The other main element of a state–business alliance is to ensure that profits are used to boost productive investment, to expand output and exports. There would be no investment if profits were used to increase executive salaries or returned to shareholders as dividends. During the early stages of industrialization there is a need for the state to co-ordinate complementary investments (Rosenstein-Rodan, 1943; Scitovsky, 1954) so that interdependent investment projects are implemented at the same time. A simple example is that of a steel mill and a shipbuilding industry; the steel mill supplies inputs to the shipbuilding industry. Neither can be profitable without the other. Contracts could be negotiated and signed between the steel mill and shipbuilding firms to establish production and agree to buy/sell a particular amount of steel, but such contracts are likely to be too costly to draw up and monitor. The solution to investment co-ordination in 1960s and 1970s Taiwan was for state enterprises to take over production in sectors where the efficient scale of production was very large; production was very capital intensive (risky and costly) and where linkages to downstream enterprises were high. These sectors included petroleum refining, petrochemicals, steel and other basic metals, shipbuilding, heavy machinery, transport equipment and fertilizer (Wade, 1990:179).

The problem with generalizing the state–business model to other developing countries is that relatively unusual political pre-conditions are required for a state to be able to implement such policies. A state is needed that can be 'developmental', defined as 'states whose politics have concentrated sufficient power, autonomy and capacity at the centre to shape, pursue and encourage the achievement of explicit development objectives, whether by establishing and promoting the conditions and direction of economic growth, or by organizing it directly, or by a varying combination of both' (Leftwich,1995:401). Many of these pre-conditions take us into the realm of the deeper determinants of growth. Adrian Leftwich (1995) compiled a list of various political factors that between them gave some developing countries the capacity to be developmental.

First, the state had a politically-driven desire to promote growth and the capacity to do so. The desire often comes from the executive head, surrounded by a small elite of senior politicians who share the motivation to promote growth. Examples often discussed include President Masire in Botswana, President Lee Kuan Yew in Singapore, and President Park in Korea. Some leaders have had completely different motivations, such as Mao Tse-tung to impose a communist society on China, or the current leadership of North Korea to build a nuclear weapon. Other leaders have aspired only to enrich themselves and their supporters by confiscating and redistributing wealth from rival groups.

Second, these elites and state institutions had sufficient autonomy and independence from the demands of special interest groups to focus relentlessly on promoting economic growth. In non-democratic developmental states the major source of autonomy has been a seizure of power by an elite; in Taiwan the 1949 KMT takeover, in South Korea the 1961 military coup led by General Park, and in Indonesia the New Order of General Suharto in 1966. These were followed by the elimination or marginalization of opposition groups that had previously enjoyed wealth and power. The autonomy of formally democratic developmental states, such as Singapore, Malaysia, and Botswana, has been derived from the dominance of a single political party.

The third factor was the competence and insulation of an economic bureaucracy characterized by selective and meritocratic recruitment. These differed from typical developing country bureaucracies in their real power, authority, technical competence, and insulation from short-term political pressures in shaping development policy.

The fourth factor was that state power and autonomy was consolidated early in the development process. In East Asia large landlords were destroyed through programmes of land reform, especially in Taiwan and Korea. In Singapore the initially politically powerful Chinese business class was weakened by relying on foreign investment through MNCs. In Latin America development was hindered by powerful agricultural landlords, an emerging middle class and deeply entrenched foreign business. Chapter 9 discusses the argument that certain colonial countries (particularly the Japanese in South Korea between 1910 and 1945) made a much greater effort than others (such as the Belgians in the Congo) to construct a strong state and bureaucracy.

A fifth factor has been the widely perceived legitimacy of even non-democratic developmental states. This has supported government policies for long-term economic growth, even though it implied the population would not benefit in the short run through higher consumption and wages. Some authors have explained this as a sort of culturally ingrained respect for the government and its leaders. Others have argued that government legitimacy was hard won, based on promises to promote the rapid economic growth and industrialization that would make certain countries more secure in the dangerous world of the Cold War. In the 1950s Japan felt threatened by Russia, South Korea by North Korea and Taiwan by China.

Foreign direct investment

There is a longstanding presumption among dependency writers (see Chapter 13) that the most important consequence of FDI is not the initial investment it brings to a developing country, but rather its longer term drain on resources. This argument is known as the 'drain of surplus theory'. In the long term FDI will cause profits, royalties, expatriate wages and various license fees to flow back from the developing country host to developed countries. In recent years MNCs have often been accused of enhancing this process by paying low wages to developing-country staff and manipulating accounts and prices to avoid paying taxes. Even developed countries are not immune to this process. The internet firm Google, for example, despite having revenue in the UK of £2.6 billion in 2011, paid only £6 million in tax.

There is little evidence to suggest that FDI in general is a mechanism by which the richest countries target the poorest developing countries. Most FDI occurs between developed countries. Eighty percent of US investment goes to other high income countries. The EU in the late 1990s held 39 per cent of the world stock of FDI, the US 19 per cent, Hong Kong 6.6 per cent, China 5.8 per cent, and Singapore 1.5 per cent. By comparison all of Sub-Saharan Africa held only 1.7 per cent of the total (Wolf, 2004). A common contemporary image is that of the FDI-created sweatshop in developing countries; a foreign-owned factory paying low wages and violating local safety laws. Pessimists argue that MNCs make employees in developing countries poor by paying them low wages. An argument with more support is that MNCs pay low wages because of existing poverty and low wages. Studies show that, on average, FDI firms pay 10 per cent more than the going wage, and affiliates of US MNCs sometimes pay a premium that ranges from 40 to 100 per cent (Bhagwati, 2007:216). MNCs also tend to invest more in developing countries with better working conditions. An analysis of outward investment by US corporations showed a greater share of US investment in countries that ratified more International Labour Organization (ILO) workers' rights (Bhagwati 2007:220).

A related debate concerns the 'race to the bottom', wherein developing countries compete to host FDI by offering greater tax/environment/labour concessions than rival hosts. Much of the benefit of the investment is thus transferred back to the MNC. The success of countries such as Ireland and Singapore in attracting FDI has masked the lack of benefits to the hosts. Ever-extending tax concessions for FDI in Singapore meant that, by the 1990s, no tax was paid on the profits from almost two-thirds of Singapore's manufac-tured output, and three-quarters of direct exports. Foreign investors received cheap access to land purchased by the government under compulsory powers. For example, the Jurong Town Corporation, owned by the Singapore govern-ment, leased land at very low cost to incoming industrialists for 30 years, frequently with an option to renew for a further 30 years. If firms wished the government could provide purpose-built factories. The government also provided modern infrastructure including a port, airport, telecommunications, roads and a mass rapid transit system. From the early 1980s the government began to spend heavily on education and training geared to the labour/skills needs of FDI firms (Ermisch and Huff, 1999; Huff, 1999). Many argue that this problem intensified during the 1990s, as the Singapore strategy of zero tax and infrastructure subsidies was copied elsewhere, such as in the Republic of Ireland, in Subic Bay in the Philippines and in Malaysia. MNCs have also been adept at exploiting unintended loopholes in tax laws to avoid paying taxes even in developed countries. In 2012/13 Amazon UK had sales of £4.2 billion on which they paid taxes of only £3.2 million. Amazon.co.uk has classified itself as a service provider to its Luxembourg business Amazon EU to which it pays large fees, so reducing its UK profitability and tax liabilities. The large profits earned by the Luxembourg business are subject to much lower rates of taxation than those prevailing in the UK.

FDI that leads to the development of linkages in the host economy is more likely to promote growth than FDI that is highly dependent on imported inputs, and exports most of its output. This latter type of FDI creates what is known as an enclave, in which the FDI may have no linkages with the domestic econ-omy. Chinese investment in Africa has in recent years raised concerns about enclave effects. Chinese firms offer good quality infrastructure projects with a

25–50 per cent discount compared with other foreign investors. They achieve this through lower margins, access to cheaper financing, almost exclusive employment of Chinese staff (often living in worse conditions than the local population), use of imported Chinese materials with little local sourcing, use of standard designs and little attention to environmental impacts. Such FDI is not likely to generate many linkages with the domestic economy (Kaplinsky *et al.*, 2007). At the other extreme FDI may create demand for the output of local firms (backward linkages) that strengthens local supply industries. To ensure that inputs supplied reach the necessary quality, FDI firms may transfer technology to local firms (a vertical linkages effect). FDI studies consistently find pre-conditions that are crucial for these linkages to emerge. Examples include a highly-educated local labour force and existing technical capabilities among existing and emerging domestic producers. Government rules, such as mandatory local content requirements, have been used to ensure that FDI firms purchase a certain proportion of inputs from local suppliers. Although East Asian states were successful in deliberately promoting such linkages (Hobday, 1995) such regulations are now largely prohibited by the rules of the World Trade Organization (WTO). Other linkage effects work through technological transfer. Local firms may adopt technology used by FDI firms through imitation or reverse engineering (the demonstration effect). This latter linkage has also been made harder by the tightening of WTO rules and requirements on patents and copyright.

There is a longstanding suspicion that technology from developed countries is likely to be 'inappropriate' for developing countries and that this will limit the potential gains from any imitation or reverse engineering. The assumption is that technology imported from developed to developing countries will be expensive, capital intensive and demand skilled labour. This pattern fits the particular requirements of developed countries that have the resources to finance expensive investment projects and the skilled labour to operate them. Transplanted to a developing country such technology will then generate little employment for the mass of unskilled/semi-skilled labour. The technology will be too complex for the more limited absorptive capacity of domestic firms in developing countries, thus limiting learning benefits for the rest of the economy and leading to long-term dependence on imported rather than domestically produced inputs. In practice these negative assessments are too extreme.

Several empirical studies provide evidence of positive technology spillovers (Grossman and Helpman, 1991a; Kokko, 2004; Chuang and Lin, 1999; Aitken and Harrison, 1999; Saggi, 2002). Workers trained by an FDI firm may transfer knowledge to a local firm (knowledge spillover effects) or start their own firms (the labour-turnover effect). A famous study of this process is that of Rhee (1990) – who studied the textile sector in Bangladesh. In 1979–80 the Korean firm Daewoo provided intensive training for 130 workers from a single Bangladeshi textile firm Desh. Within several years 115 of these workers had left to set up their own textile firms, which led to a massive transfer of skills and learning. By 1985 more than 700 garment export manu-facturing factories had emerged in Bangladesh. Rhee calls this the 'catalyst model of economic development'.

Key points

- Investment is defined as 'the forgoing of present consumption in order to create an asset that will generate an expected future return'.
- Investment can be broken down into physical and human capital.
- It is important to distinguish between net and gross investment.
- Investment can impact on economic growth either directly through expand-ing the capacity to produce, indirectly through facilitating the acquisition of new technology, or through its influence in boosting demand.
- Investment has a more significant and robust link with economic growth than any other factor of production.
- The investment–growth link is likely to be stronger in developing countries and weaker than the productivity–growth link in developed countries, owing to diminishing returns to investment.
- There is no agreement on what policy measures are best to promote invest-ment, some emphasize freeing the market, others that there is an important role for a pro-active state to mobilize and allocate resources to investment.
- There are important pre-conditions for the government of a developing country to successfully promote productive investment.
- There are many examples of failed efforts by governments to boost investment.
- Scholars like Karl Marx and John Maynard Keynes placed investment at the centre of their work on economic development.
- Some argue that Foreign Direct Investment is a useful/important means of supplementing domestic investment, but others disagree.

Chapter 4

Population and Economic Growth/ Development

Many people assume that investment is always and everywhere a good thing; the opposite assumption is often made for population growth. A tabloid newspaper reported in late 2013 that the 'UK population could DOUBLE to 131 million within a century'. Two-thirds of this increase, it suggested, would result from immigrants and their children. Looking at a longer time span makes the numbers certainly look less dramatic. The population of the earth took 10,000 years to increase from 5 million to 730 million in 1750. Over the next two hundred years the total increased to 3 billion, then doubled again to 6.4 billion in 2000. Current forecasts suggest that the population will peak at 11–12 billion in 2100, and that 90 per cent of the increase will take place in current developing countries. By 2050 the population of Pakistan, for example, is forecast to increase from 160 million to 340 million and India from 1 billion to 1.6 billion. As a proportion of the global total the population of Europe is expected to decline from 12 to 7 per cent and Africa to rise from 13 to 22 per cent.

Thomas Malthus (see Box 4.1) predicted that untrammelled population growth would bring social and environmental catastrophe.

In the late 1960s a book by Paul Erhlich entitled *The Population Bomb* (1968) forecast that the 1970s would be characterized by global mass starvation and the food surplus countries (particularly the US, Canada and Australia) would face the appalling choice of who to save. The disaster never came. Since Ehrlich's book was published the population of the world has doubled and the incidence of famine has declined sharply. Ehrlich missed the impact of science applied to agriculture. During the Green Revolution of the mid-1960s higher yield crop varieties were developed and agricultural inputs such as fertilizer, pesticide and irrigation were improved. These changes enabled a sustained growth of agricultural output based on improving the productivity (yield) of land so freeing food production from a dependence on without bringing ever more land into cultivation. It wasn't just luck that saved us from global starvation. There appears to be a systematic relation between economic and population growth, whereby economic growth first increases, then slows the rate of population growth. This is known as the demographic transition. The rate of world population growth has been slowing decreasing since the 1960s, falling from about 2 per cent

Box 4.1 Malthus and population catastrophe

Thomas Malthus wrote 'An Essay on the Principle of Population' in 1798. He argued that population growth and economic change were essentially unrelated. Economic output (then principally agriculture) would increase arithmetically (so many extra tonnes of corn per year) and population geometrically (so many percentage points per year). Population would thus outstrip food supply and cause famine. The resulting rise in mortality (termed by Malthus a 'positive check' on population) would restore food supply per capita. More food would stimulate fertility and the growth of population would resume. This periodic lurch into hunger crises, he argued, could only be prevented by a rise in the age of marriage to slow the rate of population growth (a 'preventive check'). Malthus didn't anticipate the impact of the Industrial Revolution, the beginnings of which many scholars have dated to his era. The application of industrial-scientific principles to agriculture enabled 'a vast increase in output which enabled British farming in the 1830s to supply 98 per cent of the grain for a population between two and three times the mid-eighteenth century size' (Hobsbawm, 1995:48). Malthus also failed to see that population and the economy were intimately linked. Population growth could have negative, but also positive, impacts on economic growth.

to about 1.1 per cent per annum by 2014. Scholars now realize that population growth can be good or bad depending on the context in which it occurs. The optimistic work of Ester Boserup challenges the pessimism of Paul Erhlich.

This chapter examines how population growth affects economic growth and how the latter affects fertility and mortality (the demographic transition). Of all the chapters in this book (except perhaps Chapter 6 on education and health) this chapter is the one where economic issues (growth) are mostly tightly bound up with broader issues of human development (fertility and mortality). The chapter concludes with a discussion of government policy related to demography using insights derived from a catastrophic but often forgotten form of mortality, that of 'missing women'.

Population and economic growth

Population growth, by supplying a potential labour force, is a proximate determinant of growth. Higher fertility increases (with a delay) entrants to the labour force whilst declining mortality reduces exits. The links between population and economic growth are shown in Figure 4.1.

Figure 4.1 *Population growth as a proximate determinant of economic growth*

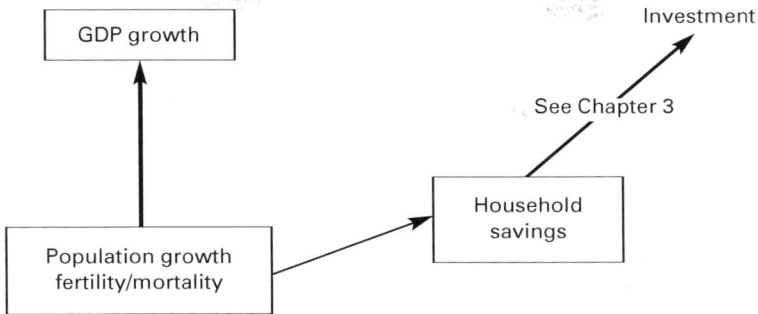

Population: the basic concepts

The total fertility rate (TFR) measures the number of children born to a woman during her lifetime if at each age she were to bear children in accordance with the currently prevailing age-specific fertility rate. For simplicity the TFR is calculated assuming that there will be no future changes in age-specific fertility rates so the measure will inevitably be an overestimate in those parts of the world where fertility rates are likely to continue falling. The mortality rate is the number of deaths per 1,000 per year of a defined population, infants, children, or adults. Migration is the difference between arrivals and departures in a particular geographic region. So population growth is the total impact of fertility minus mortality and net migration.

Migration has a big influence at certain times. Between 1820 and 1920 60 million people migrated from Europe to the Americas, Australasia and Southern Africa. Britain in the 2000s experienced its biggest wave of inward migration since the seventeenth century. An estimated 500,000 people migrated from Poland to the UK when Poland joined the European Union (EU) and border restrictions were lifted. Migration is not relevant for the world as a whole, and does not have the same systematic relationship with economic growth as fertility and mortality, so is usually left out of demographic models.

Population growth and the economy: the negative

Numerous theoretical arguments link rapid population growth to adverse economic outcomes. Families may reduce savings to sustain consumption for each household member. For the whole economy, lower savings reduces the pool of investible resources which must be more thinly spread. For example increasing primary school places rather than deepening education into secondary and tertiary levels. High fertility (repeated pregnancies) may undermine the health of mothers and their ability to work outside the household to supplement household income. Rapid population growth will initially increase the dependency burden (defined as the ratio of the population under 15 and over 64 to the population of working age) by increasing the relative number of children. In Nigeria, for example, around half the population are under 15. In developed countries the dependency burden is instead the result of declining fertility and mortality, leading to a relative increase in the population aged over 64. In Sweden 20 per cent of the population are over 65. Either version of dependency will place a greater demand at the aggregate level through taxation and at the household level on those working to finance the consumption needs of the non-working. Dependency burdens may be less relevant in the poorest developing countries where children can enter the labour force at an early age and older people continue working and are less likely to take up golf at 65.

Some scholars have suggested that rapid population growth causes deforestation and desertification, as people are pushed onto marginal land to sustain subsistence production. This argument misses the real causal chain. The true drivers of environmental problems are changing demand patterns from the wealthy (recall the discussion of changing diets in Chapter 1) to a more meat-intensive diet (which can lead to clearance of land for farming), or technology (the chainsaw, not an impoverished peasant, most ruthlessly clears forest) and inequality (the average US person consumes 350 times as much energy as the average Ethiopian). This last point is supported by Molinas (2010), who separates the impacts of population growth, economic growth and technology on carbon emissions in India between 2003 and 2030 (which he forecasts will double during these dates). Population growth will play a relatively marginal role. Population growth, he forecasts, will account for just 26.83 per cent of total increase in CO_2 emissions. The fast growth of the Indian economy is the main cause, accounting for 131.7 per cent of the increase in CO_2. Technological change is likely to offset 58.53 per cent of the increase in CO_2 until 2030. He notes that population growth in China will contribute less than 10 per cent of the increase in Chinese CO_2 emission over the same period.

Population growth and the economy: the positive

Population growth can benefit economic growth. Ester Boserup (1965) argued that population growth can stimulate technological change. She argued that a dense population was needed to utilize modern transport facilities, provide labour for labour-intensive rice-based agriculture, and provide all the development benefits of urbanization. Models of 'endogenous technological change' have shown how higher population growth spurs technological change (Grossman and Helpman, 1991; Aghion and Howitt, 1992). They have given mathematical and theoretical rigour to the earlier arguments of Boserup. This result comes from the non-rivalry nature of technology which means that the cost of inventing technology is independent of the number of people using it, whilst the likelihood of invention increases with the population (and consequent number of inventors).

Early in the demographic transition the proportion of children in the population will be increase, this in turn will reduce the share of working-age adults, and so reduce the growth of per capita income. Over time those children will move into the labour force and the population will comprise an increasing share of working-age adults and the early demographic burden will become a demographic dividend. The demographic dividend can boost economic growth through three mechanisms. The first is labour supply. Children born during high fertility years enter adulthood and become productive workers. Women in particular are then more likely to enter the labour force as a declining fertility rate gives them the freedom to do so. The second impact is through savings (and so the resources available for investment). Working-age adults have the potential to save more, whilst the increase in life expectancy associated with the demographic transition gives more time to save and more incentive to do so (longer retirements). The third is human capital. Lower fertility allows families to increase educational expenditure on each child. The demographic dividend is a temporary phenomenon and will disappear as the bulge of working-age adults retires. Data from 78 Asian and non-Asian countries for the years between 1965 and 1990 show no significant relationship between overall population growth and that of GDP, but growth of the working-age (15–64 years) population did have a positive and significant impact on per capita GDP growth. Between 1965 and 1990 the working-age population in East Asia grew 2.39 per cent per annum faster than overall population growth (1.58 per cent) and growth of the dependent population (0.25 per cent). These results imply that population dynamics can explain one-third of the total growth rate in East Asia (Bloom and Williamson, 1998).

Part of the rapid growth in China over the past three decades can be explained by demography. After rapid population growth in the early 1960s, and subsequent sharp falls in fertility, a bulge of young people entered the labour force during the 1980s and 1990s. During these decades the working-age population grew by 2.5 per cent annually. With rural to urban migration included, the urban labour force grew by more than 4 per cent per annum. By 2000 70 per cent of the Chinese population were between 15 and 64; significantly higher than the average for all developing countries. Over these years the Chinese economy successfully absorbed much of this extra labour into export-oriented manufacturing industries. This demographic dividend is now grinding to a halt, leading some to think that economic growth in China will slow. Growth of the working-age population is likely to have ceased by 2015. The only source of labour force growth will then be migration from rural areas. It is estimated that the number of Chinese over 60 years of age will increase from 128 million in 2000 to 350 million in 2030. India is also experiencing a delayed though similar demographic dividend. India is now one of the youngest countries in the world. In 2000 one-third of the population were below 15 years of age and another fifth were aged between 15 and 24. The population aged between 15 and 24 increased from 175 million in 1995 to 210 million in 2010. This demographic dividend has created a large and growing labour force.

At most a demographic dividend offers only a potential for increased economic growth. There is no guarantee more people entering the labour force will generate more employment and more output. First, the population must be able to leave the household and be available to work. In India cultural norms prevent women from leaving the household to do paid work. In 2004/05 female labour force participation rates in urban areas were only 15 per cent and showed almost no increase from the previous decade (Chandrasekhar *et al.*, 2006:5059). Second, work must be available where people are. Chapter 11 discusses how industry is most likely to be located close to raw materials or urban markets, or in coastal areas. Historically people have tended to populate the most fertile farmland. Some of the highest population density in Africa is in the Great Lakes area (Rwanda, Uganda and Burundi). Migrating from there and crossing borders to work in the richer coastal areas of Kenya and South Africa is very unlikely for the vast majority of the population. In China, by contrast, perhaps one hundred million people have migrated from the poor interior areas to the rapidly growing coastal regions. China is a single unified nation so people don't have to cross international borders. China also has good infrastructure and a high degree of cultural uniformity such that people can more easily communicate and blend in once they have migrated for work. Third, those entering the potential labour force must be sufficiently educated. Subsistence agriculture requires little education, but most other forms of employment do. Literacy is generally required even in a dingy backstreet factory. A survey of young women working in casual, informal exploitative conditions in small-scale textile production (in Tiruppur, India) found that 99.7 per cent of them were literate (Neetha, 2002). Chapter 6 shows just how poor the education system is in many developing countries. Fourth, the relationship between available cheap labour and long-term economic growth is more complicated in practice. An increasing supply of young labour could make labour markets more competitive, reducing wages and encouraging domestic and foreign firms to set up production facilities, thus increasing employment. The Chinese export boom after 1980 was based on employing reasonably well-educated people at low wages, and using labour-intensive methods to produce cheap manufactured goods for export. A completely different dynamic could also be possible. More people and lower wages may reduce the incentives for firms to use more modern technology. Why, for example, utilize modern and expensive machinery in a knitwear factory if there is a queue of people willing to stitch by hand? More people could lead to an economy being stuck in low-technology, labour-intensive, low-skill production methods and being unable to shift to a more dynamic growth path based on high-technology, capital-intensive and high-skill production methods. Some historians have argued that the abundance of slaves available in ancient Greece in the fourth and fifth centuries BCE to work on farms, mines and in households gave the poets, historians and philosophers the freedom to wander the streets of Athens pondering life. At the same time this ready availability of slaves also meant there was never any real incentive to introduce new labour-saving or output-boosting technologies into agriculture or industry. If slavery was good for philosophy it wasn't good for technological change. Other historians have argued that the rapid ascent of the US to technological leadership at the end of the nineteenth century can be explained in part by its scarce and expensive labour. Low wages in the US were never an option. Wages had to be high to induce people to invest the time and effort for labour to travel across the ocean from the cities and villages of Europe. The abundance of land meant migrants if treated badly or paid poorly could always head west and become family farmers. According to this view American factories were compelled to introduce modern, labour-saving technology. The more rapid adoption of the production line, most famously by the Ford Motor Company after 1913 could then be explained less as a result of American ingenuity than as a response to the difficult labour market conditions faced by entrepreneurs.

The demographic transition

Three main stages of demographic transition lead a country from high-mortality/high-fertility to low-mortality/low-fertility. Some scholars add a fourth stage characteristic of very high income countries, where fertility can fall below mortality and lead to (before immigration) population decline. The fertility rate in Italy, for example, is now only slightly greater than one child per woman. Without migration the population will fall by around 25 per cent by 2050. This chapter covers the first three as those being most relevant to developing countries.

Stage one: high mortality, high fertility and slow population growth

In a developing country poor working conditions, bad sanitation and nutrition and lack of basic health care lead to low life expectancy. Mortality is high in the very young and in those at vulnerable moments in the life-cycle such as childbirth. Fertility rates are also high. Many will depend upon subsistence agriculture, which offers productive employment even to young children. In traditional agriculture women can also combine bearing and caring for children. The lack of insurance for parents in old age and high child mortality necessitates high fertility to ensure that sufficient children survive into adulthood to care for the parents. Even today in China more than half of the elderly live with their children, usually a son. Insecure property/land rights place a premium on having children (especially sons) for physical protection.

Catastrophic mortality from famine and illness is common during the first stage. Nineteenth-century India, for example, faced recurrent famine. 5 million to 8 million died in 1876–88, 2 million to 4.5 million in 1899–90, and in the last famine before independence in 1942–3 2 million to 4 million died in Bengal. During the late nineteenth century famine caused life expectancy in India to drop to roughly 22 years. In the district of Berar this famine raised the infant mortality rate (IMR) to 415 infant deaths per 1000 births, and life expectancy fell to 9 years (Dyson, 2005). Epidemic disease also has devastating effects. In the Indian state of Bombay in 1918, influenza reduced life expectancy to about 6 years. The virus killed millions across the world, in both developed and developing countries. Bubonic plague, introduced into Bombay by ship in 1896, caused 12 million deaths in the years to 1921. Throughout the nineteenth century British efforts at famine relief in India were poorly organized. Some administrators believed that free markets could deal with the problem; that food scarcity would raise prices, giving farmers and traders an incentive to transport supplies to famine threatened areas. Some administrators were concerned that spending on famine relief would make the problem worse in the long run by stimulating population growth. The Famine Commission Report of 1880 and the Famine Reports of 1898 and 1901 established administrative procedures and systems of relief which played a role in reducing the effects of famine, especially after 1901 (Dyson, 2005).

During this first stage the high rates of fertility and mortality more or less cancel out such that population growth tends to be slow. India during the nineteenth century was typical. Population growth averaged around 0.5 per cent per annum; this trend was dominated by those sharp year-to-year fluctuations.

Stage two: mortality declines, fertility remains high and population growth accelerates

In the second stage mortality falls rapidly. Mortality can be significantly reduced in the poorest developing countries through simple medical interventions and behavioural changes. Cheap and easy health-care treatments are introduced and reduce death from disease and those transmitted via the faecal-oral route through contaminated water causing diarrhoea and dehydration. For example, treatment for diarrhoea is generally easy, through oral rehydration therapy (a mixture of sugar, salt and water), and prevention is simple through regular hand washing with soap and boiling drinking water. For measles, which in the poorest countries is a substantial cause of morbidity and mortality, a single dose of a cheap vaccine is enough to give lifetime protection. Such treatments are affordable even for the poorest countries and await only the understanding, will and minimal finance to introduce them. In the poorest developing countries three-quarters of rural households cook with unprocessed solid fuels such as dried animal dung, crop residues, wood, charcoal and coal. These produce hazardous emissions when burnt in inefficient traditional stoves in poorly ventilated households and so are often most dangerous for women and children at home. Household air pollution is strongly linked with acute respiratory infection in children, and chronic obstructive pulmonary disease in adults. The problem can be tackled cheaply through education and the provision of improved stoves.

In the decades after the 1950s developing countries reduced levels of mortality more quickly than the developed countries had done in the past at similar income levels. 'The worldwide decline in mortality after WWII happened because two hundred years of progress against mortality in the now-rich countries was rapidly brought to bear on mortality in the rest of the world' (Cutler *et al.*, 2006:107). Such treatments were introduced rapidly across the developing world after 1950, often under the auspices of donor organizations. Examples of the rapid and successful diffusion of new treatments include penicillin (discovered in 1927), sulfa drugs (1932), streptomycin (shown to treat tuberculosis in 1943) and chloroquine (shown to treat malaria in 1943). By the 1950s the medical profession had accumulated much low-hanging fruit waiting to be exploited in developing countries. In India the National Malaria Control Programme was introduced in 1953 when the annual incidence of malaria was estimated to be 75 million with 800,000 deaths. By the late 1950s annual incidence had dropped to 2 million, with around 150,000 deaths. In Sri Lanka, between 1945 and 1955, mass spraying of insecticide to kill mosquitoes reduced the crude death rate from malaria by 50 per cent. This measure was estimated to have saved more than 250,000 lives and opened up large areas of farmland to cultivation (Gray, 1974:21).

East Asia passed rapidly through the second stage of the demographic transition. Between 1960 and 1992 mortality declined rapidly. Life expectancy increased from 61.2 to 74.6 years, driven by declines in mortality among younger age groups. Reasonably rapid growth of agricultural output improved general nutrition (Bloom and Williamson, 1998). In China life expectancy rose by nearly 30 years after 1950 and in Africa life expectancy rose more than 13 years from the early 1950s to the late 1980s,before declining due to AIDS/HIV.

The relationship between life expectancy and income has shifted during the twentieth century. For countries with per capita annual incomes between $100 and $500 life expectancy was around 10–12 years higher in the 1960s than in the 1930s. This was the low-hanging fruit effect, which was largely independent of income and accounted for around 75–90 per cent of the growth in life expectancy for the world as a whole between the 1930s and the 1960s (Preston, 2007).

Fertility remains high in the second stage of the demographic transition. Insufficient time has elapsed for fundamental structural change in the economy, such as urbanization or industrialization, so economic benefits and ample labouring opportunities remain for (illiterate) children in subsistence agriculture. Women can still combine household and agricultural labour with child bearing and rearing, and children provide a form of insurance in the parents' old age and security for the household. In India the TFR remained at around six children per woman between the 1880s and 1950s (Dyson, 2005:21).

With high fertility and falling mortality population growth accelerates, and in many post-war developing countries reached 3–4 per cent annually. Mortality took longer to fall historically in the now-developed countries that had to learn from scratch the efficacy of such public health interventions rather than watch and learn, so they never experienced population growth much above 1.5 per cent per annum.

Box 4.2 Potatoes: The First Wonder Food

An earlier shift in the relationship between income and mortality resulted from the introduction of potatoes from the New to the Old World after 1492. Potatoes were nutritionally superior to previous (before c1700) staple crops. They provide nearly all the important vitamins and nutrients necessary to life (Nunn and Qian, 2011:599). Humans can be healthy on a diet of potatoes supplemented with dairy (providing vitamins A and D, which potatoes lack). An acre of potatoes yields approximately three times more energy than an acre of wheat, barley or oats. Old-World population growth after 1700 was more pronounced in regions suitable for potato cultivation. Careful statistical analysis shows that introduction of the potato can explain 26 per cent of the increase in Old World population and 34 per cent of the increase in Old World urbanization between 1700 and 1900 (Nunn and Qian, 2011).

Stage three: mortality continues to decline but at a slower rate, fertility begins to fall rapidly, population growth rates slow down

The third stage of the demographic transition sees mortality falling more slowly. Rising incomes change the pattern of mortality and we see an increase in 'diseases of affluence'. In India deaths due to 'accidents and injuries' increased from 3.9 per cent of the total in 1966/67 to 9.5 per cent in 1994/95, which is probably due to greater mechanization of factory production, and lifestyles and traffic accidents. The share of non-communicable diseases in rural mortality rose from about 35.9 per cent in 1969–71 to 54.9 per cent in 1994–95, as bronchitis and asthma, heart attack, cancer, and paralysis (including strokes) all became more important contributors to mortality. In urban areas coronary heart disease is closely related to changing lifestyles. The shift from rural to urban living increases exposure to toxic industrial chemicals, and various contaminants such as airborne lead from motor vehicles. In Delhi, for example, the number of cars increased by 12 per cent annually during the 1990s. More sedentary lifestyles, and diets involving a high intake of saturated fats, meant by the late 1990s an estimated 10 per cent of women in Delhi were obese and another 25 per cent overweight. The 1998/99 National Family Health Survey (NFHS) survey found that 28 per cent of males over the age of 15 years chewed tobacco, and 29 per cent smoked. The figures were increasing among women and had reached 12 and 2.5 per cent respectively (Visaria, 2005). When life expectancy reaches about 65 further reductions in mortality are much harder, more expensive and slower. They require more expensive medical treatments for cardiovascular disease and cancers, and lifestyle changes, such as more exercise, less smoking and a healthier diet. In India life expectancy has continued to increase, though at a diminishing rate, from (for males) an average of 36.8 years in the 1950s, to 44.0 in the 1960s, 50.0 in the 1970s, 55.5 in the 1980s and 60.8 in the 1990s (Dyson, 2005:21).

Fertility falls rapidly in this third stage. Increasing female literacy typically associated with economic growth has three effects on fertility. First, female education can reduce desired family size through greater autonomy of women in defining their fertility goals, accepting modern social norms, and a reduced dependence on sons for social status and old-age security. If the probability of a new-born child reaching adulthood is 75 per cent a mother who wants the risk of having no adult son to be less than 5 per cent has to bear three sons, which would require six births on average. If sons and daughters are considered equally valuable and parents want to avoid ending up with no children then three births are enough. If the probability of survival to adulthood rises from 75 to 80 per cent, two births are enough. Thus the combination of son preference and high child mortality may be important causes of high fertility. Second, female education generally reduces child mortality as educated women can better access medical treatments. They need to plan for fewer births to achieve a desired family size. Third, female education may help to achieve the desired number of births by giving knowledge of, and access to, contraception, and by increasing a woman's bargaining power within the family. Statistical evidence shows that women's education and child mortality are the most important factors explaining fertility differences and levels of son preference (Drèze and Murthi, 2001; Murthi, 2002). Male literacy usually has a much smaller negative effect on child mortality (independently of female literacy). Rising incomes may make children more affordable, but other factors related to higher incomes are likely to have the opposite effect. Urbanization is likely to reduce fertility because children are less able to contribute to household production and are more difficult to supervise by parents in urban employment. Rising disposable incomes and savings will reduce the need to have children to provide security in parents' old age. Urbanizing, industrializing economies typically implement legal changes to prohibit child employment and promote school attendance. This is usually reinforced by rising benefits from education. Urban sweatshop factories offer higher incomes than do subsistence agriculture but generally require literate workers. Considering fertility decisions as a form of investment, household returns can be maximized by having a small number of educated children rather than a large number of uneducated children.

In India the TFR fell rapidly from the 1960s onwards, from a peak of over 6, and dropped roughly 1 child per decade to reach 3.5 in the 1990s (Dyson 2005:21). Higher literacy, greater availability of healthcare, and higher incomes lead to a lower TFR. India has experienced average GDP growth of around 5 per cent a year between 1950 and 2000, and slow employment growth, particularly of women. TFR fell less quickly than in East Asia where economic growth, industrialization, and (especially) women's employment growth were far more rapid after 1950.

An odd pattern of fertility decline has emerged in contemporary India. In survey evidence between 1992 and 2005 it has become clear that the main contribution to the overall fertility decline in the majority of Indian states came from illiterate women. This seems to contradict the central place often given to education in empowering women in household, employment and fertility decisions. During these years contraceptive use rose more steeply among illiterate women than currently married and educated women. This was not just catching up, as, by 2005/06, 10 out of the 17 major states had higher contraceptive use among illiterate women than the average rate for all women (Bhat, 2002; Arokiasamy *et al.*, 2004; Arokiasamy, 2009). It is probably wrong to conclude that female education is no longer important for reducing fertility. An indirect influence of education is more likely. Uneducated women are likely being influenced by the fertility behaviour of educated women; what could be called positive externalities at the community level (Arokiasamy *et al.*, 2004). Increasing school attendance by the children of illiterate parents is also likely to be important. This suggests that couples have begun to reduce their family size in order to invest more in child schooling and such aspirations have increased through observation of the beneficial effects of education among wealthier others. There is evidence of higher school enrolment and attainment of primary education among children of parents who are using contraception (Bhat 2002).

The strength of the standard economic incentives in driving demographic change can be seen in Africa. A study by Caldwell and Caldwell (1987) argued that Sub-Saharan Africa would see a stubborn culturally-motivated resistance to fertility decline. They suggested that a cultural-religious system sustained and rewarded high fertility. In Europe and in Asia falling fertility has been concentrated among women over 30, but in Africa the main contribution has been among younger women. Studies showed a steep rise in the use of contraception in Nigeria in the late 1980s, much of it linked to the campaign against AIDs. Better education in Ado-Ekiti (South-west Nigeria) and Ghana from the 1980s led to a dramatic shift in the behaviour of single, and now better educated, young women, who wished to postpone marriage and pregnancy to consolidate their careers and earning capacity. In a context of widespread premarital sexual activity the mechanism was both abortion and increased use of modern contraception (Caldwell *et al.,* 1992).

New findings from demographic and health surveys carried out in the early 1990s showed that birth rates had fallen substantially across much of West, Central and Eastern Africa. The decline in Zimbabwe was dramatic, with a fall in TFR of two children per woman in ten years. In Senegal fertility declined due to a later age at first marriage. Survey evidence suggests that fertility in Kenya started declining from a TFR of more than 8, from about 1960 in urban and about 1968 in rural areas. Across 19 countries in Western, Eastern, Central and Southern Africa there is clear evidence of fertility decline, mostly in urban areas before 1975 and in rural areas about ten years later (Garenne and Joseph, 2002). Despite this 'progress' there is still a long way to go. In 2011 total fertility was 4.5 in Kenya, 6.0 in Nigeria, 5.0 in Senegal and 5.4 in Tanzania (World Development Indicators, 2013). There is little explanatory power in Sub-Saharan Africa for income which was not growing during this period for much of the region.

As with the second stage, the third stage of the demographic transition was rapid in East Asia. There was a sharp improvement in female education, infant mortality and employment, together with rapid GDP growth, urbanization and industrialization. Total fertility rates in rapid-growth Asia in the early 1950s were similar to those of India in the mid-1960s; ranging from 4.4 per woman in Hong Kong to more than 6 in Taiwan, China and Thailand. By the mid-1980s fertility had fallen to 1.4 in Hong Kong and, by five children per woman, to only 1.7 in Taiwan and slightly more than two in Thailand and China (Naughton, 2007:166).

Demography and government policy

Since 1945 population policies of governments and donors have greatly changed. William Easterly has recently argued that much of this effort was useless. I criticize below his optimistic concept that investing in people is enough, through a discussion of the phenomenon of missing women which shows that perverse demographic outcomes may occur as a result of cultural norms even in the context of rising 'investing in people'.

Since 1945 developing-country governments (and donors) have intervened actively in family planning. In 1951 India was the first country to adopt a national population policy. Pakistan, South Korea, China and Fiji did so during 1960–62 and many other developing countries had done so by the late 1960s and early 1970s. Despite the lingering legacy of Malthus, governments have not uniformly tried to reduce population growth. In 1976, 40 out of 156 countries (both developing and high income) had policies to lower fertility, and 14 to raise fertility. In 1984, at the International Conference on Population in Mexico City, a majority of African delegations reversed their previously pro-fertility approach. In 1996, 80 out of 179 countries still had policies to lower and 23 to raise fertility. Policies have broadened over time from a narrow perspective on supplying and promoting contraception use to concerns with the role and status of women in the household, and society more generally. The 1994 International Conference on Population and Development in Cairo saw an important shift in emphasis from population control towards sexual/reproductive health (Tsui 2001).

Perhaps the most famous contemporary demographic story is that of China. The government of China launched its first family planning initiative in 1971. It promoted later marriage by raising the legal minimum age of marriage, and encouraged longer spacing between births, and reduced fertility. The TFR declined from 5.8 in 1970 to 2.7 in 1978. By the late 1970s there were renewed concerns. Those born in the baby-boom years during 1962 to 1971 were due to enter childbearing age during the late 1980s and early 1990s. In September 1980 the government pre-empted this anticipated surge in population growth by passing the One-Child Policy, aiming at a stable population of 1.2 billion by 2000. The policy penalized families having two or (especially) more children. After 1984 the government renounced forced sterilization/abortion and often allowed a second child if the first was a girl. Single-child couples had access to various privileges including preferential access to day care and schooling. Penalties on families having a third or fourth child were equal to the annual income of many households, and if families were unable to pay they risked having their belongings confiscated or house knocked down. Debate continues about the real impact of this drastic policy. Hong Kong, Singapore and Taiwan share a common culture and language with China but not the one-child policy. Like China these countries have experienced substantial fertility decline, probably caused by rising education among women, economic growth and urbanization. Without coercion the Indian states of Kerala and Tamil Nadu achieved faster reductions in fertility than China in the 1980s, relying instead on improvements in health and education, of women and children in particular (Drèze and Sen, 1995:82). Other influences in China evolved in a direction that would have been expected to promote low fertility even without the one-child policy. For a low-income country China has very high female labour force participation, high female educational attainment, striking educational aspirations for children, good access to health and contraception, and a relatively good social security system. Studying these trends led Hussain (2002) to conclude that the urban TFR in China in the 1990s would probably have been below the replacement rate even without a birth-control policy.

William Easterly mocked all such government and donor efforts to reduce population growth by direct intervention, or as he put it, 'The most unprepossessing candidate for the Holy Grail of prosperity is seven inches of latex: a condom' (2001:87). Easterly argues as follows. The belief that making more contraception available will reduce fertility is inconsistent with the fact that people respond to incentives. Why would people risk a birth and lifetime of child-raising expenses to avoid paying $0.33 (an estimated international price) for a condom? 90 per cent of actual fertility is explained by the desire for it. People have more children because they want to and have an incentive to do so (as explained above under stage two of the demographic transition). The way to slow population growth, as demonstrated by these empirical findings, is to invest in people; more education, child and maternal health, more opportunities for employment.

The phenomenon of missing women

I consider the Easterly argument too optimistic. The phenomenon of missing women is a catastrophic form of mortality and is not being solved by 'investment in people'. Missing women are defined as the 'additional number of females who would be alive if there had been equal treatment of the sexes among the cohorts that are alive today'. The demographic transition theorizes that mortality falls when income and GDP grow. The phenomenon of missing women has worsened with rising incomes. A more extended discussion of the phenomenon of missing women can be found in McCartney and Gill (2007).

Many factors influence the biological sex ratio. These include race, timing of conception, whether the mother smokes, whether parents are both right-handed, whether pregnancy occurred during a war, hormonal factors, and the incidence of Hepatitis B (Sieff, 1990; Oster, 2005; Jha *et al.*, 2006). These factors tend to cancel each other out and the normal biological male–female ratio at birth is around 0.952. Since the first all-India census in 1901, the proportion of males in the population has increased. In India as a whole, between 1901 and 1991, the male/female ratio increased from 1.029 to 1.079. Within this overall trend, the male–female ratio by the early 2000s varied widely by state: from high figures in Haryana (1.161), Punjab (1.145) and Uttar Pradesh (1.109) in the north, to low figures in Kerala (0.945) and more generally in the southern states (Dyson, 2001:342). India experienced rapid economic growth in the 1990s and 2000s, with rising urbanization, improved health and education, but the problem of missing women intensified. The 2011 Indian census showed some improvement in the overall sex ratio, as the life expectancy of women continued to increase (older women living longer) and adult female mortality increased faster than male. A striking fact was that the child sex ratio (CSR), boys/girls, in the 0–6 year range continued to rise, from 1.079 in 2001 to an all-time high of 1.094 in 2011 (John, 2011).

The problem of missing women has appeared in other 'successful' developing countries experiencing rapid GDP growth, urbanization, improved education and health, and in some cases rising employment of women. In China the male–female ratio showed little change during the communist-Maoist era, being 1.073 in 1953 and 1.070 in 1982, but then increased greatly to 1.208 in 2000 (Naughton, 2007:171). Virtually all of this was accounted for by a rise in the sex ratio at birth, indicating that gender selective abortions were the likely driver. In South Korea the sex ratio at birth increased to above 1.10 in the early 1990s (Park and Cho, 1995), although due to a very low overall fertility rate the demographic impact was smaller than elsewhere. By the mid-1990s global estimates of missing women ranged from 60 to 101 million (Klasen and Wink, 2003:8). The total estimated figures for missing women are larger than the combined death tolls of both world wars (Klasen and Wink, 2003:264).

It is important to examine the motives for this catastrophic mortality to gauge what, if any, policies could improve the situation and expose Easterly's argument that 'investing in people is enough'. A *preference for sons*, in the absence of other factors, cannot explain it. Acting on the desire to produce more sons will lead to higher fertility but not change the gender balance of the population. Some couples will achieve the desired number of sons early and so have small families, while others will have larger families including more girls. Deliberate intervention is needed to alter the gender balance.

This is not a matter of *religion*. Muslim Pakistan and Confucian China both have a problem of missing women. The two Indian states with the highest male–female ratios Haryana (predominantly Hindu) and the Punjab (predominantly Sikh and Hindu) have a tiny share of Muslims (Drèze and Sen, 1995:ch7). Predominantly Islamic Bangladesh has witnessed a sharp reduction in fertility levels, a surge in female wage employment outside the household, and declining male/female ratios over the last twenty years (Kabeer and Mahmud, 2004).

While *poverty* may contribute to the phenomenon of missing women, it is insufficient to explain the adverse sex ratio trends in South Asia. In India there has been steady economic growth throughout the twentieth century, and poverty has steadily declined from the 1970s/1980s onwards, but the male/female ratio has consistently risen. Village-based field work consistently shows a negative relation between wealth/income and chance of survival for females in South Asia (Sen and Sengupta, 1983; Krishnaji, 1987; Vlassoff, 1991; Agnihotri, 2000; Jejeebhoy and Sathar, 2001; Harris-White, 2001). In some exclusive Delhi neighbourhoods – the boy/girl ratio is 1.256 (Manhoff, 2005:902). According to the 2001 census, the Punjab had the most abnormal sex ratios of any state in India, despite being among the most developed states (Kurian, 2000), with very low levels of extreme poverty (Shergill and Singh, 1995). In China and South Korea rising sex ratios have been associated with rapid economic growth and declining poverty.

In general, *rising incomes* are associated with development. The status of women is often assumed to improve with development, but cultural factors may intervene. Sanskritization refers to the practice in India of adopting high-caste cultural norms. These norms include the prohibition of widow remarriage, the adoption of a vegetarian diet, purdah (the withdrawal of women from paid employment outside the home), and dowry payment at marriage. With rising household incomes and falling poverty in India after the 1980s, low-caste households have been able to afford these high-caste norms. This has increased the economic burden of women upon the household, as they are withdrawn from wage labour and require dowry payments. There is good long-term evidence of this process in India. During the twentieth century, male–female ratios among low-caste groups converged with those of high-caste groups, as the low castes adopted adverse high-caste norms (Drèze and Sen, 1995). Economic development, improved communications and the spread of aspirational-celebrity media seem to be increasing the speed of diffusion of these Sanskritic norms from the north to the south and from high- to low-caste groups of India (Rajan *et al.*, 2000). Marriage is almost universal for women in South Asia and the bride is expected to bring a dowry. Although dowry demands are illegal in India, the law is seldom enforced (Ulrich, 1989; Vaz and Kanekar, 1990). Dowry has spread into southern India, where bride-price used to be the tradition (Heyer, 1992; Rahman and Rao, 2004). A common excuse for dowry is that it compensates the groom's family for a non-working wife who won't contribute to household income. If this were the case, we would expect to see an inverse relationship between female earnings potential (participation in the labour force or level of education) and dowry levels. In fact the exact opposite is true. In general as the earnings potential of a woman increases, so does the level of her dowry. There is no evidence that an educated woman is regarded as a more worthy economic asset by the husband's family. Instead, she is regarded by the husband's household as a suitable match for a better educated and consequently 'more expensive' man. A better educated woman will have to pay a higher dowry. The result is that educating a girl child will perversely increase the economic burden she places on her natal household. In Andhra Pradesh, a high-caste US-based IT worker could expect a dowry of $120,000. The practice of dowry is best explained by cultural factors; it favours, and is favoured by, a culture in which brides are viewed as vehicles for the procreation of children, for social prestige, for ensuring a male lineage and for the transfer of wealth. Dowry is an important symbol of the economic standing of the bride-giving family and can determine the family's future social standing (Srinivasan and Lee, 2004; Srinivasan, 2005). There has been a sharp increase in the real burden of dowries across India (Rao, 1993; Sharma, 1994; Vindhya, 2000; Srinivasan, 2005) and dowries can cause destitution in households with marriageable daughters (Deolalikar and Rao,1998).

As discussed earlier in this chapter, *education* has a significant impact in reducing the overall incidence of child mortality (Beenstock and Sturdy 1990; Klasen and Wink 2002). As with rising incomes, rising female literacy in the context of a pre-existing culture of son preference can generate a perverse outcome. Female education raises the likelihood of women being employed in remunerative work outside the household. The inability to combine such work with child rearing increases the opportunity cost of fertility, so reduces fertility and with it the option to have more children to ensure the birth of a son, so a woman may then became more likely to resort to gender-selective abortion, deliberate neglect, or culling of female children to ensure they have the desired number of sons. This is of striking relevance in India, where over the 1980s the fertility rate did fall by more than the desired number of sons (Das Gupta and Bhat, 1998:76). There is evidence to support this argument. According to recent fieldwork in Haryana, abortions were more common among women with education beyond higher secondary education, high living standards and husbands in better paying jobs (Unisa *et al.*, 2007).

The increasing availability of *sex-selection techniques* in India has made it easier for people to satisfy a preference for sons. Ultrasound can indicate the sex of a foetus early enough in pregnancy to permit legal abortion (Jeffrey *et al.*, 1984). Private clinics offering sex-selection techniques first appeared in 1982–83 in Delhi, Amritsar, and Bombay (Sudha and Rajan, 1999). Within three years, sex selection had become available in hundreds of larger cities and dozens of smaller towns in the north and northwest of India. By the early 1990s, the now portable technology had spread to rural areas in northwest, and urban central India (Sudha and Rajan, 1999). By 2000, ultrasound sex identifications were being openly advertised with the slogan 'spend Rs 500 ($10) now to avoid Rs 500,000 (dowry) later'. Sex-selective abortions have rapidly become an accepted norm in Indian society, especially among the educated (Arora, 1996; Basu, 1999). In Gujarat, Haryana and the Punjab, the sex ratio at birth for children was

1.231, 1.838 and 1.167 for mothers who received ultrasound imaging as part of a pre-natal check-up (Arnold *et al.,* 2002). Despite a 1996 law that made it illegal for the sex of children to be divulged to parents, and a 2001 Supreme Court order for states to enforce the ban on using ultrasound to determine the sex of a foetus, estimates of sex-selective abortions range from 100,000 to 500,000 per annum (Arnold *et al.*, 2002; Bhat, 2006; Jha *et al.*, 2006). Ninety per cent of the estimated annual total of around 5 to 6 million abortions were performed in unregistered (illegal) facilities. The exact number motivated by sex selection can only be guessed at. A survey in Haryana found that 18 per cent of women had had abortions, of which more than one-third were for sex selection (Unisa *et al.*, 2007).

Sex-selective abortions are only a partial explanation for the imbalance in the sex ratio. Excess female mortality in India continues until the age of 35 (Ravindran, 1995). Female mortality soon after birth (female infanticide) continues to be the dominant way to remove female children in India. Rough estimates for 1981–91 indicate that there were up to four times as many excess female deaths taking place after birth as before birth (Das Gupta *et al.,* 1998:90). The male/female ratio in the 0–6 age group has continued to rise (Dyson, 2001). Except for Kerala, the cohort of young children has become more male in every state. Between 1982–83 and 1992–93, the all-India child mortality was 43 per cent higher for girls than for boys; in Haryana and Punjab it was 135 and 81 per cent higher, respectively (Arnold *et al.*, 2002:304). Much fieldwork shows that female infanticide is prevalent in contemporary India (Gardner, 2003). In the late 1980s almost 10 per cent of female births in Tamil Nadu resulted in infanticide (George *et al.*, 1992). This practice continued into the 1990s (Chunkath and Athreye, 1997; Sudha and Rajan, 1999). In 2000, in the Salem district of Tamil Nadu, 42 per cent of infant deaths were reported to be due to 'social reasons' (Srinivasan and Bedi, 2007:859). In the 0–6 age range the sex ratio in the same district had reached 1.175 boys to every girl. This was despite the fact that Tamil Nadu has relatively high literacy, low infant mortality, good education and basic health care.

Excess mortality among girl children also results from long-term neglect and discrimination. The intra-household allocation of 'life-sustaining' resources can be thought of as an investment decision. Because male children, later in life, are more likely to get (better) paid work, allocating resources to them will maximize the return on the household investment. After the neonatal period, excess female infant mortality can stem from biases in the household allocation of survival-related goods, such as nutrition and medical care. In India, there is noticeable discrimination against girls in breastfeeding and in access to nutritious foods such as milk and fats (Das Gupta, 1987; Pebley and Amin, 1991). Provision of medical care is also significantly biased in favour of boys. Expenditure on medical care and clothing in the Punjab is significantly higher for boys (Alderman and Gerler 1997). The maximum differentials in the allocation of medical care occur in the first two years of life, the period in which most child deaths take place (Das Gupta 1987). In South Asia, boys are more likely to be taken to doctors (Chen *et al.*, 1981; Alderman and Gertler, 1997) and to be immunized (Arnold *et al.*, 1998; Hazarika, 2000; Mishra *et al.*, 2004; Koolwal, 2007).

Numerous scholars, such as Caldwell and Caldwell (1987), have placed cultural factors at the centre of their explanations for demographic change and have underestimated the role of economic incentives. Governments and donors have in consequence rather naively considered the supply of (rather than demand for) modern contraception to be a constraint on reducing fertility. William Easterly's recommendation that 'investing in people' is enough is equally mistaken. The case of India shows that aspects of the fertility decision and consequent human welfare can be strongly influenced by cultural norms.

Key points

- Population growth, by increasing the labour force, is a proximate determinant of growth. Higher fertility may increase (with a lag) entrants to the labour force or lower mortality and reduce exits from it.
- Empirical studies show that population growth has both positive and negative impacts on economic growth.
- Growth of the labour force has a strong positive impact on economic growth (the demographic dividend), but is insufficient on its own to boost growth.
- Growth affects fertility and mortality through the demographic transition.
- Three stages of demographic transition are relevant to developing countries. During the first stage there is high mortality, high fertility and slow population growth. In the second stage mortality declines, fertility remains high and population growth accelerates. In the third stage mortality continues to decline, but at a slower rate, and fertility begins to fall rapidly, leading to slower population growth.
- Since 1945 direct government (and donor) interventionist policy related to demography has expanded greatly. Differing policies have sought either to increase or reduce fertility rates.
- Missing women is a catastrophic form of mortality. The demographic transition theorizes that mortality should reduce with income and GDP growth, but the phenomenon of missing women has worsened with rising incomes.
- Missing women are 'the additional number of females who would be alive if there had been equal treatment of the sexes among the cohorts that are alive today'.
- Global estimates of missing women range from 60 million to 101 million for the mid-1990s. The total estimated figure for missing women is larger than the combined death tolls of both world wars.
- The phenomenon of missing women shows how the relative life chance of women can worsen even with rising incomes, urbanization, and education. Investing in people is not enough to achieve favourable demographic outcomes. Longstanding policies related to demography may have perverse outcomes in certain cultural contexts.

Chapter 5

Technology and Economic Growth

The general pattern of economic growth over the last few decades that we noted in Chapter 2 was: rapid in East Asia; moderate in South Asia; and slow or negative in Latin America and Sub-Saharan Africa. These patterns are paralleled by the success in absorbing technology from the rest of the world, showing that technology has a close link with economic growth. The question of causation, however, is a difficult one. Do new technologies provide new goods and services for export, raise productivity and reduce costs, thus driving economic growth, or does a rapidly expanding economy create the wealth and resources to purchase and create new technologies? New technologies can help a country overcome diminishing returns to investment, permitting sustained economic growth and enabling society to avoid the trade-offs associated with scarce resources. Nevertheless, any act of technological creation is closely linked to destruction; of older technologies, of traditions and existing patterns of employment.

Technology and economic growth

We saw in Chapter 2 that growth in developing countries is typically based on accumulating more factors of production and growth in developed countries is more often productivity (TFP)-based. This section gives a theoretical explanation for this pattern. Growth based on investment is likely to run into diminishing returns (see Figure 3.2) and increased productivity will be necessary to sustain growth once a country reaches a higher, developed-country income level. Although productivity can be driven by many different factors a key constraint on long-term productivity growth is the ability to introduce new technologies into the process of production (see Figure 5.1).

Technology: the basic concepts

Sustainable growth and catch-up

Figure 5.1 shows that in an economy with a fixed level of capital stock, quantity of land or labour, technological change (shown as point A) leads to higher output, land yield or labour productivity. This gives us a big and optimistic idea; that technological change can make growth sustainable, when as

Figure 5.1   *Technology and economic growth*

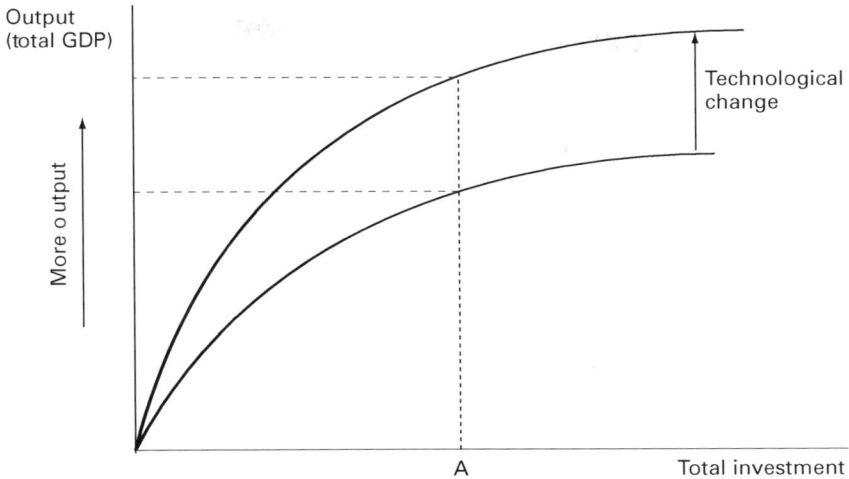

Figure 5.1 shows it would otherwise run into diminishing returns, as at point A there is little scope left to raise output by further increases in total investment. A second implication is that the effort by developing countries to catch up with average income levels in developed countries becomes harder. Catch-up is no longer just a case of mobilizing resources to boost investment – which Chapter 3 showed was the key policy recommendation by a generation of development economists working in the 1940s and 1950s. Catch-up now also requires that developing countries absorb new technologies from developed countries. Boosting the rate of investment may be difficult for developing countries but they are likely to find it much harder to acquire new high technology given its complexity, cost, and protection by patents and copyrights.

Technology and more of everything

The thick lines in Figure 5.2 are called the production possibility frontier. This shows the maximum output that can be produced in an economy at a point in time when using all available factors of production. Moving along the frontier by re-allocating factors of production between economic sectors (perhaps by labour migrating from the rural to the urban economy) shows the quantity of agricultural output that must be given up to increase output of industrial production. A second way of representing technological change is to shift the production possibility frontier outwards. Figure 5.2 shows that technological change allows a country to avoid the trade-offs associated with scarce resources and here to consume more of the output of both agriculture and industry.

Figure 5.2   *Technological change*

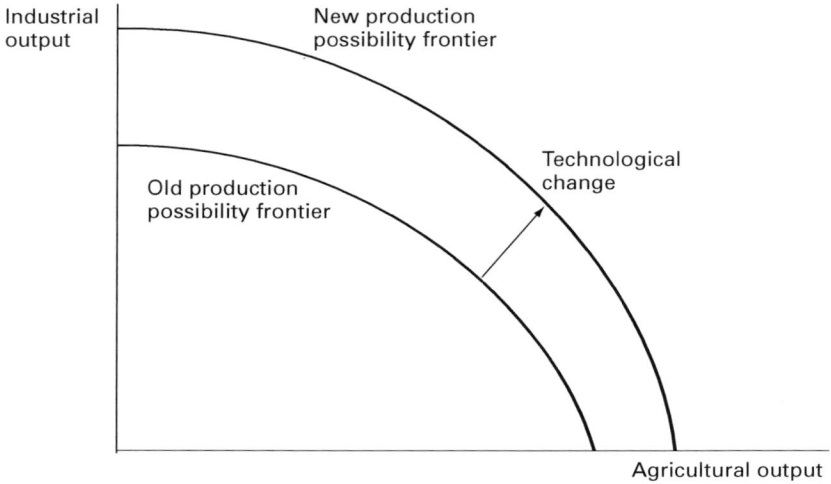

Biased technological change: the green revolution and industrialization

Technological change can be biased such that it favours one sector of the economy more than others. Figure 5.3 shows technological change biased towards the agricultural sector. A good example of this was the 'green revolution' of the mid-1960s when the application of science to agriculture boosted

Figure 5.3   *Technological change: the green revolution*

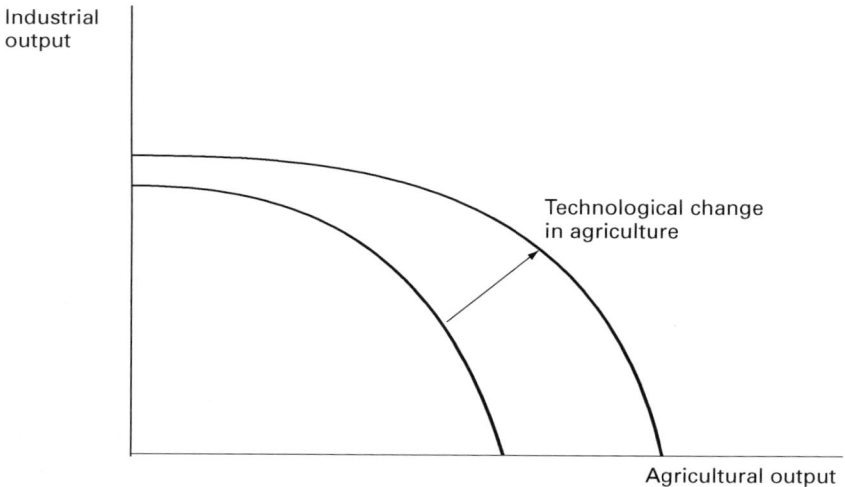

Figure 5.4 *Technological change: industrialization*

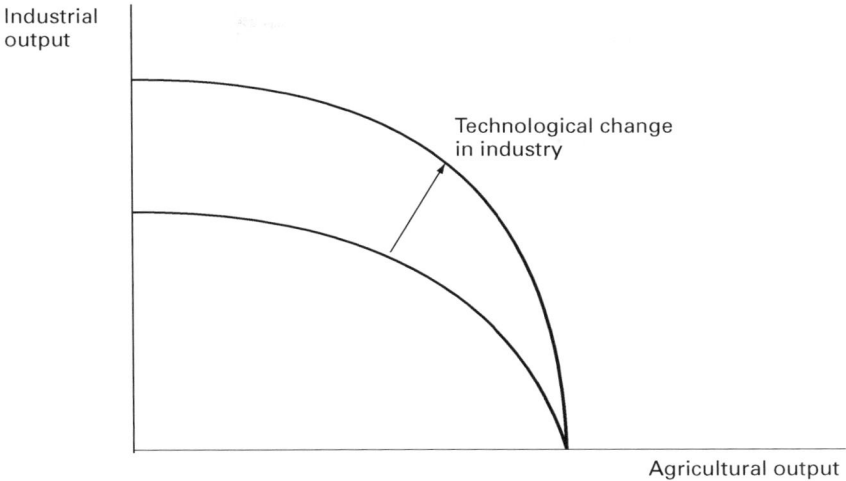

agricultural output in many developing countries through new seed types, and better fertilizer and pesticides.

Figure 5.4 shows technological change biased towards industry. There is a general belief that technological change is likely to be more rapid in industry than agriculture, and this is one reason why economic development is often associated with industrialization. An historical example would be the series of innovations which raised productivity in the British textile industry in the eighteenth century (see the Introduction).

Technological change and losers

Technological change is likely to create losers, such as those whose skills become obsolete or who lose employment as a task becomes mechanized. There can sometimes be a gender dimension. When agricultural or industrial work is mechanized and becomes a more skilled occupation, female labour is often replaced by male labour. The organization and political influence of the losers can be important in determining the feasible pace of technological change. Those who oppose technological change are often known as 'Luddites'. This is in memory of a movement that started in Nottingham, England in 1811 and spread rapidly over the next two years. The participants (allegedly led by a Captain Ludd) smashed wool and cotton mills, believing that mechanization had deprived them of employment and left people destitute. The rising was brutally suppressed by the government and many of the participants were executed or transported to Australia.

Between 1750 and 1850 the British political system continued to give consistent support to innovators and those winning out from technological change (Mokyr, 1990:256). Across Europe resistance to new technology came from guilds of skilled artisans fearful of unemployment. This led on occasion to complete bans on inventions when established interests were threatened. The Ribbon loom was resisted Europe-wide in contrast to its more rapid adoption in Lancashire, England after 1816.

Technological change as cumulative, dead-end, complementary and transformative

In seventeenth-century England the high price of wood- and water-based energy created incentives to expand the use of coal as an alternative energy source. This in turn required deeper mines and so stimulated technological efforts to develop machines to pump water out of mines. This promoted the development of steam- and water-driven power sources and in turn metallurgy, chemistry, mechanics and civil engineering. Technological change was in this case cumulative: one problem led to a long chain of technological progress. By contrast in the Middle East and North Africa, the camel replaced wheeled transport after the invention of the camel saddle in approximately 100 BCE. This may have then been a rational decision given the geographical demands of two thousand years ago but it reduced subsequent incentives to build roads and railroads and so was ultimately a technological dead end (Mokyr, 1990; Easterly, 2001). New technologies can be complementary to each other, whereby one invention raises the rate of return to others or a new technology may destroy the old. If complementarity dominates the effect is similar to increasing returns: one invention will make others more likely, meaning that inventions will tend to be highly concentrated in time and space. Examples have included the English cotton industry after the 1760s or Silicon Valley in the US in the 1980s and 1990s. This will lead to a pattern of economic divergence as the wealthier and more technologically advanced countries or regions experience more rapid technological change, productivity increase and economic growth.

Key transformative technologies have included steam power in the 1760s, electricity in the 1870s, atomic energy in the 1950s and computing technology in the 1980s. However, it was the expansion of the railways, argues Christopher Wolmar, that was a key 'transformative' technological driver in modern social, economic and military history. The Liverpool to Manchester railway, opened in 1830, was more advanced than any of its predecessors, being double-tracked, entirely powered by steam and capable of carrying traffic, including passengers, in both directions. The ability to quickly transport fresh dairy produce, vegetables, meat and fish helped revolutionize the diets of ordinary people. In the 1840s the Leipzig–Dresden railway began to encourage industrialization and economic interdependence among the German states. In 1846 the railway companies agreed to centralize administration which made state boundaries less relevant and so contributed to the political unification of Germany. Railways also contributed to territorial unification in more brutal ways. In 1870 at the Battle of Sadowa, Prussia was able to carry its field army of 285,000 men over five railway lines to concentrate them on the frontiers of Saxony and Bohemia in five days. Austria then had only one line of rail and it took them 45 days to assemble 210,000 men (Wolmar 2009:ch4). The German victory contributed to its own territorial expansion and nation building. In 1857 railways were used to transport troops to suppress the Indian Mutiny and preserve the British Empire. In 1871 the Gottard railway opened up Switzerland for travel during the winter months and created a new line to Italy, tripling German exports (mostly coal and iron) to Italy in less than five years and revolutionizing patterns of European growth and development. In the nineteenth century the US government played a vital role in promoting and regulating railway schemes, providing financial aid and free route surveys. As railroads spread westwards into new territory, government provision of land grants became the principal means of supporting railways, and compulsory purchase, known as 'eminent domain', gave the railroad freedom in the selection of its route after the charter was obtained. In the UK, by contrast, the route had to be approved by Parliament, putting landowners in a strong position to hold out for large compensation payments (Wolmar, 2008, 2009).

While case studies such as these illuminate the sequence of cause and effect, they do not explain the origins of the railways. Why was Britain the pioneer of railways? How was the state in the US but not in the UK able to intervene so effectively to promote the growth of the railways? If technological change in railways was the initial spur for economic growth, as argued by Wolmar, where did the necessary finance come from? Another problem (discussed in the Introduction) is that these sort of big one-story explanations have problems (or usually completely ignore) comparing the merits of alternative one-story explanations such as the introduction of the potato (Nunn and Qian, 2011), rising costs of military technology (Bean, 1973), or time keeping and clocks (Landes, 2000).

Technological change in economic theory

Simplified models of technology transfer assume that technology is freely available to all countries/firms, who select the technology that best suits domestic wages and the availability of savings for the necessary investment. According to this argument, countries with abundant low-wage labour would be more likely to select labour-intensive technology, which can be either costlessly absorbed, or else any learning period is predictable and automatic (Lall, 1992, 1994). The graphs illustrated earlier in this chapter suggest that firms or countries can easily move along curves as technology changes. This approach to technology assumes that the activity of innovation is completely distinct from gaining mastery of technology or adapting it to different conditions (the only differences between countries are assumed to be factor price ratios).

In reality markets within which International Technology Transfer (ITT) takes place are subject to various market failures. First, there is asymmetric information. Since technology suppliers cannot fully reveal their knowledge without undermining the profitable basis of their trade, buyers cannot fully determine the value of the technology before buying it. Second, legally enforced intellectual property rights tends to give owners of new technologies substantial market power which can be used to exploit buyers to boost their own profits. Third, there are likely to be externalities in the process of learning. The adoption and mastery of new technology by one firm may act as a signal to other firms who then adopt the same technology. These wider social benefits of the initial learning to other firms will not be accounted for by the pioneer firm. Firms may even choose not to engage in learning that can easily be replicated, given this will make the subsequent market more competitive and less profitable. Fourth, contrary to the simple models, many technologies are tacit, meaning that firms have more knowledge about their own technology and may know little about alternative technologies even within their own industry, and a period of learning is necessary to master any new technology.

Different technology structures have different implications for growth. Demand for high-technology products tends to rise rapidly in world markets (known as a more income-elastic demand), which offers more potential for rapid export growth (see Chapter 8). High-technology products also offer greater potential for spillover effects in terms of creating new skills and learning. Simple technologies are also vulnerable to being replaced by new technologies and the entry of lower-wage competitors to the market. As noted earlier, although technological change can be complementary it can also be destructive and render earlier technologies obsolete.

There is strong empirical evidence in support of these arguments. Between 1985 and 1998 world exports of primary products grew by 3.4 per cent per annum, low-technology manufactured exports by 9.7 per cent and high-technology manufactures by 13.1 per cent (Lall, 2000:344). These differential growth rates resulted in significant changes in the structure of world trade. The share of resource-based exports fell from 23.7 per cent of world exports in 1985 to 17.3 per cent in 1998; low-technology and medium-technology exports remained stable (18.6 per cent and18.8 per cent and 40.9 per cent and 38.9 per cent respectively); and high-technology exports increased (from 16.8 per cent to 25.1 per cent) (Lall 2000:351).

Given these market failures there may be a valid case for government intervention to promote 'infant industries'. Industries or firms that have the potential to be competitive (the infant can grow up) need nurturing through the process of learning. This nurturing is known as 'industrial policy'. In relatively simple labour-intensive activities based on standardized and easily available technology (such as garment assembly) the wage-cost advantage of developing countries may offset the learning costs completely, making nurturing unnecessary. In more technologically complex activities with greater demands on skills and linkages with other sectors, the learning process may be long and uncertain. Protection against imports or the provision of subsidies may give space for firms to learn without facing the potentially destructive consequences of competition from established producers. Such help may also, perversely, reduce the incentive to learn by removing the pressure of competition. Any such industrial policy must provide offsetting incentives in the form of performance requirements that are carefully monitored and enforced, such as an obligation to meet export targets (Lall, 1992).

The process of learning to reach the production frontier is often slow, risky and costly. Learning by doing may imply a lengthy and unpredictable period of losses as firms learn and adapt technology to make it more appropriate to developing-country conditions. In theory, private capital markets could fund firms through the period of learning. In practice uncertainty, risk and illiquidity mean private capital will be reluctant. This is especially relevant when economies are industrializing and the economy is undergoing profound structural changes, where past history is a poor guide to the future. The state then has a vital role in both inducing and facilitating learning by the private sector. Without such state prompting, firms in developing countries may simply compete on the basis of sweated, unskilled labour, and producing simple products more cheaply. Such a *low road* of development may be an ideal path for a single firm but there are likely collective and dynamic benefits from following a *high road* of competition based on learning, productivity, skills and upgrading (McCartney, 2011).

Case studies of technological change

The general finding from the case studies reviewed here is that technological change is not automatic, that the same technology can be utilized to dramatically different levels of efficiency in different developing countries. The role of the state is important in boosting the pace of technological diffusion but (as in the case of Maoist China) appalling mistakes are possible.

Our first case study shows that availability of technology is less important than the efficiency with which it can be utilized. There is reasonable evidence from the nineteenth-century textile industry that many key industrial technologies were able to diffuse quite rapidly. This case study shows that availability of technology was less important than the efficiency with which it could be utilized. By the early nineteenth century Britain had developed a specialized export-orientated machine-building sector within its cotton industry and by 1845 some of these firms were exporting at least 50 per cent of their production, providing a complete package of services to customers including technical information, machinery, construction expertise, managers and skilled operatives (Wolcott and Clark, 1999; Clark, 2007). In Japan, with access to this same technology, output per worker nearly trebled between 1907 and 1935, while in India over the same years it showed no change (Clark, 2007:347). India failed to efficiently utilize this basic technology, and its mills employed up to five times as many workers as were needed. This failure has been blamed on enduring workplace conflict and mistrust which resulted in undisciplined labour with high absenteeism requiring higher employment to compensate for low labour productivity while maintaining output levels (Clark, 2007:363).

The case study of Malaysia between 1971 and 1990 shows how responding to market incentives may leave a free-market economy stuck with low levels of technological competence. Here GDP grew by an annual average of 6.7 per cent, with the share of manufacturing in GDP increasing at the expense of mining and agriculture. Early exports were concentrated in processed natural resources such as rubber, tin and palm oil. The growth of non-traditional manufactured exports started in the 1980s with the entry of US electronics firms. The share of manufactures in total exports rose from 12 per cent in 1970 to 71 per cent in 1993, when they reached $34 billion (Lall, 1995a). There was long a concern about the learning associated with this 'technological transformation'. Malaysia's export of electrical and electronic products after the mid-1970s contrasted with the more typical export focus on garments, footwear and toys in other developing countries. By the 1990s Malaysia was the world's largest exporter of semi-conductors and among the largest exporters of disk drives, telecommunications equipment, audio equipment, calculators and colour televisions. Production, however, was very labour-intensive and based around the manual assembly of imported components, so it was less 'high-tech' than at first appeared. The sector was based more on low wages than high skills and was heavily dependent on imported components and technology from parent companies in South Korea and Japan. This meant that net exports (subtracting those necessary imports) were much less impressive than the headline figures suggested (Lall, 1995b). This was labelled by Kunio (1988) as 'Ersatz (or fake) capitalism'. What appeared to be successful upgrading into new and higher technological production masked a profound technological dependency on foreign firms (see Chapter 13 on the Dependency School) and generated few benefits to the host economy.

By comparison in South Korea there was a deeper and longer process of industrial learning. This case study illustrates a dramatically successful process of state-led industrialization and upgrading. Exports of electronics from South Korea increased from US$2.0 billion in 1980 to US$20 billion in 1991. The electronics industry in South Korea had its origins in the late 1950s with the production of simple vacuum tube radios and the 1960s as US multinational corporations (MNCs) set up wholly-owned factories to assemble semiconductors using cheap local labour. The industry quickly (and unlike those in Malaysia) moved to joint ventures with Japanese firms that, crucially, included technical assistance. Matsushita and Sanyo provided general technical assistance to Samsung and Goldstar after 1961 to produce transistor radios. Samsung sent 106 Korean workers to Japan for training in electronics production. During the early 1970s Goldstar and Samsung acquired technology through subcontracting arrangements with Japanese firms and also by licensing technology without the direct involvement of the foreign firm. This was strikingly difference from the dependence on imported technology and components in Malaysia. Finally, by the 1980s electronics in South Korea saw the growth of local capabilities and diversification of exports into high-quality precision engineering products such as hard disk drives, PCs, camcorders, and semiconductors. In 1983 Sanyo withdrew from its joint venture with Samsung and in 1987 NEC withdrew from its link with Goldstar Electric. By the 1990s the industry had shifted towards advanced electronics and information technology based on in-house research and development (R&D), the acquisition of overseas high-tech firms and more equal technology partnerships with leading foreign companies (Hobday, 1995).

Continual technological upgrading in electronics and other industries in South Korea did not occur automatically. Firms were pushed to upgrade through a state industrial policy. The Korean state chose several industries at a time as 'priority sectors' and provided subsidized credit and foreign exchange, state investment funds, preferential tax treatments (such as tax holidays and accelerated depreciation allowances), import protection and entry restrictions. The most important policy tool was the use of 'policy loans' (subsidized interest rates and priority access to credit) which accounted for nearly 60 per cent of total bank loans made between 1962 and 1985 (Chang, 1993:143). Empirical studies of industrial policy have generally found them to have been a success. Korean infant industries have in general tended to mature – as shown by domestic costs of production dropping below world costs of production. In the 1970s this occurred in iron and steel, electrical machinery, precision instruments, and non-industrial chemicals (Lee, 1997:1275–7). An important feature of Korean industrial policy was the tight performance-monitoring system. All firms in the 'promoted' industries were required to report not just on export performance but also on performance in other areas such as absorbing new technologies and research efforts. Failure to report/false reporting could result in fines and imprisonment. The commitment of the political leadership to exports (and truthful reporting), especially during the rule of President Park in the 1960s and 1970s, signalled to private businessmen that if they were to obtain government help (or avoid penalties) in the long run, they had to boost exports. The important political pre-conditions for a state to be developmental and enforce such conditionalities were discussed in Chapter 3.

In Sub-Saharan Africa there has been a generalized slow diffusion of technology from abroad. Between the 1970s and 1990s Africa did not experience a Green Revolution in agriculture and had the lowest uptake of high-yield variety (HYV) seeds in the developing world. This was partly because the thrust of technological changes was not appropriate for African conditions and Africa has lacked the capabilities to adapt such technology for local conditions. Worldwide, HYV research has focused mainly on wheat and paddy rice, while Africa produces maize, sorghum, millet and tubers (such as cassava, coco yams and sweet potatoes). Between 1980 and 2000 food production per capita actually fell by –0.1 per cent per annum in Sub-Saharan Africa, while increasing by between 1 and 2.3 per cent in Latin America, the Middle East and Asia. This was associated with a much lower share of agricultural land planted with modern varieties of seeds (23 per cent in Sub-Saharan Africa compared with 50–80 per cent in the other three regions (Sachs et al 2004:138).

From the early 1950s to 1978, despite its low-income status, **China** pursued a high-technology strategy. The state mobilized enormous resources, creating elite research institutes such as the Chinese Academy of Sciences. Government expenditure on R&D peaked in 1964 at 1.7 per cent of GDP – a very large share for a low-income country. Military technology 'successes' included the atom and hydrogen bombs and intercontinental missiles. Not all technological efforts were successful, however. The 'Great Leap Forward' of 1958, was supposed to be a strategy of 'appropriate technological change', or as Mao called it, a 'strategy of walking on two legs', whereby rural and urban industrialization would take place at the same time. Rural industry, Mao argued, offered a means of reducing underemployment in rural areas and saved on transport costs. Steel production, much of it in small-scale rural industry, (known as backyard furnaces) increased from 4.5 million tonnes in 1956 to 18.7 million tonnes in 1960. Targets were even more ambitious, 50 million tonnes for 1960, rising to 80–100 million tonnes by 1962. The rural workforce lacked the relevant skills for industrial labour and output was of inevitably poor quality. There are many anecdotal stories of huge quantities of sub-standard steel rotting away in rural areas. The effort led to a disastrous misallocation of resources. Labour was pulled out of agriculture to work in rural industry (industrial output almost doubled between 1957 and 1960) to such an extent that agricultural output plummeted by around one-third. Up to 30 million people are estimated to have died in the ensuing famine.

Chinese yields in key agricultural crops such as rice, wheat, and corn surpassed world levels by the mid-1990s. This was achieved by little mechanization (tractors),very labour-intensive techniques, a great deal of fertilizer and land irrigation networks which in turn were created by the massive labour mobilization campaigns of the Maoist era (Naughton, 2007:265). Per capita grain output increased from 300kg in 1955–57 to 400kg in 1984. This was based on an indigenous technological effort to replicate many technologies that had been pioneered in the West. In the 1950s China built an agricultural research network that linked local services up to the Chinese Academy of Social Sciences at the apex. This was complemented by the world's largest seed production and distribution system. By 1957 1,400 seed stations and 1,900 breeding and demonstration stations had been created across China (Bramall, 2009:221). There was a complementary massive expansion of rural infrastructure. Starting in the early 1950s, irrigation projects were built by labour mobilized by collectives during the slack season. The irrigated areas grew from 16 million hectares in 1952 to 36 million in 1975 (Naughton, 2007:259). There were some notable technological gains. These included the introduction in 1961 of hybrid maize, extended so successfully that by 1990 about 90 per cent of the area sown was using this hybrid variety. Hybrid rice was introduced in 1976 and by 1990 it was sown in more than 40 per cent of rice-growing areas. The yield of the latest dwarf varieties of wheat in Sichuan in the late 1970s was around 300kg per sown mu, far above the 70kg achieved from traditional varieties, and rice hybrids yielded 500kg per sown mu compared with 200kg from the traditional seeds (Bramall, 1993, 2009).

A paradox of appropriate technological change: preventative interventions and a vaccine for malaria

Both economic theory and empirical evidence suggest we should have been very pessimistic about the possibility of private-sector pharmaceutical companies engaging in medical R&D relevant to the needs of developing countries. In the case of malarial vaccines those pessimistic views would have been wrong. The vaccine market is now dynamic as never before and developing countries appear to be among the principal beneficiaries.

Mortality declined worldwide after World War II because medical progress in developed countries was transferred to developing countries (Cutler *et al.*, 2006:107). These were relatively low-technology public health interventions, related to water supply, removing disease vectors (such as anopheles mosquitoes that carry malaria or rats that carry lice), the use of antibiotics, and widespread immunization. Diffusion of this kind does not always offer such evident benefits. Technology that may be well suited to a developed country with an abundance of skilled labour (and relative shortage of unskilled labour), good infrastructure (roads, power supply), low-cost capital (an efficient financial system), and a temperate climate may be unsuited to the conditions of developing countries. Since around 95 per cent of patents are produced in developed countries, there is a long-standing presumption among development economists that the thrust of technological change is likely to be biased towards the conditions prevailing in developed countries.

Furthermore, the disease environment in developing countries differs systematically from that in developed countries. This can be explained by a mixture of differences in geography and in the prevalence of poverty. Infectious and parasitic diseases account for one-third of the disease burden in low-income countries (nearly half in Africa) and only 3 per cent of the burden in high-income countries. Many diseases occur almost exclusively in developing countries. These include Chagas disease, dengue, ancylostomiasis and necatoriasis (hookworm), Japanese encephalitis, lymphatic filariasis, malaria, onchocerciasis (river blindness), schistomiasis, leprosy and pertussis (Kremer, 2002:71). The disease burden in developed countries consists mainly of non-communicable conditions such as cancer and cardiovascular disease.

Not surprisingly medical research is biased towards more profitable developed-country diseases. Profits are largely determined by the size of a potential market, which in turn will be a product of the prevalence of a disease and also the disposable income of those affected. In practice income has been the dominant determinant. This has led to what is known as 'the 90/10 problem' where 90 per cent of R&D is focused on health issues predominantly relevant to the richest 10 per cent of the world's population (Chataway and Smith, 2006:16). The impact is striking. Of the 1,233 drugs licensed worldwide between 1975 and 1997, only 13 were for tropical diseases: five of these came from veterinary research, two were modifications of existing medicines, and two were produced for the US military (Kremer, 2002). In 1992 only 0.2 per cent of global health-related R&D was conducted on diarrhoeal disease, pneumonia and tuberculosis, which between them constituted 18 per cent of the total global disease burden. Between 1975 and 1996 patents related to tropical diseases constituted only 0.5 per cent of total pharmaceutical patents (Lanjouw and Cockburn, 2001:272, 285). Even for diseases that affect both rich and poor countries, research tends to focus on delivery systems that are more appropriate for use in rich countries. It would be more appropriate for research/technological change to focus on drugs that can be delivered in a few (rather than repeated) doses by personnel with little medical training and that are not transported using expensive refrigeration.

Market failures in medical research face developed and developing countries alike. Technological change with the associated R&D expenditure leading to new knowledge has the characteristics of a public good. 'A good is a (pure) public good if, once produced, no one can be excluded from benefiting from its availability. Public goods usually also will be non-rival. (Nicholson, 1995:815). This implies that knowledge, once produced, can often be relatively easily copied (non-exclusionary) and by any number of firms or individuals (non-rival), which reduces the incentives to undertake the original research. Glaxo (India), for example, was beaten to its launch of Zantac (an anti-ulcer drug) by seven competitors selling cheaper generic products. A patent or copyright is an artificially created barrier to entry to ensure the (temporary) monopoly of an innovator, to provide a reward (monopoly profits) as a stimulant to undertake R&D and offset this market failure. At the end of the 1980s, forty countries worldwide did not grant patents on innovations in the pharmaceutical industry. This changed dramatically in the early 1990s through the auspices of the WTO. The 1994 Agreement on Trade Related Aspects of Intellectual Property Rights (TRIPs) required least developed countries to join the rest of the WTO members in providing 20-year patent protection for pharmaceuticals by 2006. It was argued that although patent protection would lead to higher prices, this would be offset by an increased incentive for R&D. It was, however, unclear whether developing countries would benefit in net terms, partly because of the lags between granting patent protection (which raises prices) and the benefits of R&D filtering through (a long and uncertain process).

Wu (2000) found that stricter protection of intellectual property rights (IPRs) increased technology transfer by MNCs, specifically to China, while Lai (1998) claimed that because patents would reduce the ability of firms in developing countries to slow technological diffusion. This tightening of patent protection under the WTO in the early 1990s forms an interesting case study. The results relevant to developing country diseases are pessimistic. In the early 1990s patent applications for malaria, leishmaniasis, and chagas fell and leprosy showed no change. In the early 1990s publications in the scientific literature concerning malaria and leishmaniasis increased, while those related to Chagas showed no change (Lanjouw and Cockburn 2001:273, 278).

For state-owned pharmaceutical firms in developing countries, producing their own vaccines would create significant challenges in development and clinical trials. The fixed start-up costs of production in pharmaceuticals are high. New combination vaccines based on combining several antigens have significantly increased the complexity of production. Vaccines are biological products based on living organisms that are heat-sensitive and have fixed shelf lives. Capital investment for a new production facility is currently around €300 million to 500 million (Taylor *et al.*, 2009). Vaccine registration and manufacturing facility inspection standards are constantly being raised. During development of the vaccine Infanrix hexa in the early 1990s around 5,000 subjects were required for clinical trials, tens of thousands for the subsequent development of cervarix, and 100,000 for post-license follow-up commitments (Taylor *et al.*, 2009:5). As costs increased the number of private vaccine suppliers in the US dropped from 20 in 1970 to five in 2006 (Srinivas, 2006:1742). In 1994 the top ten companies in the industry held 28 per cent of the total global pharmaceutical market and by 1999 this had risen to over 43 per cent (Nolan, 2001). Few developing countries will be in a position to compete.

The most pessimistic view of medical R&D in relation to developing countries suggests that technological change is likely to be inappropriate, resources will be targeted to high-income profitable markets, tightened intellectual property rights are likely to hinder the diffusion of relevant technology, the complications described above will hamper production, and the medical sector will continue to be plagued by market failures. On the contrary, however, the vaccine market is more dynamic than ever and developing countries appear to be among the principal beneficiaries.

Around 120 different vaccines are now available, with 80 products in late-stage clinical testing, 30 of which target otherwise untreated diseases. A malaria vaccine has gone to Phase III clinical trials. Several candidates are going through similarly advanced trials for dengue fever. Merck and Co have teamed up with the Wellcome Trust to develop more affordable and heat-stable vaccines appropriate to conditions in developing countries (Wechsler, 2010:1). Even the pessimism about localized production was misplaced. In 1986 there were seven suppliers of four internationally procured vaccines, none of which were in developing countries. By 1996 there were 14 producers for five internationally procured vaccines, seven of which were based in developing countries (Srinivas, 2006). In India a dynamic pharmaceutical industry is adapting vaccines for local markets by reducing cost, sensitivity to periods out of cold storage and vulnerability to rougher transport conditions (Lanjouw and

Cockburn, 2001). Such appropriate technological change has enabled Indian pharmaceutical firms to export 60 per cent of their vaccine output to other developing countries (Srinivas, 2006:1756). In 1988 there were 350,000 reported cases of polio and endemicity in 125 countries, and elimination of polio now seems likely, with 1997 reported cases in 2006 and endemicity affecting just four countries by 2008 (Taylor *et al.*, 2009).

The development of a vaccine for malaria and even its physical delivery to developing countries will be just the start. The development of oral rehydration therapy to treat diarrhoea was a very low-cost, simple and appropriate technology but diarrhoea remains a significant cause of infant mortality. Other cheaply treated significant causes of mortality include tuberculosis and respiratory infections (Kremer, 2002:107; Cutler *et al.,* 2006) and diarrhoea, particularly in infants. Up to 50 per cent of children in some developing countries do not receive the basic vaccinations that are part of the World Health Organization's (WHO) Expanded Programme on Immunisation and three million lives are lost annually. In some countries (Congo, Nigeria and Somalia) coverage rates of the most basic vaccines declined dramatically over the 1990s (Bloom *et al.*, 2005). Approximately 25 per cent of people worldwide suffer from intestinal worms, though annual or biannual treatments with virtually no side effects cost less than $1 per year (Kremer, 2002). As discussed in Chapter 6 there is a pervasive problem in translating even (very low) public expenditure and programme objectives into real health gains in developing countries (Chaudhury *et al.,* 2006; Filmer *et al.*, 2000: 208–11). While a large majority of urban household heads in one survey of urban-slum India understand the purpose and role of cholera vaccines, a substantial minority still never boil water (Whittingdon *et al.*, 2009:402). Education, information and persuasion remain crucial.

Despite these gloomy prognostications global malaria deaths were reduced by an estimated 38 per cent between 2001 and 2010. Ten African countries as well as most endemic countries in other regions reduced malaria cases and deaths by more than 50 per cent. The key behind this unexpected success was a huge increase in donor financing of relevant R&D and related delivery systems. In December 1998 the Roll Back Malaria (RBM) Partnership was launched with leadership from the WHO, UN Children's Fund, World Bank and UNDP. Between 2000 and 2009, 84 from 100 endemic countries worldwide received donor assistance for malaria control. This changed the nature of incentives facing health care research, dissemination and health care providers. Massive donor funded investment in related R&D has provided relevant technology for developed countries de-linked to small low income markets. Newly developed insecticide treated bed-nets (ITNs) are now far longer-lasting and in need of less re-treatment. UNICEF became one of the largest net procurers of bed-nets and globally purchased 164 million nets between 2000 and 2010. As a result of this guaranteed demand global annual production of nets increased five-fold from 30 to 150 million between 2004 and 2009. By the end of 2010, 19 African countries received enough nets to satisfy 80 per cent + of their estimated need.

ITN use among children younger than five years increased dramatically across Africa from 2 per cent in 2000 to around 38 per cent in 2010. Improved technology in Rapid Diagnostic Testing (RDT) even in remote rural areas and provision of related equipment and training have permitted more accurate diagnosis and hence correct and quick (so more effective) treatments for those infected with malaria (Roll Back Malaria, 2011).

MNCs and technology transfer

From independence until the mid-1970s many developing countries viewed MNC investment with suspicion. It was widely regarded as exploitation of the local economy and the establishment of foreign monopoly control, hence as a form of new or 'neo' colonialism'. In 1973 the military coup in Chile was backed by foreign firms angered that the government of Salvadore Allende had nationalized copper mining. In the 1960s the Indian government, in the belief that scarce resources were being lost through royalty payments to MNCs for technology use, prohibited FDI in certain sectors and restricted royalty payments and conditions of technology transfer in others. In response to these restrictions, Coca-Cola and IBM stopped production in India in the late 1970s.

Since the 1980s, there has been a much greater acceptance and even enthusiasm worldwide for FDI, and policy has reflected this enthusiasm. Of 145 regulatory changes made by 60 countries in 1998, 94 per cent created more favourable conditions for FDI (Gorg and Greenaway, 2004:171). In many cases interventions have gone beyond liberalization; and have provided substantial public subsidies for FDI. Ireland offers a corporate tax rate of 12.5 per cent to all manufacturing firms locating there. In India the 1990s saw full-scale liberalization of trade policy and rules governing MNC activity; and 100 per cent foreign ownership was permitted in the sensitive energy sector. Inflows of FDI increased from $200 million in 1991 to $3.2 billion in 1997 and over $20 billion in 2005/06.

Developing countries hope that encouraging FDI will result in the import of more advanced foreign technologies and will promote technological spillover for local firms in various ways: the demonstration effect (local firms may adopt MNC technology through imitation or reverse engineering); labour turnover (workers trained by MNC may transfer knowledge to local firms or start their own firm); and vertical linkages (MNCs transfer technology to firms that are potential suppliers of intermediate goods or buyers of their own products). Negative horizontal spillover effects may occur if MNCs siphon off domestic demand or bid away skilled labour from domestic firms (Saggi, 2002). While happy to benefit from the low wages and access to raw materials and markets of developing countries, MNCs tend to leave core R&D work in their high-skill developed-country head office with its extensive links to universities and research institutes/laboratories. The resulting preference for transferring the more low value added aspects of production is likely to limit the amount of learning and spillovers from FDI (Kumar and Agarwal, 2000). There is an important question here. Do joint ventures or wholly-owned foreign subsidiaries exhibit higher levels of productivity growth than local firms and is there is there any evidence of spillovers to local firms occurring from these foreign entrants? There is a significant problem with answering these questions. If FDI is attracted towards industries that are already successful then any observed correlation between the presence of foreign firms and the productivity of domestically owned firms will overstate the positive impact of FDI. One study (Aitken and Harrison, 1999) using annual survey data on more than 4,000 Venezuelan firms between 1976 and 1989 found (i) a positive relationship between increased foreign equity participation and subsequent firm performance; (ii) that FDI was attracted to higher-productivity sectors; and (iii) that productivity in other domestically owned plants seemed to fall as FDI entered a sector. This negative spillover the authors interpreted as being due to domestic firms losing market share to foreign firms. The net effect though was very small. Although these results show that there can be benefits from FDI, there is no evidence supporting technology spillover from foreign firms to domestically owned ones.

Other studies, however, have found evidence of positive spillovers. MNCs in Taiwan created substantial backward linkages to local components suppliers or assembly services in personal computers, sewing machines, sports shoes and bicycles. Growth of component and other intermediate-goods producers in turn created a forward linkage to final-goods producers, drawing in both more MNCs and more domestically owned firms (Hobday, 1995). A famous example of FDI as a dynamic catalyst in promoting rapid industrialization is that of Bangladeshi textiles in the late 1970s (Box 5.1).

It is clear that the impact of FDI depends on the circumstances of the particular case. This means that government policy has an important role in maximizing the net benefits FDI to host countries. Policy needs to go beyond simply opening up a country to FDI and keeping governmental fingers crossed that all goes well. Studies have found that the magnitude of positive spillovers depends on local endowments of education and skills, the technological capability of local firms and the quality of infrastructure (Lall, 1992; Pantibala and Pedersen, 2002; Gorg and Greenaway, 2004; Li and Liu, 2005). A study of the determinants of the local content ratio (value of locally sourced inputs and raw materials to total sales) of 272 Japanese electronics manufacturing affiliates in 24 countries found that the local content is positively affected by the quality of infrastructure and by joint ventures between the Japanese-owned and domestic firms (Delderbos *et al.,* 2001).

The state also has a potentially more strategic role. A government industrial policy that targets particular types of technology with subsidies or other forms of support can promote technological transfer and domestic learning. Higher-end technologies such as R&D investment generate more spillovers than low-end operations such as data-entry and call centres (Pantibala and Pedersen, 2002). Enforcing an export obligation on FDI is also important. FDI attracted

Box 5.1   Spectacular spillovers: textiles in Bangladesh

Perhaps the most spectacular example of FDI leading to positive spillovers is that of the South Korean firm Daewoo investing in the textile sector of Bangladesh. In the mid-1970s restrictions on garment exports from South Korea to the US and other OECD markets did not apply to Bangladesh (then a marginal exporter of textiles). The Desh Garment Company was founded in 1979. Daewoo signed an agreement to assist Desh with technical training (six months in Korea), purchase of machinery and fabric, plant start-up and marketing. In return Desh were to make royalty payments to Daewoo equal to 3 per cent of its sales (Rhee, 1990). The crucial and unusual aspect of the FDI was the agreement to train 130 workers at Daewoo's Pusan plant in South Korea. These workers 'received some of the most intensive on-the-job training in garment production ever seen in the history of LDCs' (Rhee, 1990:337). The emphasis was on actual experience of running a factory that produced world-quality exportable goods and transferring relevant skills in production, marketing and management. At Desh average monthly exports increased from US$70,000 in 1985/86 to over $5 million after two and a half years. 115 of the original 130 trained workers left Desh, most to set up their own firms, and they became a powerful medium for transferring know-how throughout the entire garment sector. In 1985, before the US imposed quotas on Bangladeshi garment exports, there were more than 700 garment-manufacturing factories in Bangladesh exporting $300 million of garments. Rhee (1990) calls this relation 'the catalyst model of development'. The success of the model owed much to the peculiar conditions of world trade at the time, in the late 1970s and early 1980s, including the Multi-Fibre Agreement (MFA) limiting textile exports from many developing to developed countries to protect domestic industries in the latter. By the late 1970s South Korea was reaching its quota limits and shifting into more high-technology sectors. China was still embroiled in an ideologically charged struggle for political control after the death of Mao and remained largely closed to international trade. India was still promoting self-sufficient growth focusing on import substitution in heavy industry. Bangladesh, hitherto considered a development disaster by many experts, was not subject to any textile quotas – few ever thought it was likely to successfully export manufactured goods. So Daewoo had an incentive to transfer production to Bangladesh and with it, the skills necessary to successful produce and export textiles. And Bangladesh offered low-wage labour, no restrictions on exports and no competition from China or India. Such circumstances are unlikely to be replicated in the world economy in the near future.

by high domestic tariffs to produce for the domestic market in a developing country can lead to negative spillovers by contributing to the efficiency costs of import substitution, that is, producing something because subsidies make it profitable rather than because it can be produced efficiently (Brecher and Diaz-Alejandro, 1977). If the aim of FDI is to avoid tariff or quota restrictions on the import of fully assembled/final goods, then limiting production to simple assembly operations may be the most cost-effective activity for the FDI firm, but will limit potential technology and learning transfer to the host economy (Delderbos *et al.*, 2001). Empirical evidence shows that FDI has a positive effect on economic growth in export-promoting countries and no significant effect in import-substitution countries (Balasubramanyam *et al.,* 1996). The more passive enabling factors, such as good education and infrastructure, have been supplemented by more coercive policy interventions. Japan, South Korea and Taiwan all mandated local content requirements to rapidly increase the proportion of local inputs used in the production process and so increase domestic linkages.

Key points

- Technology can overcome diminishing returns to investment and permit sustainable economic growth.
- Technology can be biased, cumulative, dead-end, complementary and transformative, and can create both winners and losers.
- Economic theory ranges from treatments of technology as a public good that is freely available to all countries and firms to a focus on the profound market failures within which technology transfer takes place.
- Case studies generally find that technological diffusion and learning is by no means automatic and that the same technology can be utilized to dramatically different levels of efficiency in different developing countries. The role of the state is important in boosting the pace of technological diffusion but (as in the case of Maoist China) appalling mistakes are possible.
- Over the last decade there has been a dramatic improvement in the quality and availability of interventions to reduce the transmission of malaria, and recent progress towards a malaria vaccine. Massive donor funding for R&D and other relevant interventions have contributed to change the innovation incentives, and this technological change is expected to be of enormous benefit to developing countries.
- There is considerable debate as to whether FDI generates wider spillover benefits to the domestic economy, including the diffusion of new technologies. The empirical evidence is ambiguous.
- There is an important (potential) policy role for the government in boosting the net benefits from FDI.

Chapter 6

Education and Health

The question of education and health in relation to economic growth can be confused, not by the issue of causality, where the evidence is relatively clear, but by means and ends. There is clear evidence that education and health both cause and are caused by economic growth. This is good news for policy-makers, as promoting education is likely to have a positive impact on economic growth and so provide the resources for governments and house-holds to further expand education (as well as incentives to do so if the growth creates well-paid jobs that require a good standard of education). Society can float upwards on a virtuous circle of education and rising incomes. However, the opposite is also true. Poor education and slow economic growth could become locked together in a vicious embrace.

This chapter notes some of the research that shows both education and health are important *means* to promote economic growth. A healthy and educated labour force will raise labour productivity, attract FDI and facilitate the diffusion of new technologies. Education and health are also desirable *ends* of development. Education is linked to the ability to participate in a literate society, to personal empowerment and to the ability to live a life that one values. Health, freedom from repeated morbidity and pain, and an extended life expectancy are self-evidently good things. The link between health and education as proximate determinants of growth and as measures of wider aspects of development give them a centrality in debates about economic development. However, some scholars feel there can be conflicts between the means and the ends. Education focused on personal fulfilment (art or philosophy) may not be the best at promoting economic growth (engineering, numeracy, literacy). There is also the question of education for whom? Perhaps the promotion of economic growth needs a few highly educated scientists rather than mass literacy? And what if people utilize a first-rate education to work in a job that is personally profitable but socially destructive – the accusation made against many bankers and hedge fund managers in the last few years? The questions and answers are complicated and many of them are introduced in this chapter.

Education and health in developing countries

Education

Literacy is a widely discussed measure of human capital; shows both how much human capital exists at a point in time and how quickly it is rising; and is a component of the widely used Human Development Index (HDI) published by the UNDP since 1990. Table 6.1 shows literacy rates in various middle- and low-income countries in the late 2000s. Although there is a general tendency for richer countries (for example, Brazil, Russia) to have higher literacy rates than poorer countries (India, Bangladesh), there is an enormous range of outcomes. Sri Lanka and China, for example, which at the end of the 1970s were outliers in various other indicators of human development, have high rates of literacy despite being poor developing countries. In most parts of the world male literacy is much higher than female literacy, reflecting greater access of male children to schooling and probably more learning through interaction in work and social life outside the household. In some cases the enormous gap between male and female literacy (28.6 per cent in Pakistan, 24.4 per cent in India) is an indication of more general gender discrimination. In all cases youth literacy rates (15–24-year-olds) are higher and in some case much higher than in the population overall. This reflects recent improvements in education and is a guide to the likely future (positive) evolution of literacy rates. In some cases the difference is substantial. Female youth literacy in India, Pakistan, Sierra Leone and Uganda is around 20 per cent higher than female literacy in the population as a whole.

Table 6.1   *Adult and youth literacy rates*

Country	Year	Adult literacy rates (15+ years)			Youth literacy rates (15–24-year-olds)		
		Total	Male	Female	Total	Male	Female
Bangladesh	2010	56.8	61.3	52.2	77.0	75.5	78.5
Pakistan	2009	54.9	68.6	40.3	70.7	79.1	61.5
Sri Lanka	2010	91.2	92.6	90.0	98.2	97.7	98.6
India	2006	62.8	75.2	50.8	81.1	88.4	74.4
China	2010	94.3	97.1	91.3	99.4	99.5	99.3
Brazil	2009	90.3	90.2	90.4	98.1	97.4	98.7
Russian Federation	2010	99.6	99.7	99.5	99.7	99.6	99.7
Ghana	2010	67.3	73.2	61.2	80.8	81.7	79.9
Sierra Leone	2010	42.1	53.6	31.4	59.4	69.1	50.1
Uganda	2010	73.2	82.6	64.6	87.4	89.6	85.5

Source: Data compiled from *World Development Indicators* (2013).

The literacy data in Table 6.1 are based on relatively simple writing or read-ing tests. Whether a person is functionally literate – and can comprehend the written language sufficiently to engage with the demands of an urbanizing, industrializing society – is a more demanding criterion. The reality of poor-quality developing-country education systems means that even completing nine years of schooling does not guarantee functional literacy. Internationally comparable test scores that roughly approximate to functional literacy reveal significant variations. In Japan, the Netherlands, South Korea and Finland less than 5 per cent of tested students fall below the literacy threshold. Data from developing countries shows that a large proportion of students are functionally illiterate, including Peru (82 per cent), Saudi Arabia (67 per cent), Brazil (66 per cent), Morocco (66 per cent), South Africa (65 per cent), Botswana (63 per cent) and Ghana (60 per cent) (Hanushek and Woessmann, 2009). In many developing countries the share of any cohort that completes lower secondary education and passes at least a low benchmark of basic literacy in cognitive skills is below 10 per cent. This demonstrates that the education deficits of developing countries are even larger than indicated by the better-known liter-acy scores.

Health

Chapter 1 discussed in some detail measures of health in developing countries; these include malnutrition, low body mass, height and life expectancy. Table 6.2 shows three indicators for the state of health, two representing inputs (spending and doctors) and the other an outcome (mortality). A very clear pattern of enormous inequalities in both inputs and output measures of health

Table 6.2   *Health indicators in developed and developing countries, 2011*

	Afghanistan	Burkina Faso	Ethiopia	Sweden	Switzerland	United States
Health expenditure per capita (current US$)	48.2	38.6	13.8	5418.8	9247.8	8467.0
Physicians per 1,000 people	0.2			3.8	3.9	2.5
Mortality rate under-5s per 1,000 live births	101.2	108.1	71.9	3.0	4.4	7.3

Source: Data compiled from *World Development Indicators* (2014).

emerges when the three poor countries (Afghanistan, Burkina Faso and Ethiopia) are compared with three developed countries (Sweden, Switzerland and the United States).

These health inequalities have been narrowing, even as income gaps between developed and developing countries have been widening. Table 1.3 (see p. 29) showed that the difference in life expectancy between the developed West and the rest of the world was zero in 1000 CE, reached a peak of 22 years in 1950 and declined to 15 years by 2002.

Education, health and economic growth

Education affects growth through its impact on labour as a factor of production. Time spent in formal education reduces the labour supply, particularly of young people. Education is also linked to fertility, mortality and migration which will influence the quantity of labour through demography. Educated workers are likely to be more productive themselves and will make it easier for productivity-enhancing technology (likely to need skilled labour) to diffuse throughout an economy. Education may also have indirect impacts on growth, for example through public debate and discussion that improve the functioning of democracy and hence the quality of government policy-making, which many argue will have a positive impact on productivity. FDI may be attracted to countries offering investors a higher stock of human capital, and technological spillovers from FDI are then likely to be higher in countries with a better stock of education. Health has very similar impacts. A healthier labour force will increase the effective labour supply by reducing time off work and increasing

Figure 6.1   *Education, health and economic growth*

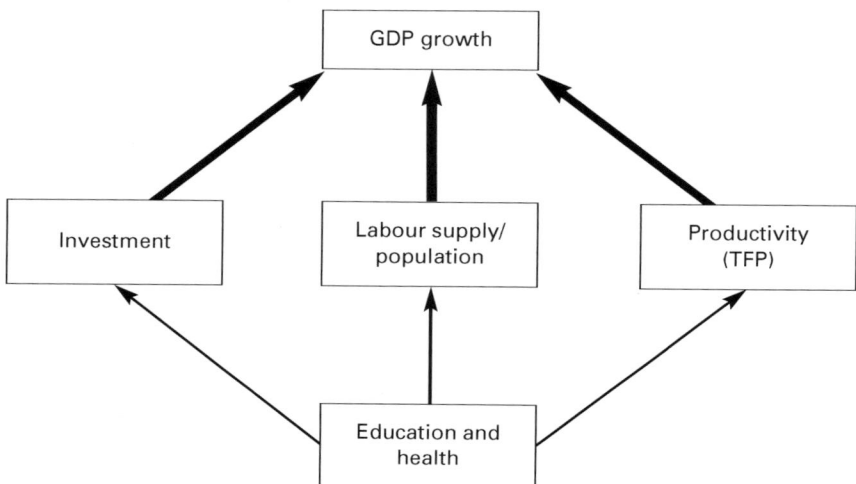

the ability to expend either mental or physical effort while at work. Health will contribute to human capital formation through increasing school attendance and on-the-job learning at work, so increasing productivity. There is also some evidence that FDI will be attracted to countries with better health facilities. These links are shown in Figure 6.1.

From growth to education and health

Although the main focus of this chapter is how education and health impact economic growth the pattern of reverse causation is also important. Growth in general promotes both education and health, so a virtuous circle between economic growth and human development is at least theoretically possible. The causal mechanism, however, is complicated and uncertain.

Across a broad cross-section of countries higher income per capita is associated with lower infant mortality and higher life expectancy. There is strong evidence that the positive relationship between income and health is causal, such that 'wealthier nations become healthier nations'. A study shows that differences in country growth rates over three decades explain roughly 40 per cent of the cross-country differences in mortality rate (Pritchett and Summers, 1996). Growth was also found to strongly positively impact on child malnutrition in a study of weight-for-age data based on food consumption in 12 countries and aggregate data from 61 developing countries (Haddad *et al.*, 2003). There are of course outliers. Child malnutrition rates, for example, are little different in Kenya and South Africa despite the latter having GDP per capita eight times higher than the former.

It is likely that GDP growth improves health directly and indirectly via increased public and private/household spending on goods that directly/indirectly improve health. Evidence using inter-country comparisons shows that GDP growth leads to increased life expectancy, mainly through its impact on the incomes of the poor and also by raising resources and enabling public health expenditure to increase (Anand and Ravallion, 1993). There is, however, no guarantee that the resources created by economic growth will be funnelled by the government into public services rather than infrastructure for business or imported consumer goods for urban elites. In some countries (South Korea and Hong Kong) resources generated by economic growth *were* invested in health inputs, so life expectancy increased rapidly. In other countries (Brazil) similarly rapid economic growth was not so closely associated with more health inputs and life expectancy rose more slowly. This finding also raises the possibility that governments or households can increase spending on health inputs even at low incomes. The low cost of vaccinations and the low wages of the nurses who administer them have enabled some poor developing countries (Sri Lanka, pre-reform China, and Costa Rica) to achieve very rapid reductions in mortality without much economic growth. An interesting finding here is that almost all of China's post-1945 reduction in infant mortality happened prior to 1980. During the rapid economic growth that occurred after 1980 there was relatively little progress in further reducing child mortality. In India also growth after 1990 was accompanied by a decline in infant mortality improvement rates (Drèze and Sen, 2002).

Other evidence of links from growth, such as expenditure on food, is harder to interpret. Data from a relatively poor, malnourished sample of 240 households in rural south India in the mid-1970s show that food expenditure increased one-for-one with income (Behrman and Deolalikar, 1987). This does not, however, imply that higher incomes will lead to more/better nutrition so improve health. Food can be purchased for its appearance, status, odour or convenience. Even at low levels of household income considerable weight is given by households and individuals to such attributes as taste rather than nutrition in food. The ambiguous nature of nutrition as a measure of development and its sometimes perverse relation with economic growth was discussed in Chapter 1.

The social health gradient shows that higher incomes are associated with higher health status even in developed countries. The two most influential investigations of the social health gradient in the UK are the two 'Whitehall Studies' of British civil servants conducted in 1967 and 1985–88. The first study found a steep negative relationship between employment grades and health outcomes, including mortality from various diseases such as heart and respiratory disease, and cancer. With reasonably well-paid and secure jobs, the health findings for the civil servants in this sample were not related to unemployment or poverty. The follow-up study (of 10,000 civil servants) in the mid-1980s found no decline (even a widening in some cases) of the gradient. For men between 40 and 65 there was a four-fold increase in the risk of mortality in the lowest relative to the highest employment grade. The gradient remained despite continued national efforts to equalize health care access for all through the free National Health Service. The hypothesized explanations for this seeming paradox include the work-related stress, monotony of work and lack of control over work that may characterize working patterns among lower employment grades (Smith, 1999:159).

Although there is less empirical work on how growth affects education, there is some evidence that economic growth increases the expected return from and so incentives to acquire education (Bils and Klenow, 2000).

From education to economic growth

Education can increase the human capital of the labour force and so boost labour productivity, increase the innovative capacity of the economy, facilitate the diffusion and transmission of knowledge and so finally increase GDP. A theme running through efforts to quantify the impact of education on growth is the problem of measuring human capital (Mankiw *et al.*, 1992:418–19). Education investment takes the form of direct spending (by the individual, family and state) and indirect costs (forgone earnings). Much schooling is provided free at the point of use and there is an inherent difficulty in measuring the output or productivity of a teacher. A common measure used in much statistical work is the share of the population in secondary school. This fails to measure the quality of education (influenced by teacher absenteeism), those instances where official enrolment rates are very different from the actual number of children in school or workplace learning on the job.

Many of the benefits from education are non-material and fall on those other than the person receiving education (what are called externalities). All of these will be hard to capture in any statistical test of the link between education and growth. Among the many examples are that women's education impacts fertility (Drèze and Murthi, 2001), children's education (Bhat, 2002) and child health (Haddd *et al.*, 2003). Education also enhances the ability of an individual to participate in wider social processes. A person may benefit from education through reading, communicating, arguing, being able to choose in a more informed way and being taken more seriously by others, all of which may be independent of that person's income. Work by Craig Jeffrey (2012) on education in North India shows that parents often value education for their children in the belief it will give them the social awareness, confidence and good manners to be more socially mobile. All these findings see education not just as a means to an end, with humans as inputs into the process of production, but also as an important end goal of what makes a good society.

Nevertheless, studies have found a consistently positive relation, in both developed and developing countries, between education and higher individual incomes. One such study used data for 1994 to 1998 from 23 countries that participated in common educational testing of adults between the ages of 16 and 65 (Hanushek and Woessmann, 2009). An obvious conclusion is that expanding education should boost GDP. And, if there are positive externalities from the individual acquisition of education (as discussed above), then total incomes should rise even more.

Empirical results at the aggregate level of the entire economy often fail to find these positive effects. One influential study found that the growth in educational capital had a negative relationship with the growth of GDP and productivity (Pritchett, 2001). The result persisted if only developing countries were used, all observations from Sub-Saharan Africa were excluded and when using different estimates of educational capital. These extra tests implied that the result was 'robust' and did not depend on a few odd examples or an unusual historical time period. Iqbal and Zahid (1998), studying education and growth in Pakistan, find that various measures of education including primary, secondary and high-school enrolment are either insignificantly or negatively related to GDP growth.

There are three possible explanations for this paradox – sometimes called the 'Pritchett Dilemma'. First, that education does raise individual productivity but that labour is allocated to jobs that pay a good salary but are socially wasteful activities such as working in an inefficient or corrupt public sector. Second, that the expansion of the supply of educated labour when demand is stagnant could cause the rate of return to education to fall rapidly. In many

African countries the expansion of education has exceeded the growth of wage employment leading to declining returns to education. Third, that the quality of schooling may be so low that it fails to raise cognitive skills or productivity.

There is ample evidence that the quality of education in developing countries is often very poor. A proxy measure for education quality is teacher absenteeism. The Public Report on Basic Education (PROBE, 1999) provided the first serious evidence-based study of the quality of primary schooling in India. It was based on a survey of schooling facilities in 242 villages in five North Indian states (Bihar, Madhya Pradesh, Rajasthan, Uttar Pradesh and Himachal Pradesh) in 1996. PROBE found poor school infrastructure: 26 per cent of schools did not have a blackboard in every classroom, 52 per cent had no playground, 59 per cent no drinking water, 89 per cent no toilet, 59 per cent no maps/charts, and 77 per cent no library. In half of the schools surveyed there was no teaching activity at the time of the observations, though often teachers were physically present. Another survey of teacher absence in rural India in 2003 was based on three unannounced visits to each of 3,700 schools in 20 major states. The study found that on average 25 per cent of teachers in government primary schools were absent from school on a given day and of those teachers present only half were found to be teaching (Kremer *et al.,* 2005). The results from surveys when enumerators made two unannounced visits to primary schools (and health clinics) in Bangladesh, Ecuador, India, Indonesia, Peru and Uganda showed that averaging across countries, 19 per cent of teachers (and 35 per cent of health workers) were absent (Chaudhury *et al.,* 2006:92). Together these results imply that around two-thirds of employed teachers are not teaching at any particular moment during the school day.

The best type of data for 'education quality' would be comparable direct measures of the quality of education. There are only a few such examples. One measure of cognitive skills is for children enrolled in the ninth grade in 288 schools from the Indian states of Rajasthan and Orissa. The results show that 42 per cent of enrolled children in Rajasthan and 50 per cent in Orissa are unable to 'show some basic mathematical knowledge'. Since secondary enrolment in India is only 53 per cent, the performance of the median child (which includes those not enrolled in school) is certainly considerably worse. Results of the top 5 per cent of performers in these two states are comparable to those in high-income countries, though the average child in both states studied is being badly failed (Das and Zajonc 2010).

Using this new research the link between student achievement tests and economic growth has been re-examined internationally. One study uses data between 1960 and 2000 with a sample of 50 countries that have comparable quality measures and data on GDP growth. The measure of the quality of education, a simple average of the mathematics and science scores in international tests of school children, has a statistically significant impact on the growth of real GDP per capita. Adding educational quality (to a model that only uses initial income and years of schooling) increases the share of variations in economic growth explained from 25 per cent to 73 per cent. Sharp changes in test scores are also associated with fluctuations in growth between 1975 and 2000. These results are robust and still hold many different sub-samples, including OECD compared with non-OECD countries, and above and below average income countries in 1960. The results persist if all ten observations from East Asia with its rapid growth and high levels of education are dropped. If the scores are divided into those reflecting basic literacy and the top 5 per cent in the sample, both thresholds enter the model significantly, indicating that both improvements in basic skills (broad basic education for all) and having more high achievers are significantly related to economic growth (Hanushek and Woessmann, 2009).

Education policy

Among the many alternative policies for improving the quantity and quality of education in developing countries are universal primary education, improved transparency, efforts to promote teacher attendance, empowering parents and the local community, and private-sector provision.

Education and market failures

There are market failures in the provision of education. Education (as discussed above) can have wider social benefits (externalities or spillovers) such as reduced fertility, the improved functioning of democracy and more rapid take-up of vaccinations. These benefits will not be taken into consideration in the decision by a household over whether one of its members should acquire more education. This may necessitate government efforts such as making schooling up to a certain age compulsory, to ensure the widespread take-up of at least primary education. Education is also a merit good. Relying solely on the market to provide education for a price will likely leave the poorest in society under-supplied. There is widespread support for the idea that at least literacy and primary education should be supplied by right to all citizens of a country regardless of their income levels. There may also be a case for quality control by government in the form of licensing of schools, teachers and examination boards to overcome any difficulties that parents would have in trying to ascertain the same information.

Universal primary education

There is overwhelming evidence that simple physical expansion of educational facilities and increased spending per student does not lead to clear increases in children's learning achievements. The vast expansion of resources devoted to education in the OECD countries between the early 1970s and mid-1990s produced no improvement in educational attainment scores. There is, unfortunately, no relationship between schooling outcomes and expenditure per pupil, expenditure as a fraction of GDP, or pupil/teacher ratios even when controlling for parental education (Hanushek and Kimko, 2000).

The Education for All (EFA) initiative and the MDGs promoted by international donors as well as the policy pronouncements of various developing-country governments are all pushing for universal primary education. Many African countries have come close to achieving universal primary education (UPE) at various points during the past half-century, though the hoped-for social and economic benefits have not materialized. Box 6.1 discusses the failure of such

Box 6.1   Universal primary education in Tanzania

In the late 1970s Tanzania raised the gross primary school enrolment rate to 98 per cent; by 2000 it had declined to less than 60 per cent. UPE became a euphemism for poor-quality education. There were insufficient high-school graduates to staff the expansion which meant that less than 50 per cent of teachers reached the minimum qualifications set by the Education Ministry. Of those children completing the seven years of schooling around 80 per cent failed the final examination. Since 2000 there has been a new drive to achieve UPE in Tanzania through the heavily donor-supported Primary Education Development Programme (PEDP) and since 2004 an accompanying programme to expand secondary education. The emphasis was again on quantity and expanding physical capacity to accommodate numbers. The government claimed that the national net enrolment rate had increased from 59 per cent in 2000 to 95 per cent in 2005, implying an extra 3 million children in primary school. As with previous efforts the new drive to UPE has been associated with a reduction in the standard of qualifications required for teachers. This was not surprising, given that the number of new teachers required in 2008 represented over 40 per cent of secondary school graduates in 2006. New teacher training colleges did open but shortages remained. The pupil/teacher ratio increased from 46:1 to 60:1. The evidence on education (as opposed to teacher) quality is mixed. Drop-out rates remained high, reaching nearly 40 per cent in some regions. In 2002–03 over 20 per cent of pupils repeated the fourth standard, the year in which students sit the first set of public examinations. There has, though, been an improvement in quality as judged by the Primary School Leaving Examination (PSLE) results, with the pass rate increasing from 19.9 per cent in 1999 to 40.1 per cent in 2003. Although the aspiration was universal education there exist very large inequalities in enrolment rates between poor and rich households and urban and rural areas (Wedgwood, 2007). A reason to be positive this time is that the incentives to acquire primary education are more apparent. Data from the 2000/2001 Tanzania Integrated Labour Force Survey (ILFS) showed that primary graduates earned double the wages of those with no education. Education in Tanzania has also been found to have a positive impact on productivity in agriculture and a negative impact on fertility. This indicates that the labour market for those with post-primary education is not saturated which was one of the concerns raised by Pritchett (2001). This latter effect may have been due to economic liberalization which has raised the return to education in urban areas.

efforts in Tanzania in the 1970s and more recent successes. Increased provision of primary education in the 1970s and 1980s was frequently followed by regression during the 1990s. Filmer (2007) estimates that very large increases in the availability of schools would have little impact on school attendance. Other factors like the demand for education or the perceived quality of education are likely to be contributing significantly to low levels of school attendance.

Improved transparency

Between 1991 and 1995 there was a three-fold real increase in public spending on basic education in Uganda, which had no effect on official enrolment data or the quality of education. The reasonable suspicion was that these funds were being misappropriated. This extra expenditure had led to higher teacher salaries which tripled in real terms between 1991 and 1995. About 20 per cent of government spending on primary education was non-wage expenditure in the form of per-pupil grants, of which schools received on average only 2 per cent, and at best less than 30 per cent, the bulk being retained by local government officials and politicians. In practice two-thirds of the non-wage expenditures of schools in the early 1990s was raised through parental contributions. While teachers were well aware of how much they should be earning, there was little general knowledge about the existence of the per-pupil grant. The information problem was tackled in a novel manner. The central government published monthly reports in newspapers of how much had been transferred to schools and required primary schools to post public notices on all inflows of funds. This promoted accountability, and preliminary evidence from an evaluation of the information campaign shows a sharp increase the share of grants reaching schools and being spent on educational materials (Ablo and Reinikka, 1998; Reinikka and Svensson, 2004).

Teacher absence

Teacher absence undermines any efforts to ensure quality rises with greater provision of school places and enrolment. Without teachers present pupil attendance at school cannot translate into learning. Fieldwork suggests two major explanations for teacher absence: poor quality of learning infrastructure, and the politics of interest groups.

Surveys of education (and health centres) in Bangladesh, Ecuador, India, Indonesia, Peru and Uganda show that good-quality infrastructure (presence of a library, running water, electricity and covered classrooms) reduced absence from schools. Presumably such schools were nicer places in which to teach. Teachers were also less frequently absent in schools where the parental literacy rate was high, which probably implies some combination of greater demand for education, political influence and monitoring ability by parents, a more pleasant working environment for teachers (children better prepared), or selection effects whereby educated parents choose schools with low absence rates

(Chaudhury *et al.*, 2006). Higher-ranking staff such as headmasters and doctors were more often absent than lower-ranking ones. The bigger problem, though, was the lack of accountability among teachers/medical staff to other groups (parents and pupils/health service users). Many developing countries have highly centralized and formalized government systems for recruiting teachers and health workers. Such workers are typically unionized and so politically influential. Recruitment, salaries and promotion are largely determined by educational qualifications and seniority, with little scope for performance-based pay. Disciplinary action is rare and teachers and doctors almost never fired. The main sanction is transfer to an undesirable location, though one study found that only in 18 of 3,000 cases was a teacher reported to have been transferred for repeated absence (Chaudhury *et al., 2006*).

One possible solution is to improve the technical ability to monitor teachers combined with attendance incentives. The NGO Seva Mandir implemented a teacher incentive programme in government schools in rural villages of Rajasthan, India. Before the study in August 2003 teacher absence was about 35 per cent. In September Seva Mandir gave 57 randomly selected schools a camera and instructions for one student to take a picture of the teacher and other students at the start and close of the school day. The cameras had a tamper-proof date and time function. Each teacher was then paid a bonus for attendance exceeding a specified number of days per month. In 56 comparison schools, teachers were paid a fixed rate for the month. The programme resulted in immediate and long-lasting (four years later) improvements in teacher attendance rates. Teacher attendance was tracked over 30 months; programme schools had 21 per cent absence, compared with 42 per cent in comparison schools. This experiment showed that teachers are responsive to financial incentives. There was strong evidence that once in school, teachers also increased teaching time. Classroom contact time increased by an estimated 30 per cent in the treatment schools. Pupils in the treatment schools were also more likely to later switch to a government primary school which required them to pass a learning competency test. This was evidence that the quality (as well as quantity) of education had increased (Duflo *et al., 2012*). Despite the evident success of the programme there is doubt about the extent to which this policy can be replicated. Government teachers tend to be politically powerful and would be unlikely to agree to be subject to such close monitoring. An example in the section on health (see p. 142) of a similar programme applied to nurses in Rajasthan shows how the scheme was undermined by politics.

Empowering parents and communities

An alternative is to give greater control to potential beneficiaries (maybe parents in the case of education or the local community in the case of health services). There are two pre-conditions for such a scheme to work. First, beneficiaries must demand the service so they have an incentive to monitor service providers. Second, beneficiaries must be able to influence providers, for example by punishing absence. The latter may be particularly difficult in practice. Switching to an alternative (private) provider will be constrained by affordability and such a shift is unlikely to have much impact as salaries are paid to service providers by the state or central government regardless of how much service they actually provide. Many control strategies are possible, ranging from putting the beneficiaries in charge of hiring and firing the providers or deciding how much they should be paid, to more limited proposals, such as having the beneficiaries monitor and report provider absence. Making teachers accountable to a school committee/body of parents is the standard example. The beneficiaries may be better informed about shirking if they come from the same community as the service provider, and to the extent that the service is valuable to beneficiaries they should be more willing to reward or punish the agent. In Udaipur, Rajasthan, a member of the community was paid to check once a week on unannounced days, whether the auxiliary nurse-midwife assigned to the health sub-centre was present in the centre and if not there, whether she could be found in the village. A parallel system (a monthly visit by a member of the survey team on the same day) confirmed that this system of local monitoring was properly implemented. External monitors and community members found similar absence rates (44 per cent and 42 per cent). The problem arose with the use of this information – paradoxically, local committees made no attempt to impose an external reward system for the nurse-midwives based on this monitoring. A similar scheme in Kenya, where members of the community monitored and reported on teacher absence, had a similar negligible impact.

In many cases people have long-established low expectations about public service provision so households have little desire to invest time and energy in hopeless efforts to improve them, and in any case have long ago opted instead for the private sector. This is happening in India where between 1993 and 2002 95.7 per cent in urban and 24.4 per cent of the increase in total primary school enrolment occurred in private schools (Kingdon, 2007:186). A similar pattern is occurring in health services with even the poorest turning to private provision. Incentives are therefore needed alongside efforts to increase the demand for public services, to ensure the continuation of worthwhile monitoring. This may include incentives for children to attend school such as direct cash payments or school meals. A scheme in Kenya that awarded scholarships for girls based on national end-of-year test results reduced teacher absence in programme schools by about one-third (Banerjee and Duflo, 2004).

Private-sector provision

It is claimed by some that public-sector services in many developing countries are irredeemably broken and we should look instead to the private sector. In much of the developing world responsibility for education has been transferred to the private sector through the rapid growth of private schools rather than through planned reform. Studies have found even the poorest parents have exercised the exit option, moving their children en masse from free government schools to the private sector. In a private school teachers are accountable to the manager (the headmaster who can fire them) and through him to the parents (who can withdraw their children). In a government school, controversially, the chain of accountability is much weaker, as teachers have a permanent job with salaries and promotions not related to performance. There are concerns that private schools are inequitable because they charge high fees so will exclude the poorest and that private schools are of low quality. Analysis of fieldwork on private education for the poor in Ghana, Nigeria and India has revealed some surprising results. Schools in selected parts of these countries were visited to check facilities and the activities of teacher and pupils were given a standardized ability test. The research also collected data on background variables of pupils such as household income, years of parental education, caste/tribe, religion and parental motivation. The results found that though the proportion varied, private schools enrolled a clear majority of children, ranging from 60 to 75 per cent of the total. There was no enrolment difference by gender. Fees were affordable: in India, for example, for the 4th grade they averaged around 3–4 per cent of the monthly wage for a breadwinner on the minimum wage and in Africa around 12–20 per cent of the minimum wage. The majority of these schools also offered free or reduced rate places to children. In Hyderabad, India around 75 per cent of private schools offered free or concessionary places amounting to nearly one-fifth of all private school places. In both countries private primary school teachers were more often teaching and absenteeism was lower than in their government counterparts. In Hyderabad more than 90 per cent of teachers were teaching in private schools compared with 75 per cent in government schools. In each of the studies private schools consistently achieved higher test results than government schools. In Hyderabad mean scores in mathematics were about 22 percentage points higher in private schools than in government schools and the advantage was more pronounced for English (not unexpected as private schools were more likely to be English-medium). In Lagos State, Nigeria the mean advantage over government schools was between 14 and 19 percentage points in maths and between 22 and 29 percentage points in English. Assuming that children of wealthier and more educated parents are more likely to attend private school we need to make an adjustment to these raw scores to find the value added by private education. After controlling for these effects the differences were reduced, though still large and in favour of private schools. Finally, private schools provided more cost-effective education. Average salaries were more than three times higher in government than private schools and in all studies class sizes were found to be smaller in private schools. The results showed that the per-pupil teacher cost is nearly two and a half times higher in government schools (Tooley and Dixon, 2006).

Conclusions

It is evident that no single policy solution can improve teaching quality. Poor education is more likely to occur in low-income and rural areas or when parents have low levels of education, implying a risk of a vicious circle of poverty and poor education. Central control over appointments and job security led to absenteeism in various developing countries. Teacher attendance can be significantly increased by close monitoring and financial incentives but this will be difficult to implement when service providers are politically influential. More central spending on primary education led to declining quality in Tanzania and decentralized funds in Uganda went missing without proper local information and accountability. Three institutional features form a coherent reform programme for education: competition introduced by private-sector participation; decentralization of responsibilities to give schools autonomy in making decisions related to teaching methods and hiring/firing of staff; and features such as regular centralized exams that provide information on student progress, increasing transparency and making schools and teachers ultimately accountable to citizens and administrators. But these are not isolated policies that can be introduced separately. Local autonomy without strong accountability may be worse than doing nothing if politically influential teachers then abandon their classrooms. Accountability without choice will put little pressure on schools to improve. Choice cannot be exercised effectively without good information about school performance (Hanushek and Woessmann, 2009).

Health and economic growth

There are very significant problems with measuring health status but evidence does show that health is linked to economic growth. There are no clearly agreed priorities to improve health outcomes.

Measuring health

Measuring health presents even greater difficulties than measuring educational attainment. Comprehensive clinical evaluations of health are generally too expensive for developing countries to include in large-scale surveys so small samples tend to be used. In the household surveys that have generally been used, respondents are usually asked to rate health on a scale from excellent to poor, which cannot account for the complexity and diversity of individual health status. 'Good' health may not mean the same thing to all people and self-evaluations reflect perceptions of health which are likely to be influenced by the extent of current and prior use of healthcare. Those individuals who have little prior experience with the healthcare system (the poorest) usually report themselves as being in good health.

Some studies use data from health facility records to create a disease-oriented definition of the health status of a population, but in low-income countries those using such facilities tend to be from higher-income households and not even those with the worst health. Various surveys have asked whether an individual has experienced illness or specific symptoms (such as fevers, diarrhoea, or respiratory problems) during a prior reference period. Again such surveys are difficult to interpret as the notion of an illness or symptom will differ between respondents. Survey evidence generally finds that the poorest people have better health status. In Ghana and the Côte d'Ivoire the likelihood of adults reporting an illness is positively associated with education and per-capita household expenditures. Reported morbidity is even much higher in the US than in the poorest state of India, Bihar (Sen, 1998). In some circumstances individuals may claim to suffer from an illness in order to become eligible for health-related benefits. The number claiming Disability Benefit in the UK, for example, increased from 1.1 million in the early 1990s to 3.2 million in 2012, with no recorded increase in other aspects of ill health. Asking how many days of normal activity were lost to ill health may reduce the impact of such errors. Here the better educated whose opportunity cost of time is high will have less incentive to miss work/school activities but the measure will be impacted by fluctuations in employment and spells of unemployment due to economic reasons.

Health status can also be measured by output, including anthropometric measures such as height, weight and body mass index (BMI). The BMI is the ratio of weight (in kilograms) to height (in meters) squared. A prime-age male in the US has an average BMI of about 25. BMI is relatively easy and cheap to collect through surveys that include fieldwork data on height, weight and sometimes arm circumference. BMIs are considerably lower in poor countries, averaging between 21 and 23 in the Côte d'Ivoire for example. Values below 18 or above 30 have been associated with higher adult mortality (Strauss and Thomas, 1998). Undernourished babies tend to be born with low birth weight which is then associated with a greater risk of coronary heart disease, strokes, diabetes, and hypertension 50 or 60 years later (Smith, 1999; Cutler, 2006). Improvements in maternal and child health inputs may only impact health outcomes with a very long lag. Although it does not help us to measure the impact of current health policy, current health status can be considered a summary measure of health inputs over an individual's entire life, providing a more comprehensive measure of lifetime well-being than current income or current capabilities.

Health and growth

Survey evidence finds that healthier workers (admittedly there is a problem in defining and measuring a 'healthy' worker) are physically and mentally more energetic, more productive and earn higher wages. Rising longevity may increase the incentives of individuals to acquire education and save for retirement, so increasing the pool of resources available for investment. The latter effect is likely to be temporary as the saving boom lasts one generation and will then be offset by the consumption needs of the elderly once population aging occurs. FDI is more likely in environments where the labour force has good health. Endemic diseases can deny humans access to land or other natural resources as occurred in much of West Africa prior to the successful control of river blindness (see Chapter 11 on the disease impact of tropical geography). Healthier children have higher rates of school attendance and improved cognitive development. An adult's illness may result in the poor health or death of a previously healthy child due to a decline in care or reduced family income.

Evidence from cross-country growth regressions suggests that the initial health of a population is a large and robust driver of economic growth. One extra year of life expectancy has been estimated to raise long-term GDP per capita by about 4 per cent. There will also be feedback effects if the higher incomes resulting from better health are invested in health-augmenting inputs such as more regular medical care. For any given initial income level, countries with lower infant mortality rates in 1965 experienced higher economic growth between 1965 and 1994 (CMH, 2001:23).

The health–wealth relationship holds even in developed countries. In the US across all age groups in 1984 those in excellent health had 74 per cent more wealth than those with fair or poor health. It is not clear, however, whether healthier households are wealthier because higher incomes lead to better health or whether poor health restricts a family's ability to accumulate assets through paid employment or because of rising medical expenses. There is evidence that the impact of new and severe health problems on savings is significant; the average wealth reduction is about US$17,000 or 7 per cent of household wealth. Medical expenses (most of which are insured) were not the leading cause of wealth loss which was more closely related to its impact on labour supply and expenditures associated with illness such as transport and care arrangements which are typically not reimbursed by insurers (Smith, 1999).

Chapter 11 looks at the incidence of malaria as a problem of geography, specifically as a health issue. The average income of countries without intensive malaria was five times higher than those with and between 1965 and 1990. GDP growth was 2.3 per cent in countries without intensive malaria, 0.4 per cent in countries with. A number of growth accelerations can be dated from the eradication of malaria, including Greece, Italy and Spain from the early 1950s, Taiwan in 1961, Jamaica 1958 and the southern US from the 1950s (Gallup and Sachs 1999). A malarial index has a strong negative association with income levels even after controlling for other determinants of income (Gallup and Sachs 2000). Unlike other important diseases such as TB and diarrhoea (linked to inadequate sewage, unsafe drinking water, and substandard housing), malaria is not so clearly a direct consequence of poverty, its extent and severity is more strongly determined by climate and ecology. The mechanism through which malaria impacts on economic growth is not clearly understood or measured but probably revolves around the impact of repeated infections (morbidity) on school and labour force participation (rather than mortality), the costs to a household for treating repeated infections, the long-term impact of cognitive development of children exposed to infection in the early months of life, chronic anaemia, and an impact on tourism and FDI. The malarial link is likely to decline owing to the recent successes in reducing the mortality and morbidity associated with the disease (see Chapter 5 on the development of a malaria vaccine).

Some (more micro-) studies quantify the causal link between health and growth through school attendance and the productivity of classroom learning and so ultimately through the more efficient formation of human capital. A 2003 study in Sri Lanka shows that better childhood nutritional status has a positive and statistically significant impact on school test scores, and that children with hearing problems and illnesses that cause them to miss school perform significantly worse in tests (Wisniewski, 2010). An experimental study found that children in schools where pupils were given de-worming treatments had higher attendance and also that higher attendance was noted for untreated children within the treated schools. This latter result suggested a 'school attendance positive spillover effect' from treated to untreated children (Kremer and Miguel, 1999).

Health policy

Significant market failures in health care are: the public goods nature of many public health measures; externalities in medical care; the failure of demand and supply to work as in other markets; and the systematic breakdown of health insurance.

Population-based public health interventions include addressing communicable disease, large-scale vector control (such as spraying against mosquitos), provision of large-scale sanitation facilities, collection and analysis of data and mass media campaigns. These are near-perfect examples of *public goods*. It is not possible to quantify individual benefits of public goods and charge a market price for them, as even those not participating will benefit from the reduced incidence of disease. The difficulty in charging for public goods means they are likely to be under-supplied in a free market. The public good of communicable disease control also has equity implications as poor people suffer from such illnesses more than rich people.

Another market failure in health is that of *externalities*. 'An externality occurs whenever the activities of one economic agent affect the activities of another agent in ways that are not reflected in market transactions' (Nicholson, 1995:802). If one person is vaccinated or if one country promotes a national programme, beneficiaries will be other individuals or neighbouring countries whose risk of exposure to the disease will be reduced. Private individuals will not account for the external benefits of their decisions so a market is unlikely to provide sufficient vaccinations. There is good empirical evidence of this in developing countries. The economic benefits in urban-slum Calcutta of a typhoid-cholera vaccine were almost four times the cost of delivery (Whittingdon *et al.*, 2009). A survey in Tigray, Ethiopia estimated the gains to households from the free provision of a malaria vaccine to be twice the value of income losses and treatment costs incurred by households because of the disease (Cropper *et al.*, 2004). Basic vaccinations were found to have a significant effect on the ability of children to acquire education in the Philippines (Bloom *et al.*, 2005:33).

A third important market failure is that *demand and supply* in health care cannot operate as in other markets. In most markets suppliers have an incentive to supply good-quality products or services to ensure repeat demand and a reputation for quality. Consumers have an incentive to invest in acquiring information on the quality of goods or services to help ensure they make good consumption decisions. Consumers of health care (the sick) typically lack the necessary information to make a judgement on the quality of treatments so have to depend on medical professionals to determine their demand. This implies that the same individual (often the doctor) would determine both demand (the doctor's diagnosis) and supply (writing a prescription for treatment) in the market. There are evident opportunities for doctors and pharmacists in developing countries to collude and push expensive and unnecessary treatments onto patients. The captive nature of consumers gives an important role to government in regulating quality but regulatory standards in many developing countries are very low, as attested by the proliferation of poor-quality medical treatments. Only 52 per cent of private-sector doctors in one sample in Delhi held the required medical degree (Das and Hammer, 2007). The most extreme cases have been the development of (bogus) domestic cures for AIDS given semi-official government sanction in Kenya and South Africa.

The *systematic breakdown of the health insurance market* is a consequence of imperfect information. Only the most ill or those vulnerable to the condition for which they are seeking insurance are likely to insure themselves (adverse selection). The insurance company is less able to observe health status than the individual seeking insurance (asymmetric information). Once insured, people may take fewer precautions to prevent illness such as not exercising to reduce blood pressure when costly medicines to control the problem are available and covered by insurance (moral hazard) and insurance companies will go bankrupt. In the absence of insurance almost everyone is exposed to catastrophic loss of income in case of serious illness. In India out of pocket payments (OOP) form a disproportionately large component of total health expenditure; they include direct payments for consultations, diagnostic testing, medicines, and transportation (Sakthivel, 2005). In 2004–06 the average direct health expenditure on outpatient care per treated person in rural areas was nearly 20 per cent of total household expenditure (30 per cent for the poorest consumption class) and 13 per cent in urban areas (Baru *et al.*, 2010), largely financed from households' own resources and borrowing. Nearly 29 per cent of the households surveyed in Udaipur, Rajasthan identified health expenditure as their major source of financial stress (Banerjee and Duflo, 2007). In 2005–06 OOPs alone caused an estimated additional 3.5 per cent of the population, or 35 million people, in India to fall below the poverty line.

One common solution is for the government to provide health care to all and fund it through the tax system, so in effect making insurance compulsory and having the healthy subsidize the unhealthy. The following sections discuss policy interventions for developing countries that go far beyond a narrow focus on improving health care.

Nutrition
Mortality from tuberculosis in developed countries declined by 80 per cent before there was any effective treatment of the disease. Some have argued that nutrition was the historical key to improved health and mortality (Fogel, 1997). Contrary evidence, however, shows that calorie consumption actually declined after the seventeenth century in England and the pattern of consumption (a switch to tea and sugar) actually worsened in nutritional terms (see Chapter 1). This is compounded by phenomenon of 'missing women' in India and beyond (discussed in Chapter 4) where it is common to find even in income-rich, food-abundant households that women and children show poor nutritional outcomes (Mukhopadhyay, 2012).

Public health
If economic growth were the sole reason for improved health, countries would over time move along the Preston Curve, which traces the positive relation between GDP and life expectancy. For a given level of income people today live longer than they did in the past. China in 2000, for example, had the income level of the US in the 1880s but the life expectancy of the US in about 1970 (about 72 years). Preston (1975) calculated that about 85 per cent of the increase in life expectancy between the 1930s and 1960s was a result of factors other than rising incomes. Big efforts to promote public health in developed countries did not really begin until the wide acceptance of the germ theory of disease in the 1880s and 1890s. There were subsequently dramatic reductions in water- and food-borne diseases such as typhoid, cholera, dysentery and non-respiratory tuberculosis. These diseases were virtually eliminated in the US by 1970 and one study shows that water purification can explain half of the mortality reduction in the US in the first third of the twentieth century (Cutler and Miller, 2005). There have also been big achievements in public health interventions in developing countries. Since the 1920s one hallmark of the Chinese communist government's approach to health care has been the mobilization of the populace to maintain public hygiene, immunization and to fight parasitic diseases. These efforts have improved levels of public cleanliness and by the 1960s ensured that yellow fever, diphtheria, polio and smallpox were marginal concerns. Despite only a modest improvement in per capita food consumption between 1956 and 1978 there were striking gains in average

nutrition caused by a more equal allocation. Another good example of a successful public health campaign was the National Malaria Control Programme introduced in 1953 in India based on large-scale spraying of DDT. Within five years the annual incidence of malaria dropped from 75 million cases and 800,000 deaths, to 2 million cases and 150,000 deaths. Other improvements in public health have included filtering and chlorinating water supplies, building sanitation systems, draining swamps, pasteurising milk, and mass vaccination campaigns. They also include micro-changes made by individuals but often encouraged by the public sector such as boiling bottles and milk, protecting food from insects, washing hands, ventilating rooms and keeping children's vaccinations up to date.

As a country begins to urbanize and industrialize it is likely that public health measures become more important. High mortality in cities can be effectively tackled by focusing on the delivery of clean water, removal of waste, and campaigns to improve personal health practices. This was discussed in the context of the second stage of the demographic transition in Chapter 4.

Vaccination and medical treatment
The first important medical interventions were vaccines. Variolation (the introduction of smallpox scabs from previous victims to bodies of the healthy) was introduced to Europe from Turkey and to the American colonies by African slaves in the early eighteenth century. Since the late nineteenth century there has been a steady stream of new vaccines such as rabies (1885), plague (1898), dipthheria (1923), pertussis (1926), tubercolosis (1927), tetanus (1927), yellow fever (1935), polio (1955 and 1962), measles (1964), mumps (1967), rubella (1970) and hepatitis B (1981). Chapter 5 discusses very recent efforts to develop a vaccine for malaria. The morbidity consequences of these diseases was high but the available historical data suggests that in the now-rich countries direct mortality from these diseases had declined to low levels (except for tuberculosis) before these vaccines were introduced. Something else, perhaps nutrition, perhaps public health, was more important. Antibiotics (such as Sulfa drugs and penicillin) developed in the 1930s and 1940s were the first of a new wave of medical therapies and had a dramatic impact on mortality. By 1960 mortality from infectious diseases had already declined to its current level in developed countries.

The near-eradication of smallpox, once thought to be impossible, represents an enormous success of medical intervention. The elimination of measles, which was still killing 800,000 people every year in 1998, is possible if global vaccination levels can be raised. Malawi, where 20 per cent of the population had no access to health service and less than 50 per cent had access to safe water, committed itself to high levels of routine measles immunization in the early 1990s; by 1999 no children's deaths due to measles and only two confirmed cases were reported in the country. The WHO, with donations from NGOs and the global pharmaceutical industry, are aiming at the global elimination of seven other diseases (Chagas disease, guinea-worm disease, leprosy, lymphatic filariasis, neonatal tetanus, iodine deficiency disorders and blinding trachoma).

The development of new treatments for diseases prevalent in developing countries is important but the main problem is *not* a lack of suitable treatments. Diarrhoeal disease and respiratory infections are the first and fourth leading causes of deaths worldwide but are rapidly and easily treatable with oral rehydration therapy (a mixture of salt and sugar to prevent dehydration) and antibiotics respectively. Infectious diseases such as whooping cough, tetanus, polio, diphtheria and measles kill more than a million children each year worldwide and have all been nearly eliminated in developed countries by existing cheap vaccine treatments. By the late 1990s avoidable mortality still accounted for about 87 per cent of total deaths among children up to the age of five in low- and middle-income countries (CMH, 2001). The National Family Health Survey in India for 1998–99 found that almost 20 per cent of children aged three years and under had suffered a bout of diarrhoea during the two-week period prior to the survey. While most women are aware of the importance of providing sick children with extra fluids and oral rehydration therapy, only about half suffering children had actually been treated. Measles remains a substantial cause of morbidity and mortality in India but only about half of children between 12 and 23 months were reported to have been immunized in the mid-2000s (Visaria, 2005).

Successful health programmes in poor countries such as the eradication of smallpox and the near-eradication of polio have been top-down campaigns run from outside the country by international organizations such as the WHO or UNICEF (Cutler *et al.*, 2006:109). The problem here is that such campaigns are very different from what is needed to improve general health care on a sustainable basis. With most developing countries spending less than US$10 per capita, per year on health care, how can they accomplish anything worthwhile? Case studies from Brazil (Box 6.2) and China (Box 6.3) offer good examples of successful and low-cost health interventions relying on incentives, motivation and information rather than large investments.

Hospital care
Sustaining mortality reduction in developed countries is more closely associated with expensive hospital care. In the US, mortality from cardiovascular disease due to medical advance has declined by over 50 per cent since 1960, and such reductions account for 70 per cent of the seven-year increase in life expectancy between 1960 and 2000. Around 20 per cent of this increase is a result of reduced infant mortality through improved neonatal medical care for low birth-weight infants (Cutler, 2004).

In many developing countries the public budget for health care is principally absorbed by public hospitals staffed by doctors expensively trained and using costly medical technologies. However, even when treating urban elites there is widespread evidence of poor-quality medical care. One study directly observed doctors (some medical school graduates and others untrained) in

Box 6.2 Community health care in Ceara, Brazil

Ceara in north-eastern Brazil introduced the Health Agent Programme (Programa de Agentes de Saude or PAS) in the late 1980s. After a few years of operation Ceara's PAS had contributed to a sharp reduction in infant deaths, from 102 per 1,000 (one of the highest in Latin America) to 65 per 1,000 in 1992. The programme tripled vaccination coverage for measles and polio, from 25 per cent of the population (the lowest in Brazil) to 90 per cent. By 1993 health agents were visiting 850,000 families (roughly 65 per cent of the state's population) in their homes every month to provide assistance with oral rehydration therapy, vaccination, prenatal care, breastfeeding and child growth monitoring. The programme costs averaged US$2 per capita, compared with the approximately US$80 per capita cost of the existing health care system. Eighty per cent of these costs represented payments to health agents (earning the minimum wage of US$60 per month) who worked under temporary contracts without job security or fringe benefits.

The scheme was not based on decentralization. The central state maintained a strict control over the hiring and payment of the health agents (the opposite conclusion to the one we reached earlier in this chapter about the importance of local control over teachers) who worked for nurse-supervisors hired by the local municipality. The state government created a sense of calling around these jobs through a rigorous process of meritocratic selection and training, constant publicity and regular publicized prizes for good performance. To be chosen for the job of health agent was like being awarded an important prize in public. Newly hired workers began their jobs strongly influenced by the prestige accorded by the selection process. Workers often took on tasks voluntarily that fell outside their job descriptions, an ambiguity that seems to have made supervision of workers even more difficult, but now there were also pressures to perform from the community. Central publicity campaigns empowered local communities to monitor performance of the health workers. This demonstrated that effective local monitoring is possible even with centralized hiring (which again contradicts our discussion of education earlier). In urban clinics nurses had traditionally been regarded as inferior to the doctors. Now each nurse was supervising/training an average of 30 para-professional agents and felt herself an important local personage. By enhancing the status of nurses as professionals the programme turned a large number of potential resistors into ardent advocates: 'In creating an informed and demanding community, in other words, the state had initiated a dynamic in which the mayors were rewarded politically for supporting the programme. In doing so, the state had contributed toward replacing the old patronage dynamic with a more service-orientated one' (Tendler and Freedheim, 1994:1776).

clinical practice in Delhi, India. Only 52 per cent of private-sector 'doctors' sampled held the required Bachelor of Medicine and Bachelor of Surgery (MBBS) degree. In tests only 30 per cent of public-sector doctors were able to ask the appropriate questions to gauge a medical condition from the symptoms declared by a patient, but less than 10 per cent then did so when observed

Box 6.3 Barefoot doctors in China

By the 1960s and 1970s the Chinese were achieving better health outcomes than many countries with much higher incomes. One reason was the strong emphasis on preventive efforts. In most developing countries government-provided health care is based on an urban curative hospital-centred system and the majority of medical professionals are concentrated in the cities, wielding sufficient political power to resist any shift in emphasis or simply absent themselves from practice if formally posted to rural areas – remember those absent doctors, nurses and teachers discussed earlier. After 1968 China popularized a programme first developed in 1958 in Shanghai. Prior to 1968 intermediate medical schools graduated doctors after three years and higher-level institutions trained physicians for six or more years. Both types of personnel were highly trained and expensive and so too scarce to staff China's several hundred thousand village cooperative health programmes. An alternative 'barefoot doctor' model based on training of 3 to 6 months began to be promoted. These health workers provided limited curative services such as post-natal care, advice on boiling water, vaccinations and some pharmaceuticals. By 1976 there were an estimated 1.5 million such barefoot doctors in post and 85 per cent of villages had a health clinic staffed by trained barefoot doctors (Lampton, 1978; Riskin, 1991). Life expectancy in China increased from 36 years in 1950 to 64 years in 1979. The infant mortality rate in rural China fell from 73 per 1,000 in 1963 to 40 in 1978, while the average for the other poorest developing countries was 97 per 1,000 (Riskin, 1991; Bramall, 2009). The most valuable lesson from the Chinese model is that healthcare provision suited to the particular conditions of a developing country can achieve a significant impact at relatively low cost. The exact Chinese-style model owed much to the particular conditions of Maoist China, which would be difficult to replicate. In China during the 1960s and 1970s agricultural land was owned and managed by rural collectives (massive centrally directed state-owned farms) so it was possible for the local state to allocate the locality's labour power to mass health campaigns such as vaccinations when needed. Few developing countries have the characteristics (strong central state able to mobilize the rural population and impose its will on elite urban health groups) which could make the Chinese model feasible (Lampton, 1978).

interacting with actual patients. In contrast, private non-MBBS doctors knew the right question to ask only 20 per cent of the time, but achieved the same level in practice. Private doctors, who are directly accountable to the patient, make more effort but tend to over-prescribe medicines that are not effective to please the patient (Das and Hammer, 2005). These problems in delivering healthcare, especially primary healthcare, are related to bad incentives. When private providers do not turn up to their clinics they do not get paid. Public healthcare providers are paid by salary, not monitored by supervisors, cannot be fired or have pay reduced under any circumstances, and have lucrative alternative work in the private sector (Hammer *et al.*, 2007).

The poor receive low-quality care from the private sector because doctors do not know much and low-quality care from the public sector because doctors do not do much. These results suggest that poor-quality medical services for the poor are a result of both incentives and competence of providers. For the private sector any solution is likely to come from improving information to consumers and greater regulatory oversight by the state which together can help to reduce demand for excessive and inappropriate treatment.

Mortality reduction in rich countries, where most deaths are from cancers and cardiovascular diseases (Cutler *et al.*, 2006:107) is closely associated with expensive hospital care. There is a widespread view in developing countries that the existing allocation of health resources in curative care in hospitals is inappropriate and that a reorientation of government spending to primary health care would bring about health gains and cost savings. Some of the inspiration comes from the 'barefoot doctors' model (Box 6.3). There are problems with this argument. Advocates of primary health care often assume that the public sector can deliver whatever the government (or some international donor) decides ought to be delivered. The argument then jumps to the idea that if government supplies the right things then patients will receive the right things (here primary health care). There is, however, little empirical support for the link between more spending on primary health care activities and greater access to primary health care services, or for the argument that greater access to primary health care facilities reduces mortality (Filmer and Pritchett, 1999). In general socioeconomic (rather than healthcare) characteristics explain nearly all of the variation in mortality rates across developing countries. Studies show that virtually all of the cross-country variation in child mortality can be explained by six variables (average GDP per capita, a measure of the distribution of income, level of female education, a dummy variable for predominantly Muslim countries, an index of ethno-linguistic diversity, and a set of dummy variables for regions). Public expenditure on health as a share of GDP has only a small and statistically insignificant impact on child mortality (Filmer and Prichett, 1999).

In 1977, for example, a very intensive maternal and child health and family planning programme was started in a set of treatment villages in the Matlab region of Bangladesh. In the treatment area mothers and children were visited every 15 days by a female health worker. Mortality rates among children did fall but this was attributed almost exclusively to measles immunization, not primary health care more generally (Koenig *et al.*, 1991). Another example is a study based on unannounced visits to 150 health facilities in Bangladesh. Here, depressingly familiar results in terms of staff absence were found. But important for the pro-hospital argument was that primary/village facilities performed worse than urban hospitals. Again absence rates of staff were around a quarter with highly trained physicians showing the highest rates of absenteeism. Absenteeism was very high in small rural posts where it reached 74 per cent. These empirical results suggest that enhancing health outcomes is not simply a matter of providing additional funds or increasing access to primary health care services and services (Filmer *et al.*, 2000).

In India at least there is no obvious shortage of primary health care facilities. A survey of health facilities in rural Rajasthan finds that infrastructure is operational. The average household is within 2 km of the nearest public facility and qualified medical personnel are employed by the government to staff them. Yet, the system fails to deliver good care and patients prefer the more expensive private sector. In an intervention to try and address nurse absence the Indian NGO Seva Mandir used time-clocks to monitor attendance of nurses at small rural health clinics. The government used the attendance data with a specific schedule of fines and penalties (introduced for this programme) to determine the wages for any nurse. In the first six months the incentives led to dramatic improvement in attendance (doubling by some measures). After the first six months the local health administration deliberately undermined the incentive system by allowing more exempt days for nurses and not sanctioning them for absences. After sixteen months there was no difference between the absence rates in treatment and comparison centres, both reaching around 60 per cent. These results show that nurses, like other public service providers, are responsive to properly administered incentives. But they also show that ensuring nurses come to work is a low priority for the local health administration and incentive systems can be quickly distorted where sufficient political will is lacking. Resources are not the main limitation and pumping in more money without attendant reform to reduce absenteeism will not solve the underlying problem (Banerjee *et al.*, 2008). The root problem here was that there was no countervailing pressure working through the political system to actually deliver better-functioning primary health care.

Large hospitals may offer advantages not often considered by advocates of primary health care. Peer monitoring among a larger staff often leads to better attendance. A significant determinant of attendance is whether doctors/nurses are able to live in a nearby town (hospitals tend to be in larger urban areas). These results and research more generally show that doctors tend to appear for work where they have colleagues to work with as well as equipment and opportunities to use their skills and education. Together these factors mean that hospitals are a plausible second-best solution in the absence of functioning universal health insurance programmes and can potentially provide protection for all against financially catastrophic loss (Hammer *et al.*, 2007). Box 6.4 shows how the presence of hospitals combined with affordable forms of insurance can make a big difference.

Donors

The Commission for Macroeconomics and Health (CMH) chaired by Jeffrey Sachs in 2001 costed a range of health interventions that would by 2015 (among many other aims) raise the worldwide coverage of immunization from 70 per cent to 80–90 per cent, skilled birth attendance from 45 per cent to 90 per cent, diarrhoea treatment from 52 per cent to 80 per cent, tuberculosis treatment from 44 per cent to 70 per cent, and malaria treatment from 31 per cent to 70 per cent (CMH, 2001:54). The costs included the 'full economic price of

Box 6.4 Community health care insurance in Senegal

Community-based health insurance schemes have proved successful in Senegal when linked to hospital-based medical care. This example is of a poor rural-agricultural region (Thies) with a high incidence of poverty, malnutrition and bad health conditions. For a sign-on fee and a monthly payment (equal on average to 2 per cent of household income) the scheme pays for the cost of hospitalization (while individuals still have to contribute to the costs of surgery). Membership has a strong positive effect on the probability of going to hospital and members pay hospital expenses averaging less than half the amount paid by non-members. Without insurance a single stay in hospital can lead to expenditure equalling more than 25 per cent of the household's annual budget. This study shows that community financing through pre-payment and risk-sharing reduces financial barriers to health care. Despite the insurance scheme, access to health care even among members of the scheme was still strongly and positively related to household income. This scheme was also contingent on the existence of a viable health care provider (the hospital of St Jean de Dieu) that was able and willing to offer support for the schemes (Jutting, 2004).

providing the health interventions, including the direct costs of medicines and health services, capital investments, complementary management and institutional support, and investment in training new personnel'. This would require by 2015 an additional $13 per person per year (2002 US$ prices) in developing countries, an increase of more than 50 per cent, which would be sufficient to ensure a 'decisive drop in avoidable deaths' (CMH, 2001:56). The total was very small compared with spending per person in high-income countries, which in 2001 was more than $2,000 per person per year. By the early 2000s almost all middle-income countries were already spending sufficient resources to ensure universal access to essential health services, but this aim was undermined by large inequalities within society and a lack of access by the poor to public health services. The CMH also argued that at least $3 billion a year should be allocated towards R&D on health priorities of the world's poor, of which $1.5 billion should be for R&D for new drugs, vaccines, diagnostics, and intervention strategies against HIV/AIDs, tuberculosis, reproductive health and other priority health conditions of the poor.

Assuming that some revenue could be raised domestically, the spending gap was estimated at $38 billion a year by 2015. The progress made in combating malaria (see Chapter 5) reveals this approach can sometimes work. The malaria initiative was based on a top-down drive to promote and disseminate appropriate interventions such as bed-nets and data collection. The more general problem with this big-push donor plan is that it ignores almost everything discussed in this chapter, especially the lack of any clear link between expenditure and health outcomes. The CMH never did make clear how they would engage with the incentives, motivation and poor information that characterize failures in service delivery in so many developing countries today, nor clarify the link between expenditure and health outcomes.

Key points

- Education affects growth via its impact on labour through fertility, mortality and migration.
- Education can increase the productivity of labour (by forming human capital) and so impact growth via TFP.
- Education may also have indirect impacts on growth, such as the effect of public debate and discussion on the functioning of democracy and the quality of government policy-making, which many argue has a positive impact on TFP.
- Investment may be attracted to countries offering investors a higher stock of human capital.
- Health contributes to human capital formation through increasing school attendance and on-the-job learning at work, increasing TFP.
- Progress in the provision of education and health in developing countries has narrowed the gap with developed countries in measures of education and health achievement over the last fifty years.
- Despite measurement and data problems, empirical work shows clear links from both education and health to economic growth and from economic growth to education and health. This suggests that there can be a virtuous circle with improvements in growth and these human measures of development.
- Public service delivery (of education and health) remains very poor across many developing countries.
- There are striking market failures in both education and health.
- Education policy needs to focus on choice and competition, decentralization and increased accountability of schools to improve their performance.
- A range of possible interventions focus on different aspects of the health problem, and are debated in terms of their comparative impact. Those discussed in this chapter are nutrition, public health, medical treatment and vaccination, hospital care and donor-funded schemes.

PART II

Patterns of Long-term Economic Growth and the Deeper Determinants of Economic Growth

After discussing the proximate determinants of economic growth in Part I we may be tempted to start listing desirable policy reforms. Perhaps the country of our particular concern needs more investment, better education and more hospitable domestic laws for FDI to make it easier to attract new technologies from overseas. Of course we recognize the complexities of education. We can't simply will a better and more inclusive school and university system into being. So after a lot of study we may decide the Finnish education system based around highly qualified teachers, a flexible approach to learning and small class sizes is the one to emulate. So far so good but that is not enough. We need now to turn to Part II which analyzes the five deeper determinants of growth: the underlying deep structures which influence the proximate determinants and through them economic growth. These are colonialism, institutions, geography, culture and openness. We noted in Chapter 6 that the education system in India was very bad. We cannot then jump to the policy decision of importing the Finnish model and hope for quick improvements. The Indian education system, for example, is influenced by those deep determinants: perhaps India's colonial history is responsible for the elitist pattern of good education for a tiny few and poor education for the mass of children; or India's culture sees education as unsuitable for the low caste of the population; or perhaps India is simply not open enough to the ideas and debates from the rest of the world to give education an appropriate richness.

Chapter 7 explores the data and debate about the centuries-old origins of contemporary patterns of income inequality. Did the income gap between today's developed and today's developing countries emerge in 1750, in 1500 or even earlier? Chapter 8 shows how economic growth, whether over the recent or historical past, impacts on the structure of the domestic economy. The first deeper determinant discussed is colonialism in Chapter 9. It comes first because, arguably, its influence works through the other four deep determinants of growth: through institutions (importing them from the colonizer or maintaining indigenous institutions); through geography (colonial rulers drawing borders); through culture (whether ethnic divisions existing today are a product of the colonial experience); and through openness (typically exposing the colony to trade and openness with the colonizer at the cost of trade and openness with the rest of the world). Chapter 10 explores the deeper determinant widely assumed by many scholars to be the most important: institutions. Institutions influence economic growth through their impact on the incentives to invest in physical (or human) capital or through stimulating technological diffusion or innovation and through this total factor productivity (TFP). The most widely discussed institutions are the political system and property rights. Chapter 11 discusses geography. An adverse disease environment may undermine health and so the acquisition of human capital through schooling or learning on the job. Being landlocked and isolated from international trade may reduce the incentives for entrepreneurs to invest in export-oriented sectors. Adverse weather conditions may directly influence the agricultural output of land. The availability of natural resources may influence output directly (exporting oil) or indirectly (good soils boosting output from agriculture). Chapter 12 finds that culture influences whether countries are open to ideas and innovation from overseas and considers how countries cope with the changes associated with economic growth, urbanization and innovation. Culture may affect the supply of labour via prohibitions on women working outside the household or attitudes to labour affecting labour productivity and so TFP. Culture may also affect investment by influencing attitudes related to savings. Chapter 13 explores how openness can influence economic growth through its impact on the supply of labour (immigration or migration), the supply of capital (FDI or the drain of surplus), through changing the incentives to invest (expanding domestic productive capacity to export onto world markets) or influencing productivity (through competition from the world market, exposure to new ideas and the ability to import technology from the rest of the world).

Chapter 7

The Great Divergence since 1750

The fact that there are large inequalities in the contemporary world economy is the central fact of our current economic existence. But when did these inequalities emerge? Some scholars argue that much of the now developing world had incomes little different from now-developed countries as recently as 1750. Inequality, it is claimed, is not long-standing or natural but is the result, perhaps, of better economic policies in the now-developed countries, which suggests poor countries should learn from developed countries what policies work. Or perhaps the experience of colonialism which drained wealth that promoted economic growth in the now-developed countries suggests a moral case for massive amounts of aid to rectify that historical guilt? This chapter finds that Western Europe did not have a particularly high (by historical standards) standard of living in 1750, but it was rising and then already had a significant lead in per capita incomes over the rest of the world. This lead was based on a long history of significant improvements in production, trade and transport technologies in Europe. The lead goes back to as early as 1500 CE or even 1350 CE. Whether this technological dynamism of Europe was indigenous or imported from outside misses the most important point. Over the long term the origin of innovation is less important than receptiveness to ideas, whatever their source, and the ability to build on ideas in a cumulative manner. This is an important lesson for contemporary developing countries, where the conditions of access to technology developed elsewhere, such as the activities of MNCs (Chapter 3) or regimes of intellectual property rights (Chapter 10) are crucial influences on long-term economic growth.

Europe in 1750: stagnation or growth?

There is good evidence that GDP per capita in Europe in 1750 CE was low but also that there had been significant improvements in production, trade and transport technologies in Europe in the centuries after 1000 CE. There is a related controversy about whether average incomes in Europe in 1750 were higher than those prevailing elsewhere, particularly in China and Japan.

Europe in 1750

Western Europe in 1750 had a level of GDP that was not impressive by long-term historical standards. It was little different from other civilizations at their peaks, including the Arab Caliphates in the tenth century, China in the eleventh century, or India in the mid-seventeenth century (Bairoch, 1993). In fact by the mid-eighteenth century Europe was only just returning to the income levels it had achieved in the first century under the rule of the Roman Empire. Between 300 BCE and 14 CE the population of Peninsular Italy had increased from 3.9 million to 7 million and GDP per capita (1990 dollars) from $425 to $857. Contributory factors characteristic of the Roman Empire included: law and order; literacy; new agricultural products such as vines and olives; urbanization; bridges and road networks; a common currency and increasing monetization; international trade improved by harbours and shipping; elimination of piracy; and increasing specialization in production and trade. The Empire in the first century had large cities, including 350,000 people in Rome, 216,000 in Alexandria and 90,000 in Antioch. Between 14 CE and 1000 CE the population of Italy fell to 5 million and per capita income (1990 dollars) to $450 (Maddison, 2007). This decline was due to the collapse of the Roman Empire, the replacement of urban civilization with self-sufficient, relatively isolated, illiterate rural communities and the virtual disappearance of trading links between Western Europe, North Africa and Asia.

Few would disagree that after 1750, 'the West' diverged dramatically from 'the Rest'. Pritchett finds that 'Divergence in relative productivity levels and living standards is the dominant feature of modern economic history' (1997:3). He estimates that between 1870 and 1990 the ratio of per capita incomes between the richest and poorest countries increased by a factor of approximately five. It is something of a simplification to think of the 'Rise of the West' as a single homogeneous process; rather, it is a complex set of sub-stories. One big study, for example, chronicles 'four systemic cycles of accumulation', among countries comprising the West: the rise of the Genoese to dominance from the fifteenth to the early seventeenth centuries; a Dutch cycle, from the late sixteenth century through most of the eighteenth century; a British cycle, from the latter half of the eighteenth century through the early twentieth century; and a US cycle, which began in the late nineteenth century (Arrighi, 2010). Large parts of the European economy also underwent noticeable relative decline from the sixteenth century onwards, including Spain, Portugal and the old manufacturing centres of Europe from Flanders through western and southern Germany down to northern Italy (Wallerstein, 1980:179). While acknowledging this pattern, for the sake of simplicity this chapter either focuses on England as the first industrial nation or considers Western Europe as a whole as 'the West'.

The paradox of long-term stagnation in Europe

If incomes in Europe were indeed not very impressive in *c.*1750, we have a puzzle. In the centuries before 1750 there were obvious and significant improvements in production, trade and transport technologies in Europe. Between 1000 and 1500 the heavy plough, open fields, the three-field rotation system in agriculture, modern horse harness and nailed horseshoes were widely adopted in Western Europe. The silk industry emerged in the twelfth century and had greatly expanded in southern Europe by 1500. In 1000 CE ship design in the Mediterranean was little different from that in 0CE. Subsequently there was dramatic advance in the technology of trade and transport. By the thirteenth century the most important innovations were the magnetic compass with 32 directional points the sternpost rudder replacing trailing oars for navigation, the Arab lanteen sail (which could be set at an angle to the mast and allowed sailing under a wider range of conditions) and the Venetian sandglass to measure time more accurately. Charts with an accurate indication of ports, anchorages, tides, depths, and winds began to appear. By the fifteenth century there had been further progress in navigation through the use of charts and the pole star, the quadrant was developed which made judgements of latitudes and distance sailed more accurate, and the nautical mile became the standard measure of distance. In 1615 John Napier invented logarithms to better calculate a ship's course. In 1714 the British government offered a £20,000 prize for an accurate invention of a means to measure longitude which was achieved in 1760 with the invention of the chronometer by John Harrison (Maddison, 2007).

Nef (1934) argues that there was a long history of rapid industrial growth in England dating from the mid-sixteenth century. There was rapid growth in the output of coal, salt, glass, and ships and industrial commodities such as aluminium, soap, gunpowder, and metal goods – much produced by large-scale industry. The annual output of a coal mine before the middle of the sixteenth century rarely exceeded a few hundred tonnes and much of the mining was done casually by manorial tenants. By 1640 collieries producing between 10,000 and 25,000 tonnes of coal, representing an investment of many thousands of pounds, and employing sometimes hundreds of miners, had become common in the Midlands, the north of England and Scotland.

Gregory Clark (2007) uses a Malthusian mechanism to reconcile this apparent paradox of low incomes in the mid-eighteenth century. Until the late eighteenth century, argues Clark, all technological advances stimulated higher fertility and so increased the rate of population growth, without generating any gains in per capita incomes. In 1800 English farm workers spent 75 per cent of their income on food (including 44 per cent on basic starches and bread) and the rest on the basics of shelter, heating, soap, light, clothing and bedding. Using these numbers and measuring income as the wage in pounds of wheat for unskilled labourers, Clark finds that real incomes were no higher in seventeenth-century Britain than in Ancient Babylonia (1800–1600 BCE, Classical Athens (408 BCE), or Roman Egypt (250 CE). It was only after 1770 that Western Europe, led by Britain, broke with Malthusian stagnation. The population of England tripled by 1860 and still real incomes rose. Such findings, though exciting, are comprehensively dismissed by other scholars, notably Robert Allen. Allen *et al.* (2007), examining real annual earnings of labourers in six cities in Europe and Asia, found that real wages in north-western

European cities remained at relatively high levels (in southern England, for example, never dropping to basic subsistence levels) and then increased steadily after the seventeenth century. Contrary to Clark's assertion that there was no improvement in the standard of living for 100,000 years before 1800, Allen (2008) notes that historical data on height shows living standards in 1700 were higher than in forager or agricultural societies in the distant past. There is also widespread evidence of an emerging mass market in Europe from the seventeenth century onwards for imported manufactures such as Chinese porcelain and Indian calicoes, for books, mirrors, crockery and watches.

We can conclude that incomes in Western Europe were not very high in 1750 but had been growing slowly over the previous centuries. This thesis is supported by the careful statistical work of Angus Maddison, which shows that per capita GDP in Western Europe increased by 0.29 per cent annually between 1000 CE and 1500 CE and by 0.4 per cent between 1500 and 1820 (2007:81).

Comparative incomes in 1750

If Western European incomes were (if low) growing by 1750, when did the gap between today's developed and today's developing countries start to emerge? Did Western Europe already have a significant lead on the eve of the Industrial Revolution around 1750? Those who argue the lead only emerged after this time emphasize the revolutionary importance of industrialization in Western Europe as the primary cause of current inequalities in world incomes. Those who argue Europe already had a lead in 1750 emphasize the importance of revolutions in European commerce, trade and science in the sixteenth and seventeenth centuries or even earlier.

Bairoch (1993), arguing that there was not much difference in average income levels between today's developed and today's developing countries around 1750, finds that incomes in the richest regions of the world economy (Western Europe and parts of India, pre-Colombian America, Africa and China) were only around 40–60 per cent higher than in the rest. Pomeranz (2000) offers more specific indirect evidence in support of this finding and argues that consumption of everyday luxuries and life expectancy were little different in England and China in 1750 and infers from this that incomes must have been broadly equivalent, but there are both data and conceptual problems with this evidence. Pomeranz (2008:138) argues that per capita output of cloth in England and the Yangzi Delta (12.9 pounds) in 1800 translated into roughly equal levels of consumption. Pomeranz here makes the assumption that all the cotton produced in the delta was consumed there, even though elsewhere he notes that much of the cloth was sold in the rest of China to pay for food crops. A study by Maddison (1971) finds similar evidence for India but a more careful consideration of it leads to a very different conclusion. He shows that during the sixteenth and seventeenth centuries in India there was a thriving luxury handicraft industry producing high-quality cotton textiles, silks, jewellery, and weapons. Most of this went to domestic consumption. This did not indicate high incomes for ordinary people but instead a (Mughal) state that was able to squeeze revenue from agriculture and with it the incomes of the poorest agricultural workers and divert it to consumption by the upper classes. Maddison estimates that the various taxes on agriculture and land were equivalent to a third or more of gross crop production and represented about 15–18 per cent of GDP which was large by European standards of the time. Income distribution is notoriously difficult to estimate but must be considered when trying to draw inferences about typical standards of living.

Pomeranz (2000) also argues that China had more freely functioning factor markets than did Western Europe after 1500 and that this implied higher incomes in China. Land was freely alienable (marketable) in China in the mid-1500s and by comparison entailed (constrained to be inherited by a direct descendent and not sold) in much of Western Europe. He also argues that long-distance migration of labour exceeded 10 million people in China between 1600 and 1800, but in Western Europe it was constrained by the enduring feudal obligations that tied labour to land. Others disagree strongly with these conclusions. Roberts (1985) argues exactly the opposite, suggesting that by 1500 most of Western Europe was experiencing a 'general liberation' of the economy marked in particular by a free(er) market and price mechanism. Landes (1998) notes that by 1500 there were few serfs left in north-western Europe and the labour market was correspondingly free(er). Either way the problem with using this as proxy evidence for income comparisons is that free markets are not and never have been enough to generate income growth. This book makes a clear case throughout that markets need be combined with other factors such as good institutions, the plunder from colonization, a scientific revolution, or many other factors to generate long-term economic growth.

Wages are commonly used in this debate as a proxy measure for more general living standards. Parthasarathi, for example, argues that eighteenth-century South Indian labourers had higher and more stable wages than their counterparts in Britain. Wages, though, cover only a small fraction of the (employed) population and miss the poorest (subsistence peasants), the richest (lords living on rents) and the indeterminate (self-employed living on profits). So in reality the link between wages and general living standards is much more uncertain than many economic historians allow for.

Parthasarathi finds that in Britain a textile worker's weekly earnings bought 40 to 140 pounds of grain and in South India between 65 and 160 pounds of grain equivalent (1998:84). When adjusting for weeks of employment Parthasarathi argues that this increases the advantage of South Indian textile workers who had more consistent work. To support this latter point he finds a 1739 quote from an employee of the English East India Company who suggested that 'the demand for South Indian cloth was greater than all the weavers in the country could manufacture' and also that rice cultivation barring a few unusual years between 1725 and 1735 was 'a very secure enterprise'. Given that later Parthasarathi criticizes the implicit prejudice and ignorance of travellers' negative comments on India it is not clear how or why we should trust so much to the judgement of this positive (British) commentator. In making his case that rice cultivation was 'secure' he argues that harvest short-falls in South India were highly localized and did not lead to the kinds of crises common in Britain. This evidence is belied by the occurrence of famine well into the nineteenth century, even after the construction of the railway system. More than a million people died in Orissa in 1865–66, the Deccan in 1876–78, North-West Provinces in 1877–78, and in the countrywide famine of 1896–97. Empirical evidence for contemporary India shows that the monsoon is highly variable and through its impact on agricultural output influences all-India industrial growth (Gadgil and Gadgil, 2006). Parthasarathi excludes data on wages in London, which, by dropping the most dynamic (the population of London increased from 50,000 in 1500 to 1million in 1800) and high-wage corner of the English textile industry, leaves average wages in the rest much lower.

The traditional view of Japan is of a country that isolated itself from the outside world in the 1630s, fearing the influence of foreign Jesuit missionaries and the growing (300,000 by the mid-sixteenth century) number of Christians. Between 1639 and 1853 only the Dutch were allowed to trade with Japan and even they were confined to a small artificial island in the harbour of Nagasaki. This, it is argued, left Japan cut off from technological progress in printing, textiles (silk and cotton), military equipment and agriculture. In June 1853 a US navy contingent of four warships entered Tokyo Bay with a request from the US President for a treaty of friendship and commerce. In March 1854 the US returned with nine ships and Japan agreed a treaty which opened two ports to foreign ships for supplies and repairs. Soon after, Japan signed treaties allowing widespread trade with numerous Western nations (Maddison, 2007). The traditional narrative is that the following era (known as the Meiji Restoration) from the mid-1860s saw the Japanese state force modernization from above. Reforms included the establishment of a professional army and civil service, formal legal equality between different social classes, the protection of private property, compulsory primary schooling and the expansion of the university system. By the 1880s the state was responsible for about 40 per cent of all capital formation, some of which went into infrastructure (railways, telegraph, roads) and much into directly productive enterprises (mills to produce cotton and silk, factories to produce bricks, cement, glass, and mines). Once established, many of these enterprises were sold to the private sector (Maddison, 2007). The conventional view that Japan successfully industrialized by emulating the West has been challenged by revisionists who argue that Japan had built a foundation for the agricultural and industrial growth that occurred from the 1870s onwards. There is good evidence of significant growth in agricultural production before the 1850s. Land productivity increased due to innovations in fertilizer use, increased rice varieties, more irrigation to spread paddy agriculture, greater regional crop specialization and multiple cropping, and an increase in cash-crop production including cotton, rape seeds, indigo and silk (Hanley and Yamamura, 1977; Yasuba, 1986).

There is no evidence (as with the case of Mughal India discussed above) to suggest that feudal dues increased after the middle of the Tokugawa period to siphon off higher yields to benefit landlords (Yasuba, 1986). The share of GNP received by the elite was probably declining (Hanley, 1983) and population was more or less constant over the nineteenth century. Together these factors imply that increased rice production would raise the net income of the peasantry. There was also considerable diversification of employment and output in the rural non-farm economy with increased production of cotton cloth and improvements in sericulture in rural areas, especially after the 1830s (Yasuba, 1986). It is reasonable to suppose that standards of living were higher in 1868 than some research has allowed for but the further step to argue that they were higher than in Western Europe is difficult to sustain.

Some scholars have concluded that the standard of living in Japan in 1850 was indeed higher than in most of Western Europe (Hanley, 1983). These scholars illustrate a common problem with the use of indirect evidence and specifically here confuse the relation between income and nutrition. Hanley points to various pieces of evidence that indicate ordinary Japanese people had a fairly good diet. In the late 1870s, he notes, most were eating a diet based on a mixture of unpolished or crudely polished rice with barley, buckwheat and various millets, which is more nutritious than polished rice. This may be evidence for good nutrition but it is not evidence for high incomes; indeed it is common for standards of nutrition to worsen with rising incomes (see Chapter 1), and the incidence of beriberi rose towards the end of the nineteenth century in Japan as machine-milled rice (a product of a more urban-industrial economy) was introduced. Wider welfare indicators, such as the fact that buildings were usually no more than one and a half stories high giving a population density much below the largest cities in Europe and well-maintained (by local government) streets, bridges and water supply systems, simply describe a well-managed pre-industrial city, and are not evidence of rising incomes. Although Japan (and possibly China) had a high quality of living in the nineteenth century, the evidence is consistent with this occurring at lower levels of material income than in much of Western Europe. Rising incomes in eighteenth- and nineteenth-century Britain were accompanied by the growth of fetid slums and worsening health conditions among the urban population or what the English Romantic poet William Blake termed 'the dark satanic mills'.

Pomeranz states that life expectancy in the late pre-industrial era in China was almost 40. This, he argues, was broadly equivalent to that in England and indicates that average incomes must likewise be similar. There are very significant conceptual and empirical problems with this claim. These figures are for persons who survived to at least six months. An estimate of life expectancy for China in the 1920s that includes infant mortality gives an average of only around 20 years. By comparison life expectancy at birth in England for 1800–10 was 44.8 (Brenner *et al.*, 2008). Other estimates of life expectancy in

Japan of around 40 (Hanley, 1983) are also likely to be a significant over-esti-mate. Again, the records Hanley used did not account for infant mortality (those who die at age zero), which in 1800–50 in Japan was around 300 per 1,000 (comparable with developing countries in the 1950s), so life expectancy estimated from this would have been about 34.7 years or five years shorter than Hanley estimated or the British level of 40.4 in 1854–58 (Yasuba 1986). The argument of Pomeranz and Hanley also ignores the common observation that life expectancy can fall alongside industrialization and urbanization. Eric Hobsbawm (1995:206) notes that the average life expectancy at birth in the 1840s was twice as high for agricultural labourers in Wiltshire or Rutland as for those in Manchester or Liverpool.

These works by Clark, Pomeranz and Parthasarathi and others together rely on indirect comparisons based on scattered output, consumption, or demo-graphic data. Far more systematic and comprehensive is the enormous effort by Allen *et al.* (2007) to estimate wages in eighteenth-century China and compare them with existing estimates for Western Europe. Data taken from Imperial Ministry records, merchant account books, and local gazetteers includes wages of unskilled male workers on government building projects in Beijing, unskilled port labour hired by European trading companies in Canton, and wages of daily earnings of men working as calenderers pressing cloth in the textile industry in Suzhou. These more comprehensive series are then compared with a broader range of 264 scattered wage quotations from many sources in different parts of China. They then define a consumption basket that represents the bare minimum for survival. The basket provides 1940 calories per day mainly from the cheapest available carbohydrate. In Shanghai, Canton, Japan and Bengal this was rice, in Beijing it was sorghum, in Milan polenta, and in North-west Europe oats. The basket also includes some beans, small quantities of meat or fish and butter or oil. These baskets were derived from detailed consumption surveys in Japan and China from the 1920s and 1930s. The cost of the baskets was calculated using prices from a huge variety of sources and adjustments were made for the length of the working year. Allen *et al.* (2007) compare daily wages of unskilled workers in London, Amsterdam, Leipzig, Milan, Beijing, and the lower Yangzi in the eighteenth and nineteenth centuries and find that wages in Amsterdam and London were significantly higher than in the rest of Europe and China. Overall European wages rose rapidly in the nineteenth century and after 1890 Japanese wages also began to rise, while Chinese wages changed little over the entire period. During the eighteenth century unskilled labourers in major cities of China and Japan had roughly the same standard of living as their counterparts in central and south-ern Europe but were significantly below those in Western Europe.

These measures of real wages are likely to underestimate increases in living standards in Western Europe after 1600. Long-run changes in living standards were explored by Allen *et al.* through real wage indices using an unchanging consumption basket. This is not a realistic assumption. Tea and coffee were available in limited quantities before 1500. Tea consumption reached England via Holland in the 1650s and during the eighteenth century English tea consumption increased by a factor of 400. Coffee reached Europe via Venice in 1615, and by the mid-seventeenth century coffee houses were popular across Europe. In 1500 sugar was available from a variety of sources (sugarcane, sugar beets, sorghum, honey etc.) but only in small quantities at prohibitive prices. By the 1790s roughly 10 per cent of the household budget was spent on tea, coffee, sugar and treacle by poor, working-class households, even during recessions, illustrating the high value assigned to these new commodities. For the poor a cup of sugary tea could reduce feelings of hunger, give a short energy boost and serve as a substitute for a hot meal. By the end of the eighteenth century previously luxury goods had been transformed into those for mass consumption. In 1800 the European continent as a whole imported 120 million pounds of coffee, 125 million pounds of tobacco, 40 million pounds of tea, and 13 million pounds of chocolate. Volume effects were reinforced by price falls. One series shows the real price of sugar falling from 32 pence per pound in 1600, to less than 15 pence by the 1650s and 5.7 pence in 1850, and the price of tea falling from 614 pence per pound in 1690 to 54 pence in 1850.

Table 7.1   *Per capita GDP levels, 1500 and 1820*

	1500	*1820*	*Growth rate*
Dynamic countries and regions	**1990 US$**		
Belgium	875	1,319	0.13
France	727	1,135	0.14
Germany	688	1,077	0.14
Italy	1,100	1,117	0.00
Netherlands	761	1,838	0.28
Portugal	606	923	0.13
Spain	661	1,008	0.13
Ireland	526	877	0.16
United Kingdom	714	1,706	0.32
All Western Europe	798	1,245	0.14
Brazil		646	
Mexico		759	
US	400	1,257	0.35
Less dynamic countries and regions			
China	600	600	0.00
India	550	533	–0.01
Japan	500	669	0.09
Russia	499	688	0.10
Eastern Europe	496	683	0.10
Egypt	680	475	0.00

Sources: Data compiled from Maddison (2006:436–7, 444, 465, 473, 520, 558); Bolt and van Zanden (2013).

Hesh and Voth (2009) use a method from the microeconomics of consumer theory to calculate how much of their income consumers would have been willing to forgo in 1850 to keep access to tea, sugar and coffee. They calculate the import of these goods was equivalent to 15 per cent of income. This result suggests that these supposed 'luxuries' had big consequences for the well-being of the English population. The measure of real wages using an unchanging consumption basket is inappropriate in trying to capture the transformation of consumption patterns that occurred during the eighteenth century.

Table 7.1 uses per capita GDP data to show the gap between Western Europe and the rest of the world by 1820. It also reveals that Western Europe had already established a significant advantage in terms of per capita incomes by 1500 and then experienced more rapid economic growth up to 1820. If a gap already existed around 1750, when did it emerge?

Comparative incomes in 1500

In 1500 GDP levels per capita were already higher in much of Western Europe than the rest of the world (see Table 7.1). The two principal explanations for this gap are the Diamond thesis, which focuses on geographical differences between Eurasia and the rest of the world in 11,000 BCE, and the Brenner thesis, which argues that agricultural changes in England after 1350 were responsible.

Urbanization and the Diamond thesis

Jared Diamond (1998) uses the conquest of the Americas by the Spanish to illustrate the differences in technology and political organization that marked the gap between Western Europe and 'the Rest' in 1500. In 1532 168 Spanish soldiers under Pizarro defeated 80,000 soldiers and the largest and most advanced state in the Americas. The conquest pitted steel swords, armour, guns and horses against stone, wood and bronze clubs. In addition to the military advantage, smallpox, measles, influenza, typhus, and bubonic plague played a decisive part in the conquest by ultimately killing an esti-mated 95 per cent of the native population of the Americas. These differ-ences, captured by Diamond in the title of his book, *Guns, Germs and Steel,* originate around 11,000 BCE, which marks the beginnings of village life in a few parts of the world. Food production was a prerequisite for the develop-ment of those guns, germs and steel. Settled agriculture is a pre-condition for the emergence of urban life – a single acre can feed 10–100 times as many as hunter-gathering. Along with urban life come more specialized occupations and the bureaucratization of life that stimulates the technological develop-ment and literacy necessary to ultimately produce steel. Even in the contem-porary world there is a strong relationship between income per capita and urbanization.

The earliest crops, such as wheat, barley and peas, which were domesticated around 10,000 years ago, evolved from wild ancestors that occurred naturally in Eurasia, particularly around the Fertile Crescent in the modern Middle East. These had many advantages; they were already edible, gave high yields in the wild, were easily grown merely by sowing or planting, were easily stored and were self-pollinating (Diamond, 1998:92). These crops were then more easily diffused from East to West across Eurasia. Across Eurasia the climate and growing season are similar, but they change significantly, heading south into Africa. Further diffusion from Eurasia was also hindered by the Sahara to Sub-Saharan Africa and the Atlantic and Pacific Oceans to the Americas. Possession of domesticated livestock was also important: such animals fed more people through meat and milk, and by pulling ploughs and providing manure for fertilizer helped raise agricultural yields. Large animals were the main means of land transport, including the horse in Eurasia and the camel or llama in North Africa and Arabia and the Andes. Infectious diseases like small-pox, measles and flu originated as human diseases from mutations of similar germs that had affected animals. It was the availability of domesticable plants and animals that ultimately explained why urbanization, literacy and steel weapons developed earlier in Eurasia.

The Diamond thesis is based on the premise that the areas that urbanized after 11,000 BCE were still the most urbanized around 1500 CE and this gave them the guns, germs and steel to engage in conquest and launch modern economic growth, so becoming today's developed countries. There is a funda-mental problem with the Diamond thesis. There is little evidence that urbaniza-tion rates were significantly higher in Western Europe in 1500 than elsewhere. The Diamond thesis assumes a process of emerging urbanization being locked in by 11,000 BCE and continuing ever since, whereas in fact there has been a 'reversal of incomes' between 1500 and 1995. The most urbanized civiliza-tions in 1500 (the Mughals in India, Aztecs and Incas in America) were among the richest, while those in North America, New Zealand and Australia were less developed. By 1995 the situation had reversed.

Looking at more specific data shows there were examples of high levels of urbanization and big cities in the now-developing world (not expected, given the Diamond thesis). China had many cities larger than any European city before London in the eighteenth century. It has been estimated that 22 per cent of Japan's population in the eighteenth century lived in cities and only 10–15 per cent in Western Europe (Pomeranz, 2000; Hobson, 2004). In mid-seven-teenth-century India Agra, Delhi, and Lahore had populations of 500,000+ and urbanization in cities of 5,000+ reached 15 per cent of the population of the sub-continent. Even earlier, in 1500 the East had larger cities, including Istanbul with 700,000 inhabitants, Cairo 250,000, Calicut 500,000, and Angkor had declined from its peak of 150,000. Paris then had a population of 150,000 (Frank 1998). Ferguson writes elegantly that Western Europe in 1411 'would have struck you as a miserable backwater, recuperating from the ravages of the Black Death ... bad sanitation ... incessant war ... internecine warfare … quarrelsome kingdoms … anarchic wilderness' (2012:2), while in 1411 the Chinese were building the Grand Canal and the Forbidden City. If, as Diamond suggests, urbanization leads to at least guns and steel it is not clear why warriors from urban Angkor or Lahore were not heading West to conquer Europe. The answer lies not in the urban world but in the rural economy of Western Europe.

Social and property relations and the Brenner thesis

Pomeranz argues that growth across Europe and Asia in the eighteenth century coupled with a limited supply of land and the rising demand for food and raw materials pushed countries into ever more labour-intensive methods to compensate. Europe sustained growth beyond 1750 because it gained access to American colonies that supplied sugar and grain for food, cotton for fibres for manufacturing, and timber for heating that together enabled England, then Europe, to save on the extra acres and additional labour otherwise required to produce them. There is persuasive evidence refuting this pessimism and explaining the English lead in around1500 as due to an earlier revolution in agriculture.

Brenner *et al.* (2002) argue that in England the system of social/property relations underwent significant change after 1400 and was radically different to that in the Yangzi Delta during the Qing dynasty (1644–1912). This economic and social revolution in English agriculture paved the way for higher incomes in 1500 and subsequent income growth and urbanization.

Peasants in the seventeenth-century Yangzi Delta had no land ownership rights, possessing instead various customary forms of ownership or secure tenancy. One such customary right in China was that of peasants to inherit land. This meant that landlords effectively could not vary rents in accordance with market conditions or remove tenants. Fixed rents and lack of exposure to market competition reduced the incentives for landlords and tenants, respectively, to raise the productivity of agriculture (Brenner *et al.*, 2002:614). Fertility was high and so land holdings fragmented between generations. The average size of family holdings fell from 1.875 acres in 1620 to 1 acre in 1850.

In Europe the Black Death (1348–49) had caused a radical transformation of social/property relations in the countryside. The sharp drop in population (by an estimated 25–60 per cent) led to a shortage of labour and forced landlords to offer concessions to peasants to persuade them to remain working on their land. This shifted rural agricultural relations to a commercial lease basis in a competitive land market, creating a class of direct producers who did not own the land but were compelled to produce competitively and efficiently to survive economically. Those who weren't efficient faced losing their tenancy to those who were. In England commercial tenants could not bequeath the land they farmed to their (multiple) children which supported the rise of ever larger farms. Land was entailed so would pass intact to the eldest son of the landlord. By 1800 English farms were on average ten times larger than in the late Middle

Ages, double those in 1600 and 130 times larger than farms in the Yangzi Delta (Brenner *et al.*, 2002).

In the Yangzi peasants had to increase yields (output per unit of land) to maintain consumption levels on ever smaller plots of land and did so through increasing labour inputs. Higher output per unit of land was achieved at the cost of long extra hours of labour such that between 1600 and 1800 grain output per capita fell by 30 per cent. In England large farms were able to use animals and nitrogen-fixing fodder crops (sainfoin, clover and turnips) that both supplied feed and increased soil fertility. Between 1500 and 1750 agricultural and labour productivity in England rose by between half and two-thirds (Brenner *et al.*, 2002). In England fewer people were required to produce sufficient food, enabling the migration of labour from agriculture into manufacturing. The share of the population in towns of more than 10,000 people increased from 5.5 per cent of the labour force in 1500 to 24 per cent in 1800. More agricultural output led to falling grain prices, freeing wages to be spent on manufactured consumer goods. Between 1600 and 1750 the population in England increased by 40 per cent, the population working outside agriculture by 80 per cent and real wages by between 35 per cent and 40 per cent (Brenner *et al.*, 2002). Evidence from Bairoch (1993) is consistent with the Brenner thesis and shows that until the early 1820s wheat imports into England were negligible and even by the 1840s what imports were only 12 per cent of consumption, most of which came from Russia and Prussia, not the Americas.

In the Yangzi Delta all available arable land was being cultivated by around 1800, and traditional methods of production were unable to further raise output. The outcome was a subsistence crisis marked by falling life expectancy for males caused by steadily increasing child and infant mortality.

The origins of the Western lead

A related debate asks whether the West's lead at the beginning of the sixteenth century was internally generated or came from borrowing technology developed elsewhere. It is important to note, however, that the historical ability to diffuse and utilize ideas and technology productively is what typically distinguishes successful growth stories.

One traditional historical drama centring on Britain is that of the 'heroic entrepreneur'. This view argues that from the eighteenth century a series of innovations transformed the British cotton sector and gave rise to the modern factory system. These innovations included the Spinning Jenny (1766), Arkwright's Water Frame (1769), Crompton's Mule (1779), Cartwright's Power Loom (1787) and the Self-Acting Mule (1830) (Roberts, 1985). 'Some time in the 1780s, and for the first time in human history, the shackles were taken off the productive power of human societies [and represented a] sudden, qualitative, and fundamental transformation' (Hobsbawm, 1995:28–9). By 1850 the cotton textile industry had been completely transformed. Of the

375,000 employed in the industry nearly 90 per cent were in formal factory-based production. The industry was extensively mechanized with 21 million spindles and 250,000 power looms being driven by 71,000 horsepower of steam (Inikori, 1989). This explanation begs the question of why Britain was so innovative in the decades after the 1760s.

Traditional 'internal' arguments hold that 'much of the dynamism of the West rests on what was done in the Middle Ages to prepare its material, institutional, cultural and psychological foundations' (Roberts, 1985:73). David Landes (1998) traces the achievements of the 'heroic entrepreneur' to a long tradition of intellectual freedom going back to medieval Europe where the authority of the church was limited by competing secular authorities (kings and free cities) and religious dissent from below. This facilitated the rise of rational investigation, learning and experiment within Europe. The first European university was established in Bologna in 1080 and by 1500 there were 70 such centres of secular learning in Western Europe, largely free from church control. Gutenberg produced his first book in Mainz in 1455 and by 1500 there were 220 printing presses and Western Europe had produced 8 million books. By the mid-seventeenth century the 'scientific revolution' had been firmly established in North-western Europe, culminating in the 1687 publication of Isaac Newton's *Principia Mathematica*, which put forward theories of motion and gravitational attraction that were consistent with the motions of the known universe. The new techniques of Descartes, von Leibniz and Newton were valuable for expressing theories in mathematical form. New instruments were developed, including telescopes, microscopes, thermometers, barometers, and clocks. New bodies, such as the British Royal Society, the French Académie des Sciences, the Paris Observatoire and the Royal Greenwich Observatory provided fora for the dissemination and discussion of scientific results (Landes, 1998; Maddison, 2007).

A second internal explanation for the origin of the Western lead revolves around good institutions promoting investment and innovation. North and Thomas (1973) argue that the establishment of property rights accounted for 'the rise of the West'. The English monarchy was defeated in the Civil War of the 1640s and again in the Glorious Revolution of 1688 and the exercise of arbitrary and confiscatory power by the Crown was subsequently curtailed through greater judicial independence, and ultimately the supremacy of Parliament. The long-term consequences were the increased security of property rights, greater incentives to undertake long-term investments and ultimately the onset of the Industrial Revolution. France and Spain had absolutist monarchies that took longer to create a legal system and property rights existing independently of the Crown.

The alternative 'external' view is that the East enabled the rise of the West through the two processes of diffusion and assimilation/appropriation. In this view, first, Easterners created a global economy and global communications network between 500 and 1500, and second, the more advanced Eastern 'resource portfolios' (ideas, institutions and technologies) spread to the West through these networks where they were assimilated in a process of 'oriental globalization'.

The early Abbasid caliphs (661–1258), who ruled much of the Middle East and North Africa from their capital at Baghdad, played a pioneering role in sponsoring secular learning in the Middle East. They created libraries and observatories in Baghdad which produced translations of Greek and Indian works on philosophy, mathematics and medicine. As scholarly activity in Baghdad declined during the twelfth century and disappeared with the Mongol invasion, intellectual leadership had passed to Muslim Spain (Maddison, 2007). The 'external' view argues the European agricultural revolution (discussed above) was preceded and influenced by one in the Islamic world between 700 and 1100. This revolution was stimulated by a systematic effort by the Abbasid caliphate to collect and diffuse knowledge about botany, agriculture and pharmacology. Ease of trade and travel allowed new crops such as sugar cane, cotton, rice, hard wheat, sorghum, taro, indigo, oranges and eggplants to diffuse westwards. More settled political conditions and access to credit allowed for investment in improved irrigation, water storage in cisterns, and water-lifting technology, which in turn permitted a more intensive use of land (Maddison, 2007).

The financial innovations (in banking, insurance and accounting) associated with the commercial revolution after 1000 CE in Europe have often been credited to Italy. In reality, argues Hobson (2004), they were all derived from the pre-Islamic or Islamic Middle East. Likewise, he argues, the voyages of the Portuguese in the fifteenth century merely followed earlier Afro-Asian exploration. The African Cape, for example, had been rounded in the mid-fifteenth century by the Arab navigator Shihab al-Din Ahmad Ibn Majid, who eventually reached the Mediterranean via the straits of Gibraltar. Key features of Portuguese shipping such as sternpost rudders, triple-mast system (with square and lanteen sails) had long been characteristic of Chinese shipping and could have been learned by European visitors to China or by observation of Chinese ships in Africa and the Middle East. Hobson also argues that the origins of printing lay not with Gutenberg in 1453, but with sixth-century China and four-teenth-century Korea. The learning of Europe was nothing particularly special. As early as 978 CE a single Chinese library contained 80,000 volumes (which was exceeded only by some Islamic libraries). By 1100 China became the global centre of pioneering innovations encompassing military technology (metal-barrelled guns, cannons), agricultural technology (seed-drill, horse-drawn hoe, horse-powered threshing machines, crop rotation, the Rotherham plough), and industrial technology (iron, steel, cotton, steam engine, blast furnace). In all cases, Hobson argues, the technology was originally developed in the East (mainly China) and diffused west. Hobson's claims are certainly bold: 'After 1000, the major technologies, ideas and institutions that stimulated the various Western commercial, production, financial, military and navigational revolutions as well as the Renaissance and the scientific revolution, were first developed in the East but later assimilated by the Europeans' (Hobson, 2004:22).

Counter-arguments have been advanced by other scholars. In a review, Hall (2007:149–150) agrees that Hobson presents 'an exceptionally stimulating and elegantly stated polemic' but that his historical picture 'stands an exaggeration that sometimes becomes wild'. Blaut (1993) had earlier argued that the argument attributing all technological dynamism after 1500 as wholly internal to the West is 'ultimately a coloniser's model of the world in that it legitimises colonialism and domination by the inventive to teach the non-inventive'. In his exhaustive efforts to demonstrate that all modern technologies in *c*.1700 had been developed in the East and were assimilated by the West, Hobson perpetuates this error in another guise. His efforts to demonstrate diffusion are generally tenuous and based on assertions without substantive supporting evidence. For example:

No-one knows where the origins of the heavy plough lay. It is often assumed that it was the Slavs who first developed the plough around 568 but it reached them from an unknown probably eastern source.

The technology of the European military revolution was derived from the East and diffused across to the West through a long chain of transmissions.

It is striking that Tull's basic principles of the seed-drill, outlined in his book *Horse-Hoeing Husbandry* (1733) were almost a word for word reproduction of those laid out in the original Chinese manuals dating back to the 3rd century BCE.

Almost all of these aspects of the Italian machines resembled the earlier Chinese models down to the time when Lombe visited Italy.

The great advantage of first England then the rest of the West lay in an ability to utilize inventions successfully whatever their origins. This could perhaps be due to a mixture of openness and culture (discussed in more detail in Chapters 12 and 13). This distinction has long been a crucial concept in tales of growth and development. This claim will not come as a surprise to anyone familiar with the story of rapid growth of South Korea and Taiwan in the 1960s or Thailand and Malaysia in the 1970s or China in the 1980s. These growth stories were based on utilizing innovation and technology from elsewhere to manufacture cheap exports. The key difference between the West on the one hand and China, India and the Islamic countries on the other, whether around 1500 or around 1750, is that only in the West did learning generate a self-sustaining process that brought about modern industrialization and economic growth. An example is that of iron and steel. In both these industries India was a technological leader until at least the eighteenth century with 10,000 furnaces producing the famous Wootz steel which was exported to Persia (Frank, 1998). Steel was used to produce swords and other luxury products for the nobility but never achieved growth through mass-market expansion, continuous technological change and reduced costs. In iron manufacture the

Box 7.1 How do we imagine a giraffe?

Erik Ringmar says that it was 'a cultural predisposition in favour of the extra-European and the exotic, and not some impersonal imperative that prompted the far-flung ventures of the Renaissance [colonialism after *c*.1500]. There would never have been money to be made in commodities such as spices, pearls, silk, teak, and tea but for this predisposition' (2006:377). He cites the giraffe as an example. Giraffes (then otherwise unknown) were presented to Lorenzo de'Medici in Florence in 1486, to King Charles X of France in 1827 and to the Chinese Emperor in 1414. In fifteenth-century Italy the giraffe was a new and exotic creature. 350 years later huge crowds turned out to see the giraffe on its 900-km walk to Paris. A noted zoologist named Geoffroy introduced the animal with a lecture at numerous local scientific academies along the way, and in Paris the giraffe was presented to the monarch together with a scientific tract. The Beijing giraffe arrived at a court that saw itself in 1414 as the most sophisticated civilization on earth where tributes to the Emperor from surrounding states would be magnanimously reciprocated by even more lavish gifts in a process demonstrating submission, generosity and the splendour and virtue of the Emperor. According to Ringmar, there are three basic cultural models here: a Renaissance model of outward-looking curiosity (Florence); an Enlightenment model of outward-looking self-sufficiency (France); and a Confucian model of inward-looking self-sufficiency (China). These models had implications for action. The Florentines went out into the world full of curiosity and a will to satisfy a booming European market in exotic goods. The French lived in a universe based on science and rationality related to what they perceived to be a world of irrational superstition outside. The Chinese self-confidently closed themselves off from the rest of the world.

Chinese learned to use coal and probably coke (as against charcoal) in blast furnaces for smelting iron, producing 125,000 tonnes of pig iron by the late eleventh century. This was not achieved in Britain for another 700 years, while in China the coal, coke and iron industry fell into disuse (Landes, 1998, 2006). Europe's willingness to benefit from innovation and opportunity is demonstrated in a curious comparative story about the giraffe (Box 7.1).

As Roberts (1985) puts it, in Western Europe a 'cumulative process was at work. Knowledge was built on knowledge and lack of information stimulated further investigation. The work of the great explorers and geographers was part of the more general transformation in European culture loosely called the Renaissance'. In Europe the mechanical clock undermined religious authority by making the town clock the symbol of secular municipal life. The clock contributed to the rise of the modern factory system by allowing industry to measure productivity in relation to units of time and thus to strive to maximize productivity. The Chinese, by contrast, treated time and its measurement as a confidential privilege of monarchy. Islam used clocks for prayer and they never contributed to a wider public sense of time. Printing was invented in China in the ninth century and was in general use by the tenth century, though publication remained dominated by government controls over the spread of printing presses and the content of publications. In Europe printing in the vernacular broke the monopoly of Latin but Muslim countries were opposed to a printed Koran for much longer (Landes, 1998). Between 1405 and 1431 the Chinese undertook seven major naval expeditions to explore the waters of Indonesia and the Indian Ocean – the first in 1405 comprised 317 vessels and 28,000 men – but further maritime enterprise was banned by the Ming court. Some argue that the rising power of merchant traders was being perceived as a threat to the scholarly court bureaucrats so ocean-going trade was abandoned by an authoritarian monarchy with the power to enforce such a decision (Landes, 1998). The Portuguese voyages of discovery, by contrast, were cumulative. In the medieval period the Portuguese pushed down the coast of Africa, reaching the Senegal River by 1450 and the Congo by 1485; in 1498 Vasco De Gama rounded the Cape and reached India. Within a few years Portugal was trading regularly with the Malabar Coast, had built ports there, and dominated Indian waters; soon after a Portuguese squadron appeared in Canton (Roberts, 1985). This Portuguese success was the result of decades of exploration and extension of navigational possibilities in the Atlantic. The Portuguese were not innovators but very successful at learning. As Portugal faded as a naval and colonial power in the late sixteenth century they were replaced by the Dutch and later the English.

Hobson (2004) argues that this notion of a ban on and subsequent decline of naval trade in fifteenth-century China is a myth for three reasons. First, many private Chinese merchants ignored the ban by relocating to other parts of the region in order to export products back to China. In the first half of the sixteenth century Chinese merchants spread to all parts of South-east Asia, dominating this trading network into the nineteenth century. Second, not all private trade was banned and much of it was officially sanctioned in three key ports – Macao, Changzhou in Fukien province and Suzhou in Shensi province – and later through Amoy, Ningbo and Shanghai. Finally, as most of the world's silver ended up in China, the economy must have been well integrated into the global economy through a consistently large trade surplus (Hobson, 2004). If true then this argument makes the China problem even more of a puzzle. If China was so open to trade why did its technological innovativeness slow down so dramatically in the fifteenth century? Why did the Chinese fail to learn from superior European science and technology once they were exposed to it from the sixteenth century onwards?

Thinking about learning as a cumulative process helps us to answer this question. China was the self-proclaimed Celestial Empire; first in the world in its own eyes in terms of age, experience, cultural achievement, moral and spiritual superiority. This cultural triumphalism, argues David Landes, made China a bad learner. Chinese scientific enquiry tended to look back at its own writings to confirm there was nothing new from outside, so China had no tradition of 'standing on the shoulder of giants'. China also lacked the organizations that made for a cumulative process of finding and learning, such as schools, academies, learned societies, challenges and competitions. There was a tendency to let the findings of each generation slip into oblivion with limited diffusion, and lack of replication and testing (Landes, 2006:17). Europe certainly had its similar moments, when practitioners of medicine revered the ancient learning of Greece, or philosophers and theologians tried to impose a standard view of the world through the dictates of the Catholic Church. The difference lay in the evolution of these views and efforts in Europe (Landes, 1998). The gifted in China had fewer incentives than their equivalents in the West to acquire knowledge about the universe and skills in mathematics and science. In China after the Qin unification in 221 BCE the state was ruled by bureaucrats. Civil service examinations were instituted during the Sui dynasty (589–617), and during the Song dynasty (960–1275) bureaucrats were selected through competitive civil service examinations. Government service was the most honourable and worthwhile occupation. The basic readings for the civil service examinations were the Confucian classics with a total of 431,286 characters that took six years to memorize. Other philosophical, historical and literary works were needed as a basis for writing poems and essays in the examination. This was not the learning relevant for modern scientific research (Lin, 1995).

Key points

- Western Europe did not have a particularly high (by historical standards) standard of living around 1750, but it was rising.
- By the mid-eighteenth century Europe was only just returning to the income levels it had achieved in the first century under the rule of the Roman Empire.
- Western Europe in 1750 had a significant lead in per capita incomes over the rest of the world.
- Western Europe probably had a lead as early as 1500.
- In the thousand years to 1750 there were obvious and significant improvements in production, trade and transport technologies in Europe.
- The Diamond thesis that the gap that existed in 1500 can be traced back to 11,000 BCE is not convincing.
- The Brenner thesis that social and economic change originated in English agriculture after 1350 is more persuasive.
- Some scholars argue that the East created a global economy and global communications network between 500 and 1500 CE, and also that more advanced Eastern ideas, institutions and technologies diffused to the West through these networks.
- The debate about whether technological dynamism of Western Europe was indigenous or imported from 'the East' misses the most important point. Over the long term the origin of innovation is less important than receptiveness to ideas, whatever their source, and ability to build on ideas in a cumulative manner.

Chapter 8

Economic Growth and Economic Structure since 1750

The previous chapter placed inequality into an international perspective and showed how average incomes between countries are affected by centuries of even small differences in economic growth. This chapter looks at one aspect of what growth does within the domestic economy. We have seen in earlier chapters how economic growth may impact on measures of health, education, nutrition and happiness. This chapter confines the discussion to the economic, in particular economic structure.

Economic growth has a systematic impact, not just on average living standards, but also on inequality and the relative contributions of agriculture, manufacturing and services to both employment and total GDP. Some economists (known as structuralists) have argued that economic structure is not simply something that changes in response to economic growth but is itself a key determinant of growth. Structuralists believe that industry has the advantage over agriculture for sustaining rapid long-term economic growth. Developing-country governments generally have a very disappointing record of successfully promoting industrialization as part of a strategy to promote rapid economic growth. Nevertheless, it has been characteristic of the most successful stories of growth in the twentieth century, such as South Korea and more recently China.

Conceptualizing structural change: The Lewis model and inequality

There are two broad and influential ways of conceptualizing structural change: the transition from the traditional to the modern most famously encapsulated by the Lewis model; and the relation between growth and inequality, likened to an inverted U by Simon Kuznets.

From the traditional to the modern: the Lewis model

Arthur Lewis's 'Economic Development with Unlimited Supplies of Labour' (1954) is regarded by many as the founding document of development economics. Much subsequent work has been an extension, qualification and criticism of this original paper (Findlay 1980:64). Lewis argued that traditional economic theory's concern with the efficient allocation of a given quantity of resources

166

was not appropriate for developing countries. As development was enlarging the stock of resources, concern had to be with investment and growth. Lewis divided the economy of a developing country into two sectors: modern-capitalist and traditional-subsistence – not, as many have assumed, industry and agriculture. Labour he argued is available to the capitalist sector at a wage determined by earnings or consumption in the traditional sector. The key implication is that abundant unskilled labour in the traditional sector ensures an effectively unlimited supply of labour to the capitalist sector at a wage just above its existing subsistence-level earnings. Using modern machinery and factory-based production methods the capitalist sector has a higher productivity per worker than the traditional sector. The surplus of output over wages is captured by the capitalists as profit. If the capitalist reinvests a part of this profit the capitalist sector will grow, absorb more labour and generate more profit. This process will slow down and halt when the capitalist sector has absorbed all the surplus labour; wages will then rise, while profits and so the incentive to invest will decline. Structural change, according to the Lewis model, sees profit-seeking investment driving a traditional-subsistence economy towards a modern-capitalist one. This process is accompanied by rising inequality as wages remain fixed and the share of profits in national income increases.

There are various theoretical and empirical critiques of the Lewis model. One long-standing critique is that Lewis assumes that food flows from the traditional agricultural sector to the capitalist industrial sector at a fixed price, while any rise in price (shift in the terms of trade) may undermine capitalist profits. This critique is mistaken: the capitalist sector in the model could very well comprise modern productive farms mass producing cheap food – as Lewis does make clearer in various other works. A second and more serious criticism is a seeming contradiction at the heart of the model linking investment and demand. Capitalists are assumed to appropriate and reinvest the rising share of profits, which leads to an expansion of the capitalist sector. If workers are all earning wages just above subsistence, then who is going to consume the rising modern-sector output? It may also be the case that capitalists do not invest their surplus in 'productive capacity' but instead divert resources to investments in agricultural land, ostentatious consumption, urban real estate, and capital flight (Hunt, 1989). Then where does the investment and growth come from? Third, the persistence of unemployment and underemployment in the shanty towns and *favelas* of the developing world indicates that workers are not automatically absorbed by the expanding capitalist sector as suggested by the model, but that they migrate from rural areas, often to a between-sector limbo in an informal sector waiting for a modern-sector job. Fourth, in practice wages do not obligingly wait at subsistence levels until the labour surplus has been fully absorbed. In India, for example, trade unions won strong employment rights for workers in the early 1950s that protected formal-sector employment, raised wages and slowed down the transfer of labour to the modern/formal sector. Forty years later there were only around thirty million modern/formal-sector workers in India and around 93 per cent of total employment remained in the traditional/informal sector (Bhalotra, 1998).

Inequality: the Kuznets inverted U

A second important structural change that occurs with development is that of inequality. In a 1955 paper, Simon Kuznets asked whether inequality in the distribution of income increased or declined as a country experienced economic growth. The likelihood of increasing inequality (a rising share of profits in national income and stagnant wages) was implied if not discussed in detail in the Lewis model. Kuznets used data for the US, England and Germany showing that rising inequality during the early stages of the Industrial Revolution was reversed after the 1920s. For example, the income share of the bottom quintile in the US increased from 13.5 per cent in 1929 to 18 per cent in the mid-1940s. With a small sample and unreliable data Kuznets admits that the attempt to discern any trend 'comes perilously close to pure guesswork' (1955:6), but he nevertheless drew some plausible and influential hypotheses from his findings. The early tendency to widening inequality, Kuznets argues, can be explained by the concentration of savings among the wealthiest house-holds. In 1955 the top 5 per cent of income units in the US accounted for nearly two-thirds of savings and so accumulated the bulk of income-yielding assets. The shift from agriculture to industry will permit households that migrate early to take advantage of high incomes in the industrial sector. Kuznets suggested that incomes from services, professional and entrepreneurial sources (rather than accumulated property income) would tend to increase their share of total incomes over time. Continued migration from the agricultural sector would reduce returns in urban industry and gradually equalize them across the whole economy (there are parallels with the Lewis model). Any remaining differences in incomes would then be determined by individual excellence rather than inherited position, or as Kuznets put it, inequality would be undermined by the 'the dynamism of a growing and free economic society' (1955:11).

Kuznets' proposition concerning the rise then fall of inequality, which has since become known as 'the inverted U-shaped hypothesis', has been subject to much subsequent testing, some scholars finding that sustained growth will eventually reduce inequality, others that a decline in inequality will either take decades or require supporting policies (Randolph and Lott,1993). The model cannot account for some recent inequality stories such as the dramatic lurch into inequality in Russia, where the range of incomes between the top and bottom decile rose from a multiple of 4.5 in December 1991 to 13 in mid-1994 (Nolan, 1995:295). There is a heated contemporary debate about whether government policy can master this process and enforce 'pro-poor' economic growth such that economic growth disproportionately benefits the poorest.

The role of agriculture in structural change

The share of GDP or employment accounted for by agriculture typically declines relative to other sectors during the course of growth and development.

Historical case studies of China and Japan, however, provide support for the idea that the agricultural sector can have a positive role to play in promoting wider economic growth.

Lewis and Kuznets both believed that the role of the agricultural sector was likely to decline as a poor developing economy experienced economic growth. This decline would occur in both the share of the total labour force and the share of total GDP accounted for by agriculture. This structural change can be explained by both demand and supply factors. On the demand side Engel's Law states that as incomes rise above subsistence the share of income spent on food declines and that on manufactured goods rises (a higher income elasticity of demand for manufactured relative to agricultural goods). The basic idea is that, unlike the demand for manufactured goods, the demand for food is limited by the size of one's stomach, though the contemporary global 'obesity crisis' seems to suggest the size of stomachs may not have been as limited as originally thought. On the supply side, the productivity and output growth of agriculture is limited by the availability of land and possibilities of increasing returns to scale, but manufacturing faces no such constraints. Increasing returns to scale is a particular case where output increases by more than the multiple of factors of production. For example, if all factors of production are doubled, output more than doubles. At most agriculture can grow by 3 per cent or 4 per cent per annum, while China has sustained manufacturing output growth of 10–15+ per cent for nearly thirty years.

The theoretical discussion in the previous section is borne out by empirical evidence. Table 8.1 shows that the widespread decline in agriculture's share of GDP across Latin America, Africa and Asia, has been most rapid in the rapidly

Table 8.1   *Agriculture's share of GDP in selected Asian, African and Latin American countries, 1960, 1980, 2000 and 2010*

	Agriculture, value added as a % of GDP			
	1960	*1980*	*2000*	*2010*
Bangladesh		31.6	25.5	18.6
Bolivia		19.0	15.0	12.9
Brazil	20.6	11.0	5.6	5.3
Burkina Faso	39.8	29.4	29.3	35.4
Côte d'Ivoire	47.9	25.9	24.2	22.8
Ghana	45.2	60.1	39.4	29.8
Indonesia	51.5	24.0	15.6	15.3
India	42.6	35.4	25.1	18.0
South Korea		16.2	4.6	2.6
Malaysia	34.3	22.6	8.6	10.4
South Africa	11.2	6.2	3.3	2.5
South Korea		16.2	4.6	2.6

Source: Data compiled from *World Development Indicators* (2013).

growing countries such as South Korea and Malaysia. The share remains at high (though declining) levels for poorer countries such as Burkina Faso, Ghana and India.

An impoverished traditional sector is a great advantage to the modern sector in the Lewis model. Here low wages in subsistence agriculture provide a cheap labour force available to the modern sector. Bruce Johnston and John Mellor published a classic paper in 1961 challenging the pessimistic view of agriculture. They accepted the widespread view that a declining share of agriculture in both output and employment is a necessary characteristic of economic growth. But they argued that agriculture can make five principal contributions to economic development. First, growth and urbanization requires a substantial increase in the output of agricultural products to meet the consumption demands of a growing urban labour force. If food supplies lag demand the result is likely to be a substantial rise in food prices and when over half of total expenditure (in a typical poor developing country) is spent on food this is likely to generate political tension and/or pressure for increased wages. Higher wages can then reduce industrial profits and slow the cycle of investment and industrial expansion identified by Lewis. Second, the expansion of agricultural exports is a crucial means to raise foreign exchange earnings to import the necessary capital and desired consumer goods. Third, the labour force for manufacturing must be drawn from agriculture so requires productivity growth to enable the agrarian labour force to produce more with fewer people. Fourth, as the dominant sector of a developing country, agriculture is the most important source of savings and tax revenue to fund the public and private investment required for infrastructure, education and industrial investment. Fifth, rising incomes of the farm population may be important to stimulate industrial expansion through higher consumer demand. However there is an inevitable conflict between agriculture as a source of capital (withdrawing savings to be invested elsewhere) and agriculture as a source of market demand (leaving incomes with agricultural households to be spent on consumption).

A good example is the case of 1980s China. While we may associate economic growth in China with the cheap manufactured goods that fill up the households of the world, agriculture was crucial to this outcome. Agriculture contributed to more general economic growth in China in the 1980s and 1990s in terms of those various linkages discussed by Johnson and Mellor. Despite the collectivization (the takeover of small privately owned farms and their amalgamation into large state-run farms) of Chinese agriculture in the mid-1950s, patterns of growth were broadly typical of any developing country. Between the early 1950s and mid-1990s the share of agriculture in GDP declined from 50 per cent to 20 per cent, though as late as the early 1980s, 80 per cent of the population still lived in the countryside. Rural reforms (revolving around a shift from large collectives to small family farms) in the late 1970s led to growth of agricultural output by nearly 8 per cent per annum between 1978 and 1985. This boosted farming incomes and had a dramatic impact on rural consumer demand. Rural assets were then distributed in a fairly egalitarian manner so increased output tended to boost the disposable incomes of the large rural population. Farmers spent a high proportion of incremental income on (then) new consumer durables, such as TVs, shoes, watches and bicycles. In the 1950s around 70–80 per cent of total state revenue came from taxing agriculture and by the mid-1980s it was still around 50 per cent. Agricultural exports were long the dominant source of foreign exchange in China, providing more than 80 per cent of the total in the1950s and still about 40 per cent by the 1980s (Yao, 2000). This provided much of the foreign exchange to import the capital goods and oil necessary for rapid industrialization. A similar story can be seen in nineteenth-century Japan (Box 8.1).

Box 8.1 Agriculture and Japanese economic growth after 1858

The story of Japan during the Meiji era (after 1858) is commonly regarded as a case study of the positive impact of agriculture. Agricultural output growth (2.0 per cent per annum) consistently outpaced population growth (0.9 per cent). Between the 1880s and 1920 there was a five-fold increase in silk cocoon production and a seven-fold increase in the output of raw silk which supplied an important export industry. During these same years labour productivity in agriculture doubled, which eased the transfer of labour (particularly young women) into the urban-industrial economy as fewer workers in agriculture were required to produce a given output. Agricultural growth did not require much investment and so scarce savings could be channelled to investment in industry. Between the early seventeenth and mid-nineteenth centuries the number of rice varieties increased from 177 to 2,363 – an example of appropriate innovation. Another major innovation was the increasing use of locally produced fertilizers like dried fish and oil cake to supplement scarce natural organic sources. Through a land tax the state extracted a large revenue from agriculture to channel into industry, education and infrastructure. This was done through a land tax. The land tax was initially set at 3 per cent of the (annual) assessed value of land in 1873 (later lowered to 2.5 per cent). The tax was payable regardless of how the land was being used which gave owners an incentive to bring waste or fallow land into production (Bird, 1977). Since the tax was fixed according to the value of land, once paid all surplus output remained with the farmer/landlord which provided a strong positive incentive to produce. By comparison a 50 per cent income tax would have siphoned off half of any increased output and would probably have undermined incentives to expand output or produce more highly valued crops. In the early 1870s the land tax raised nearly 90 per cent of central government revenue, and even though by 1911 the economy had diversified the share was still nearly 30 per cent. The key requirement to implement the tax was a strong and competent state that was able to accurately measure land value from an elaborate survey begun in 1875 and completed around 1881. Very few developing countries have the equivalent capacity even today (see Chapter 10 on the bewildering state of land registration in contemporary India for a contemporary comparison).

Agriculture in the contemporary world

Most contemporary debates around agriculture lack any sort of historical perspective. Some argue for a big pro-agricultural push, boosting infrastructure investment, agriculture-relevant R&D in bio-technology and fertilizer, expansion of rural credit, seed distribution and electrification. Some propose direct policy intervention such that agricultural growth benefits small poor farmers. Such policies are often implemented through Fair Trade organizations, and might include the provision of seed and credit to small farmers, and support services such as marketing and cold-storage facilities.

Others argue that amalgamating small plots to permit large-scale commercialized and mechanized agriculture is the only way to sustain growth. The increasing size of supermarkets in developed countries means that small farmers have to provide standardized quality, appearance and detailed product labelling often beyond their resources. Related to this view is the perception that structural change will continue to be the dominant trend, and governments and NGOs should act to facilitate the movement of people out of agriculture into industry (and possibly services) through rural to urban migration and education, rather than trying to preserve a picturesque and photogenic small-scale agriculture. This rather bleak (if realistic?) picture sees the loss of rural livelihoods as a pre-condition to gaining better-paid urban jobs. This is discussed in Chapter 10 in the section relating to 'accumulation by dispossession'. Yet other scholars, citing high prices of foodstuffs and other agricultural products in world markets over recent years, suggest there are now long-term profit-making opportunities in farming and more sustainable livelihoods in the sector.

The role of industry in structural change

A shift from agriculture to industry has been a characteristic feature of many contemporary and historical stories of growth and development, though deindustrialization is now common among the most developed countries; examples include Latin America in the 1980s and Russia in the 1990s.

Much of the early work on economic structure was conducted by Hollis Chenery. Chenery (1960) conducted empirical work on 38 countries between 1950 and 1956. He found that for every 1 per cent increase in GDP, output in the manufacturing sector grew by 1.44 per cent. As per capita GDP rose from $100 to $1,000, his data showed that industry's share of total GDP rose from 17 per cent to 38 per cent, while primary production (agriculture, forestry and mining) declined from 45 per cent to 15 per cent. The pattern of industrial output also changed over time. When GDP was $100 per capita Chenery found that 68 per cent of manufacturing output consisted of consumer goods and only 12 per cent investment goods and by the time income levels had reached $600 the figures were 35 per cent and 43 per cent respectively. Chenery and Taylor

Table 8.2   *Industry's share of GDP in selected Asian, African and Latin American countries, 1960, 1980, 2000 and 2010*

| Country | Industry, value added as a % of GDP | | | |
	1960	1980	2000	2010
Argentina		41.2	27.6	30.9
Bangladesh		20.6	25.3	28.5
Botswana	13.4	50.7	52.6	45.0
Brazil	37.1	43.8	27.7	28.1
Chad	9.5	8.9	11.3	
China	44.9	48.2	45.9	46.7
Denmark		27.2	26.8	21.8
Germany		41.1	30.5	27.9
Ghana		12.3	28.4	19.1
Hungary	59.0	47.1	32.4	31.0
India	19.3	24.3	26.1	27.6
Japan		39.0	31.1	27.4
Kenya	18.2	20.8	16.9	18.6
South Korea	18.6	36.6	38.1	38.8
United Kingdom		40.7	27.3	21.6

Source: Data compiled from *World Development Indicators* (2013).

(1968) found structural change was slower among countries rich in natural resources (they included Venezuela, Malaysia and Iraq in their sample). This effect was only pronounced in countries with GDP less than $1, 000 per capita.

Table 8.2 shows some interesting sub-stories within the general industrialization picture. The share of industry in GDP tends to be higher in richer developing countries, such as Argentina or Brazil, than in Chad, Ghana or Kenya. Countries that had adopted a communist/socialist economic model (Hungary and China here) tended to have extremely high shares of industry in GDP by 1980, as this type of economic system placed great emphasis on promoting industry through extensive state intervention. The highest-income countries, such as Denmark, Japan, Germany and the UK have all experienced sustained deindustrialization since 1980 (a declining share of GDP accounted for by industry). Countries in Latin America, such as Argentina and Brazil, experienced very sharp falls in the industry share after around 1980, associated with the profound economic crisis in the region during the subsequent decade.

The rapid industrialization of South Korea after 1960 was driven not by the changing pattern of consumer demand as suggested by the basic theory described above, but rather by state intervention. After the 1961 coup of General (subsequently President) Park the overwhelming priority of the government was to expand exports, particularly of industrial goods. Large firms were assigned orders (politely called targets) by Ministry officials. If they succeeded they gained various tax and credit benefits and easier/cheaper access to new technology. Much of this effort required the growth of consumer demand to be deliberately suppressed. For example, colour TVs were first marketed abroad and domestic sales were not allowed until 1980, as was true of phonographs and portable telephones. In May 1973 Korea shifted from general export promotion to the targeting of heavy and chemical industries (HCI). These industries included steel, heavy machinery, automobiles, industrial electronics, shipbuilding and metals. Cheap credit was targeted to these preferred sectors (Harvie and Lee, 2003).

The socialist system (the USSR, Maoist China, Eastern Europe until 1989 and a few others) promoted an even more extreme form of industrial growth. Investment in China in 1981 was 28 per cent of GDP, which was then more than twice that of other developing countries; 80 per cent of this total went to heavy industry. Between 1952 and 1978 industrial output grew by 11.5 per cent per annum, the share of industry in GDP rose from 18 per cent to over 40 per cent (heavy industry accounting for half of the total), and that of agriculture fell from 51 per cent to 28 per cent. The growth of heavy industry was reflected in the creation of new industries such as electricity generating equipment, chemical fertilizer and motor cars (Nolan, 1995; Naughton, 2007).

While South Korea used extensive government intervention to guide the market, in China the state abolished the market. Resources were allocated according to a central plan whereby firms were given instructions to produce so many tonnes or units of output utilizing a certain quantity of inputs. The very success of diversification eventually overwhelmed planning. Central planners in Beijing identified 600 different varieties of industrial product while in the USSR in the 1970s there were 60,000 separate commodities (Naughton, 2007:62). The communist planned economy produced waste on a grand scale. The system abolished production for profit (a key socialist criticism of the

---

Box 8.2 From socialist industrialization to socialist deindustrialization

Structural change does not always happen patiently and relentlessly in the same direction. One example is that of Russia in the late 1980s. Russia experienced what has been described as 'explosive' deindustrialization. Between 1989 and 1991 national income fell by 34 per cent, comparable to that of the US or Germany between 1929 and 1932 during the Great Depression. National income (which was measured differently to GDP in socialist Russia) then fell by another 30 per cent in 1992, 10 per cent in 1993 and 25 per cent in 1994. In 1994 alone the output of the machine-building industry fell by more than 40 per cent (Nolan, 1995:295). This collapse Nolan blames on the disintegration of the state and Communist Party and the consequent inability of planners to ensure the flow of inputs and outputs throughout the USSR's wide mutually interdependent state-owned industrial sector. 'The process was substantially the result of appalling policy errors by the Soviet leadership' (1995:298).

capitalist system) but could not replace it with production based on need, and much of the resulting output was unwanted junk. A central justification of planning was that it could look ahead, focus on deliberate aims and achieve a more co-ordinated pattern of industrial growth. The system did not manage to abolish the boom and bust associated with capitalist market economies. National income in China dropped by around 35 per cent in the early 1960s (the Great Leap Forward) and by 13 per cent between 1966 and 1968 (The Cultural Revolution) (Nolan, 1995). While socialist industrialization was dramatic, in some cases socialist deindustrialization (see Box 8.2) was even more so.

The role of services in structural change

A shift to services, once a feature of the highest-income countries, has now become general in countries of all income levels.

If the highest elasticity of demand at high income levels is in service-sector activities, such as retail, leisure, education, finance and media, the corollary is that economies can expect to shift from industry to services at these income levels. Not only is there evidence for this, but this shift seems even more generalized, with a significant increase recorded in the service-sector share of GDP after 1980 in all countries (Table 8.3). The world economy is now dominated by services, in contrast to the old idea that developed countries exported manufactured goods and developing countries agricultural goods. In high-income

Table 8.3   *Services' share of GDP in selected Asian, African and Latin American countries, 1960, 1980, 2000 and 2010*

| Country | Services, value added as a % of GDP | | | |
	1960	*1980*	*2000*	*2010*
Argentina		52.4	67.4	59.1
Bolivia		48.6	55.2	49.9
Brazil	42.3	45.2	66.7	66.6
Burkina Faso	39.6	50.1	46.1	41.7
Côte d'Ivoire	39.0	54.4	50.9	50.0
Germany		56.5	68.2	71.2
India	38.2	39.9	50.8	54.4
Japan		57.9	67.4	71.5
Malawi	39.6	33.7	42.5	49.9
Morocco		50.5	56.0	55.0
Pakistan	38.2	45.6	50.7	53.4
Senegal		59.9	57.6	60.2
Uganda	35.0	23.5	47.7	50.3

Source: Data compiled from *World Development Indicators* (2013).

countries such as France, Germany and Japan the share of the service sector exceeds 70 per cent, and in the UK today around 80 per cent of employment is in the services sector.

Certain characteristics of service sector output make measurement and analysis problematical. It is difficult to identify what constitutes the service activity in any particular sector such as banking. Quality and productivity are difficult to measure. Would a teacher who took on more students in a class be raising their productivity levels or diluting their effort? (Banga, 2005). Market prices are not available for publicly provided services such as education or health so it is difficult to put a value on the output or consumption of those services. Some worldwide growth in the service sector is illusory. Industrial and other firms have increasingly used specialist sub-contractors to deliver services they previously provided themselves, such as legal, accounting and security. The practice of what Bhagwati (1984) called 'splintering' may lead analysts to overestimate the decline of industrial relative to service-sector output.

A surprising tale in recent economic history has been the rapid growth of output and exports from the service sector in India. Between 1950 and 1980 'normal' structural change occurred in India, with industrial growth exceeding that of agriculture and services. During the 1990s service growth was been more than double that of industry or agriculture, or of overall GDP (Gordon and Gupta, 2004:29) and after 2003 service sector growth touched 10 per cent per annum. In 1990 low-income India's service sector achieved very close to the average share predicted by its income level, but by 2010 that share was around 55 per cent of GDP which would be expected in an upper-middle income country (Gordon and Gupta, 2004:7). In India the fastest-growing service sector in the 1990s was business services (including IT) with growth averaging nearly 20 per cent per annum; other sectors such as telecommunications and banking also experienced rapid growth.

A policy case study: structuralism

Structuralists argue that the structural features of the economy do not passively change with economic growth over time but are rather a key determinant of economic growth potential. This implies that economic structure is both determined by and is a driver of growth; a common presumption is that industry is the sector best able to promote long-term economic growth.

Structuralism: the theory

In a hugely influential article in 1950, Raul Prebisch divided the world into 'core' countries producing industrial goods and 'periphery' countries producing agricultural goods. He stated that the shift from agriculture to industry is desirable but may not even happen without some deliberate policy efforts by government. Prebisch argued that these demand-and-supply factors caused the terms of trade (see below) to move against the periphery: the price of agricultural goods would fall relative to manufactured goods. Rigid domestic wages in core countries (protected by tight labour markets, regulations and trade unions) would prevent export prices falling as productivity increased in export-oriented manufacturing industries. This would cause developed countries to absorb productivity gains in industry as higher wages and profits. Competitive markets, the unlimited supply of labour and flexible wages in periphery countries would lead to productivity gains in agriculture being reflected in lower export prices which would benefit importers in core countries. Prebisch further argued that due to the low-income elasticity of demand for agricultural goods on world markets (Engel's Law), developing countries are likely to experience a slow growth of export revenue over time. Technical innovations such as fibre optics replacing copper in telephone communication or artificial rubber replacing natural rubber may even generate absolute declines in the demand for some raw materials. At the same time developing countries tend to be heavily dependent on imports of capital goods and inputs for industry and agriculture, and luxury branded consumer goods.

The ratio of prices of primary to manufactured products is known as the 'terms of trade'. Many scholars have argued that the terms of trade declined between the 1950s and 1990s (Thirlwall and Bergevin, 1985; Sapsford and Balasubramanyam, 1999; Mayer, 2002). Not all agricultural products have been subject to declining relative prices. Jamaican Blue Mountain coffee for example costs up to $20 per cup in Japan and in early 2002 was being priced at $6,000–8,000 per tonne in London markets compared with $1,200 per tonne for Arabica coffee (Kaplinsky, 2005). More recent evidence suggests that this 'terms of trade pessimism' may have been fundamentally altered as a result of the 'China effect' (Box 8.3).

Nicholas Kaldor (1967, 1968) formalized many of the arguments of early structuralists like Prebisch and added to them the concept of 'dynamic economies of scale' to make an influential case for the 'superiority of manufacturing'. Dynamic economies of scale are a particular form of increasing returns to scale. Here, as producers accumulate experience in production they improve in skills and capabilities so learn to produce with more efficiency. Over time average costs will decline and productivity increase.

The relationship between the rates of growth of industrial output and GDP is captured in Kaldor's First Law. This states that the faster the rate of growth of industrial output in the economy, the faster will be its GDP growth. Data for nearly 50 countries and across 29 Indian states for the 1990s support the First Law (Dasgupta and Singh, 2005, 2006). Kaldor's Second Law states that there is a strong positive correlation between the growth of industrial output and the growth of productivity in the industrial sector. Evidence for this can be seen in Chapter 1 where it was shown that rapid industrial growth after around 1960 in Japan, South Korea and Taiwan was associated with rapid growth of productivity. The slowdown in industrial and GDP growth after

---

Box 8.3 'The China effect'

China is relatively resource-poor, and its rapid growth, based on the export of manufactured products, has been very import-intensive. Between 1998 and 2003 China accounted for 96 per cent of the increase in global demand for steel, 99 per cent for nickel, 100 per cent for copper, and 76 per cent aluminium. Between 2002 and 2004 the price of hot-rolled coil steel rose from $140/tonne to more than $500/tonne (compared with a previous post-war peak of $400/tonne), a direct result of growing Chinese demand. The other side of the 'China effect' has been surging Chinese exports of manufactured goods. Between 1993 and 2000 there was more than a 10 per cent decline in China's terms of trade in manufactures, particularly in computers and office equipment, telecommunications equipment and semi-conductors, the sectors in which China's participation in world trade has being growing most rapidly. Some commentators believe this surge in raw-material prices has fundamentally changed the nature of the world economy to the permanent benefit of (African?) exporters of raw materials. Others argue it is only a temporary effect that will last only as long as China's growth is so raw material-dependent and the upgrading in China towards more high-technology and skill-intensive manufacturing sectors will reduce this effect over time.

1973 was again associated with a slowdown in productivity growth, particularly in the developed countries. Kaldor's Third Law is that faster growth of output in the industrial sector leads to faster growth of productivity in the whole economy (due to the operation of Verdoorn's Law) because of dynamic economies of scale. There is evidence that productivity growth by country and also across different Indian states varies positively with the expansion of the industrial sector (Dasgupta and Singh, 2005).

Together the Second and Third Laws show that countries with a high growth rate of industrial sector growth will have a relatively high growth rate of productivity in the economy as a whole. These laws show that the industrial sector is the dynamic centre of technical change and productivity growth. A more industrialized country will experience an increasing lead over non-industrial countries. Economic success in the post-war world was typically associated with rapid industrialization.

Structuralism: the debate

While Lewis (1954) argues that in order to facilitate the transfer of labour from the traditional to the modern sector, there must be no increase in wages, many structuralists argue that higher wages help expand the domestic market and by making labour more expensive create an incentive to introduce productivity-enhancing mechanization. Structuralists do not generally accept the automaticity of structural change modelled by Lewis. They tend to argue that the working of market forces can lead to developing countries being locked into declining sectors (agriculture) and consequently often argue in favour of government intervention to manipulate relative prices (tariffs, taxes, multiple exchange rates) and to push the allocation of scarce resources (finance, capital, foreign exchange) into priority areas (industry).

The case for promoting the industrialization of the periphery rests partly on a historical analysis of trends in the terms of trade and predictions about their likely future path. The selection of the starting year in calculating the terms of trade is important. Prebisch's late nineteenth-century data showed a long-term decline in raw-material prices. It is difficult to determine, however, how much these declines were losses to primary product producers and how much a reflection of sharply falling international freight costs during the same era. The fall in international commodity prices after the 1950s was biased by the very high prices of commodities in 1950 induced by the Korean War (1950–53) and their subsequent collapse. Changes in quality and product innovation and their impact on the value of manufactured exports are also difficult to account for (as noted later by Chang). The income terms of trade can improve (that is, total export revenue can rise) if productivity and output in export industries increases faster than the decline in the price of those exports.

Structuralists argue that growth in the periphery countries depends on demand from the core countries. Akin and Kose (2007) used a dataset of 106 countries for the period 1960–2005 to examine the nature of these global linkages. They found that the North *has* played a dominant role in explaining growth dynamics in the rest of the world, but also that the more successful developing countries ('the emerging South') are breaking away decisively from this dependence. Between 1960 and 1972 the emerging South was heavily dependent on Northern markets and 60 per cent of its exports consisted of primary commodities. Between 1986 and 2005 the share of primary exports from the emerging South declined to 17 per cent and the share of manufacturing exports increased to 74 per cent. There has also been an increase in trade flows among the emerging South countries, with economic interactions between the North and emerging South evolving from dependence to interdependence (Akin and Kose, 2007:25). A clear indication of this has been in recent years when despite recession and stagnation in the North many South developing countries have sustained rapid growth.

The slowdown in manufacturing growth is one of the key explanations for the end of the 'golden age of capitalism' after 1973. For many developed countries (and even developing countries) the 1980s saw not just a slowdown in manufacturing growth but a situation of deindustrialization (a fall in the share of manufacturing employment or an absolute fall in such employment). Deindustrialization for some represents a pathological state preventing the economy from being able to achieve its full potential of economic growth and full employment. This view was developed in relation to weaknesses of British manufacturing in 1970s and 1980s (Singh, 1977) but later seemed relevant to similar processes in much of Latin America and Africa over the 1980s and 1990s. Deindustrialization is now occurring in several developing countries at lower levels of per capita income than observed historically in today's developed countries. In the past this historical turning point occurred at per capita incomes of US$ 10,000; it is now estimated to take place at $3,000 in some countries (Dasgupta and Singh, 2006). Table 8.2 shows this process has occurred in both Ghana and Botswana since 2000.

A key argument of the structuralists has been the link between manufacturing growth and export potential. For example, even in the 2000s, despite the manufacturing sector falling to 15 per cent of GDP in the UK it still accounted for 60 per cent of total exports. It has been long recognized that services are less tradable than manufactured goods, since they have to be consumed at the place and moment of their creation. A haircut, for example, cannot be produced, stored and then traded at long distance. Technological change, however, has now facilitated international trade in services such as education, law, accounting and back-office functions. Trade barriers in services generally do not take the form of import tariffs, but quantitative restrictions on international trade in services are often applied to providers of services rather than services per se. Doctors, for example, are not generally free to practise their profession in different countries. Service industries are also sometimes supported through explicit or implicit subsidies especially in construction, communications and transport (Banga, 2005). This kind of policy constraint is tackled by the WTO who in recent years have turned their attention to the liberalization of trade in services.

Kaldor placed manufacturing at the centre of his analysis, in terms of its effects in driving both GDP and productivity growth. The case of India illustrates how things have changed. Technological change and greater tradeability of services means rapid productivity growth in the sector is now possible. TFP growth in the service sector was 3.9 per cent per annum in India between 1993 and 2004 (Bosworth and Collins, 2008:54). There is strong evidence that service-sector growth has had a positive impact on productivity growth in Indian manufacturing (Banga and Goldar, 2004:13). There are also indications that agriculture and industry in India have become more intensive in the use of inputs from the service sector (Sastry *et al.,* 2003). Together these findings imply that service-sector growth can drive growth elsewhere in the economy.

The conventional theory is that deindustrialization in developed countries is caused by the internal factors (demand and productivity effects) discussed in this chapter. Some argue that cheap manufactured imports from developing countries displacing domestic production and employment are responsible. This suggests that, rather than being a natural process, deindustrialization can be facilitated by too much openness to trade, and trade protection may be necessary to preserve the dynamic industrial heart of an economy. Living standards and economic dynamism may then really be threatened by Chinese manufactured exports. Rowthorn and Ramaswamy (1999) used annual data for 18 industrial countries between 1963 and 1994 to test the impact of international trade on economic structure. They disagreed with the more pessimistic view and found that among developed countries, of a total of 350 million jobs, about 7 million were lost because of developing-country competition and about a million were created by additional exports to the south. This net loss of 6 million jobs was less than one-fifth of all the manufacturing jobs lost because of deindustrialization since 1970.

The 'naturalness' of deindustrialization is supported by evidence that as per capita incomes exceed a certain level the income elasticity of demand for services exceeds that for manufacturers. So at very high income levels the highest income elasticity for demand is found in service-sector activities, such as retail, leisure, education, finance and media. Chang (2011) argues that we are not living in a post-industrial age. The falling share of services in output and employment is not due to slow output or demand growth but to the falling relative prices of manufactured goods, due to increased productivity in manufacturing. Manufacturing, Chang states, is still more tradeable internationally and still has greater scope for productivity gains, and so industrialization continues to be crucial for any developing country seeking to raise living standards. This does not, however, mean that all governments should launch state-led industrialization drives. Only a few developing countries have succeeded in this; for every successful South Korea there is an unsuccessful Ghana.

Key points

- Two important ideas of long-term structural change are the Lewis model and inequality.
- Agriculture's share of GDP or employment typically declines relative to other sectors during growth and development.
- Agriculture, long neglected as a declining sector, can have a positive impact on long-term economic growth.
- A shift from agriculture to industry has been a characteristic feature of many contemporary and historical stories of growth and development.
- Deindustrialization is now common among the most developed countries; there are particular examples in Latin America in the 1980s and Russia in the 1990s.
- A shift to services, once a feature of the highest-income countries, has now become general in countries of all income levels.
- Contrary to earlier concerns, the rapid growth of the services sector can have a positive impact on long-term economic growth in many contemporary developed and developing countries.
- Economists known as 'structuralists' argue that the structural features of an economy do not merely passively change with economic growth but are rather a key determinant of growth. In particular industry has advantages over agriculture for promoting long-term economic growth.
- Some have argued that the 'China effect' has changed the nature of the global economy and there are now more permanent advantages to relying on exports of raw materials.

- Three laws developed by Nicholas Kaldor show that the industrial sector is the dynamic centre of technical change and productivity growth.
- Many case studies show that government-led efforts to promote industrialization in developing countries do not generate sustained and rapid long-term economic growth.

Chapter 9

Colonialism

Most people agree that the subjugation and subsequent domination by one country of another is a bad thing. This simple moral question has obscured a deeper understanding of the nature and impact of colonialism. The bigger question is whether studying the colonial experience helps us to understand centuries of economic growth and their manifestation in contemporary global economic inequalities? This chapter explores various accounts of the influences and impact of colonialism. Acemoglu *et al.*'s settler/extractive typology is too crude, as case studies of colonialism in India, Korea, and Nigeria demonstrate. Although Marxist thought has long since disappeared from mainstream economic discussion, it offers a rich seam of academic writing and analysis that illuminates the impact of colonialism. The key thematic debates about the impact of colonialism on development in the colonies are the drain of surplus, deindustrialization, diversity and isolation, and human development.

Colonialism and economic growth

Colonialism has influenced growth at a proximate level through policies relating to investment, education and land during the colonial era. Colonial rulers, for example, have been widely blamed for inadequate spending on health and education. During the post-independence era colonialism has also impacted on deeper determinants of economic growth (see Figure 9.1). Colonial powers drew borders and left some countries landlocked (see Chapter 11) or left legacies of conflict as international borders ran through traditional tribal or linguistic groups. Colonial powers either left behind institutions that they had imported from the home country or propped up indigenous institutions (see Chapter 10). After the 1950s many neo-Marxists or dependency scholars linked FDI and openness to colonialism, arguing they had been key mechanisms of domination and exploitation (Chapter 3 and 13).

The diversity of colonialism

The experience and impact of colonialism have been diverse. The Acemoglu *et al.* thesis states that the geography of the colonized country had the determining impact on the nature of the colonial experience. Various case studies show that the nature of the colonizer was also an important influence.

Box 9.1 The complex nature of colonialism

Naive discussion tends to divide the contemporary world up into now-developed countries (assumed to have been the colonizers) and now-developing countries (assumed to have been the colonized) and to discuss the impact of the former on the latter. In reality much of today's developing world conquered large empires; the Egyptian, Persian, Ottoman, pre-Colombian American and Mughal empires lasted centuries. One of the greatest colonial expansions was that of the Arab world into North Africa, Spain and parts of France after the death of Muhammed in 632 CE. Much historical colonization was conducted among today's developed countries. Europe established numerous internal empires such as what is now France under Charlemagne in the eighth and ninth centuries, under Louis XIV in the sixteenth and seventeenth centuries and under Napoleon in the nineteenth century. Southern and South-eastern Europe is today relatively wealthy by world standards but as part of the Arab and Ottoman empires has been a colony longer than a colonizer.

The nature of colonialism has differed enormously across time and space. Ten million people are estimated to have been killed as a consequence of Belgian colonization of the Congo in the nineteenth century, but a study of heights derived from military recruitment records and other sources suggests that physical welfare improved during the British colonial period in Kenya and Ghana (Moradi, 2008). The economic effects have differed greatly. Many scholars accept that British colonial rule led to the deindustrialization of India in the seventeenth and eighteenth centuries but many likewise agree that the Japanese colonial state promoted rapid industrialization in Korea. Lal (2004:33) describes the varying motivations behind imperialism: 'revenue maximising objectives of a predatory state' (ancient Mesopotamia); 'the search for glory' (Alexander the Great, Julius Caesar, Genghis Khan); 'expanding the territorial area of empire to keep nomadic predators at distance' (Chinese, late Egyptian, Roman); 'booty and Christian conversion' (Spanish and Islamic); and 'trade and commerce' (British and Dutch).

It is difficult to argue there was any single motivation behind the expansion of the British Empire. The extremely decentralized nature of its administration left policy-making up to the discretion of colonial administrators and soldiers on the spot: 'The role of history, of the British Empire, in all this is clear to see. Accidents and decisions made on a personal, almost whimsical, level have had a massive impact on international politics. The empire ... [had a] belief in the individual action of its servants, with very little supervision and without any real central philosophy' (Kwarteng, 2011:140).

The Acemoglu et al. thesis

Acemoglu *et al.* (2001) argue that geography determined the nature of colonialism, which in turn had long-lasting effects on institutional development. According to their thesis, there were two types of colonial state: 'extractive states' where the motive was to extract natural resources using cheap forced

Figure 9.1 *Colonialism as a deeper determinant of economic growth*

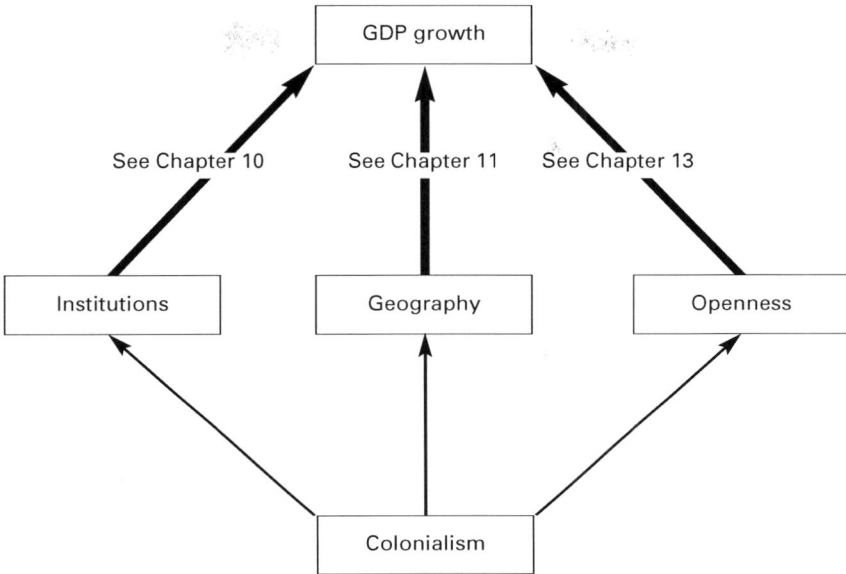

labour; and 'neo-Europes' or 'settler colonies' where colonial policy tried to replicate European institutions with an emphasis on private property and checks on government power. The former group was exemplified by the Belgian colonization of the Congo; the latter included Singapore, Hong Kong, Australia, New Zealand, Canada and the US. The colonization strategy chosen was influenced by the feasibility of settlement. Where the disease environment (see Chapter 11 for a more extended discussion on the geography of disease) was not favourable to European settlement, the formation of extractive states was more likely. Their final point was that these colonial institutions tended to persist after independence.

In their statistical work, Acemoglu *et al.* (2001) used data on the mortality rates of soldiers, bishops and sailors stationed in the colonies from the seventeenth to nineteenth centuries. There is a strong negative relationship between GDP per capita today and historical settler mortality in a sample of 75 countries. The result is robust to the inclusion of controls for the current disease environment, including the prevalence of malaria, location in Africa, life expectancy and infant mortality, and the current fraction of the population of European descent.

The most significant problem with the Acemoglu *et al.* thesis is that it is not a direct test of the impact of colonial rule. The results only show that settler colonies ended up with higher per capita income and better property rights a century or so later. Other explanations are compatible with this same result: perhaps settlers were young, ambitious, entrepreneurial and better educated

and this, not good institutions, led to subsequent economic growth? Others
have supported this alternative explanation with in-depth case studies. For
example, the difference between the export structure of Uganda (primary products) and Zimbabwe (manufactures) is explained by the skills, capital and
experience brought by European settlers and by the pro-industry policies that
this facilitated from the 1920s onwards (Wood and Jordan, 2000). Another
problem is that the distinction between settler and extractive colonies is too
crude. Alternative distinctions could be between plantation economies in
which land was operated by foreign companies and settler colonies where
farming was conducted by European settlers; or between 'poor peasant
colonies', such as French Sudan (now Mali) or Tanganyika (now Tanzania),
where poor soil quality prevented the profitable production of export crops,
and fertile agricultural exporters such as Ghana, Nigeria, Senegal, and
Uganda, where output was in the hands of small-scale African rural capitalists
(Austin, 2008). Finally, if the colonial experience was the key determinant of
subsequent economic growth, how can we account for the variation in income
levels among countries that were never colonized? The dispersion of incomes
within the colonized sample (103 countries colonized by the major western
European powers before the twentieth century) is little different from the non-
colonized sample (the 60 countries not colonized, such as Finland, Ethiopia
and Mongolia) (Rodrik *et al.,* 2002).

The extractive state: the Belgian Congo

The colonial experience formed extractive institutions which persisted after
independence and led to continued arbitrary dictatorial rule and ultimate
economic disaster. The most extreme case was the Belgian Congo, which
closely fits the model of Acemoglu *et al.* The country had existed for a century
before the arrival of the Portuguese in 1491, with a chief chosen by an assembly of clan leaders, and an elaborate civil service (Hochschild, 1999:8). Full
sovereignty over the core of the state was gained in 1884 in exchange for one
piece of cloth per month to the two main chiefs. The Belgian Congo was the
personal 'property' and dictatorship of King Leopold II (1835–1909), and its
control by Belgium was ratified at the 1884 Berlin conference without the
involvement of any Congolese. It was abundant in natural resources including
ivory, palm oil, timber and copper. In a brutal extractive process, the colonial
state compelled the cultivation of cash crops through forced labour; the harvest
was sold and distributed by the government at fixed prices. 'Congo state officials (1890s) and their African auxiliaries swept through the country on ivory
raids, shooting elephants, buying tusks from villagers for a pittance, or simply
confiscating them.' (Hochschild, 1999:118)

Villagers failing to meet production and procurement quotas risked flog-
ging or mutilation. Exports of rubber increased from 100 tonnes in 1890 to
6,000 tonnes in 1901 and ten million people are estimated to have died in that
export effort. The Congolese had no rights to own land, no political voice, and

were subject to urban curfews that prevented their freedom to travel. Without checks the system gave absolute power to European officials:

> For a white man, the Congo was also a place to get rich and to wield power. As a district commissioner, you might be running a district as big as Holland or Belgium. As a station chief, you might be a hundred miles away from the next white official; you could levy whatever taxes you chose in labour, ivory, or anything else, collect them however you wanted, and impose whatever punishments you wanted ... here one is everything! Warrior, diplomat, trader! (Hochschild, 1999:136)

There was little or no investment in human capital. At the time of independence in 1960 there were only 30 Congolese university graduates, no doctors, no secondary school teachers and no army officers (Meredith, 2005). The post-independence era preserved the extractive nature of the state through its dominant figure, President Mobutu:

> Aside from the colour of his skin, there were few ways in which he did not resemble the monarch who governed the same territory a hundred years earlier. His one man rule. His great wealth taken from the land. His naming a lake after himself. His yacht. His appropriation of state possessions as his own. His huge shareholdings in private corporations doing business in his territory. (Hochschild, 1999:304)

The mixed colonial state: British India

The origins of the British colonial state in India lay in the rise of the East India Company in Bengal after 1757, which culminated in the British Crown taking over the sovereignty of India between 1858 and 1947. Per capita income growth was 0.2 per cent per annum in the fifty years before independence. Net investment during colonial rule never exceeded 2–4 per cent of GDP. In 1950, modern industry contributed only 6–8 per cent of national income and employed only 2.3 per cent of the labour force (Sivasubramonian, 2004). At independence life expectancy was only 30 and the Bengal famine had just killed three million people. In 1951 84 per cent of people (92 per cent of women) were illiterate (Mukherjee, 2007). In an address to Oxford University in 2005, Manmohan Singh, then Prime Minister of India, argued that the British colonial experience did have some benefits, including notions of the rule of law, constitutional government, a free press, a professional civil service, modern universities, the judiciary, legal system and police, the English language and the modern school system (Maddison, 2007). In fact, British colonialism in India contained aspects of both the extractive and settler models described by Acemoglu *et al.*

The British colonial government set up many European-style state institutions with an emphasis on private property and checks on government power.

Civil service reforms began with the creation of an exam-based system in 1853 and culminated in the creation of the Indian Civil Service (ICS) in 1892. This was a professional service recruited via a highly competitive exam and subsequently governed by an internal merit system that largely eradicated nepotism and patronage. From 1922 onwards it became possible to take the exam in India, making it more accessible to Indian recruits. The British–Indian balance had reached near parity by 1939 (Roy, 2002: Kohli, 2004). The political reality below the apex of the 1,000 officers of the ICS was very different. As colonial rule spread in the eighteenth and nineteenth centuries the British secured their influence by making a variety of arrangements with local notables who then collected taxes and maintained order. In the Punjab, for example, rural military and landlord elites were allowed to dominate various legislative councils and political parties in return for ensuring social stability (Yong, 2005:309). This indirect system of rule through local alliances limited the colonial state's ability either to be extractive or to set up European-style institutions (Kohli, 2004).

Tax revenue was too limited to be called extractive and spending too low to support settler-type institutional development. Public expenditure during the first half of the twentieth century averaged 10 per cent of GDP; more than half of this was spent on running the state itself (the military, civil service, legal framework and judiciary) and a further 20 per cent was spent on irrigation projects. By 1900/01 only 4 per cent of the budget was spent on health and education. The tax base was pre-modern. Tax revenues initially came from land and opium taxes, replaced over time by taxes on salt and customs duty. An income tax was levied in the 1860s, withdrawn and re-introduced several times over the subsequent decades.

The first major British conquest in South Asia was the Mughal province of Bengal in 1757, then already a settled peasant economy. The history of British rule can be read as a series of efforts to create property rights to promote productive agriculture while also attempting to maintain social and political stability. These two objectives proved impossible to reconcile and led to the creation of conflicting sets of rights, more contradictory than Acemoglu's extractive or settler type. The Permanent Settlement of 1793 imposed an obligation on local landlords (known as *zamindars*) to make a fixed annual payment to the state. Revenue beyond this could be kept and *zamindars* were granted the formal right to buy and sell their revenue-collecting authority (Khan, 2010). It was hoped *zamindars* would make efforts to improve the productivity of agriculture, knowing they could keep any extra revenues.

The colonial state in India lacked traditional sources of power and authority which made the maintenance of social order a major concern, especially after the rebellion of 1857. After 1857 the state tried to avert further threat to its rule by passing legislation to protect tenants and strengthen their rights to avoid discontent and instability. This legislation included the Rent Act of 1859 and Tenancy Act of 1885. These acts strengthened the rights of small landlords who were the tenants of the larger *zamindars* (Khan, 2010). By 1880 in the

Punjab considerable amounts of land were being taken over by moneylenders in lieu of mortgage defaults. This undermined the landowning castes that the British traditionally relied on for political support, revenue and military recruitment. The 1900 Punjab Alienation of Land Act forbade the passing of land from agricultural to non-agricultural castes (Ali, 2003). This left India not with extractive or settler-type institutions but with a bewildering, complex and overlapping variety of property rights. Single pieces of property could be simultaneously subject to claims based on formal ownership, informal purchase, tenancy, inheritance, sub-letting and actual occupancy. This has been a key long-run problematic legacy of British colonialism in India and has hindered the transition of a small-scale agricultural economy to one based on the amalgamation of plots for large-scale mechanized agriculture and the transfer of land usage for urban industrialization (Khan 2010).

There is good evidence that colonial institutions did persist into the post-colonial era in India, in accordance with the predictions of Acemoglu *et al.* But, contrary to Acemoglu *et al.*, it is not possible to characterize India as solely extractive or settler. Those areas where the British had strengthened the tax-collecting authority of traditional landlords underperformed those areas where property rights were given to individual cultivators until long after independence. The reason is probably that in areas where the British government gave property rights to a few landlords, political and legal institutions were more extractive and were used for the benefit of the few as compared with non-landlord areas where property rights were given to the mass of cultivators (Banerjee and Iyer, 2005; Kapur and Kim, 2006).

This mix of settler and extractive efforts can also be seen in infrastructure. Between 1860 and 1920 the number of railway-track miles increased from 838 to 37,029 in British India (Hurd, 1975; Habib, 2006:42). The impact of the railways in integrating British India as a single economic entity was famously praised by Karl Marx. Railways promoted the growth of European-style institutions and organizations. The railway-based postal system was started under Dalhousie (1848–56) and the number of letters and packets carried increased from 85 million in 1869 to 1,043 million in 1914. The Indian National Congress, which eventually led the independence movement and became the first ruling party of independent India, met for the first time in Bombay in 1885, relying on the railways to bring delegates from the provinces. The growing Indian press depended on railways for their circulation. They railways connected up the main metropolitan areas and helped to create a national market for bulk goods. There is good evidence that fluctuations in commodity prices and inter-state/regional price differentials both declined over the course of the nineteenth century and that this process was explained by the expansion of the railway system (Hurd, 1975; Habib, 2006:41). The railways also enhanced the extractive powers of the state. The motivation for railway building was not benevolence but to ensure (after 1857) that troops could move quickly from ports to the interior, between urban areas and to the borders with Afghanistan to meet a supposed Russian threat. The railways also assisted in extracting agricultural resources for export. This process was so thorough that average grain consumption in India was lower in 1950 than it had been in 1900.

The absent colonial state

Direct rule occurs when colonial officials run all but the very lowest levels of the administration. Indirect rule occurs when governance is entrusted to members of the local elite under the supervision of imperial governors. It often incorporates indigenous institutions and not simply individuals into the system of colonial rule.

If the Congo exemplified an extractive colonial state and India a complex mix, the state in Nigeria and Kashmir could be best described as 'absent'. Nigeria was created from highly diverse pre-existing political entities. These comprised in the North the Sokoto caliphate, in the South-west the Lagos consulate and dozens of small-scale Yoruba kingdoms and in the South-east small-scale tribal communities. The caliphate in northern Nigeria had some organization, a common religion and a written language. In the rest of Nigeria political structures were highly fragmented and based around a widely dispersed subsistence peasantry. The British did not set up 'extractive' or 'settler' type institutions, but rather reinforced weak centralization and indirect personal rule (Kohli, 2004).

In Nigeria there was no attempt to develop a tax system. Of the 2–3 per cent of GDP raised from taxation, most arose from foreign trade, especially alcohol. There was minimal economic growth (about 0.5 per cent per annum) in per capita terms between 1900 and 1930, based mainly on the export of cash crops (palm oil, groundnuts, cotton and cocoa). By the late 1930s only 12 per cent of children were receiving any education, literacy was only 2 per cent in the north and by the early 1950s Nigeria had only 1,000, mainly Yoruba university graduates (Kohli, 2004). The British had only a minimal physical presence in Nigeria including 3,000 soldiers, 4,000 police (and 80 officers) and one civil servant (over 400 in total) for every 100,000 Africans. World War II drew off personnel from the British colonial state, and the further devolution of administration from the minimal centre to the three regions was formalized by the 1954 constitution. At independence in 1960 the nationalist movement was, not surprisingly, divided along the personalistic, tribal, ethnic and regional basis of colonial rule (Kohli 2004). In the 1959 elections in the run-up to independence, three ethnic parties, none of whom had a national majority, each won majorities in their home region, which proved 'wildly destabilising and a perfect recipe for ethnic conflict' (Kwarteng, 2011:303).

Kashmir is another example of indirect colonial rule and 'a classic case of extending the empire by franchise, a way of allowing local rulers the freedom to do what they wanted so long as everything was quiet externally and trade routes remained safe and secure' (Kwarteng, 2011:96). After the Indian Mutiny of 1857, the valley of Kashmir was sold to the family of Gulab Singh, who became the hereditary Maharaja. The promotion of a Hindu Maharaja in a state with a predominantly Muslim population created inevitable tensions in the run-up to Indian independence, as the Hindu elite tried to maintain their dominance in government and the economy.

Typically, studies of indirect rule have focused on detailed case studies; there is at least one interesting exception, a study by Lange (2004) which examines the impact of direct versus indirect colonial rule in 33 former British colonies. The extent of indirect colonial rule is measured by the relative number of officially recognized court cases presided over by local chiefs rather than British colonial officers. The results show that the extent of indirect colonial rule in 1955 was strongly and negatively related to the World Bank governance indicators (state effectiveness, stability, corruption) in 1997–98 (Lange 2004). The case study of Burma shows that the one thing worse than indirect rule is having no indirect rule at all.

In Burma the problem was not that the British set up an extractive state or that they relied on indirect rule through traditional authorities, but that they abolished all aspects of the indigenous state structure and replaced them with nothing: 'The monarchy had been abolished. The court and religious authorities had been largely eradicated or marginalised ... which ... ensured there were no leaders of Burmese society" (Kwarteng, 2011:198). This political vacuum was an open invitation to the communists and the military in the years immediately after independence. Elsewhere colonialism had also crushed emerging feudal states in Africa. The French wiped out the large Muslim states of the Western Sudan and Dahomey, and kingdoms in Madagascar. The British eliminated the emerging states of Egypt, Mahdist Sudan, Asante, Benin, the Yoruba kingdoms, Swaziland, Matabeleland, Lozi and East African lake kingdoms (Rodney, 1972). The persistent tribalism of Africa can be partly understood as a result of this destruction. The loss of emerging state formations deprived the region of the institutions and organizations that could have supplanted tribal loyalty with a broader national identity.

A comparison with the historical experiences of France and Botswana is instructive. At the beginning of the nineteenth century France contained many different languages, ethnicities and local allegiances; only a few people spoke French or owed any loyalty to the central state, and many straddled international boundaries. It was the expansion and consolidation of the central state, and the related imposition of a uniform educational curriculum, a national language and symbolic national symbols such as the French flag and national anthem, 'La Marseillaise', dating from 1792, that led to the creation of France. Gradually Provençals on the French side of the border came to see themselves as French and those on the Italian side came to see themselves as Italian. A similar process has taken place in (economically successful) Botswana over last 50 years. The Tswana assemblies (*dikgotla*) were the origins of the modern state. Although in theory these were assemblies of adult males where public issues were discussed and which ordinary tribesmen were expected to attend, in practice they were dominated by an inner circle of influential citizens, and were highly centralized and manipulated to obtain the people's consent. The Tswana state had clear rules stipulating how the chiefship was to be inherited and these were used to remove bad rulers and allow talented candidates to become chief. This culture promoted the executive powers of the state in pre-independence Botswana. Those executive powers included the appointment of state personnel and command over the military, both of which prevented the emergence of rival institutions to the state (Maundeni, 2001). The post-independence leaders of Botswana (in particular the first two presidents, Seretse Khama and Quett Masire) have often been praised for their vision, lack of corruption and strength of purpose. But good leadership is better considered as a product of the deeper determinants of growth, or as an 'intrinsic part of the historical divergence of Tswana's political institutions' (Robinson, 2009:4). The Tswana institutions persisted and evolved because Botswana was a colonial sideshow largely ignored by the British, and unlike Nigeria had strong indigenous state structures.

Developmental colonialism in South Korea

Korea became a Japanese colony in 1910. Much writing on South Korea argues that rapid economic growth under a strong state only began with the shift to export promotion under the incoming military government of Park after 1961 and denies any continuity with the colonial period. Others disagree: 'South Korea under Park Chung-Hee fell back into the grooves of an earlier origin and traversed along them, well into the 1980s' (Kohli, 1994:1270). The colonial story does not fit with the Acemoglu *et al.* thesis. In Korea settler-type colonialism set up extractive institutions but used them to promote long-run growth and some aspects of development (notably education). The post-colonial state continued with this model, freed from the burden of the benefits of economic growth being drawn away to Japan.

In the second half of the nineteenth century, the Korean state was unable to collect taxes. The monarchy was dominated by independent factions of aristocratic state officials who manipulated the legal system to enable themselves to extract a surplus from agriculture. According to Kohli (2004:27), the impact of Japanese colonialism (1910 to 1945) was 'more intense, more brutal, and deeply architectonic in comparison with European colonialism'. Korea was seen as a long-term integral part of 'Greater Japan' and colonialism was based around settlement to more closely integrate the two countries. The aristocratic state was abolished and replaced by a cabinet-style government run by Japanese bureaucrats. The number of police increased from 6,222 in 1910 to 60,000 in 1941. The police wore military uniforms and had summary powers to judge and punish minor offenders. The Korean state in the 1960s certainly looked much like the late-colonial state, despite the fifteen-year interlude. Though the 1950s Rhee presidency was marked by chaos, his successor General Park, a graduate of the Japanese military academy in Manchuria, was more obviously a product of the Japanese experience (Kohli,

1994). The question of whether there is a causal link from the colonial to the Park state is complicated by the fact that between 1930 and 1970 there were five different regimes in power: the Japanese, US occupation, the Rhee government, the short-lived Chang Myon government, and the military and civilian governments of Park. Each of these periods corresponded to different political alliances, different economic policies and different patterns of bureaucratic organization. It is possible to emphasize the fundamental discontinuities of the era by focusing on the transition from the colonial bureaucracy to the chaotic Rhee government. Another significant problem with tracing a causal link from the colonial to Park eras is that Koreans did not widely participate in the Japanese colonial state. While Park may have been a graduate of the Japanese military, there was little or no Korean presence at the upper levels of the bureaucracy and only 2.6 per cent of those reaching officer status in the police were Koreans (Haggard *et al.*, 1997).

Rice shortages and riots in Japan in 1918 led to major efforts by the brutal colonial state to expand production in Korea. The motive was extractive: to export rice to Japan to alleviate shortages there. The percentage of paddy land using improved seeds doubled between 1915 and 1940, eventually reaching 85 per cent. Fertilizer input increased ten times over the same period. Between 1919 and 1938 land under irrigation increased 10 per cent annually and by 1938 rice yields were around 11 per cent higher in Korea than in the US. Local police were known to have compelled villagers to switch from existing food crops to cash crops and adopt new techniques in rice production (Kohli, 2004:37). Others have critiqued this success story. Much of the growth in agriculture from the 1930s, however, was wiped out during World War II and growth tended to be concentrated in rice rather than being broadly based across the agricultural sector. The most significant break in output growth occurred after independence. Output, which had grown 1.62 per cent a year between 1920 and 1939, increased to 4.33 per cent per annum between 1953 and 1969. This was associated with policy changes implemented after independence, including land reform and an end to the extractive export-orientated approach to rice production (Haggard *et al.*, 1997). Even accepting these criticisms, a comparative perspective shows that growth of agriculture during the colonial era *was* relatively rapid, and crucially this growth was led by productivity gains which were almost unique in the history of colonialism.

Opinions differ among scholars about the pace and nature of industrial growth in colonial Korea. The average annual rate of growth in industry (including mining and manufacturing) between 1910 and 1940 was nearly 10 per cent. The motive was again largely extractive, to contribute to Japan's 1930s war economy. By 1943 heavy industry accounted for nearly half of all industrial production and by 1940 nearly 35 per cent of total commodity production originated in the industrial sector, According to Kohli (2004:48), 'The extent of Korea's industrialization during the colonial phase was both considerable and nearly unique in the comparative history of colonialism'. Haggard *et al.* (1997) argue, on the other hand, that industrial growth was relatively slow between 1918 and 1931, increasing rapidly only in the later 1930s. They also question the legacy of this for longer-term industrialization in South Korea as colonial industry was dominated by the Japanese. In 1941 the Japanese owned nearly 60 per cent of all firms in Korea and accounted for over 90 per cent of all paid-up capital. These figures were even higher in heavy and more technologically advanced sectors. The Japanese, for example, had 98 per cent of paid-up capital in the metal industry and 99 per cent in the chemical industry. The Japanese even dominated in light manufacturing, having 93 per cent of paid-up capital in food, 80.3 per cent in rice mills and 85.4 per cent in textiles. Korean firms tended to be small, and their average size even declined during the colonial period. For the top ten or fifty (South) Korean business groups in 1983 the most important start-up period was between 1945 and 1960 (Haggard *et al.* 1997:876). Colonial industrialization made little impact on employment. In 1940 only 5.4 per cent of workers were employed in manufacturing. By contrast economic growth from the 1960s was based on large, Korean-owned firms generating rapid increases in employment. In addition the areas that became North Korea housed the bulk of heavy industry. Finally, as was the case with agriculture, much of this industry was destroyed. According to one estimate total industrial output fell by 80 per cent between 1940 and 1948 and between 1945 and 1949 industrial employment declined by 60 per cent (Haggard *et al.,* 1997). But even without physical production facilities it is easier (as Germany and Japan found) to rebuild after a war using an accumulated body of modern skills, education and experience than to make an original shift from agriculture to industry. The South Korean elite were among the very few in the developing world for whom a developmental state model and industrial skills were readily available from their own historical past (Kohli, 1997).

From Marx to neo-colonialism: a changing debate

The rich tradition of thinking relating to colonialism that has come from a Marxist perspective includes works by Marx, Lenin, and the dependency scholars Baran and Sweezy, and Warren.

Marx famously argued that Asiatic society was based on a village economy and a hereditary division of labour, and lacked private property in land. Asiatic geography required large-scale irrigation works to create a flourishing agriculture and this, he argued, strengthened the powers of central government (the only organization capable of mobilizing and managing such a large investment project). The resulting strong state was then able to drain a surplus from agriculture. Chapter 7, for example, gives an estimate by Maddison (1971) that the Mughal Indian state raised taxes on agriculture and land equivalent to about a third or more of gross crop production, representing about 15–18 per cent of GDP which was large by historical European standards. The argument here is that geography determines the nature of institutions, which echoes the Acemoglu *et al.* thesis discussed earlier in this chapter. What Marx called the

'Asiatic Mode of Production' was, he claimed, stable but stagnant and had no internal progressive dynamic.

Marx believed that British rule in India destroyed this 'Asiatic society' and created the conditions for industrial capitalism. British colonialism in India, he wrote, had 'dissolved those small semi-barbarian communities by blowing up their economic basis, and thus produced the greatest, and, to speak the truth, the only social revolution ever heard of in Asia'. This social revolution may have been 'actuated only by the vilest interests and was stupid in its manner of enforcing them', but 'whatever may have been the crimes of England, she was the unconscious tool of history in bringing about the revolution'. Imperialism left England to 'fulfil a double mission in India: one destructive the other regenerating – the annihilation of old Asiatic society, and the laying of the material foundations of Western society in Asia' as 'Modern industry resulting from the railway system, will dissolve the hereditary divisions of labour, upon which rests the Indian castes, those decisive impediments to Indian progress and Indian power' (Warren, 1980).

Though colonialism may have had a progressive impact in laying the foundations of capitalism, the most influential driving force, according to Marx, was the internal dynamic of capitalism. Capitalism, he argued, has a relentless tendency to expand, both within and between countries, so if colonialism was important, trade and openness were even more so. The development of capitalism in Western Europe, he wrote, would 'compel all nations on pain of extinction to adopt the bourgeois mode of production', and the 'country that is more developed industrially only shows to the less developed, the image of its own future' (Palma, 1978).

After 1900 Lenin and others brought an analysis of imperialism more formally into Marxist thought. Lenin argued that imperialism then represented a new stage of capitalism and was linked to the changing structure of developed capitalist countries. The formation of joint-stock companies allowed firms to expand beyond the wealth of a single owner and the constraints of re-investing only earned profits. The key features of this new stage were the centralization of industrial capital, growth in the size and independence of banks (what Lenin called 'finance capital'), and the export of that finance capital (distinguished from the export of commodities). Lenin argued that the monopolization of capitalism led to an exhaustion of investment opportunities at home and so reduced incentives to innovate. The resulting motives to control and expand into new global markets prompted colonial expansion. Lenin retained the traditional Marxist view that the export of capital (and commodities) would accelerate development in the backward areas. There are numerous problems with this analysis. Lenin dated the monopolization and export of finance capital to the 1900s several decades after the rapid colonial takeover of Africa. According to his schema they should have occurred the other way round. Germany, rather than the UK and France, had the most concentrated industrial structure but a much smaller and later colonial empire. Lenin argued that monopoly capitalism was associated with stagnation in the developed countries; in fact there *was* rapid economic growth between the 1880s and 1910. Lenin argued that technological change would stagnate during the monopolization phase; in fact there was a new dynamic phase of scientific-technological change after 1890 based on electricity, chemicals and the internal combustion engine.

Around 1920 Marxist thought embraced a new vision of capitalism in 'backward nations'. The power of traditional dominant classes (the indirect rule discussed earlier in this chapter) in the backward countries was now seen to be preventing the transformation of internal structures which capitalist development/industrialization both needed and brought about. In contrast to many contemporary concerns, colonialism was supporting rather than undermining traditional indigenous social structures. But it was also propping up the power of rural landowners for political reasons and was influenced by industrialists in the home country who wanted no competition from producers of manufactured goods in the colonies. In 1957 Paul Baran wrote *The Political Economy of Growth,* the first major Marxist work to study underdeveloped countries. He argued that capitalism was no longer an engine of growth in developing countries. The centralization of capital that produced murderous imperial competition in Lenin's work was associated by Baran with corporate lethargy. Monopolization, argued Baran, led to large firms squatting on markets protected from competition from new entrants by their enormous size and domination of markets; these firms also used this market power to restrict output globally, raise prices and protect profits. Consequently, Baran argued that much of the drive to pursue technological innovation would disappear. At the centre of Baran's worldview was an alliance between the developed country and a feudal ruling class in developing countries. The latter, he believed, had been created and/or sustained in power by developed countries and ultimately served to prevent growth. The strength of feudal groups allowed them to maintain traditional modes of surplus extraction and fritter the results away on conspicuous consumption such as large homes, fine dining and servants, rather than investing in modern industry.

Later, Bill Warren returned to classical Marxism and revived the argument that colonialism was a 'powerful engine of progressive social change' (1980:9) and was/is a pioneer of capitalism. He returned to the views that colonialism was progressive because it was linked to the penetration and spread of capitalism into non-capitalist parts of the world. Third-world nationalism, he suggests, can explain the 'ideological dominance of the underdevelopment fiction' (1980:8) whereby colonialism and its alleged harm provide a fictional unifying element for disparate nationalist groups by giving them someone to blame for any economic or social problems.

In the 1950s only the US, UK and France were major investors in developing countries but by the 1960s there was sharp competition between US, Japanese, and European enterprises for access to developing countries (Warren, 1973). In the 1960s developing countries were still dependent on developed-country technology but the conditions of their access in a post-colonial world were increasingly competitive. Warren argued that by the 1970s there were favourable prospects for capitalism in many developing countries, there had been a loosening of relations of dependence in the global economy and there was clear empirical evidence of rapid industrialization. Independence broke the monopoly of the colonial power and the then Cold War allowed developing countries to play off capitalist states against each other, communists against capitalists, and individual firms, especially those from different national origins, against each other.

Oil companies were long seen as the archetypal exploiting MNC and so were the subject of neo-Marxist polemics:

Nothing compares with this 'black gold' as a magnet for foreign capital, nothing earns such lush profits, no jewel in the diadem of capitalism is so monopolised, and no businessmen wielded the global political power of the great petroleum corporations. Standard Oil and Shell seat and unseat kings and presidents, finance palace plots and coup d'états, have innumerable generals, ministers, and James Bonds at their command, and make decisions about peace or war in every field and every language. (Galeano, 2009:157)

The reality was very different. Soon after independence developing countries began to assert control over foreign firms, including oil companies, located in their territories. Examples included the forcible nationalization of oil in Iraq, and British assets in Uganda and in Egypt (the Suez Canal). Linkages within developing countries have almost universally increased through more widespread refining and processing of raw materials, such as copper, iron and bauxite, in the country of extraction (Warren, 1973). In both minerals and fuels developing countries retained an increasing share of profits over time; their share of profits on crude oil rose from 10–15 per cent in the 1920s to about 85 per cent in 1972. In Chile taxes paid by large copper companies rose from under 10 per cent of the value of the product in the 1920s to about 30 per cent in 1964. Tax charges on the Zambian copper industry from 1965 significantly reduced the net outflow of profits and by the late-1960s Zambia received about 80 per cent of the international value of the product (Warren, 1973).

By other measures, such as trade diversification (judged by the geographical destination or the commodity composition of exports), controls on FDI (including the widespread nationalization of resource-based enterprises), structural change (including a reduction of the enclave features of FDI) and development of greater backward linkages, economic power steadily became more dispersed (Warren, 1980). The leading sector for post-World War II developing countries has been manufacturing for the domestic market. In Pakistan, for example, between 1951–52 and 1954–55, 96.6 per cent of total growth in manufacturing was met through import substitution and near-total domestic self-sufficiency was achieved in sectors such as sugar, cotton, matches and edible oils (McCartney, 2011:42). A large number of developing countries after the 1960s built capacity in heavy industry, including iron and steel, petrochemicals, lorry-making, aircraft industries, locomotives, cement, electrical machinery and heavy non-electrical machinery. The net result was that the balance of power shifted away from the dominance of a few major imperialist countries towards a more even distribution of power. Imperialism declined as capitalism grew (Warren, 1973:41). Many have argued this trend was reversed with liberalization, particularly of trade and FDI in the 1980s and 1990s and that MNCs have regained control over many developing countries.

Colonialism and development: the debate

The key thematic debates about the impact of colonialism on development in the colonies are the drain of surplus, deindustrialization, diversity and isolation, and human development.

Colonialism and the drain of surplus

Lenin argued that the export of capital from developed to developing countries characterized colonialism and exploitation. The more enduring argument has been that a drain of surplus has been a key mechanism enforcing economic stagnation in colonized countries.

Between 1609 and the beginning of the eighteenth century, the Dutch gained control of most of the Indonesian archipelago but did not rule directly except in Batavia-Java. This allowed them to achieve an effective monopoly of trade. They enforced the delivery of spices and other crops at low prices and managed to prevent the growth of alternative indigenous industries. Data up to 1939 showed persistent trade surpluses (exports to the Netherlands exceeding imports), which is an approximate measure of the transfer of surplus to the Netherlands. The influential Indian historian Irfan Habib argues that what came to be called the 'tribute' or 'drain of surplus' was the primary objective of the British conquest of India (2006:23). In the eighteenth century the East India Company converted tax revenue from the conquered areas into goods and shipped them overseas. The excess value of British imports from East India over exports was around £4 million per annum by the late eighteenth century. With the advent of more settled colonial government, the tribute/drain became composed of 'home charges' such as the expenditure on the Secretary of State's establishment of British staff, pensions paid to British officials, and expenses incurred on using the British Indian army on campaigns outside India. Habib argues that British investment in Indian railways was deliberately distorted to generate 'excessive' profits. Land for railway companies was given free by the government and investors were also guaranteed a return of 5 per cent on capital paid at a fixed exchange rate (2006:36). The result was an excess of exports over imports which amounted to 30 per cent of total imports between 1868–69 and 1882–83, and above 20 per cent thereafter. This constituted around 3 per cent of the national income of British India and half of domestic savings (Bagchi, 1982; Habib, 2006). The problem with these measures of 'drain' from Indonesia or India is that investment is generally value-creating, so generating an excess of profit over initial investment does not necessarily indicate an absolute drain.

Debates related to the drain of surplus have been revived in recent decades, especially after the beginning of the debt crisis in the early 1980s. The Jubilee Debt Campaign estimated that in 2011 the poorest 36 countries in the world (with GDP per capita below $975) had external debts of $133 billion and total external debt for all developing countries was $4.9 trillion. During that year developing countries paid $620 billion servicing those debts (www.jubileedebtcampaign. org.uk). In 2011 the OECD estimate that members of their Development Assistance Committee (DAC) provided net aid to developing countries of $133.5 billion, a 2.7 per cent reduction over the previous year.

Colonialism and deindustrialization

A long-standing critique of colonialism is that of deindustrialization. There is widespread evidence that the proportion of people working in Indian manufacturing fell after the late eighteenth/early nineteenth century (Bagchi, 1976), and that many established industries, such as Kashmiri shawls, Bengali silk and handloom jute weaving disappeared (Habib, 2006:98). This occurred alongside the tightening grip of British colonialism after the 1750s. The railway system and other infrastructure was, according to this critical view, less about promoting development, and more about facilitating extraction by converting India into a market for British manufactured exports and extracting raw materials for British industry. During the eighteenth century calicoes and other manufactured textiles had represented 60–70 per cent of India's total exports, but by 1820 13 million square metres of cloth were imported into India, rising to 2,050 million in 1890. Raw cotton accounted for 12.04 per cent of exports in 1849–50 and 36.36 per cent in 1869–70. In 1862 India supplied 75 per cent of all cotton imported into Britain (Kohli, 2004; Habib, 2006).

The traditional view is that this deindustrialization was a deliberate policy by the British colonial state: while English textiles could enter the Indian market with no duties payable, Indian textile exports were subject to very high tariffs in the UK. The decline of the Indian hand paper industry has been blamed on the requirement from the 1860s that all paper required for government purposes was imported from Britain (Habib, 2006:98). A more realistic argument is that that policy was overwhelmed by the impact of industrialization and technological change in Britain. By 1830 the productivity of an English worker using modern equipment was 10 to 14 times higher for an average yarn and 200 to 300 times higher for fine yarn than Indian or other traditional workers (Bairoch, 1993:54). The traditional arguments also tend to focus on the welfare losses to Indian producers. It is often forgotten that these losses were balanced by gains to consumers. By 1850 prices of ordinary cloth had declined by 80 per cent from their 1800 levels (Roy, 2002).

There are similar arguments for Africa, but not backed by the good statistics of the Indian example. Prior to European colonialism most African societies fulfilled their own needs for a wide range of farming equipment, weaponry and clothing. In Katanga, Sierra Leone and Zambia local copper was long preferred to imported items. There was a famous brass and bronze industry in Benin and a glass and bead industry in Nupe (now Northern Nigeria) (Rodney, 1972). These nascent industries were destroyed by competition from imported manufactured goods. Rodney argues that the abandonment of traditional iron smelting in most parts of Africa was probably the most important instance of technological regression. These losses of industry and skills in Africa were extremely small if measured from the viewpoint of modern scientific achievements or by the standards of eighteenth-century England, though once lost it was impossible to progress further (1972:105). Darity (1992) (recall his argument from the Introduction) emphasized instead the role of the slave trade in diverting energies from productive endeavour.

Others argue that colonial infrastructure did not promote economic growth. The construction of the railways, in this pessimistic view, produced few positive wider growth links to the Indian economy. Apart from ballast for railway tracks and coal, everything needed for railways right down to sleepers had to be imported from Britain. Railway materials and stores accounted for 7.3 per cent of total Indian merchandise imports in 1897–98 (Rothermund, 1993; Habib, 2006). The value of India's exports quintupled between 1870 and 1914 with agriculture providing 70–80 per cent of the total, but per capita output and consumption of food crops remained unchanged or even declined from the early 1900s to the late 1940s (Bagchi, 1982; Chandra, 1982; Roy, 2002; Habib, 2006:84; Mukherjee, 2007). In Africa the pattern of infrastructure, in particular roads and railways, was based around the extent to which particular regions needed to be opened up to import–export activities or the likely need to move troops (Rodney, 1972:209). The means of communication did not facilitate internal trade in Africa; there were no roads connecting different colonies. Of the railway system in Latin America, Galeano wrote: 'The tracks were laid out not to connect internal areas one with another, but to connect production centres with ports. The design still resembles the fingers of an open hand: thus railroads, so often hailed as the forerunners of progress, were an impediment to the formation and development of a national market' (2009:199).

A big problem with all these arguments related to deindustrialization is that there was a general tendency for indigenous industrial growth to increase during the late colonial era, and this is difficult to reconcile with the thesis of an unchanging extractive colonial state. The years after 1858 saw the emergence of modern industry in India, including paper mills, breweries, flour mills, cotton and jute presses, engineering, timber mills, coffee plantations and railway companies. By 1911, of 129 spinning, weaving and other cotton mills owned by companies in the Bombay Presidency 92 had only Indian directors

(Tripathi and Jumani, 2007). During the first two decades of the twentieth century production in Indian textile mills increased from 0.6 billion to 1.3 billion yards. The coal industry imported 0.5 million tonnes in 1914 and exported 1 million tonnes in 1916. Production of steel increased from 31,000 tonnes in 1913 to 181,000 in 1918 (Rothermund, 1993). In 1914 foreign banks held 70 per cent of total deposits and by 1947 only 17 per cent (Maddison, 2007; Mukherjee, 2007:39). Likewise, Kenya experienced modest state-promoted economic growth in the late colonial era. The industrial workforce increased from 180,000 in 1942 to 440,000 in 1952 and at independence the manufacturing sector constituted 9.5 per cent of GDP. During the 1920s a number of agro-processing industries were promoted through tariffs on wheat milling and protective railway rates. The state-owned Industrial Development Corporation (IDC) acted as a finance agency providing finance, pioneer tax relief, custom duty refunds, and buildings in established industrial estates (Fahnbulleh, 2006).

Colonialism, diversity and isolation

There is widespread agreement that the borders of contemporary African states are arbitrary and that this pattern has colonial origins. Treaties among imperial powers and with local chiefs often resulted in straight lines, or the use of rivers or other geographical features previously as likely to unite as separate local populations. There are 177 African cultural or ethnic groups that are partitioned across borders, representing on average 43 per cent of their country's population (this is known as dismemberment). The Mandara of Cameroon and Nigeria, for example, have maintained a unified parallel political authority despite now living in different countries (Englebert *el al.,* 2002). A common argument is that dismemberment will increase conflict between states, especially where these borders partition previously united groups. Somalia's long-standing claims over Ethiopian and Kenyan territory inhabited by ethnic Somalis have been the cause of repeated conflict with both countries. Other examples include Morocco, Algeria, Western Sahara, Libya, Chad, Ghana, Togo and the Côte d'Ivoire. Chapter 12 discusses the 24 secessionist attempts in Africa between 1946 and 1998, most of which were linked to dismemberment. The discussion has mostly been based around specific example; one exception to this is a detailed statistical study: Engelbert *et al.* (2002) showed that there is a significant statistical relationship between colonial dismemberment and the likelihood of conflict between 1960 and 1999.

Colonialism and human development

Another area of widespread agreement is that colonial governments at best neglected welfare and at worst perpetuated genocide. The native American population declined by an estimated 80–90 per cent within the first 100 to 150 years following the arrival of Christopher Columbus in 1492. Within 50 years following contact the native Taino population of the island of Hispaniola (estimated population between 60,000 and 8 million) was virtually extinct. The population of central Mexico fell from nearly 15 million in 1519 to approximately 1.5 million a century later (Nunn and Qian, 2010). The estimated mortality from starvation and disease in British India exceeded 1 million in Orissa 1865–66, in the Deccan 1876–78, and North-west Provinces 1877–78, and in the countrywide famines of 1896–97 (when an estimated 4.5 million died) and 1899–90. The Orissa famine was clearly a pre-modern famine as crops failed in an area without roads and ports and the region could not receive supplies from outside. The 1868–69 famine in the North-west Frontier was in an area well supplied by railways, which refuted the notion that railways would automatically alleviate famine conditions. During famines, in 1875 British Indian ports exported 1.22 million tons of food grains and in 1895 about 2.49 million tons (Habib, 2006). In India, unlike the Americas, claims of genocide are rarely heard and deaths from famine are usually attributed to the ignorance or mistakes of the colonial state.

Over the longer term there was a clear (but not universal) neglect of general education in the colonies. The main purpose of the colonial education system in Africa, argues Walter Rodney, was to train Africans to help man the local administration: it was an education for subordination, exploitation, creation of mental confusion, and development of underdevelopment (1972:241). Or, as Franz Fanon argued:

> The colonialist bourgeoisie, in its narcissistic dialogue, expounded by members of the universities, had in fact deeply implanted in the minds of the colonised intellectual that the essential qualities remain eternal in spite of all the blunders men may make: the essential qualities of the West, of course. The native intellectual accepted the cogency of these ideas, and deep down in his brain you could always find a vigilant sentinel ready to defend the Graeco-Latin pedestal. (2001:36)

In 1938 in French West Africa there were 77,000 pupils from a population of 15 million. At independence the Congo had only 16 graduates from a population of 16 million. South Korea was different; the number of students attending school increased from 10,000 in 1910 to 1.7 million in 1941 and in 1945 the literacy rate reached 50 per cent. Nevertheless there has been criticism that the goal was not to instil freedom of thought and debate but to raise productivity in the labour force. More general indicators of human development in colonial Korea were pessimistic. Newspapers were suspended or heavily censored, political protest was dealt with swiftly. Wage growth lagged behind productivity gains, facilitating higher profits. Increases in food production did not lead to increases in food consumption, rather to more exports. Attempts to create unions were prohibited and there were few laws to regulate the workplace and protect workers. 80 per cent of the workers at Kyongbangs textile mill, for example, were unmarried peasant girls in their late teens, many recruited from the families who worked the lands owned by the mill owners. Discipline in the factory was severe and even extended to the conduct of personal lives and living arrangements (Kohli, 2004).

Height has been used as a long-term objective summative measure of development. Height is influenced by an individual's lifetime intake of nutrition and exposure to disease. Height is also influenced in part by genetics (tall parents are more likely to have tall children), so it is not a perfect measure. The height record of colonial armies is a little-used source providing excellent coverage across a wide population and over time. The sample of military recruits was broadly representative during the two world wars which expanded military recruitment such that in Kenya about 10 per cent of adult men (20 per cent of the wage labour force) were serving in the military. In Ghana recruitment was compulsory, with quotas for each district, and physical requirements were lowered. In Ghana the cohort of recruits born between 1905 and 1920 were taller than the cohort of recruits born between 1880 and 1893 by an average of 2cm, implying a considerable improvement in the quality of life. A major setback seems to have occurred between 1930 and 1950, after which average height gains of 0.4cm per decade resumed. In Kenya mean heights stagnated for birth cohorts between 1880 and 1920 then improved continuously for cohorts born from the 1920s to the 1980s, This evidence suggests that Ghana and Kenya experienced significant improvements in nutrition and health during colonial rule. At the beginning of the twentieth century cocoa emerged as a successful cash crop and brought an economic boom to Ghana's forest region. Other contributory factors were political stability and domestic peace, the ending of the slave trade and labour migration to the booming forest region as the British extended their rule over the inland kingdom of Ashanti and the northern Savannah after 1896 (Moradi, 2008). In industrialized countries mean heights grew around 1cm per decade. Other developing countries rarely achieved such rates. In India, for example, heights stagnated at very low levels.

The critique that education was neglected or distorted by colonialism is reflected in a more recent concern. This is the question of the Brain Drain. Developed countries offer various incentives for skilled/educated nationals from abroad (often developing countries) to migrate. The H1B Visa Programme in the US targets individuals working in sectors such as IT, finance, engineering, health care, and telecoms. It offers the opportunity to live and work in the US and eventually apply for a Green Card (permanent residence). In the early 2000s Denmark offered expatriates a special 25 per cent income tax instead of the usual rates between 39 per cent and 59 per cent. After 2003 South Korea offered expatriates tax-free allowances of up to 40 per cent of salary to cover the cost of living, housing, home leave and education. Not surprisingly, given enormous differences in living standards, such incentive programmes have motivated an enormous shift of skilled labour from developing to developed countries. (Admittedly unreliable) data from the OECD shows that in 2000 the emigration rate of college graduates was 83.4 per cent in Haiti, 49.2 per cent in Sierra Leone, 44.7 per cent in Ghana, 38.5 per cent in

Kenya, 36.0 per cent in Uganda, 31.7 per cent in Rwanda, 27.0 per cent in Vietnam and 20.9 per cent in Malawi (Docquier and Rapoport, 2011:7). It is interesting to note that these countries are a mix of the failing economically (Haiti), post-conflict (Sierra Leone and Rwanda) and those experiencing rapid economic growth (Uganda, Vietnam). Particularly affected is the medical sector in Sub-Saharan Africa where 20 per cent of medical professionals have emigrated, and in a survey of six African countries in 2003, 50 per cent of medical professionals still resident declared they were considering migration (2011:37). Critics have argued that this brain drain deprives developing countries of the skills necessary to produce and deliver services. Others have argued that skilled workers send home remittances. For example, in 2002 Pakistan, Uganda, Morocco, Guatemala and Sri Lanka all received more than 8 per cent of GDP in remittance income and all have notably high shares of skilled migration. Others have argued that skilled migrants will acquire more skills, education and savings and often return home and so become 'brain gain'. There is some evidence of this latter effect in India, though in a typical year outward migration of Indian professionals on the H1B visa is thirty times the number returning.

Key points

- Colonialism has influenced growth at a proximate level through policies relating to investment, education and land during the colonial era.
- Colonialism has also influenced growth in the post-independence era through the deeper determinants: institutions (importing them from the coloniser or maintaining indigenous institutions); geography (drawing borders); culture (ethnic divisions); and openness (typically exposing the colony to trade and openness with the colonizer at the cost of trade and openness with the rest of the world).
- The nature of colonialism was in some cases influenced by the nature of the colony. The Acemoglu thesis suggests the disease environment influenced the choice of whether the colonial state would set up extractive or settler-type institutions.
- India was not a settler state but the British did try to replicate aspects of 'good institutions' alongside extraction for their own benefit.
- The British in Nigeria and Kashmir were really an absent state, neither settler nor extractive.
- The Japanese settled in South Korea in order to more efficiently 'extract', but many argue that these extractive institutions were later turned by the independent government of South Korea into a means to promote rapid growth and development.
- There is a rich debate on colonialism from a Marxist perspective.
- There are various thematic debates about the impact of colonialism on development in the colonies; these themes are the drain of surplus, deindustrialization, diversity and isolation, and human development.

Chapter 10

Institutions

Among economists such as Dani Rodrik and particularly economic historians such as Daren Acemoglu and Douglass North, 'good institutions' are regarded as the key deep determinant of economic growth. If there is a conventional orthodoxy about the most important deep determinant – then it is institutions. Geography, goes this argument, is not unimportant but the problems manifest by bad geography can be overcome by good institutions. Tropical diseases (to pre-empt discussion from Chapter 11) are more likely to find cures if pharmaceutical firms have incentives to invest in relevant R&D, or countries that are landlocked are more likely to find investors willing to build transport links to overcome that isolation if those investors receive sufficient protection.

But institutions are also misunderstood. Douglass North defines institutions as being a mix of formal rules such as laws and constitutions and informal rules such as trust and conventions. Institutions, then, are often confused with 'organizations', which are 'groups of individuals bound together by some common purpose to achieve certain objectives', such as political parties, firms or trade unions. This chapter shows that institutions influence economic growth via the proximate determinant of investment. That investment can be in physical capital, technological innovation or human capital. How investment may (or sometimes may not) promote economic growth is discussed in detail in Chapter 3.

Institutions and economic growth

Douglass North and other economic historians have placed 'good institutions' at the centre of their explanation for the 'rise of the West' after 1500 CE. Institutions as a deeper determinant influence economic growth via the proximate determinants, one of which is investment. Good institutions may motivate investment in physical capital, technological innovation and human capital. These links are shown in Figure 10.1.

What are institutions?

Douglass North, the Nobel Prize-winning economic historian, pioneered the modern study of institutions. He described institutions as:

Figure 10.1　*Institutions as a deeper determinant of economic growth*

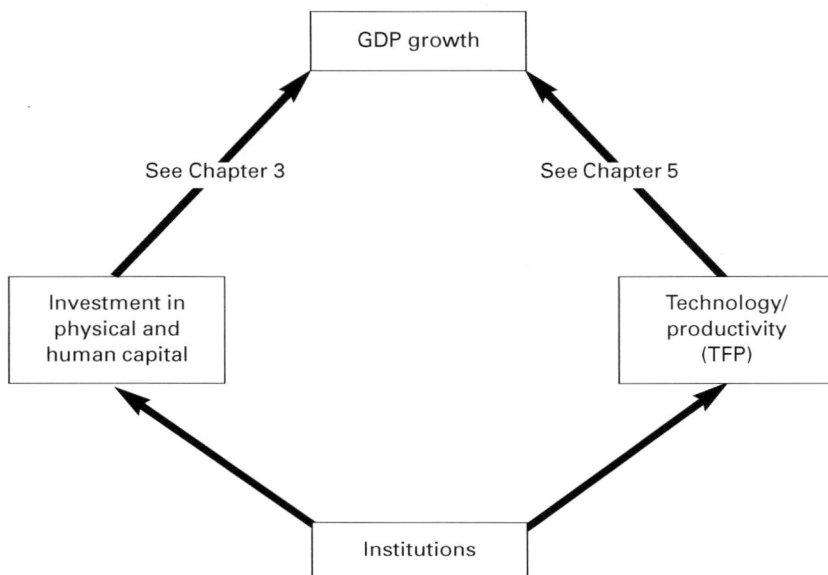

[t]he humanly devised constraints that structure human interaction. They are made up of formal constraints (e.g., rules, laws, constitutions), informal constraints (e.g., norms of behaviour, conventions, self-imposed codes of conduct), and their enforcement characteristics. Together they define the incentive structure of societies and specifically economies. (1994:359)

A constitution, for example, may set out formal rules about the circumstances under which a president may be removed from office, the laws that are not subject to legislative changes such as the right to private property or liberty, and the separation of the judiciary from the executive. Institutions can also be informal. The common practice on the London Underground of letting people off the train before trying to board makes for the more efficient running of the transport system. Formal rules are ultimately backed up by the coercive apparatus of the state, through a system of fines and imprisonment. Informal rules are supported by a variety of mechanisms, including social sanctions (being glared at may operate in the case of someone pushing their way onto a train before everyone has exited).

Institutions are often confused with 'organizations', which North defines as:

[g]roups of individuals bound together by some common purpose to achieve certain objectives. Organisations include political bodies (e.g. political parties, the Senate, a city council, regulatory bodies), economic bodies (e.g. firms, trade unions, family farms, cooperatives), social bodies (e.g., churches,

clubs, athletic associations), and educational bodies (e.g., schools, universities, vocational training centres). (1994:361)

A bank is an organization that has an important influence on economic growth through the resources it allocates to competing investment projects. Whether banks promote growth depends in part on underlying institutions. A weak legal system may lead to bank directors stealing money rather than investing it or to politicians pushing banks to lend to politically favoured constituents rather than productive businesses.

Democracy and dictatorship as institutions

There is a big debate among scholars of development about whether dictatorship or democracy is better at promoting economic growth and human development, and the relation proves to be far more complex than the simplistic sentiment that more democracy is good for everything.

Political systems are institutions; whether a country has democratic or dictatorial politics defines the rules by which individuals can acquire office, how power changes hands and the relation of the political leadership with the judiciary and citizenry. The first problem is to measure democracy. We may reasonably conclude that having frequent elections, a diverse media, free speech and rights of assembly and a viable opposition party all make for a functioning democracy, but how do we add all these variables into a single index so we can measure its relationship with income levels and economic growth? If a country has more regular elections but greater state control of the media has it become more or less democratic? One effort is by the Economist Intelligence Unit (EIU) which has been publishing a democracy index regularly since the 2000s. Countries' scores are based on the answers given by experts (though what sort of 'experts' is not made clear) to questions relating to five categories: electoral process and pluralism, civil liberties, functioning of government, political participation, and political culture. The answers are valued at one or zero and the five categories are then averaged to produce a measure of 'democracy'. Depending on its score, a country is then classified as a full democracy, a flawed democracy, a hybrid regime or an authoritarian regime. Researchers often also use an index produced by Freedom House that seeks to measure civil liberties and political rights.

These various measures of democracy do show a clear link with income per capita – richer countries are more likely to be democratic. The second problem, however, is that this positive relation says nothing about causation. Is democracy is a good political institution for promoting growth, so that democratization leads to subsequent rapid economic growth? Or is democracy something that emerges only in high-income countries? Some scholars have even suggested that the two variables are not related, that a third factor can drive both democracy and incomes. Chapter 9 examined the Acemoglu thesis which stated that a country's colonial history is an important determinant of its current institutions. Countries that experienced an extractive type of colonialism were years later likely to be poorer and less democratic than those with a legacy of settler type colonialism.

Development causes democracy

One longstanding argument sees democracy as emerging from sustained economic growth. Democracy is here seen as another aspect of a modern society, along with economic aspects such as industrialization, and social aspects such as the rise of achievement (rather than factors based on birth such as caste or kin) as the basis for personal advancement. The exact mechanism by which development gives rise to democracy is less clear. Milton Friedman, the Nobel prize-winning economist, in his 1962 book *Capitalism and Freedom* argued that it was not growth *per se* but specifically economic growth in a capitalist economic system that paved the way for democracy. Capitalism, he argued, was based on voluntary exchange so the spread of the free market would permit economic diversity and the dispersal of economic power, making it an ideal basis for a flourishing democracy. The most influential statistical representation of this relationship was by the political sociologist Seymour Lipset in 1959. The Lipset hypothesis states that various social and economic changes associated with economic growth create the conditions necessary to sustain democracy. Rising incomes give people the disposable income to invest time and effort participating in political debate and practice. Rising literacy enables people to read democratic debates in newspapers. Improved communications and concentration of the population in urban areas makes political mobilization and campaigning easier. The diversity that becomes commonplace with urbanization and market-based economic exchange will increase the tolerance and acceptability of free speech.

Rueschemeyer *et al.* (1992) argued the process was not as general as suggested by Lipset but the establishment and consolidation of democracy depended on the emerging balance of power among different classes. Economic growth that weakens the economic power of agriculture, hence of landlords, the most consistently anti-democratic class, is a crucial pre-condition for democratization. Landlords depend for their livelihoods on a large supply of cheap labour. Democracy that equalizes the right to vote (a landlord can always be out-voted by a more numerous peasantry) is a threat to their political and economic position. Economic development that weakens the economic power of landlords is a crucial pre-condition for democratization, argue Rueschemeyer *et al.* The working class and peasantry are the classes most in favour of democracy as the vote provides the promise of protection by large numbers against minority classes of capitalists and landlords. The middle classes, according to Rueschemeyer *et al.*, have a more ambiguous role. Sometimes middle classes have supported democracy to protect free speech and civil liberties (for example, South Korea in the 1980s) and sometimes they have supported dictatorship to protect their property and privilege against mobilization by the poor promising political radicalism, high taxes and redistribution (for example, Chile in the early1970s). In this view, the emergence of democracy depended on whether economic growth strengthens the working classes at the expense of landlords. Whether this process was supported by middle classes depended on factors specific to the historical experience of every country. The emergence of political parties led by middle classes that could incorporate the lower classes without an excess of radical redistribution has often been associated with middle-class support for democracy.

Democracy causes development: the new orthodoxy

During the Cold War the US was happy to support dictators. From Mobuto in the Congo to Marcos in the Philippines and General Zia in Pakistan, when dictators were pro-American they usually received financial and military backing. The rhetoric suggested such dictators were both politically useful to the US and good for development. Freed from the compromises of democratic demands, they could take the unpopular long-term decisions necessary to promote rapid economic growth. In terms of the Lipset hypothesis: urbanization, industrialization and literacy had to come first and democracy would follow later. Today, from the US to donors more generally we see a very different orthodoxy. Democracy is increasingly seen as the best means to promote growth and development, regardless of the country's geographical location or level of development (see Box 10.1).

Box 10.1 The cost of democracy: US aid in Iraq

Media reports have estimated the democracy programme over the last few years in Iraq to have cost the US more than $2 billion. Concerning their efforts to promote democracy in Iraq the US government donor organization USAID proclaims on its website:

In the northern Iraq provinces of Diyala, Kirkuk, Ninawa, and Salah ad Din, USAID has initiated new channels of communication and cooperation between communities and government. A series of meetings, conferences, and initiatives that took place in April and May 2011 brought together elected representatives, government officials, and ordinary Iraqis in a forum where local government and citizen groups could meet directly with provincial-level officials. The process allowed governors, line ministry officials, and provincial council members to learn what communities see as their top priorities and to exchange ideas on how they can improve outreach to their constituents.

As a result of the popularity and success of this initiative, the four provinces are now improving official accountability and public participation by adopting public meetings for proposed projects and budgets as official standard procedure. For the first time, constituents have an opportunity to support or oppose a measure and to propose solutions of their own.

Democracy, claims this new orthodoxy, is 'good for growth'. Free public debate ensures politicians become more aware of what public services constituents are lacking and what infrastructure is needed to promote business growth. The pressure for re-election will provide an incentive for politicians to supply them. A democratic political system by its nature is more open and transparent so voters will be more aware of inefficiencies and corruption in the political system and so be able to vote out those responsible. The ongoing debate, compromise and coalition-building associated with the practice of democratic politics is a better environment for ensuring long-term political stability. The rules of succession are clear in a democracy: when one leader loses the confidence of a majority he/she is compelled to step down and a new leader is elected. To replace a dictator is typically more complicated, especially dictators who have killed or exiled other prominent figures posing a threat to their continued rule. Democracy, by contrast, provides ample opportunities for rising figures to build a base of support before challenging for the leadership. The legitimacy of a democratic mandate may strengthen the hand of democratic leaders taking tough decisions. Democracies across Europe have been able to impose tough austerity measures (cutting spending and raising taxes) in response to the global financial crisis since 2008 by appealing to electors about the 'need for sacrifice'.

The critical response to these arguments focuses on how democracy can undermine economic growth. Democracy equalizes the right to influence the allocation of resources through the political system. As the average voter in a developing country is likely to be poor this may bias the political system towards redistribution. The resulting political threat to the property rights of business and the wealthy may reduce the incentive to undertake long-term investment. Democracy may also bias the political system towards short-term populist consumption, especially if the tenure of elected politicians is short or uncertain; for example, subsidizing rice rather than taking measures that will improve the national power supply in 25 years' time.

Olson (1993, 2000) argues the democracy/dictatorship distinction is less important than the timeframe and competition faced by the leadership. An autocrat with a monopoly of power and a reasonable expectation of surviving in office for an indefinite period (what Olson calls a 'stationary bandit') will have an incentive to promote economic growth. A stationary bandit will bear a substantial portion of losses from excessive taxation or violation of property rights. A secure stationary bandit will conduct 'theft' through predictable taxes, leaving producers with an incentive to generate incomes (Olson, 1993, 2000). Dynastic succession can reduce the likelihood of succession crises, so give dictator-monarchs more concern for the long run and the productivity of their societies (although as North Korea experiences the third generation of dictatorship, this effect is not immediately apparent). Even if the dictator has a long time horizon and hopes to bequeath power to a son or daughter there is uncertainty about what would happen when the dictator is gone. In a secure democracy with predictable succession of power under the rule of law, the adjudication and enforcement of individual rights is not similarly short-sighted. A further advantage of democracy, according to Olson, is that the promise of a dictator is not enforceable by an independent judiciary and so is never completely credible.

Amartya Sen, in numerous works including *Development as Freedom* (1999), has argued that democracy has a much broader importance than its ability to promote economic growth – which he does agree with. For Sen the expansion of freedoms is not just the principal means of development; it is also the primary end. Democracy as the ability to engage in free speech, publicly debate and conceptualize needs and be freed from the fear of arbitrary arrest is for him an important part of his definition of a good society. To ask the question 'is democracy or dictatorship better at promoting development?' is mistaken. Democracy is a crucial part of the definition of development.

Democracy and development: the empirics

Some scholars have tried to construct more sophisticated tests of the relation between political regime and economic performance. Barro (1996) tested the relation between democracy and growth. He used a panel of 100 countries for the years 1960 to 1990 and controlled for the impact of various other proximate determinants of growth such as human capital and education spending, the fertility rate, government spending, investment and the terms of trade. To this regression Barro added an index of democracy based on the ability of individuals to participate meaningfully in the political process. The results show that the democracy variable has no clear relation with economic growth. Examining the relationship between the rule of law (instead of economic growth) and democracy showed that democracy has no significant positive or negative impact on the rule of law. Barro does find, however, that schooling (particularly primary) is a strong predictor of a country being democratic; there are also positive links from income and infant mortality. This finding offers strong support for the Lipset hypothesis.

Dani Rodrik (1998a) agrees that a democratic political system has little relation with economic growth but finds instead that democratic countries have more predictable long-run growth rates and greater stability in economic performance, handle adverse economic shocks better, and that democracies pay higher wages. Typically, democracies have a wider range of decision-makers and democratic debate slows down the process of policy implementation, so such countries are at less risk of being destabilized by the policy whims of a dictator. Rodrik (1999) in a sample of over 100 countries finds that in the 1970s those with greater civil liberties and political rights experienced lower declines in economic growth in response to the sharp increase in the world price of oil. This finding is surprising as much of the argument in this section has revolved around a common assumption that a strong, perhaps non-democratic state is needed to undertake unpopular adjustment policies. The result can be explained because adjustment to shocks requires managing social conflicts and democratic political institutions can be a useful means of managing conflict. In the face of an adverse shock (such as higher world oil prices) democracies tend to be better at allocating the costs of that shock across different groups: for example, whether higher import prices should be reflected in lower wages, lower government spending or lower company profits. Collier (2010) finds that the positive effects of democracy only occur when GDP per capita reaches about $3,000; below this level democracy exacerbates political conflict and violence.

There is good evidence that democracies do better on wider measures of development. Rodrik (1998b) finds that democracies pay higher wages after taking account of labour productivity, income levels and other determinants of wages. In countries undergoing transitions from dictatorship to democracy, such as Chile, Turkey, Argentina, Brazil, Hungary, Spain, Greece and Portugal there is a significant increase in the level of wages relative to labour productivity. This case-study approach shows that the relationship runs from democracy to higher wages, not the reverse. Przeworski *et al.* (2000) find that in poor countries (below $3,000 per capita) democracies and dictatorships have similar rates of investment and productivity growth, but that patterns of growth diverge in wealthier countries. Like Rodrik they find that wealthier democracies pay higher wages; they also find democratic governments spend more on social security, health, housing, recreation and culture (2000:237). It seems that democracy increases the bargaining power of labour and pushes politicians to court workers through offering higher wages. These processes do not reduce the rate of economic growth over the longer run. Przworski *et al.* (2000) find that higher wages in democracies are offset by higher productivity of labour.

Property rights as institutions

Well-protected property rights can make economic exchange cheaper and so increase the level of income in a country. Transaction costs are the sum total of the costs of undertaking an exchange, such as selling/buying an orange. Transaction costs include comparing prices between the various sellers of oranges, measuring the attributes of the orange (taste, freshness, weight) and protecting agreements (ensuring the orange is handed over by the seller and the buyer has freedom to use it as he/she wishes). Without the protection of a legal system the seller of the orange may feel it necessary to employ bodyguards to prevent the buyer taking and refusing to pay for the orange. Good institutions reduce the transaction costs associated with economic exchange. A legally protected right to return a defective orange will enable the buyer to reduce the time and effort expended in testing the orange for freshness/quality before purchasing it.

There is no reason to suppose institutions (or even organizations) will evolve to maximize economic efficiency. North argues:

The organizations that come into existence will reflect the opportunities provided by the institutional matrix. That is if the institutional framework rewards piracy then piratical organizations will come into existence; and if the institutional framework rewards productive activities then organizations – firms – will come into existence to engage in productive activities. (1994:361)

People will opt for those occupations that offer them the highest returns on their abilities and these choices will in turn impact on economic growth. When talented people become entrepreneurs they promote economic growth and when they become rent-seekers private returns come from the redistribution, not the creation of wealth. There is empirical evidence that the number of (wealth-creating) engineers is positively and the number of (wealth-redistributing) lawyers is negatively associated with economic growth (Murphy *et al.*, 1991). Institutions may also fail to evolve efficiently. Family businesses based on informal institutions such as family and kinship networks often fail to evolve into formal institutions based on contracts and commercial law, and professionally managed firms. This represents one impact of culture on institutional change (see the discussion in Chapter 12 relating to the family firm).

The most widely studied institution is an aspect of the legal system, that of property rights. Property rights not only impact on the efficiency of economic exchange, but also on economic growth through investment and productivity. Property rights can exist over land or buildings (a title deed), over a business (share certificates), over images and trademarks (copyrights) or even over ideas and production processes (patents). Douglass North and others have argued property rights are a pre-condition for the long-term investment in and the conservation of assets that are necessary to drive economic growth. There are three principal mechanisms through which property rights impact on growth. These are incentives to invest, re-allocation of assets between users and the compulsion to use assets efficiently.

First, to undertake long-term investment in physical capital a business needs both long-term secure ownership of its factory and the certainty that profit taxes won't be raised to 'confiscate' higher profits if the investment is successful. To undertake the huge R&D costs that can run into hundreds of millions of pounds to develop a new drug or treatment a pharmaceutical company will need assurance that their drug will be protected by copyrights and not duplicated by other firms (see the discussion on WTO later in this chapter). Without well-protected property rights resources may be allocated to short-term and less productive investments such as money-lending and property speculation that can be easily shifted and hidden or sent overseas in the form of 'capital flight'. Empirical work has found that the risk of investing in Sub-Saharan Africa due to weak property rights has led to 40 per cent of the region's wealth being held overseas (Collier, 2007).

Second, defining and registering property rights makes it easier to re-allocate those rights over time to the most productive user through a market mechanism. A registry of household ownership, for example, will make it easier to locate owners, undertake a purchase and re-register the new owner.

Third, when a large proportion of inputs (fertilizer, seeds and irrigation water) and outputs (wheat and rice) are sold through the market, assets and resources must be used efficiently to make a sufficient profit, or they will be lost or sold to more efficient users.

Together these impacts on investment, re-allocation and productivity gains support the view of North and others that institutions and specifically property rights are the 'underlying determinant of the long-run performance of economies' (North, 1990:107), and consequently, 'the heart of development policy must be the creation of policies that will create and enforce efficient property rights'(North, 1995:25).

Property rights are complicated and their nature changes over time. It is no longer widely accepted, for example, that people can be property; slavery has been abolished in all countries although various forms of bonded labour continue to exist. The right to strike and withhold labour from an employer is enshrined as a basic human right in many countries and brutally suppressed by governments in others. Property rights do not always give more security and freedoms to owners in developed than developing countries. In developed countries physical property is often subject to zoning and environmental legislation and sometimes historical preservation orders. In developing countries property is often held subject to traditional claims, such as the right in many countries for people to graze animals on farmers' fields once the harvest has been collected or rights for rent-paying tenants that can be inherited.

As an economy expands and experiences the sort of structural change discussed in Chapter 8, exchange networks expand beyond traders known and often related to each other in a small local economy to a more impersonal and anonymous large market and long-distance trade. To begin with, informal institutions such as trust, personal ties and the threat of ostracism from the social group for cheating are likely to be efficient ways of minimizing the transaction costs of exchange. As the scale of production and exchange increases, formal institutions such as a codified legal system, government-backed standardized currency/weights and measures, organizations such as dedicated trading centres and lawyers to help negotiate contracts and enforce them become more important. Some personal networks based on trust do survive into the modern economy such as the Chinese or Jewish diasporas engaged in group-based long-distance trade and the rotation of credit among members. Such networks are based on the special circumstances of kinship or religion (see Chapter 12 for a comparative historical case study).

While a main focus of this chapter is *private* property rights, see Box 10.2 for important debates about the role of *collective* property rights.

Box 10.2 Collective property rights

When resources such as land are held on a common or tribal basis and subject to free and open access by all there may be little incentive to conserve those assets. Individuals will benefit from the conservation efforts of others and gain from their own use of the asset. *In extremis* each individual will have an incentive to plunder those assets before others get the chance. This is known as the 'tragedy of the commons' and is often cited as a reason why Sub-Saharan Africa, where much land and other resources are held in common, has long experienced slow economic growth (Stein, 1995). The re-establishment of a form of private rather than collective state-owned property in agriculture and industry has been cited as a key reason for rapid economic growth in China after the mid-1970s (Nolan, 1995). Nobel prize-winner Elinor Ostrom argued that collective property rights can be efficient under some circumstances. For example, when rules governing common access are well established, the group having access is clearly defined and closely tied together (often through kinship groups), the group are able to impose sanctions on those violating access rules, the resources can be easily monitored and the community are able to resolve conflicts at relatively low cost. Property rights entail two sets of costs: the cost involved in the establishment and maintenance of property rights, and the cost of negotiating and enforcing the rules of access to be obeyed by all members of the group. With private ownership the second cost is negligible. With common property, while defining ownership is easier, there are more costs associated with determining the rules of access. The relative magnitude of the two costs determines which type of property rights regime is viable (Southgate, 2002).

Evidence on property rights

There are three broad strands of evidence supporting the importance of institutions as a deeper determinant of economic growth: econometric studies, case studies and examining the results of efforts to create or strengthen property rights.

Econometric evidence

Econometrics seeks to construct a quantitative measure of institutions and relate it to economic growth whilst accounting for other growth-relevant factors. Using data from 127 countries Hall and Jones (1999) find a significant and strong association between output per worker and 'social infrastructure', which measures the extent to which individuals can capture the returns to their actions rather than those returns being lost to crime, confiscatory taxation or corruption. The index is a weighted average of five variables (law and order, bureaucratic quality, corruption, risk of expropriation and government repudiation of contracts). Knack and Keefer (1997) argue that trust (an informal institution) can facilitate economic transactions. Trust reduces or eliminates costs of written contracts, court-based litigation and protection through bribery or private security (Chapter 12 examines the role of culture in determining the level of trust). Using the World Values Survey, which contains data from thousands of respondents in 29 developed countries, Knack and Keefer find trust has a strong and positive relation with economic growth.

Rodrik and Subramanian (2003) measure the quality of institutions by a composite indicator that includes the protection afforded to property rights and the rule of law. They find this measure of institutions has a positive and significant impact on income levels. Fernandes (2009), comparing institutions in South and East Asia, distinguishes between property rights institutions (whether private property is secure from predation by the state), and contracting institutions (the effectiveness of institutions such as the judicial system in enforcing contracts or mediating disputes between private parties). He finds, first, that South Asian countries have substantially weaker property rights and contracting institutions than East Asian countries, and, second, that property rights institutions have a significant causal impact on per capita GDP across countries, while contracting institutions matter much less.

A big problem with measuring the impact of institutions on economic growth is that causality can run in both directions. Institutions may generate incentives for firms to undertake long-term investment. But institutions such as registering and enforcing property rights and maintaining an independent judiciary are costly and better afforded by a wealthy country. A study of land titling in Madagascar found that it was hard to distinguish the positive impact of property rights on productivity in rice-paddy agriculture from the reverse causation, whereby there is more incentive to invest in land titling in areas with productive land (Jacoby and Minten, 2007). Acemoglu *et al.* (2001) famously and influentially engaged with this problem by seeking a measure of institutions that was not influenced by incomes or, in the terminology of economics, was 'exogenous'. Their effort rested on three premises. First, that historically there were different types of colonial policy which created different sets of institutions. 'Extractive states', such as the Belgian Congo, did not introduce much protection for private property nor checks and balances against government appropriation; 'neo-Europes', such as New Zealand and Canada, tried to replicate European institutions with an emphasis on private property and checks against government power. Second, the colonization strategy was influenced by the feasibility of settlement. Where the disease environment was not favourable to European settlement the formation of extractive states was more likely. And third, such colonial institutions persisted after independence. Based on these premises Acemoglu *et al.* used mortality rates experienced by the first European settlers as proxy measures for current institutions in these countries. They found a strong cross-country relationship between eighteenth-century settler mortality rates and current institutions (property rights and checks against government power). Their novel methodology reduces the causality problem (current institutions cannot have influenced eighteenth-century settler mortality rates) and so lends more support to the argument that institutions have a positive and significant impact on income.

In a later paper Acemoglu *et al.* (2002b) find countries that inherited colonial extractive institutions were more likely to subsequently experience poor economic outcomes after independence. Extractive institutions do not restrain the power of elites to extract resources from society through excessive taxation, corruption or unproductive government subsidies. These greater gains from power also increase political conflict over gaining access to that power. The problem with these results, however, is that the authors do not carry out a direct test of the impact of colonial policies and institutions; they only show that settler colonies ended up with higher per capita incomes and better property rights a couple of centuries later. They present no clear evidence that this was because settler states first established stable property rights and set up limited government. An alternative story, discussed in Chapter 9, explains the very different export structures of Uganda (primary products) and Zimbabwe (manufactures) not in terms of colonial institutions but rather by the skills, capital and experience brought by European settlers to Zimbabwe from the 1920s onwards (Wood and Jordan, 2000).

Case-study evidence

Case studies can sometimes give us something close to a laboratory-style experiment to focus on the impact of institutions. Until 1945 South and North Korea had similar histories, resources, culture and geography but they ended up with very different institutions, the crucial difference being the abolition of private property rights in North Korea. Estimated per capita incomes in the late 1990s were $12,152 in South Korea and $1,183 in North Korea (Maddison, 2006). Other examples are the division between East and West Germany in 1945 and between China and Taiwan in 1949. The abrupt institutional change in all cases led to an 'immediate divergence in the way they behaved' (Ferguson, 2012:11). Historical case studies have been used to show that the establishment of property rights accounted for 'the rise of the West' (see Box 10.3).

Thinking about institutions as more than just property rights makes it much harder to conclude that good institutions are a pre-condition for economic growth. The economist Mushtaq Khan notes that measures of institutional quality based on bureaucracy, rule of law, expropriation risk and contract repudiation by government in successful East Asian countries in the mid-1980s were only slightly better than in many poor-performing countries. Fast-growing Indonesia scored the same as Burma or Ghana, and South Korea, Malaysia, and Thailand the same as Côte d'Ivoire. The corruption index created by Transparency International showed that the rapidly growing East Asian countries had corruption scores in the 1980s little different from other developing countries (Khan, 2002). This implies that improving institutions was an outcome not a cause, of rapid growth in East Asia. There is much broader

Box 10.3 The evolution of legal rights in Britain

The emergence of well-protected private property rights in Britain can be traced back to the fiscal crisis of the British monarchy in the seventeenth century. The then Stuart monarchy responded by demanding forced loans (expropriation) from the wealthy and selling monopoly rights to various royal favourites (restricting property rights). This led to a struggle with existing business and commercial groups. The English Civil War in the 1640s and later Glorious Revolution of 1688 saw a decisive victory for those opposed to the monarchy. Subsequently the exercise of arbitrary and confiscatory power by the monarchy was curtailed through judicial independence, and ultimately the supremacy of Parliament. The 'major consequence', in this view, was the increased security of property rights and subsequently the onset of the Industrial Revolution (North and Thomas, 1973). France and Spain had absolutist monarchies that took longer to create a legal system and property rights existing independently of the monarchy. The real historical failures, those who never experienced modern economic growth, were the Ottoman and Mughal Empires where property was held at the discretion and whim of the monarch and Sub-Saharan Africa where property was held communally. Quite why well-established private property rights in fifteenth-century China failed to generate similar patterns of growth as in Western Europe is a great puzzle in comparative economic growth (see Chapter 7).

historical evidence to show that now-developed countries also had poor institutions during their initial transitions to rapid growth (Chang, 2002). The UK in 1820 had a broadly similar per capita income to India today but lacked many of the institutions and organizations found today in India, including universal suffrage, a central bank, income tax, generalized limited liability, a modern bankruptcy law, a professional bureaucracy and securities legislation (Chang 2003).

The policy conclusion implied by the primacy-of-institutions argument is that improving institutions is a prerequisite for sustaining rapid economic growth. But the possibility of rapid institutional change is contradicted by the historical experience of today's developed countries. Now-developed countries experienced, according to Chang (2003), a 'long and winding road' of institutional development which took 'decades'. For example from full male to universal suffrage took France from 1846 to 1946 and Switzerland from 1879 to 1971 to achieve. The need for a modern professional bureaucracy in Britain was first discussed in the eighteenth century but only became a reality early in the nineteenth. Such slow change was often because of prejudice, the high costs of many changes (labour laws and social security) or because of the resistance from those who stood to lose out (democracy, income tax), the lack of supporting changes (the tax revenue needed to pay for professional bureaucracies) or prejudice (female suffrage) (Chang, 2003).

Attempts at registration

There have been some case studies of efforts to formally protect property rights. In the early 1990s the Indian Ministry of Rural Development launched a major initiative to register and computerize land records in 582 of the 600 or so districts in the country. It was not intended to correct mistakes in existing records, merely to register and store them. A review by the World Bank (2007) found, first, that it had simplified the system and significantly reduced the petty corruption traditionally involved in getting access to land records; second, better record-keeping improved the quality of government services to small farmers; and, third, computerization had created documents of legal ownership (collateral) which helped landowners get access to credit. Other studies have highlighted the striking diversity in the impact of the scheme. The state of Bihar lacked the capacity to implement the scheme and only 6,081 of 45,099 villages were entered (Saxena, 2005). In the state of Karnataka, by contrast, 20 million records of land held by 6.7 million farmers were computerized. The provision of land records by a village accountant in Karnataka had previously taken between three and 30 days and required a significant bribe. The request for land records at a rural IT booth after the registration effort took between five and 30 minutes and cost a minimal fixed charge. A study of the Gulbarga district of Karnataka showed there to be widespread awareness of this computerization process and a large number of those interviewed had obtained a copy of computerized information. Nearly 70 per cent of those doing so obtained their records in less than 5 minutes, for 44 per cent no bribes had been necessary, and 63 per cent of those interviewed found it easier to obtain a loan as a result (Ahuja and Singh, 2006).

Establishing property rights is in theory key to economic growth as it should facilitate the re-allocation of property rights through the market to those better able to use the assets efficiently. The Karnataka project gave easier access to credit, hence the ability to invest in one's own land, but there was no evidence that land transfers had been made any easier. In Karnataka even after registration the services of the village accountant were still needed to inspect land sales before registration changes, the process could take up to two years to complete, involved substantial bribes and there was little evidence of any progress in reducing conflicts over land ownership (Saxena, 2005; Ahuja and Singh, 2006).

In Sub-Saharan Africa ambitious donor-funded land registration projects date back to the 1950s but only 1 per cent of land is currently registered under formal property rights. Easterly (2008:97) describes property access and rights among the Luo tribe of western Kenya as:

a complicated maze of swapping plots between kin and seasonal exchanges of land for labour and livestock. Each household claims to land included many plots of different soils and terrains, on which many different crops grew [which was a] good system to diversify risk in an uncertain climate.

The traditional land patrons (*weg lowo*) would often give temporary land rights to clients (*jodak*).

State efforts to register private property rights generated conflict between the *weg lowo* and the *jodak*. The high subsequent cost of registering the change of formal titles led to the gradual re-informalization of property and to land transfers being made without recourse to formal land rights.

The WTO and the intellectual property rights debate

Another important aspect of property rights are those governing intellectual property. There is an important contemporary debate about whether intellectual property rights (IPRs) will stimulate the research in and development of technology that will be of ultimate benefit to developing countries or whether IPRs strengthen the monopoly control of technology by developed countries.

The debate about the desirability of IPRs became particularly heated after the Uruguay Round of the General Agreement on Trade and Tariffs (GATT) in 1994, the subsequent formation of the World Trade Organization (WTO) and the signing of the Trade-Related Intellectual Property Rights (TRIPs) Agreement. The TRIPs agreement tightened IPRs, giving a mandatory and uniform 20 years' patent life, placed 'tough' restrictions on compulsory licensing of patented technology by national governments, and shifted the burden of proof of infringement-of-process patent from the patentee to the alleged infringer. Under TRIPs developing countries were committed to upgrade their IPR regimes in line with developed-country standards by 2006, which gave them only six more years than developed countries.

The arguments in favour of IPRs are much like those of property rights more generally. However, survey evidence of US R&D executives finds that only in pharmaceuticals, chemicals and petroleum was patent protection necessary to stimulate many inventions (and a majority only in pharmaceuticals). In other industries, such as office equipment, motor vehicles, rubber products and textiles, primary metals and instruments, machinery, fabricated metal products and electrical equipment, patent protection was not important. This implies that more than 85 per cent of inventions would have occurred without patent protection (Chang, 2003). In such sectors professional secrecy is often regarded as more important than patents in protecting the ideas of technology developers. Much R&D is not motivated by profit. In 2000 only 43 per cent of US drugs research funding came from the pharmaceutical industry itself, 29 per cent from the US government and 28 per cent from private charities and universities (Chang, 2007). The existing patent system can encourage patent races in which different companies compete, duplicating each other's efforts and wasting resources in order to be the first to claim a patent and subsequent technological monopoly. In the past this problem has been dealt with by government intervention. The Japanese government during the high-growth era (1950s to 1980s) organized research cartels to compel industrial firms to pool their efforts and avoid the duplication associated with patent races. Once a piece of technology had been developed it was then made available for all firms in the cartel to utilize in productive competition with each other.

Of particular relevance for developing countries is the argument that IPRs will stimulate the transfer of technology from developed countries. MNCs may be more likely to bring with them new technologies if they can be reasonably assured they will not be freely copied by domestic firms. The first criticism is that IPRs are in many cases not likely to generate technological change relevant to developing countries. The pharmaceutical industry, one of the most vociferous advocates of tightened IPR protection, provides some striking examples (see Chapter 5). Around 50 per cent of total health research is conducted by the private sector, which is motivated to research diseases for which there exist markets and profits. There are distinct differences in the disease profile faced by developed and developing countries. Various diseases, such as Chagas, dengue, malaria, trypanosomiasis and onchocerciasis (river blindness) among others, are almost entirely confined to developing countries (Kremer, 2002:71). This has led to what is known as 'the 10/90 problem' where 90 per cent of R&D is focused on health issues predominantly relevant to the richest 10 per cent of the world's population (Chataway and Smith, 2006:16). Despite the tightening of patent protection under the WTO in the mid-1990s there is little indication that medical research of relevance for developing countries increased. In the early 1990s the number of patent applications for malaria, leishmaniasis and chagas declined and leprosy showed no change (Lanjouw and Cockburn, 2001:273).

Another set of arguments revolves around the distinction between innovation and the diffusion of technology. While studies have found that stricter protection of IPRs has increased technology transfer by MNCs to China (Wu, 2000) this has come at a cost. Increased protection of IPRs reduces the ability of domestic firms in less developed countries (LDCs) to imitate and adapt advanced technology for domestic use through reverse engineering (Lai, 1998). Approximately 97 per cent of all patents and the vast majority of copyrights and trademarks are held by rich countries, so strengthening of IPRs means that acquiring knowledge has become more expensive for developing countries. The World Bank estimated that following TRIPs an increase in technology licence payments cost developing countries an extra $45 billion a year. There are added costs to developing countries in the form of creating and running the legal infrastructure of an IPR system (Chang, 2007). Patent protection may have generated an incentive to invest in developing new AIDS/HIV drugs but the cost of such treatments by the mid-2000s were approximately $10,000–12,000 per patient per year. This represented 30 to 40 times the average annual income of a person in Tanzania and Uganda, while copies could be imported from India and Thailand for $300–500 or 2–5 per cent of the real thing (Chang, 2007). The constraints on technology diffusion are a very relevant concern for developing countries, as observed by Alice Amsden:

The First Industrial Revolution in Britain, toward the end of the eighteenth century, and the Second Industrial Revolution in Germany and the United States, approximately 100 years later, shared the distinction of generating new products and processes ... economies that did not begin industrialisation until about the twentieth century tended to generate neither, their products and processes being based on older technology ... [they] transformed their productive structures and raised their incomes per capita on the basis of borrowed technology. (1989:3)

Patent protection played only a minimal role during the historical experience of today's developed countries. Beginning in the 1760s, a stream of technological innovations in British textiles transformed the industry. Even during the Industrial Revolution England was not good at rewarding innovation. Leading pioneers of industrial innovation such as Richard Trevithick, George Stephenson and Humphry Davy captured very few social rewards from their enterprise; many others even died in poverty as innovations quickly leaked to imitators, leaving behind little opportunity for financial reward. The story of coal was typical, in that benefits went to consumers rather than innovators. Between the 1700s and 1860s coal output increased nearly 20 times but the real price of coal was one-third lower in the 1860s than the 1700s (Clark, 2007:237). In Switzerland, one of the most innovative centres for medical research, no patent law existed until 1888 when patent protection of mechanical inventions was first allowed. Patent law came into being partly as a response to the threat of trade sanctions by Germany for Swiss use of their chemical and pharmaceutical inventions. Only in 1954 did Switzerland acquire a patent law comparable to other then-developed countries and chemical substances still remained unpatentable until 1978. Before the 1850s many others, including Britain, France, and the Netherlands, had patent laws but allowed their nationals to take out patents on imported inventions. The Netherlands abolished its 1819 patent law in 1869 to increase competitiveness in industry (Chang, 2003).

Policy towards institutions

Policy advice regarding institutions typically revolves around a conventional view associated with the World Bank and Hernando De Soto (among others), which emphasizes the strengthening of property rights, legal reform and institutional change. A more radical alternative (accumulation by dispossession) emphasizes the need to ensure the ease of transferring property rights.

Property rights for the poor

Hernando De Soto has famously and influentially placed the creation of property rights for the poorest at the centre of his thinking on development. De Soto accepts the standard advantages of property rights and explores the process of how they come into being. The creation of property rights, he finds, is prohibitively expensive for the poorest. De Soto and his research team opened a small garment factory on the outskirts of Lima, Peru with the goal of creating a new legal business. They spent six hours a day and took 289 days to register the business. The workshop employed only one worker but the cost of the legal registration was $1,231 or thirty-one times the monthly minimum wage (De Soto, 2001:18). In the Philippines De Soto estimates that the value of real estate without formal legal ownership is $133 billion or four times the value of the 216 domestic companies listed on the Philippines Stock Exchange, seven times the deposits in the country's commercial banks, and fourteen times the value of all FDI (2001:31). While the developing world is full of entrepreneurs, they are constrained to small-scale production and trade because 'the rights to these possessions are not adequately documented, these assets cannot readily be turned into capital, cannot be traded outside of narrow local circles where people known and trust each other, cannot be used as collateral for a loan and cannot be used as a share against an investment' (De Soto, 2001:6).

Without property rights such assets are 'dead capital' (De Soto, 2001:7). He notes some historical examples of the successful conversion of dead into active capital. In nineteenth-century America settlers had been settling/improving the land frontier extra-legally for decades before the Homestead Act of 1862. This act entitled settlers to 160 acres of free land in return for agreeing to live on and develop it. Property rights here reformed to integrate the practical reality into the formal legal system. In May 1872 the US Congress passed the general mining law which incorporated recognition of miners' own laws and gave the right to anyone who improved a mine to purchase it from the government at a reasonable price.

A more recent example is that of Vietnam over the 1990s, where the government first gave a greater role to the private *control* of state-owned assets, then only gradually legalized their free *exchange*. State-owned land was initially allocated to households equally so the allocation would not be efficient in the sense of the most productive farmers receiving the most land. Legal changes in the late 1980s and early 1990s established the right to inherit, transfer, sell, lease or mortgage land use (though not full ownership) and to receive compensation in case of government expropriation (Deininger and Jin, 2003). It was hoped that this would gradually lead to the efficient re-allocation of land. This hypothesis was tested using two nationally representative, high-quality surveys which showed that between 1993 and 1998 the land market had become very active. The 1998 survey showed that 27 per cent of households sampled had received use rights to new land plots through purchase, exchange, inheritance or allocation, and 13 per cent had sold or exchanged land. There is often concern in developing economies that market failures in other parts of the economy will lead to a politically contentious concentration of control over assets such as land. For example, poorly functioning credit/financial markets may prevent small-scale farmers from borrowing to improve land or purchase equipment and new seed types. Large farmers may then accumulate land over time, not because they are more productive as farmers but because they have easier access to credit. During a drought or after a collapse in commodity prices, smaller farmers are also less likely to get access to credit or be able to run down a pool of savings to smooth consumption so are impelled to sell land at low 'distress' prices to larger owners. In this case the market failures in credit and insurance (not productivity differentials) would be driving changing patterns of asset (land) ownership. Alternatively, large landowning may be a proxy for local political influence which can be leveraged to acquire land from smaller farmers, often through non-market or coercive means (Ravallion and van de Walle, 2006).

Remarkably, the land market in Vietnam over the 1990s worked to re-allocate land to more productive farmers. Political factors such as ethnicity, connections with the local government, possession of a government job, or initial (large) landowning did not have a significant impact on subsequent land purchases. There was an increase in the share of land held under long-term rights (from 25 per cent in 1993 to 88 per cent in 1998), which was related to higher productivity. The holdings of land use certificates were found to be associated with more secure land rights and with increased irrigation investment (Ravallion and van de Walle, 2006). The land market reforms in their turn were associated with favourable macroeconomic outcomes. During the 1990s Vietnam switched from being an importer to becoming the world's second largest rice exporter. The poverty headcount ratio fell from 58 per cent in 1992–93 to 37 per cent in 1997–98 (Deininger and Jin, 2003). The increased security and greater confidence in renting out land assets facilitated the migration of labour. Between 1993 and 1998 the share of households with at least one member with an off-farm job increased from 30 to 55 per cent and the incidence of migration by household members more than doubled (Deininger and Jin, 2003). This sort of reform is not likely to work everywhere. The Vietnamese reforms were specifically in the context of transferring state assets to the control/ownership of individuals/households. Important to this result was the relatively equal initial patterns of land ownership without any great inequalities of power and asset ownership at the outset of reform and also a strong and stable state committed to a gradual reform process. In Russia privatization and marketization of state-owned assets in the late 1980s/early1990s degenerated into a system of anarchic plunder and consolidation of organized crime. This was the process that created simultaneously a massive increase in poverty and the small number of billionaire oligarchs that still dominate politics, society and the economy in Russia today.

Complementary legal reform

The World Bank, De Soto and others advise that developing-country governments should focus on the compiling, registration and maintenance of land property rights using modern technology (GPS, internet). They see property rights reform as essentially a technical matter. The 'accumulation by dispossession' view (see below) sees property rights as enmeshed in politics and relations of power. The case of Kenya showed that formal property rights registration in developing countries is often prohibitively expensive and the case of India that under certain circumstances this can be resolved. The underlying problem in India and Pakistan has not been the speed or cost of land registration but the resolution of disputes through the formal legal system.

In India the practice of law over two centuries has centred on litigation. The problem is particularly notorious and well-documented in Mumbai, where strict rent controls originating during World War I evolved into a system whereby rents are low and tightly controlled, tenants can only be removed on highly restricted grounds and tenancy can be inherited. Rising urbanization and the resulting reduced incentives to construct or maintain properties have exacerbated shortages of residential and commercial property in the city. Legal conflict arising from rent control is the largest source of litigation. In 2004 there were 36 Small Causes Courts in Mumbai and rent-control matters were the exclusive jurisdiction of all but two of them. There were 38 judges in the Bombay Civil Courts dealing exclusively with rent-control matters and only 18 judges to hear other matters. It is not unusual for conflict over property issues to remain in court for more than 25 years (Mendelsohn, 2005). In 1999 the Maharashtra Rent Control Act was passed which added to the notion of rent control the need to ensure a fair return for landlords and eased the terms on which tenants could be evicted. Large commercial tenants including MNCs were made exempt from rent control protection. The new principles were applicable only to future tenancies, hence the impact of this reform was slow in coming. The situation is similar in Pakistan. In May 2009 there were more than 100,000 cases pending before the Karachi city courts and 110 judges to try them in a city of 17 million people. Not surprisingly many people, especially in rural areas, preferred to arrange transfers and inheritance of land and property informally. In much of rural Pakistan bordering Afghanistan, the Taleban offer an alternative to the official legal system that is widely perceived to be cheaper and quicker, drawing for its legitimacy on well-established customary/community laws linked to local kinship and power relations. While legal rulings inevitably involve relative winners and losers in Pakistan because of the importance of communal peace and family prestige, care is taken to save face on all sides, and to arrange compromises and compensation rather than punishment (Lieven, 2011).

Institutional change

There is a long history of institutions transplanted from developed countries (often during colonial rule) failing to take successful root. An example is the failure of formal private property rights or democracy to function effectively in much of Sub-Saharan Africa after independence. These formal institutions lacked a supportive framework of complementary institutions and organizations such as an independent judiciary or political parties to make them work. In Sub-Saharan Africa tribal collective property rights and loyalties gradually re-emerged to replace colonial innovations in private property rights and multi-party democracy. Institutional reform needs to be carefully mapped to the existing underlying informal institutional and organizational constraints. Good examples are the US legal changes of the nineteenth century and the reform process in China after the late 1970s. China has experienced rapid economic growth over more than three decades, during which property rights were neither private, clearly defined nor protected by a clear and enforceable legal system independent of the ruling Communist Party. This did not prevent investment exceeding 40 per cent of GDP during the 1990s. If not conventionally efficient, the peculiar nature of institutions in China sustained economic growth and made reform compatible with the interests of those holding political power (Qian, 2003). Among the most important examples was an innovative type of firm ownership, the Township and Village Enterprises (TVEs). TVEs were not private but owned collectively by local communities and managed on their behalf by the local government. In 1980s China there was a strong anti-private property ideology inherited from the communist era so any private ownership was vulnerable to predation by well-connected government-linked officials. The state did attack private property during several crackdowns, particularly after the 1989 Tiananmen demonstrations. Being collectively owned by the Communist Party/local government protected the TVEs from predation. This institutional reform was underpinned by fiscal decentralization in China from the late 1970s. This decentralization hardened the budget constraints faced by local governments who were unable to rely on financial transfers from central government. This gave local governments a powerful incentive to nurture TVEs, to boost their profits and so create a revenue base with which to provide local public goods such as irrigation, roads and health care (Nolan, 1995; Qian, 2003; Mukherjee and Zhang, 2007). A second relevant incentive mechanism was that promotion through the Chinese Communist Party and government hierarchies was closely linked to the achievement of economic goals such as rapid growth of TVEs, provision of public goods, and expansion of employment (Ho, 1995). From negligible levels in the late 1970s, by 1993 there were 1.5 million TVEs, employing more than 50 million people and responsible for 72 per cent of China's industrial output and 58 per cent of industrial employment.

There are broadly two ways of nurturing institutional change: the top-down and bottom-up approaches. William Easterly labels these 'the two contrasting worldviews of institutional economics'. The top-down view of institutions sees them as determined by laws written by politicians and regulators and often pushed by international donors. The bottom-up view sees institutions as emerging from the social norms, customs, traditions, beliefs and values of individuals within a society and the written law only formalizing an existing informal practice. The top-down approach imports an institutional blueprint from more developed countries which may save the effort of inventing them from scratch. Legislation to establish a commission to regulate the domestic financial sector can probably be best borrowed wholesale from those countries that have learned how to regulate markets the hard way through trial, error and long experience. This 'blueprint' approach relies on the expertise of technocrats and foreign advisers. The alternative bottom-up approach is to utilize local knowledge to carefully fit institutional change to underlying informal institutions (Rodrik, 1999). Institutional change in the latter case is more likely to be gradual and evolutionary (Easterly, 2008:95).

An alternative view of policy implications: accumulation by dispossession

The case study of Vietnam was a very optimistic one: the market can re-allocate assets to raise productivity and improve equity. To sustain growth over the much longer term the re-allocation of agricultural assets between small farmers is not enough. Sustained economic growth in developing countries requires a shift from small-scale subsistence agriculture and petty commodity production to large-scale commercial agriculture and industry (see Chapter 8). The World Bank view is that land rights will change automatically in response to changing incentives. The greater profits to be earned in commercial agriculture or in industry will cause enterprising farmers to buy out small-scale farmers, or industrialists to buy out farmers. Peasants will derive revenue from land sales and in the longer term earn more from working on large commercial farms or industry than in previous low-technology subsistence agriculture. According to this view, any failures in the operation of land markets will be symptoms of weakly protected property rights or the ease of re-registering land by new owners. An alternative view is that such market failures are rooted in underlying political constraints and that the growth of the productive capitalist sector is likely to require non-market interventions.

There are three constraints to achieving the efficient transfer of land through freely operating land markets (Khan, 2010). First are the problems associated with clarifying property rights. Overlapping claims or rights to land (for example multiple inheritance claims in an extended family) will give multiple veto rights over sale and/or add to the transaction costs associated with the sale by necessitating negotiated agreements among multiple sellers. Second, if the initial distribution of landholdings is too fragmented even with well-defined and registered property rights, the time and effort associated with multiple purchase negotiations can be prohibitive. There is a profound market failure associated with the operation of a land market in such a situation. Once the buyer commits to buying some plots, the value of subsequent plots will increase. A single tiny plot could eventually offer its owner veto power over an entire investment project. In developed countries this problem has been overcome by the use of 'eminent domain' intervention by the state where the purchase prices can be established by reference to existing market prices in a transparent process and the land then subject to a compulsory fixed-price government purchase order. In developing countries land often lacks a market price and the gap between current land prices based on subsistence agriculture and land prices based on a future use in industry may be vast, which together make compensation a very complex and politicized process. For example, the Mahindra World City Special Economic Zone (SEZ) in Jaipur, Rajasthan, paid the state government $22,679 per acre, the land cost about $66,000 per acre to develop and long-term leases for the developed land were sold for $223,000 per acre and for residential plots for approximately $554,000 per acre (Levien, 2011). The third problem is that an efficient land market requires existing owners to sell land if the price exceeds the financial return that the land can achieve. Land in developing countries is often a source of subsistence production and so acts as insurance in case of unemployment or income loss. A vicious circle may emerge in a land-scarce agricultural economy, whereby peasants refuse to sell land without the promise of secure employment, but without access to land industry is unable to expand to offer that employment. In presence of these three problems, strengthening the property rights of existing (small-scale) holders of land may actually hinder the re-allocation of that land to more productive uses and so slow economic growth.

Both historical and contemporary case studies show that a successful transition to commercial agriculture and industrialization involves more state-backed coercion than a De Soto-style spreading of property rights to the poor. This process has been labelled by David Harvey 'accumulation by dispossession', defined as the use of extra-economic coercion to expropriate the means of subsistence or production for capital accumulation. The English enclosure movement of the sixteenth and seventeenth centuries saw 50,000 peasants (from a population of four million) forcibly dispossessed of access to common land which was transformed into private holdings and subsequently utilized for more productive sheep farming that supplied the wool to a nascent industrial export-orientated woollen textile industry (Sarkar, 2007). In *Utopia* (1516) Sir Thomas More described it as 'sheep eat men'. In Singapore land shortages began to bite in the 1960s and in response the government passed the 1966 Land Acquisition Act and later a 1973 Amendment that granted the state sweeping powers of compulsory purchase. Compensation for landowners was considerably lower than potential market prices. During the high-growth era in Singapore between the 1960s and 1980s land constituted around 80 per cent of the price of new factories, so government provision of cheap land to industry represented a major subsidy. The Jurong Town Corporation leased land to incoming industrialists for 30 years on terms reflecting low official acquisition prices with the option to renew for a further 30 years (Ermisch and Huff, 1999:28). More recently the same process has occurred in China. One estimate suggests that 20 million farmers were evicted from agriculture as a consequence of land acquisition between 1996 and 2005, enabling around 5 per cent of arable land to be transferred to non-agricultural use. This was crucial in supporting China's growth based on the export of manufactured goods. The

Chinese state has intervened brutally to support the process. China's Ministry of Public Security acknowledges that 87,000 public order disturbances broke out in 2005 alone, a large proportion of which were due to such land grabs (Sarkar, 2007).

In contemporary India accumulation by dispossession is a political process utilizing the state's coercive power to make land available for business in a context of a rural economy dominated by smallholding peasants and poorly functioning rural land markets. Formal powers of compulsory acquisition were established by the Land Acquisition Act of 1894 which enabled the state to make compulsory purchase of private assets by 'eminent domain' for public purposes with compensation linked to market prices. This law was revised in 2005 as the Special Economic Zone Act, setting a framework for state governments to acquire land for industrial estates. By 2008 404 SEZs had been approved covering 54,280 acres. Only 50 per cent of this total had been reserved for productive purposes and the rest for real estate. Many SEZs stalled after launching in response to massive political protest. These included the Salim Group's petro-chemical SEZ in Nandigram, West Bengal, the Reliance Group Multi-Purpose SEZ near Mumbai, and the $12 billion POSCO steel SEZ in Orissa (Levien, 2011). Public infrastructure projects, notably the Sardar Sarovar dam on the Narmada River in Gujarat, also attracted massive protest. In response the central government put together the first Policy on Resettlement and Rehabilitation in 2004 which was revised in 2007 after ongoing protests and emerged as the National Rehabilitation and Resettlement Policy. The aim was to more carefully quantify the costs and benefits to society at large and the impact on affected families in a participatory and transparent manner (Sampat, 2008).

Key points

- Institutions influence economic growth through incentives to invest in physical (or human) capital or through stimulating technological diffusion or innovation and through this total factor productivity (TFP).
- Douglass North defines institutions as 'the humanly devised constraints that structure human interaction ...Together, they define the incentive structure of societies and specifically economies.'
- Institutions are often confused with 'organizations', which are 'groups of individuals bound together by some common purpose to achieve certain objectives'. Organizations include such groups as political parties, firms, trade unions, churches, etc.
- The nature of the political regime is an important institution. Scholars have theorized that development causes democracy, that development causes dictatorship, and that democracy causes development.
- The empirical work linking the nature of the political regime to development is complex.

- Good institutions reduce the transaction costs associated with economic exchange.
- Property rights impact on the efficiency of economic exchange and also on economic growth through investment and productivity.
- There are three broad strands of evidence supporting the importance of institutions as a deeper determinant of economic growth: econometric studies, case studies, and analysis of the results of attempts to create or strengthen property rights.
- There is a longstanding debate about whether the tightening of intellectual property rights (IPRs) by the WTO and others is good or bad for developing countries.
- The policy implications associated with institutions are: the conventional view that emphasizes the strengthening of property rights; the importance of legal reform; institutional change; and an alternative view that emphasizes the need to ensure ease of transfer of property rights (accumulation by dispossession).

Chapter 11

Geography and Economic Resources

It seems obvious that where a country is located, its neighbours, its weather and its natural resources must influence economic outcomes. Of all the deep determinants it may seem that geography is the most straightforward to measure for the purposes of economic analysis and statistical testing. For example, average temperatures are easier to measure than culturally inspired inclinations to work hard; the availability of natural resources is easier to gauge than the strength of property rights. However obvious all this may sound, geography is only the latest and recent addition to the list of deep determinants. A very vigorous research agenda over the last decade or so led by scholars such as Paul Collier, Jeffrey Sachs, Jared Diamond and others has created a set of theoretical links to test and an excellent database on economically relevant geographical variables, and they have sought to demonstrate the link between geography and long-run economic growth. The geography hypothesis does not suffer from the problems of causation inherent in discussion of institutions in particular (whether growth leads to good institutions or vice versa). Geography is about the physical attributes of particular locations, such as access to navigable rivers, climate, soil quality and distance from coastlines etc. In statistical work the causal relations are clear because they are not caused by economic and other social variables (in the language of economists, they are exogenous). But, of course there remain deep controversies that make for a fascinating debate.

Geography and economic growth

Geography is a deeper determinant so will affect economic growth through its impact on the proximate determinants. Many of the effects of geography are likely to impact economic growth through TFP. Adverse weather conditions may directly influence the productivity (yield) of land in agriculture. Diseases associated with a tropical climate may divert resources at the household level away from investment in physical and human capital to emergency health care. Disease associated with frequent morbidity may reduce the human capital acquired through schooling or learning on the job so reduce the productivity of labour. Geography will also have an important link through another of the deeper determinants, openness. Producers in landlocked countries will face greater costs to engage with international trade and lose the benefits of facing

Figure 11.1   *Geography as a deeper determinant of economic growth*

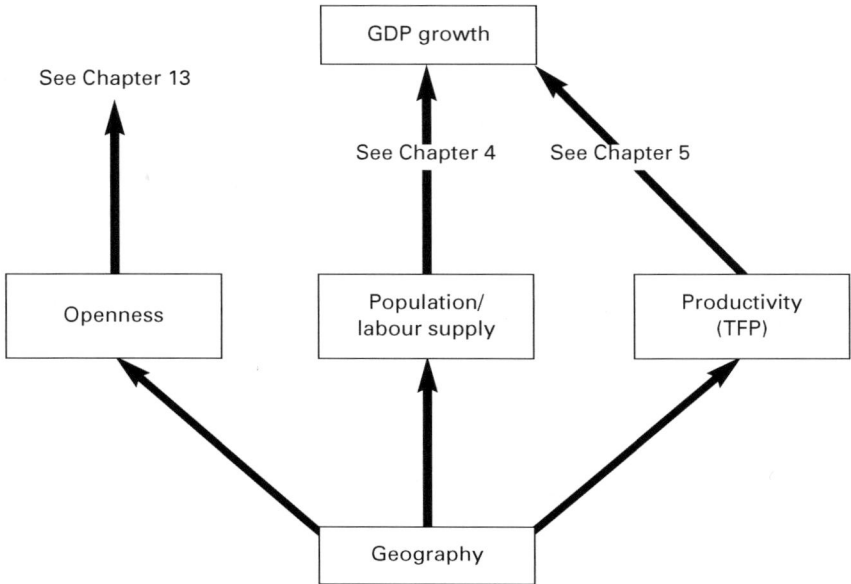

more competition on world markets and access to new technologies. These links are shown in Figure 11.1.

Geography: definitions

Geographical factors can be defined as 'physical attributes tied to specific locations', such as latitude, distance from coastlines, altitude and access to navigable rivers (fixed factors) or climate, soil quality and rainfall (slowly changing). Thankfully the statistical work for testing the impact of geography on economic growth is more straightforward. Most geographical factors are not influenced by economic growth so the direction of causation is much clearer. Chapter 10 notes that good institutions may stimulate growth but also that high income levels may be necessary to afford the court and legal systems required to protect property, so separating these two-way influences in statistical work is difficult. There are still problems in distinguishing geography as a deep determinant of growth. The original cause may be something quite different. Africa, for example, has many landlocked countries, but this is a product of how boundaries were drawn up in the nineteenth century, so what appears today as a fixed factor of geography should more properly be thought of an outcome of colonial history.

The statistics of geography: income and growth

Though there is lots of empirical evidence linking geography to levels of income and economic growth there is an important critique of the geography hypothesis – the 'reversal of fortune' thesis.

We noted in the Introduction that Robert Barro found the growth process works differently in Africa but offered no explanation as to why this was the case. More recently Jeffrey Sachs has returned to this problem. When controlling for initial income in 1980 and indicators of governance, Sub-Saharan Africa grows more slowly (by around 3 per cent a year) than other developing countries (Sachs *et al.*, 2004). The reason, he argues, is geography. The idea of geography also features prominently in the best-selling recent work of Paul Collier. Collier (2007) states there are four traps preventing sustainable economic growth in countries containing the bottom impoverished billion of the world's population. Two of those traps relate directly to geography – the natural resources trap and the trap of being landlocked with bad neighbours – while the conflict trap and the bad governance trap are both influenced by natural resources.

More than any other deep determinant of growth, evidence on geography is straightforward to come by. A global map showing GDP per capita in the mid-1990s of every country in the world reveals two clear geographical correlates of economic development. First, tropical countries (those nearer the equator) are poor and second, landlocked countries are poorer than countries with access to the coast. Nearly all landlocked countries are poor except for some in Western and Central Europe; these are deeply integrated into the large European market of low-cost trade and are easily accessible to the coast by land- and river-based traffic. These results are also supported by numbers. Countries with half or more of their land in tropical regions are almost all poor. In the mid-1990s there were 72 such countries, with 41 per cent of the world's population. Of the top thirty richest countries in the mid-1990s, only two were tropical (Hong Kong and Singapore), four were sub-tropical and 23 had temperate climates. Regions within the US, Western Europe and temperate-zone East Asia that lie within 100 km of the coastline account for 3 per cent of the world's inhabited land area, 13 per cent of the world's population, and 32 per cent of the world's GDP (measured by PPP).

There are a number of econometric studies that test the influence of various geographic variables on growth. The advantage of these is that a measure of the exact influence can be derived and compared with other factors (see Introduction). Gallup and Sachs (1999) use data from 150 countries with populations above 1 million for the period 1960 to 1990 and control for variables related to economic and political institutions. They find four variables (the prevalence of malaria, transport costs, the proportion of the population near the coastline, and coal resources per capita) explain more than two-thirds of the cross-country differences in average incomes. They obtain the same results for non-Sub-Saharan African countries, showing that the results for geography are not peculiar to Africa. The effect of the malaria variable, they find, is more important than tropical location. Bloom *et al.* (1998) examine data for 77 African and non-African countries from 1965 to 1990 and find that openness, institutional quality and public savings have a positive and significant impact on economic growth. Their results show that being located in Africa is important and that Africa experienced on average 2.1 per cent slower growth than non-African countries between 1965 and 1990. They find the key features accounting for this slower growth are: the greater share of Africa's land area being in the tropics; and the large proportion of Africa's population being located more than 100 km from the coast. A third study by Warner (2002) finds that the most important geographical variables are tropical location, remoteness from the coast or a river, and having mountainous terrain.

There are still significant statistical problems. Factors of production can migrate, and this has implications for statistical work. If labour and capital are mobile they would tend to leave areas of poor geography or low incomes. Over time factors would continue to migrate until the benefits of being located in areas of 'good geography' have been competed away, implying that there would no longer be any identifiable statistical relationship between geography and income. It is possible to overcome this problem. As many institutions tend to be reasonably similar within countries, regional data provides a way to test for the effects of geography and climate holding those institutions constant. As factor mobility is greater across regions than countries we would expect to see first, stronger effects of geography on output density (the amount of output produced in a particular area) than output per capita and second, smaller effects of geography on output per capita in regional data. Regional data on large and diverse nations (Brazil, China, India and US) finds that both of these hypotheses are correct and shows that geography has a significant effect on output density using regional/sub-national data (Warner, 2002).

Early work on geography by Sachs and others used single countries as data points so that India and the US were considered 'coastal' despite their size and diversity and the fact that large areas of land were located far from the coast. The crudity of this early work has been overcome by using 'gridded data'. This method divides the world into almost 20,000 data points rather than the 150+ country observations previously used. This approach allows us to use more finely tuned geographic data (including climate, location, distance from markets or seacoasts, and soils). The results confirm the importance of geography and find a significant positive link from temperate, climate and costal location to high economic densities (Nordhaus, 2006). Economic density is here calculated as output per capita per square kilometre.

In Sub-Saharan Africa there is a very high concentration of land in the tropics. Only 19 per cent of the entire continent's population are within 100 km of the coast, a quarter of the population are in landlocked countries, and Sub-Saharan Africa is far from core European markets. In India the mass of population is in the landlocked North-Central Ganges valley, a long way from the coast, and India is partly tropical. The US has a relatively high (38 per cent)

Box 11.1 The reversal of fortune hypothesis

If the geography hypothesis is true, geography is a fixed factor so areas of bad geography will always be poor and areas with poor geography should still be poor today (Acemoglu *et al.*, 2002a). But in the sixteenth century the Mughals in India and Aztecs and Incas in the Americas were among the richest civilizations in the world (measured by urbanization) and today's high-income countries were then much poorer.

For some scholars this reversal of fortune is a strong argument against the geography thesis. But, the reversal of fortune hypothesis is actually demonstrating that 'good geography' changes over time. Although geography *is* fixed, what constitutes good and bad geography *does* change over time. In earlier civilizations, when transport was slow and unreliable, geographical advantage came from agricultural productivity not trade. Hence early civilizations and densely populated urban areas tended to emerge in the fertile valleys around the Indus, Ganges, Nile and Euphrates rivers. In Africa dense urbanized populations emerged around the fertile Great Lakes region (Rwanda, Uganda, Burundi). The rise of Oceanic trade after the sixteenth century saw economic advantage shift, in particular to the trading ports of the European Baltic and North Atlantic. Those early civilizations based on rich landlocked agriculture were left isolated from these new sources of wealth. The meaning of 'good geography' changed again in the era of industrialization. In the early nineteenth century, before improvements in shipping technology, it was expensive to transport coal so early industrialization based on steam power was helped by a proximity to coalfields. This advantage disappeared with the discovery of petroleum refining, oil, and hydro-based power and its quick and cheap transport across the world by supertankers. The advantage of being close to the coastline has more recently been eroded by improvements in transport and communications, such as the internet.

fraction of the population within 100 km of the coast which rises to 67 per cent if ocean-navigable river systems are included, and has a generally temperate land mass (Gallup and Sachs, 1999). A big challenge to the geography hypothesis is the 'reversal of fortune' thesis (Box 11.1).

Geography and economic growth: investigating the link

There are five major mechanisms by which geography can influence economic growth: transport costs; proximity to/ownership of natural resources; state formation; human health; and agricultural productivity (including animal husbandry).

Geography and transport costs

Transport costs are similar to import tariffs: they impose additional costs that producers must absorb to penetrate export markets. Sometimes those costs can be passed on to foreign consumers. African countries are generally small suppliers of agricultural products whose prices are fixed on world markets, giving no scope to pass transport costs on, so African producers or workers will instead receive lower prices or wages for their efforts. In economic sectors where production involves importing components or inputs for assembly and re-exporting them (especially textiles and electronics) even relatively small transport costs can have a substantial impact on final costs. The very sectors characteristic of successful export-led growth stories (most often in Asia) are those where high transport costs have the most impact, giving Africa a double disadvantage.

The IMF estimates transport costs based on what the process of importing and exporting adds to the basic costs of production (freight, insurance etc.). The biggest influences on transport costs are the distance of the country from core areas of the world economy and whether it is landlocked. The data show that the median landlocked country faces 50 per cent higher transport costs than the median coastal nation (Gallup and Sachs, 1999). Not surprisingly half the world's trade takes place among countries located within a 3,000 km radius of each other. In 1990 the average distance of Sub-Saharan African countries from their trading partners was over 7,800 km. Africa is also fragmented into nearly 50 countries, each with on average four neighbours, many of which must be crossed and the costs and delays of customs clearance be borne in order to reach the coast. It costs more to transport a vehicle from Abidjan (Côte d'Ivoire) to Addis Ababa (Ethiopia) than to ship it from Abidjan to Japan.

In Sub-Saharan Africa in 1990–91 transport costs (approximated by the total net freight and insurance costs of exporting) were equivalent to about 15 per cent of the value of the region's exports. For ten countries this exceeded 25 per cent of total exports and for Somalia and Uganda it exceeded 70 per cent. Transport costs averaged 42 per cent for the ten landlocked countries in the sample and 17.5 per cent for the coastal economies. For all developing countries as a group these payments averaged only 5.8 per cent. Between 1970 and 1990 transport costs fell in Asia (from 8 per cent to 5.8 per cent) and increased in Africa (from 11 per cent to 15 per cent). Transport costs are much greater than policy-induced constraints on trade. These numbers compared with an average tariff of 0.5 per cent on exports from SSA to the US between 1974 and 1993 (Amjadi and Yeats, 1995). Data from the early 2000s show that transport costs in Africa were still almost double the world average (Naude and Matthee, 2007). Not surprisingly trade with the rest of the world is on average 60 per cent less for landlocked SSA countries (Coulibaly and Fontagne, 2005). Box 11.2 shows how Uganda's landlocked position imposes significant costs on exporters.

Geography and natural resources

In *Guns Germs and Steel: A Short History of Everybody for the Last 13,000 Years,* Jared Diamond (1998) presents the wonderfully engaging argument that

Box 11.2   Troublesome trains in Uganda

A good case study is that of the transport inefficiencies that impose significant costs on exporters from Uganda. These arise from the long and slow railway link from Kampala (Uganda) to Mombasa (Kenya) and inefficiencies at the Mombasa port. The Kampala–Mombasa route should take one week though often takes up to two months. This makes it difficult for exporters to book space on ships and departure times are often missed so goods may remain in port for long periods. Exporters are often forced to rely instead on roads, despite the high cost and increased risk of theft. The combined effect of these problems was estimated to impose an implicit tax on exports of 48 per cent in 1994. While the costs imposed by taxes on trade had been virtually eliminated, transport costs imposed a significant burden on exporters (Milner *et al.*, 2000).

geography dating back to 11,000 BCE has had a profound influence on growth and development since the sixteenth century. Diamond notes that only twelve plant species account for 80 per cent of the modern world's annual tonnage of all crops. These are wheat, corn, rice, barley, sorghum, pulse soyabean, potatoes, manioc, sweet potato, sugarcane, sugarbeet and the fruit banana. About 32 of the world's 56 largest seed grasses were historically concentrated in the 'fertile crescent' of the Middle East. California and South Africa have only one large grass seed each and Australia none (Diamond, 1998:139). In the wild these crops were already edible, gave high yields, were easily grown by sowing or planting, easily stored and self-pollinating. The earliest domesticated crops evolved from these wild ancestors. The goat, sheep, pig and cow were domesticated earliest in the regions of their wild ancestors; 13 of the ancient 14 breeds were found only in Eurasia and seven in South-west Asia. In Mesoamerica the only two domesticable animals were the turkey and dog which have a lower meat yield than those in the 'fertile crescent'. South America has only one (the llama/alpaca) and North America, Australia, and Sub-Saharan Africa none.

Diamond argues that geography affected the diffusion of crops and livestock. Food production spread rapidly along the Eurasian east–west axis from Southwest Asia, west to Europe and Egypt and east to the Indus valley (modern Pakistan) and from the Philippines further east to Polynesia. This pattern of diffusion was relatively easy. Locations on the same latitude share day length, seasonal variations and, to a lesser extent, diseases, temperature, rainfall and habitats. Germination, growth and disease resistance of plants are adapted to these features of the climate and most 'fertile crescent' crops grow well from France to Japan. Once we look south the story becomes very different. The spread of domestic animals into Sub-Saharan Africa was stopped or slowed by climate and disease, especially by the trypanosome disease carried by the tsetse fly. Similar examples of slow diffusion include the slow pace of crop exchange between Pakistan's Indus Valley and South India, food production from South

China to peninsular Malaysia, New Guinea food production into Australia or from Mexico northward to the US.

Diamond further argues that food production and domesticable animals were a prerequisite for the production of guns, germs and steel, the foundations of modern, high-income urban life. One acre under settled agriculture can feed 10 to 100 times more people than when used for hunter-gathering. The resulting increase in the density of population ultimately permitted centralized political institutions, economic specialization, social stratification and sustained wars of conquest. Domesticated animals provided the main source of protein (meat and milk), clothing (wool and hides), manure and pulling ploughs (agriculture), and the main mode of transport of people and goods (warfare and industry) up to the Industrial Revolution in the nineteenth century. The major killers of humanity throughout recent history such as smallpox, flu, tuberculosis, malaria, plague, measles and cholera are infectious diseases that evolved from diseases of animals to which people in Eurasia acquired an early immunity.

Diamond does offer persuasive evidence to explain why an army of Eurasia conquered an army and empire of South America in the sixteenth century. The argument so far remains too crude for our purposes in this book. Why was it specifically Spain that conquered the New World? Why not any other country in Eurasia such as Japan, Persia, or Russia?

A second, more specific historical example considers the very different growth experiences of North and South America. This story encompasses not just economic growth but also wider measures of development including literacy and democracy. In 1700 the most prosperous economies of the New World were in the Caribbean; in Barbados and Cuba estimated per capita incomes were then 50–67 per cent higher than in areas that later became the US. The US only established a clear lead by the nineteenth century. Explanations for this growth story have included better protected property rights or the unique entrepreneurial spirit of the US. This raises the question appropriate for this part of the book: where did such differences arise? One answer emphasizes geography: first, South America's climate was more suitable for growing sugar, which is most efficiently grown on large plantations using slave labour; and second, the North American climate was more conducive to farming of grain and hays, which is better suited to small-scale family farms. Thus geography initiated a pattern of development based on inequality and slave labour in South America and a more equal path based on family farms in North America. The second stage of the argument is that these initial conditions persisted. Equality in the North was perpetuated through the development of democratic institutions, widely protected property rights and broad-based education. The less equal South saw the consolidation of institutions that sustained a monopoly of power among a small class of elites (Sokoloff and Engerman, 2000).

The problem with this argument is the lack of generalization if we examine an even more disaggregated picture. Jamaica, for example, was part of the Caribbean sugar/slave economic system and 90 per cent of its population were slaves in 1750, but Jamaica is one of the very few countries to sustain a democratic political system since independence (in 1962) and has long had much higher levels of human development (literacy, health and life expectancy) than could be expected given its level of GDP per capita. In the sixteenth century the growth of world trade led to the intensification of coercive/feudal labour relations in Eastern Europe as landowners sought to tie down labour to benefit from exporting grain (Wallerstein, 1974:91). Grain, of course, was the same crop that was supposedly associated with small-scale, family farms and democracy in North America. Much more detailed data on the scale and pattern of the slave trade (discussed in Chapter 9) shows that all forms of slavery were negatively related to subsequent economic development, and there is no evidence that this relationship was driven by the large-scale plantation slavery that was characteristic of South America (Nunn, 2007).

A third geography-resource story focuses on why China was unable to sustain its economic lead established by the fifteenth century and why later Britain surged ahead. After the mid-eighteenth century there was a growing ecological threat to economic growth in Western Europe. In Italy, Spain, the Low Countries and Britain forest cover was down to 5–10 per cent of land area by1850 and water power was not sufficient to supply energy. The threat to energy supply, it has been argued, was overcome by the fortunate locations of coal deposits near emerging centres of European economic activity and the growing skills in exploiting them. Coal proved essential for industrial growth based on iron, steel, steam power and transport in Britain. The North and North-west of China did have substantial coal deposits but by 1600 CE the centre of population and economic activity had shifted to South China where growth was hindered by a reliance on dwindling supplies of wood (Pomeranz, 2000). This story is plausible in that it seeks to explain the contrast between growth in England and stagnation in China but it lacks strong empirical support. Coal made only a limited contribution to the Industrial Revolution in England until at least 1869 – almost a century after many scholars have dated the first signs of industrialization. Careful empirical work by Clark and Jacks (2007:46) shows that the absence of coal and so steam power would have raised production costs in British industry in the early nineteenth century by at most 10–20 per cent, so could not have been responsible for the dramatic differences in outcome argued by Pomeranz.

These three examples are of little wider use in explaining growth in different contexts and time periods. Another objection is that there is a general presumption in all three stories that having important natural resources is a 'good thing', especially if that resource can be used as an input for industry or has value in export markets. In fact some natural resources have even been labelled 'cursed'. Commodity prices tend to be very volatile on world markets and growth in those countries dependent on them for export revenue experience parallel volatility in growth. The 43 resource-rich Sub-Saharan African countries lurched from positive to negative economic growth from the 1970s to the 1980s as a resource-price boom came to a dramatic end. In general as prices fall growth decline more than cancels out prior growth economic (Collier, 2007). There are important parallels for today. Chapter 2 noted that many countries in Sub-Saharan Africa are currently experiencing a surge in growth related to high commodity prices. Coastal Nigeria is a famous example of what can go wrong with natural resources. In the 25 years to 2000, Nigeria earned some $250 billion in oil revenues, but during these years per capita income fell by 15 per cent and the number of people living on less than $1 a day increased from 19 million to 84 million.

More important than the volatility of raw material export prices is the impact of natural-resource dependence on institutional quality or what has been called 'the rentier effect'. With easy tax revenue earned from the export of raw materials, the state has less need to tax its population. In agreeing to be taxed populations typically demand that the state develop or permit mechanisms (such as democracy, transparent accounts, and a free press) to ensure taxation is reasonably fair and spent in a way that is seen as productive – on infrastructure and education, for example. With easy natural-resource revenues the government can be corrupt and buy off dissent. When such bribery can be combined with appeals to ethnic communities, competitive appeals among different politicians can result in conflict over control and access to natural-resource rents. Such electoral competition leaves the most corrupt as winners, which Collier (2007) calls the 'the survival of the fattest'. Resource rents gradually erode the good institutions, such as well protected property rights, that many argue are the foundation for long-term sustainable growth. There is good empirical support for this effect. Indicators of institutional quality measured in the 1990s (rule of law, political stability and violence, government effectiveness, absence of corruption, regulatory framework, property rights and rule-based governance) are strongly and negatively related to natural-resource dependence in 1980 across a large sample of developing countries (Isham *et al.,* 2005).

Cursed resources are not destiny. Their baleful influence can be overcome by good institutions (although this is made harder by the effect, discussed above, that natural resources can undermine institutions). Norway coped even though oil generates almost 20 per cent of GDP and 45 per cent of exports. The state oil company (recently privatized) has long been efficient, and the country recognized that oil and gas were expected to run out in seventy years, so increased investment rather than consumption by building up a stabilization fund of $850 billion (as of 2013), invested largely overseas. Landlocked Botswana is one of a few developing countries to handle its resource wealth (diamonds) well, experiencing several decades' growth of over 8 per cent after the 1970s when they were first exported.

Geography and state formation

Soon after publishing his 1998 book Jared Diamond noted that he had not addressed a conundrum. If the advantages of geography in 11,000 BCE can explain why after around 1500 Eurasia conquered Native Americans, Aboriginal Australians and Sub-Saharan Africans, rather than vice versa, why then did some parts of Eurasia (Britain, France) develop faster than other parts? Diamond explains this in terms of the political fragmentation of Europe and unification of China. All societies undergo fads or customs that make no economic sense. These are usually abandoned when their inefficiency is demonstrated by their successful adaptation elsewhere. The innovative economic dynamism China had established by the beginning of the fifteenth century was later lost (see Chapter 7). The fleet of hundreds of ships and more than 20,000 crews was abandoned in 1432 by the decision of a single emperor and was effective because China was unified under one emperor and one law. By comparison in fifteenth-century Europe Christopher Columbus was turned down by six different monarchs, dukes and princes before another took a chance and supported his 1492 trip to the Americas. Columbus had a choice of patrons in Europe; in China when the Emperor said no there was nobody else to ask. Europe was not less conservative, argues Diamond. Numerous European princes have said no to pioneering inventions and many Catholic countries tried to suppress the ideas of Galileo. But, as Diamond notes, because Europe was always divided (into 2,000 principalities after the fourteenth century), inventors had many opportunities. There was always competition – when one state tried something that worked it was adopted by other states. In 1492 when the prosperous Jews were expelled from Castile and Aragon (Spain) they sought refuge in Venice and the Ottoman Empires and carried on their commerce and trading. In 1685 when the Protestant Huguenots were expelled from France they sought refuge in England, Holland and Switzerland where they established textile production. Gutenberg hoped to monopolize his development of moveable type (as the Chinese state had done successfully) after the 1450s, but within a few years it had spread across Europe and by 1524 there were nearly 1,000 printing presses in Germany alone (Ferguson, 2012:61).

Diamond does offer an explanation for the China–Europe difference but not for changes within China. Why did the Chinese state switch to an inward-looking and conservative anti-innovation ideology after the fifteenth century? The Chinese state had a long history of leading technological change. During the Han period (221 BCE to 220 CE) governments provided peasants with the tools and draft animals to boost agricultural productivity and actively promoted the use of better ploughs. In the eleventh century state officials promoted the adoption of faster-ripening and more drought-resistant strains of rice introduced from South-east Asia. After 1000 CE the Chinese government established huge state-owned iron foundries that promoted the use of iron implements (Mokyr, 1990).

This leads us to a second question. Why was Europe fragmented and why is it still? The answer, according to Diamond, is again geography:

> Europe has an indented coastline, and each big indentation is a peninsula that became an independent country, independent ethnic group, and independent

experiment in building a society: notably the Greek peninsula, Italy, the Iberian peninsula, Denmark, Norway/Sweden. Europe had two large islands that became important independent societies, Britain and Ireland ... Europe is transacted by mountain ranges that split up Europe into different principalities: the Alps, the Pyrenees, Carpathians – China does not have mountain ranges that transect China. In Europe big rivers flow radially – the Rhine, the Rhone, the Danube, and the Elbe – and they don't unify Europe. In China the two big rivers flow parallel to each other, are separated by low-lying land, and were quickly connected by canals. For these geographic reasons, China was unified in 221BC and has stayed unified most of the time since then, whereas for geographic reasons Europe was never unified. (Diamond, 1999:13)

Military efforts continually failed to impose unification on Europe, whether Charles V of Spain after 1500, Louis XIV after 1672 or Napoleon after 1805 in France, or Hitler in Germany after 1939. The Reformation, in splintering the Catholic Church, helped facilitate the political fragmentation of Europe after 1517. Diamond is not clear why or how Europe managed to achieve something like an optimal degree of fragmentation, but he implies that 2,000 principalities was a good thing during the Renaissance – what about 3,000 or 1,000? In other parts of the world political fragmentation has not been associated with economic dynamism. Income levels in Europe collapsed with the fall of the centralized Roman Empire after the fifth century and subsequent fragmentation of Europe. The break-up of the Ottoman Empire in 1918 and its replacement with fragmented states has hardly led to competitive dynamism in the Middle East over the last century. The fragmentation of Africa, as noted earlier in this chapter, has greatly increased the costs of trading. Fragmentation has also been associated with an increased risk of conflict. Europe was devastated by wars of religion between 1550 and 1650, linked to the disintegration of the single Catholic Church and the rise of independent (Protestant) churches during the Reformation. Between 1500 and 1799, for example, Spain was at war with foreign enemies 81 per cent of the time, England 53 per cent and France 52 per cent (Ferguson, 2012:36). If we contrast the dynamism of China between 1100 and 1400, the civilization of ancient Rome from around 50 to 476 CE, or the Taj Mahal-building Mughal Empire of India in the seventeenth century with the brutalities of fragmented Europe during the Thirty Years War (1618–48), War of Spanish Succession (1701–14), Napoleonic Wars (1792–1815), World War I (1914–18), and World War II (1939–45), fragmented states do not appear to be such a good thing. And, after all, fragmented Europe was ultimately surpassed not by another more dynamic and fragmented entity but by the *United* States of America.

Geography and human health

The two-way link between health and economic growth was discussed in Chapter 6. Cholera, for example, may impact on health (and so undermine economic growth by reducing the productivity of labour) but cholera is also a disease of poverty and the poor sanitation characteristic of poor countries increases the prevalence of cholera. Although it is more prevalent in tropical countries, it does not mean we can label cholera as a disease of geography. Other arguments have downplayed the influence of geography on disease, claiming that most of the important diseases of humans and their domesticated animals are not peculiarly tropical. It is true that smallpox, typhoid, pneumonia, diphtheria, measles, bubonic plague and anthrax are found across many physical environments and their extent of variability historically has tended to reflect conditions of human poverty and crowding. But this does not mean, as Blaut suggests, that there is no 'innate unhealthiness of the tropics' (1993:78). Few agree with him, as many other diseases that are clearly products of a tropical ecology have been labelled 'diseases of geography'. The most widely discussed health issue related to geography is the prevalence of malaria. At least until recent years there was no effective prophylaxis or vector control for malaria in the areas of high endemicity. Malaria has been brought under control since 1945, mainly in temperate and sub-tropical environments where its hold was more fragile in terms of mosquito population and parasite endemicity. None of the countries with 100 per cent of their land area subject to falciparum malaria (the most virulent form) were able to eradicate it completely after 1945 (there have been more recent successes, as outlined in Chapter 5). The symptoms of malaria are bouts of fever with spikes on alternating days, headaches, malaise, fatigue, nausea and anaemia. Severe forms of the disease result in organ failure, delirium, impaired consciousness, generalized convulsions, persistent coma and death. By the early 2000s there were an estimated 200 million to 500 million cases per year, almost entirely concentrated in the tropics, and around 1 million deaths per year, 90 per cent of which occurred in Sub-Saharan Africa. Africa's malaria has been much harder to control than that in other regions due to a combination of climate and biology. The continent's temperatures, mosquito species (the exclusively human-biting Plasmodium falciparum) and humidity give Africa the world's highest malaria burden (Sachs et al 2004). Other diseases of geography (not poverty) include dengue, yellow fever, or schistosomias which are endemic in the tropical ecological zones and nearly absent elsewhere.

It is notoriously difficult to collect data related to health conditions, so estimating the morbidity and mortality costs of malaria is not easy. In Tanzania, for example, 80 per cent of all deaths occur at home, and half of those had no prior contact with medical services. The principal symptom of malaria (fever) is common to many other illnesses and accurate diagnosis requires laboratory analysis. The impact of malaria may be missed by the data as its effects only show up in related morbidity. Malaria has been estimated to account for around 60 per cent of all severe anaemia episodes in young infants in rural Tanzania, and 46 per cent of severe anaemia hospital admissions among under-5s in Kenya. Pregnant women are particularly vulnerable to malaria, experiencing an increased risk of maternal anaemia, abortion, still birth and low birth weight, due to prematurity and intra-uterine growth retardation. Low birth weight is associated with health problems much later in adult life. Malaria seems to interact with other common diseases such as measles, respiratory infections, diarrhoeal disease and malnutrition in ways that are still not well understood. Despite these data problems various small-scale studies have tried to quantify the impact of malaria. The direct costs of malaria include expenditure on prevention and treatment of malaria by households and health services. In the early 2000s evidence from Malawi indicated that expenditure on treatment was over 25 per cent of household income among very low-income households. For Rwanda it was estimated that nearly 20 per cent of the Ministry of Health budget went on treating malaria. In Kenya primary school children were estimated to have on average four episodes of malaria per year and to miss on average five days of school per episode, representing 11 per cent of the Kenyan school year. Total costs have been estimated at anything from 7 to 32 per cent of household annual income in Sub-Saharan Africa (Chima *et al.*, 2003).

A larger-scale study is the case of India in the 1950s where there were relatively successful efforts to eliminate malaria through the use of DDT (dichlorodiphenyltrichloroethane) spraying. In 1947 India suffered an estimated 75 million cases of malaria annually leading to 800,000 deaths, implying an incidence rate of 22 per cent across the whole population. The number of malaria cases (estimated using blood smear tests) fell to 100,000 per year by 1965 and statistics on causes of death indicate that the number of malaria deaths between 1952 and 1963 dropped by 91.2 and 98.3 per cent in the states of Uttar Pradesh and West Bengal. DDT was subsequently banned and though malaria prevalence remained stable in the 1960s there was a resurgence in the 1970s that peaked in 1976, though this new peak prevalence was only 1.1 per cent across the whole population. This effort to reduce or eradicate malaria was associated with a modest relative increase in income (proxied by per capita household expenditure) for working-age men but no observed increase for women. The most likely reason for this difference is that women have much lower labour force participation rates than men (Cutler *et al.*, 2010).

There is good econometric evidence to show that malaria does impact on economic growth. Gallup and Sachs (1999) examined the relation of malaria to GDP growth per capita between 1965 and 1990 using a malaria index (calculated as the fraction of the land area with endemic malaria in 1965 and the fraction of malaria cases that were Plasmodium falciparum in 1990). Their results suggest that countries with a substantial amount of malaria grew 1.3 per cent per annum less on average and that a 10 per cent reduction in malaria was associated with 0.3 per cent higher growth per year. Gallup and Sachs (2000) note that by the late 1990s 54 countries (29 per cent of the world's population) had intensive exposure to malaria and 35 of them were in Africa. The average income in countries with intensive malaria was $1,526 and in those without $8,268. A number of growth accelerations can be dated from the eradication of malaria, including in Greece, Italy and Spain from the early 1950s, Taiwan in 1961, Jamaica 1958 and the southern US from the 1950s.

Geography and agricultural output

Most Africans live in sub-humid or arid tropics without rivers and the alluvial plains that permit cheap and efficient irrigation as in much of Asia. Agriculture in Africa is consequently more dependent on rainfall, but rainfall variability is higher than in tropical America or Asia. Between 1983 and 1995, 29 countries in Sub-Saharan Africa experienced at least one year of drought which affected more than half of the continent's population, 24 suffered at least two years of drought and 14 more than three years (Bloom *et al.*, 1998). Rainfall in the Sahel (the semi-arid region south of the Sahara) has been persistently low since the 1970s, linked to changing climate and rising surface temperatures in the Indian Ocean. What rain does fall is subject to high rates of moisture loss through evaporation and transpiration due to high temperatures (Sachs *et al.*, 2004). Arguments relating to soil quality are much weaker. Heat and abundant rain do mean that tropical soils cannot accumulate organic topsoil since organic matter decomposes rapidly and is quickly lost as rainwater seeps downward in the soil. Tropical soils are therefore low in plant nutrients and subject to severe erosion. This does not mean tropical soils are inherently inferior, but that they are different. The higher rate of chemical and physical churning in humid-tropical conditions means that soil production is more rapid than in cooler climates, so soils maintain fertility from the dissolution of minerals and less from the accumulation of organic matter. Overall erosion is more serious and regeneration more rapid. In tropical climates temperatures tend to remain high during the year even at night, so plant losses of net photosynthesis (energy) are high. Many plant species are specifically adapted to these tropical conditions. These include sweet potato, yam, taro, oil palm, coffee, cocoa, tea, groundnut, cassava, banana, mango and papaya (Blaut, 1993). Tropical agriculture in some parts of the world, such as the Amazon Basin,supports very low population densities; elsewhere population densities have been extraordinarily high (in Java, Bangladesh, Barbados and El Salvador) (Blaut, 1993).

The net impact of these various effects does show a clear negative link between tropical climates and agricultural productivity. Nordhaus (2006) found that the optimal temperature for maximizing output density is approximately 12°C – much lower than the temperature typical of tropical climates. Overall tropical agriculture suffers a productivity penalty of 30–50 per cent compared with temperate-zone agriculture (Gallup and Sachs, 1999). Cotton, for example, is grown in both temperate and tropical environments and yields are much lower in the latter regions (Bloom *et al.*, 1998).

However, we should not jump to conclusions about causality. Although climate is relatively fixed agricultural technology is certainly not. The productivity of agriculture is not only determined by geography. Prior to the Industrial Revolution, in eighteenth-century East Asia 0.5 acres was enough to support a family in rice cultivation while 20 acres was required for an equivalent-sized family in England (Ferguson, 2012:26). This can be linked with the findings of Acemoglu *et al.* (2002a) that patterns of population density in the early sixteenth century were often much higher in countries that are now 'poor and tropical'. The subsequent success of temperate agriculture is in large part due to sustained efforts to expand production in developed countries. Between 1950 and 1990 annual labour productivity in developed-country agriculture rose by 5.4 per cent but in developing countries (except China) by 1.3 per cent (Skarstein, 2007:360); thanks to the massive subsidies, R&D and mechanization, developed countries could focus on temperate agriculture.

Geography: impact and policy agenda

The most important geographical factors identified in this chapter were transport costs, natural resources and health. As the impact of fixed geographical factors on economic growth has changed in the past, so it is likely to do in the future. There are a number of policy responses to geographical problems, including shifting output towards manufacturing, reducing transport costs, regional trade, aid and health care investment.

Braudel (1984:523) wrote that 'if geography proposes, history disposes'. Geography is not destiny and its effects can be mitigated or even overcome by good economic policy. An important aspect of economic development has been the shift from climate-sensitive farming towards climate-insensitive manufacturing and services. In 1820 72 per cent of US employment was on farms and by 2004 this share was only 1.2 per cent. The four tropical countries that have experienced sustained growth – Mauritius, Hong Kong, Singapore and Taiwan – were able to escape their geographical burden through export-led growth in textiles and electronics. It is doubtful whether this lesson can be copied by all developing countries. Textiles and electronics tend to be heavily dependent on importing inputs for assembly and subsequent export so are particularly vulnerable to the high transport costs associated with being landlocked. Notably all those four successful cases had easy coastal access. This problem could be partially overcome in Sub-Saharan Africa by processing local raw materials rather than importing inputs. Uganda, for example, could export roasted and branded coffee rather than raw beans and Mali could process raw cotton into textiles.

There are also many policies that can reduce transport costs even for landlocked countries. These include more efficient port facilities, duty-free access to imported inputs and capital goods, timely customs administration, physical security and reliability in warehousing, cost-effective access to international telephone and internet services, reliable power supply, flexibility in hiring and dismissing workers, and reasonable shipping costs to major ports in Europe, US and Japan (Bloom *et al.*, 1998). Geographical isolation is often policy induced. Policies that give monopolies to official national carriers (often airlines) have been adopted by many African governments but have increased freight costs. Studies of other regions demonstrate that deregulation and other pro-competition measures have reduced freight liner rates by as much as 50 per cent (Amjadi and Yeats, 1995).

One way of dealing with the problem of being landlocked is to re-orient trade to the regional economy. Efforts at regional integration have a long and unsuccessful history in Sub-Saharan Africa. There are around 30 Regional Trade Agreements (RTAs) in Sub-Saharan Africa and each country is a member on average of four. This overlapping membership generates conflicting obligations, rules and procedures. Agreements have tended to focus on (unfulfilled) promises to reduce tariff and other barriers to regional trade and neglected the lack of transport infrastructure (Naude, 2007), and there is little evidence they have increased intra-African trade. The lack of transport links between African countries is a longstanding problem dating back to the colonial era (see Chapter 9).

There is a market failure in the construction of most transport links, including railways and roads, whether oriented towards regional or global trade. Crucial external benefits arise to a landlocked country in Sub-Saharan Africa from any country lying between it and the coast investing in transport infrastructure. Improving the railway line running across Kenya to the port in Mombasa would have significant benefits for Uganda. But why should Kenya consider those external benefits for Uganda? Landlocked Malawi contributed to road rehabilitation in Tanzania to ensure better access to the Dar-es-Salaam harbour. There are other potential gains from cooperation. At present there are four different rail gauges in use in Africa, making inter-country links harder and creating different regulations relating to road transport and customs. The low existing levels of economic activity in Africa gives little incentive for governments or the private sector to invest in road infrastructure. The picture changes once externalities are taken into consideration. The World Bank proposed a 100,000 km trans-Africa road network to link 83 major African cities. The (direct) cost – $32 billion over 15 years – is small relative to the benefits (including externalities) of increased trade, estimated at over $250 billion (Naude, 2007).

Regional cooperation to provide transport links such as air traffic control, border crossings or regulations for road transport can be supported by the international donor community in various ways. Foreign aid could be targeted to the greater provision of transport infrastructure with recipient countries agreeing to binding commitments to ensure trade facilitation. The international community should help ensure implementation of and adherence to international law on the rights of landlocked countries to access to the sea. Important existing international agreements include Article V of the GATT, the UN Convention on the Law of the Sea (1982, 1994), and the UN Convention on the transit of landlocked countries (1965) (Naude, 2007).

The doubling of foreign aid announced at the July 2005 Gleneagles G-8 summit focused on infrastructure, which could eventually generate a massive construction boom in some developing countries. While potentially overcoming the high transport costs associated with being landlocked, a big donor-funded push may have a secondary effect in exacerbating problems of bad governance. Big corrupt money is likely to strengthen the politics of patronage over honest politics and the rule of law (Collier's 'survival of the fattest').

There is a need to tighten the regulatory framework in the global construction sector alongside big infrastructure aid increases.

The WHO Commission on Macroeconomics and Health (CMH) identified 49 health services that constitute a basic package of health interventions, many of which specifically target the diseases of geography identified in this chapter. These include nutrition programmes and universal access to anti-malarial nets. The cost amounts to $100 per person per year between 2005 and 2015. Given that many developing countries have a GDP per capita of only $300 and a government budget of $30 per capita, local sources could only ever pay a fraction of this. The donor need until 2015 would be $40 billion annually for Sub-Saharan Africa and $80 billion annually for the entire developing world. In 2012 total gross aid was $76 billion; after deducting payments to middle-income countries, loan repayments, emergency assistance and foreign consultants only $12 billion was given as direct budgetary support to governments. An increase in donor aid to fill this gap would represent an annual increase from 0.44 to 0.54 per cent of donor-country assistance (Sachs, 2005).

Increased aid targeted at infrastructure and health has been seen by its advocates as its own exit strategy from the poverty trap and aid dependency. With care in designing the donor–recipient process, such a commitment (not using aid for consumption) could be enforced through improved monitoring of the budget process, perhaps with the help of NGOs (Sachs *et al.*, 2004). The results of debt relief under the Highly Indebted Poor Countries (HIPC) initiative, whereby resources made available by reduced debt servicing were targeted at predetermined areas of public spending (especially social spending), have been encouraging. There are good examples of health care interventions successfully being scaled up with donor assistance. By 1974 donor-led efforts had prevented an estimated 600,000 cases of onchocerciasis (African river blindness), which made 25 million hectares safe for cultivation, and protected 40 million people from transmission. In 1988 polio was endemic in more than 125 countries; since then 2 billion children have been immunized against polio, only 784 cases were reported in 2003 and it now remains in only 6 countries (Sachs, 2005).

Key points

- An adverse disease environment may divert resources at the household level away from investment in physical and human capital to emergency health care. Disease may reduce the human capital acquired through schooling or learning on the job.
- Poor geography, in particular being landlocked and isolated from international trade and markets, may reduce the incentive of entrepreneurs to invest in export-oriented sectors.
- Adverse weather conditions may directly influence the (agricultural) output of land.

- The availability of natural resources are products of geography and may influence output directly (exporting oil) or indirectly (good soils boosting output from agriculture).
- Many of the effects of geography are likely to impact through TFP, for example, poor soils and weather reducing the yield of land, loss of schooling and work experience reducing the productivity of labour, more isolated domestic producers being less engaged with the competition and access to new ideas/technologies characteristic of international trade.
- Geography can be defined as 'those physical attributes tied to specific locations'. They may be fixed such as latitude, distance from coastlines, altitude, access to navigable rivers, or slowly changing such as climate or agricultural potential (soil quality and rainfall). In statistical work they can be considered exogenous because they are not caused by economic and other social variables.
- Adverse geography is linked to low levels of income and slow economic growth.
- There are five major mechanisms through which geography can influence economic growth: transport costs, proximity to/ownership of natural resources, state formation, human health and agricultural productivity (including animal husbandry). The most important of these are transport costs, natural resources and human health.
- The impact of geography on growth is likely to change in the future, for example, as improved communications technology reduces the penalty associated with being landlocked.
- Infrastructure, foreign aid and technological change are the key 'solutions' to deal with problems of geography.

Chapter 12

Culture

The Greek historian Herodotus, writing around 430 BCE, claimed that Greeks were exposed to more changeable weather conditions (than Asians) and were consequently more spirited, flexible and democratic. The cultural legacy of these freedom-loving ancient Greeks, argue some, is preserved today in the individualism and democracy of contemporary Europe and its offshoots in Australia, New Zealand, Canada and the US (Meier, 2009). While Socrates argued that democracy would pool ignorance, Plato believed that reasoned debate among philosopher-kings (not the masses) would lead to a better society. However, since democracy then disappeared from Europe for two thousand years until its revival inspired by the American and French revolutions, 'it takes a heroically selective reading of history to see a continuous spirit of democratic freedom stretching from classical Greece to the Founding Fathers' (Morriss, 2010:260). Measuring culture is difficult, as is examining the nature of cause and effect. Economists, nevertheless, need to measure things and give them numbers to see how they relate to economic things such as economic growth.

Culture is the deep determinant that has long made economists nervous. Any discussion of how culture affects economic outcomes risks association with now thoroughly discredited nineteenth-century views. Why did Europe surge ahead economically and colonize much of the world? Many nineteenth-century Europeans saw themselves as in some way biologically superior to people in the rest of the world, so colonialism could be legitimized as a superior race dominating an inferior race. Others argued that the explanation lay not in genetics but in culture, justifying a kind of 'cultural racism' whereby one dominant and superior culture could colonize in order to civilize an inferior culture. It is not difficult to see how such thinking legitimized many of the brutalities of colonialism and led eventually to the horrors and genocide perpetrated by the Nazi regime in Germany.

Culture and economic growth

Culture as a deep determinant of growth has its influence working through the proximate determinants. The links (see Figure 12.1) include: social capital and trust which facilitate forms of economic exchange; savings and so the pool of resource available for investment; social norms prohibiting women from working outside the household; attitudes to the dignity of labour and hard work affecting labour productivity and so TFP; the mobility of women

Figure 12.1   *Culture as a deeper determinant of economic growth*

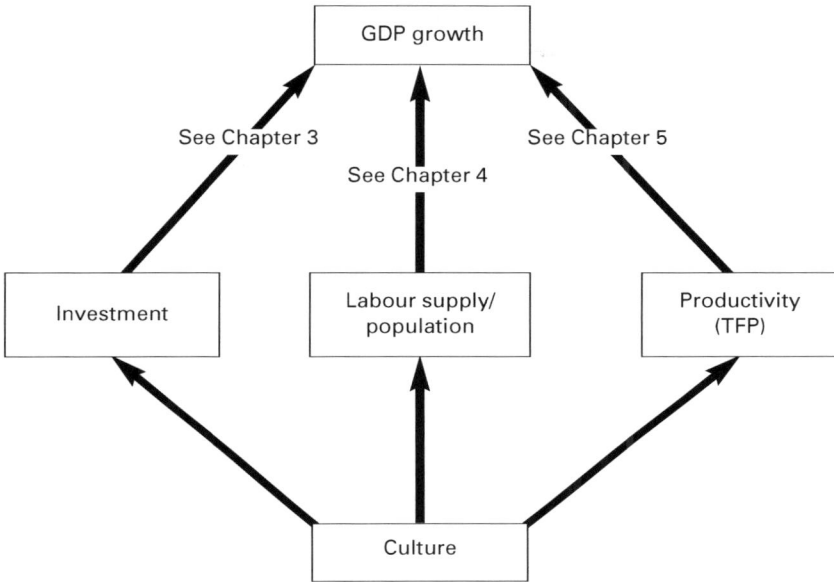

and acceptability of employing professional experts rather than family members in family firms; attitudes to social changes generated by technological change, innovation and entrepreneurship; the importance of literacy and education; and non-economic influences on fertility.

Culture can also affect economic growth through its influence on whether countries are open to ideas and innovation (see Chapter 13).

In their reluctance to engage with culture, some economists dismiss it with the assumption that all consumers and producers behave in similar 'rational' ways to maximize wages/profits. Others have nervously stepped back feeling that culture is too big and the links through which it can influence economic outcomes so numerous that it is impossible to design any sort of testable economic theories. Robert Barro's paper (1991) did not include any measure of culture. Culture is often simply derived as the residual in economic analysis: rather than being theorized from the outset, it is a measure of our ignorance. Once all the possible economic explanations for a given phenomenon have been accounted for, economists allocate what remains to 'culture'. A good example is the difference between Hindu and Muslim fertility in India, where demographic data suggest Muslim fertility is higher than Hindu. Some Hindus allege that this is evidence of a Muslim plot to take over India by becoming the majority population – a plot that is supposed to work through widespread polygamy and the rejection of contraception. The reality is less dramatic. The share of Muslims in the Indian population increased from 10.5 per cent in 1951 to 12.5 per cent in 1991. There is no difference in the occurrence of polygamy between Muslims and Hindus and fertility rates among Indian Muslims are falling rapidly. It is the wider economic and social drivers of fertility that differ systematically between Muslims and Hindus. Muslims are more urbanized than Hindus, but within urban areas Muslims disproportionately occupy poorer housing areas with lower levels of public health infrastructure and lower-paid jobs than Hindus. Muslim girls have lower levels of education than Hindu girls (Jeffrey and Jeffrey, 2002; James and Nair, 2005). Accounting for these differences shows that the socio-economic effects of child and female education, poverty, employment, urbanization, and land ownership account for the bulk of the difference in fertility levels between Hindus and Muslims. But a fertility differential still remains after these variables have been taken into account. This differential has been labelled a 'cultural impact' by demographers (Jeffrey and Jeffrey, 2002).

What is culture?

How then do we measure culture? Economists first tried to avoid the question and *not* measure it, arguing that if all the economic factors impacting something are measured and quantified, then anything that remains unexplained represents a cultural effect. However, things are improving: scholars are re-engaging with culture. Some have used ingenious statistics, such as the power of sixteenth-century German princes to influence the religious denomination of their subjects, or how religion was associated with changing city sizes in Europe after the fourteenth century. Others have turned to long-run survey data. The World Values Survey, in the words of its own website, is a 'global research project that explores people's values and beliefs, their stability or change over time and their impact on social and political development of the societies in different countries of the world'.

Guiso *et al.* define culture as 'those customary beliefs and values that ethnic, religious, and social groups transmit fairly unchanged from generation to generation' (2006:23). This definition focuses on prior beliefs and values and ignores those that are acquired during a person's life. But how do we disentangle those values that are acquired in later life from economic changes that are occurring at the same time and distinguish cause and effect between culture and economics? Some scholars have used ethnicity, race or family history as proxy measures for culture, as they are (relatively) fixed factors which may be correlated with other beliefs and values. For example, many have argued that Protestants are more individualistic than others. But these measures are inevitably very crude. Even within a group with clear rules of membership such as 'Catholic', the stated belief structure of members runs all the way from 'the ultra-conservative Opus Dei movement to left-wing liberation theology movements' (Chang, 2007). The world's major religions have evolved over many centuries, such that they can all now be interpreted in ways that are both good and bad for economic development. Hinduism, some argue, values those who renounce worldly wealth, but many Hindus also appeal to Lakshmi, the goddess of wealth and prosperity, for divine support in business life. Confucianism emphasizes hard work and frugality but also stresses the superiority of scholarship over business and conformity over individualism and innovation. Islam does not look down on trade – its founding prophet, Muhammad, was a merchant – but it has been interpreted in ways that restrict the ability of women to engage in economic activity (Chang, 2007).

Culture changes

We may be tempted to think in terms of a cultural explanation for current economic issues such as the Eurozone debt and banking crisis. We could contrast the industrious frugal Germans (with a strong fiscal/debt profile) with the ill-disciplined fun-loving Italians (who are facing a debt crisis). These stereotypes have changed. The historian of the Roman Empire, Edward Gibbon, wrote that 'the German ... passed their lives in a state of ignorance and poverty ... consumed his days and nights in the animal gratifications of sleep and food ... they delight in sloth ... these barbarians were immoderately addicted to deep gaming and excessive drinking' (1776: 235–8). Of the Italian Roman army he wrote, 'he promised never to desert his standard, to submit his own will to the commands of his leaders, and to sacrifice his life for the safety of the emperor and the empire. The attachment of the Roman troops to their standards was inspired by the united influence of religion and honour' (p. 39). As recently as a century ago the Germans were still regarded by some as being lazy, individualistic, emotional, stupid, dishonest and easy-going (Chang, 2007).

How have the respective cultures of the Italians and German changed so much? What may at a quick glance be thought of as laziness can be a product of underlying economic circumstances. Many people in developing countries work very long hours but without any sense of industrial time – there is no such thing as a 9 to 5 working day – and many are underemployed in inherently low-productivity occupations. What we call 'rational economic thinking' has developed as a result of the rise of modern corporate organizations which require the strict measurement of output, productivity and profits. When the reasonable expectation in a poor developing country is that nothing will change, there is no need to rationally plan for the future and there are few financial instruments (such as insurance or savings accounts in banks) with which to do so. Cultural habits have also tended to respond rapidly to the pressures of economic growth and development – people develop strict routines and work hard when required to do so by being employed in a modern factory. These arguments return us to the ideas of Marx, for whom culture was a reflection of underlying economic change.

One striking prediction based on a cultural analysis concerned the likely evolution of fertility in Sub-Saharan Africa. Caldwell and Caldwell argued that

Sub-Saharan Africa would show greater resistance to fertility decline than any other region in the world because of a cultural/religious belief system that sustained and rewarded high fertility. They suggested that there would be 'no declines like those of Asia' (1987:434). The crucial feature of this belief system, they stated, was the importance attached to the succession of the generations of a single family, which creates a profound taboo against dying childless.

Much of West and Central Africa has a household system structured around a mother and her dependent children. The biological bearing of children and the cost of child-raising were often separated by a high incidence of child fostering. This meant that the father was spared the financial cost of rearing children but he would still receive material benefits from children throughout his life. This cultural structure, argued Caldwell *et al.* (1992) meant the usual economics of the family and fertility did not apply. The practical results were that contraceptive use in Sub-Saharan African was very low and not likely to rise, and the 'inefficiency of African [family planning] programmes is undoubtedly a matter of lack of individual demand and culturally conditioned uncertainty of support for them among the leadership' (Caldwell and Caldwell, 1987:414–5). New findings from Demographic and Health Surveys showed that birth rates were falling rapidly; by the early 1990s a fertility decline of over 10 per cent had occurred in South-west and possibly also South-east Nigeria. This latter area was particularly significant because it was where the Caldwells had observed the social structure that they had argued would inhibit fertility decline. The mechanism behind the decline in fertility appeared to be a rapid rise in contraceptive use. In Sub-Saharan Africa female and male premarital sexual relations are widespread and so carry a considerable risk of pregnancy followed by the possibility of forced marriage or single motherhood. In most parts of the region illiterate girls are not too concerned about the former and in West Africa there is no social stigma associated with the latter. Economic growth and the increasing opportunity for women to acquire well-paid urban jobs have changed this dramatically. Girls increasingly wanted education because they aspired to urban employment. Economic incentives had trumped cultural norms.

Whilst economic incentives clearly do often change cultural norms, different cultures can react in strikingly different ways to the same set of economic incentives. An example is that of the two trading groups operating in the Mediterranean during the late medieval period, the Jewish Maghribi and the Genoese. Both groups were involved in large-scale, long-distance trade all over the Mediterranean. The Maghribis had a collectivist culture: mutual responsibility belonged to all the members of that society and everyone was expected to respond collectively to whatever transpired between any specific merchant and agent. Only those agents with a wide reputation for not cheating were hired by merchants. The Genoese began trading towards the end of the twelfth century at the same time as Genoa was experiencing rapid immigration. Over the thirteenth century the population of Genoa increased from

30,000 to 100,000. The population was diverse, with little sense of community. In this individualistic society a merchant randomly hired unemployed agents, and cultural beliefs discouraged investment in information. The historical evidence shows that social institutions emerged to reflect these cultural differences. The Maghribis invested in sharing information and the Genoese did not. Each Maghribi corresponded with many other Maghribi traders by sending informative letters to them with the latest commercial information and gossip including what transpired in relations among other Maghribis. Important business dealings were conducted in public. By contrast the Genoese were reserved, concealed information, and were jealous of business secrets. Following military and political changes in the Mediterranean both groups expanded their trade to Spain and Constantinople, each responding very differently to this economic shock. The Maghribis expanded their trade by employing other Maghribis as agents who emigrated from North Africa to the new trade centres. The Genoese tended to establish agents that were native to the other trade centre.

This example suggests that while cultures may change under the influence of economic growth and development, they do not necessarily converge and initial cultural differences have an important influence on the subsequent evolution of those cultures. This sort of process is called by economists 'path dependency'.

Weber and the spirit of capitalism

Perhaps the most influential writer on the link between culture and economic growth is Max Weber. Weber argued that the Protestant religion was good for growth and because much of Europe's population was Protestant it industrialized earliest. The key to the rise to economic dominance of Protestant North America rather than Catholic South America, according to this view, was religion. (Chapter 11 discussed the alternative view that the key difference between the two sub-continents was geography.)

Protestantism and the spirit of capitalism

Max Weber's view is captured by the title of his most famous book, *The Protestant Ethic and the Spirit of Capitalism*, first published in 1904–05. The emerging capitalism of the seventeenth century was about more than the pursuit of gain, rather 'capitalism is identical with the pursuit of profit, and forever renewed profit by means of continuous, rational, capitalistic enterprise' (Weber 1992:xxxi). Weber argued that Protestantism was particularly suited for developing this economic rationalism and profit-seeking drive; it celebrated labour and hard work as the fulfilment of a divine calling given to all individuals, and its puritanical inclinations discouraged the luxurious and idle enjoyment of wealth which would distract from a righteous life. Weber described this mix of hard work and the moral imperative to save rather than consume as 'worldly asceticism', contrasting it with Catholicism (and other religions) which sought to go beyond worldly morality in otherworldly meditation and monastic contemplation.

Many scholars disagree with the Weber thesis. There is no single 'Protestant ethic'. In its early years Protestantism was radical and anti-establishment but by the eighteenth century had built a structure as rigid as that of medieval Catholicism, so any explanation relying on religious liberty was only valid for a limited period (Wallerstein, 1974). Richard Tawney in his 1926 book *Religion and the Rise of Capitalism* rejected the link between Protestantism and the rise of capitalism, arguing instead that economic growth in England took off in the sixteenth century as the influence of religion declined and was replaced by secular-scientific attitudes. Others have argued it was not the declining influence of religion but rather the absence of religion from all matters economic that was crucial. Scholars have found support for this in the Bible, citing Jesus' dictum that people should 'give unto Caesar that which belongs to Caesar and give unto God that which belongs to God'. This separation of the human and the sacred marked a big difference between Christian and non-Christian countries. Braudel argues that 'unlike the West which clearly separates the human from the sacred, the Far East makes no such distinction. Religion is clearly involved with all aspects of human life: the State, philosophy, ethics and social relations. All fully partake of the sacred; and this is what gives them their perennial resistance to change' (1984:169). This distinction between the spiritual and secular enabled successive European rulers, even before the fragmentation of the Catholic Church after the fifteenth century, to resist the political ambitions of the Catholic papacy (Ferguson, 2012:60). Chapter 11 introduces the debate about how the resulting fragmentation of Europe into diverse states may (or may not) have stimulated competition and long-run economic dynamism in Europe.

The empirical evidence is hard to come by. Weber noted that in the manufacturing centres of France and Western Germany Protestants were typically the employers and in Switzerland Protestant cantons were the centres of manufacturing export industry and Catholic ones primarily agricultural. The only numerical analysis Weber refers to is a study of the economic activities of Catholics and Protestants in Baden in 1895 and the accuracy of these figures has been questioned.

A more recent study looks at the comparative long-run economic performance of Catholic and Protestant Europe. After the mid-1550s the many princes in fragmented Germany had the freedom to impose their preferred religious denomination upon their subjects and for most principalities no more religious changes took place after 1624. The choice of religion was imposed from above which makes it easier to examine the impact of religion on economic outcomes without having to consider questions of reverse causality (how economic outcomes influenced religion). The choice of religion was not, for example, influenced by more entrepreneurial cities choosing to become Protestant. The measure of economic development is growth of city size which has been widely used as a proxy for income growth. The study finds that there were no positive effects of Protestantism on city growth between 1300 and 1800 (Cantoni, 2010). A second study finds that there was a positive correlation between both average per capita income tax payments and the share of the labour force employed in manufacturing and services, and the share of Protestants in the total population across some 420–450 counties in late nineteenth-century Germany (Becker and Woessman, 2009).

Openness to new ideas and innovation

It has long been argued that the set piece 'event' or process in Europe that opened minds to new ideas was the Enlightenment. This was the time between the seventeenth and eighteenth centuries when superstition, ignorance and religious-inspired fatalism were supposedly replaced in the minds of Europeans by scientific attitudes, learning, and rational contemplation (see Introduction and Chapter 7).

The impact of the Enlightenment was not uniform across Europe and in part was a product of spreading literacy. The founder of Protestantism (Martin Luther) favoured universal schooling and the translation of the Bible into local languages (from Latin) to enable all Christians to read and interpret the Bible for themselves. Countries that had remained Catholic tended to respond to the challenge of this free(er) and more democratic thinking with repression. Spain, for example, imposed the death penalty in 1558 for importing foreign books without permission and banned students from foreign study except in safe Catholic universities. In 1900 3 per cent of the population of Britain was illiterate, compared with 48 per cent in Italy, 50 per cent in Spain and 78 per cent in Portugal. Religious persecution and intellectual closure was 'a kind of original sin, the effects of which only wore off by the twentieth century' (Landes, 1998).

There is strong evidence that the spread of Protestantism had a causal effect on the spread of literacy. The spread of literacy is more closely related to the distance from Wittenburg (the home of Martin Luther and centre of Protestantism) than it is to measures of economic and educational development before 1517, including the placement of schools, universities, monasteries, and urbanization. This is strong evidence that Protestantism was driving literacy rather than more prosperous/educated (hence more literate) areas being more likely to adopt the Protestant religion (Becker and Woessman, 2009).

Value of inequality versus incentives

Culture can influence political beliefs. One angle often discussed by cultural commentators is whether people prefer a dynamic unequal society or one where governments intervene to control inequalities even at the cost of some economic growth and dynamism. We leave aside for the moment the debate and evidence that shows more equal societies tend to experience faster economic growth (Alesina and Rodrik, 1994, for example). The US General Social Survey asks whether the US government should act to reduce income differences between rich and poor. On average religion is positively associated with attitudes conducive to free market and better institutions. Religious people trust the government and legal system more, are less willing to break the law, and are more likely to believe free markets are fair. The relation between religiosity and market mechanisms (incentives, competition and private property) is more mixed (Guiso *et al.*, 2003). Catholic, Protestant and Jewish respondents all have a more negative attitude toward redistribution than those with no religion and only Protestants are found to favour economic incentives at the expense of greater inequality (Guiso *et al.*, 2006).

Saving for the future

Weber's belief that Protestantism promoted a puritanical attitude to consumption and luxury is echoed by many modern economists who have argued that savings is good for economic growth as it provides a pool of resources available for investment. There is some weak supporting evidence for this. The World Values Survey finds that Catholics are 3.8 per cent more likely and Protestants 2.7 per cent more likely than non-religious people to view teaching thrift to their children as an important value. The evidence is weak because these are very small magnitudes and also the survey has no actual data on savings by particular ethnic or religious groups. Other evidence for a culture/savings link is similarly weak. The high savings in many East Asian countries (30–40 per cent of GDP) and low savings in much of Sub-Saharan Africa (less than 10 per cent of GDP) have been attributed by some to 'Confucian ethics' in the former that emphasize the importance of frugality. This slightly feeble effort is easily criticized by invoking straightforward alternative economic explanations. In East Asia, rapid GDP growth, political and economic instability, the spread of organizations (banks and post offices), and absent hyper-inflation have created long-term incentives to save. In Sub-Saharan Africa high rates of fertility are in themselves a form of savings as people seek to ensure the survival of sufficient dependents to protect and care for themselves in old age.

Conclusions

There is fairly consistent evidence in support of Weber, that Protestantism (and Catholicism a little less so) is good for economic growth. Among Protestants trust, belief in private ownership, anti-redistribution attitudes and literacy are stronger than in other religions. There are no consistent results for any other religion. There are particular problems with distinguishing the effects of belonging to a religion and participating in regular attendance/worship with the effects of group membership more generally. Does belonging to a church have any extra or different advantages from belonging to a bowling club (see below in this chapter for discussion of networks)?

Ethnicity

There are various influential works arguing that cultural diversity has been bad for economic growth. While public policies of course influence growth, this debate suggests that ethnic differences help explain policy choice, so culture becomes a deep determinant of economic growth. More polarized societies, they argue, are less able to agree on the provision of publicly provided goods and services such as roads, schools and power supply. Ethnic interest groups are likely to value only the benefits of such goods and services that accrue to their own group and discount the benefits for other groups. Different ethnic groups may have different priorities for the provision of public goods and services; for example poorer groups preferring welfare and richer groups universities.

Ethnic divisions and poor policy-making

Ethnolinguistic fractionalization (ELF) is defined and measured as 'the probability a randomly selected individual(s) belong to a different ethnic or linguistic group'. ELF is correlated with various measures of poor policy, such as black-market premiums on foreign exchange, low provision of infrastructure, low levels of basic education and poor financial development (Easterly and Levine, 1997). Although there are many ethnically diverse countries in Africa (Côte d'Ivoire, Nigeria, Ghana, Congo, etc.) the finding also holds for a sample of non-African countries. There are lots of supporting studies. The provision of certain goods such as education, roads and sewers declines with more ethnic fragmentation in US cities. Voters choose lower public goods when a significant fraction of tax revenues will be used to provide public goods shared with other ethnic groups (Alesina *et al.*, 1999). Ethnic diversity is correlated with the poor quality of government services in developing countries (Mauro, 1995). There is lower public support for higher education in US states with more religious and ethnic heterogeneity (Goldin and Katz, 1999). Primary school funding is lower in more ethnically diverse districts in Kenya (Miguel, 2000). Linguistic or religious diversity leads to greater political instability (Mauro, 1995; Annett, 1999). Ethnically diverse countries in Sub-Saharan African were more likely to be closed to trade and had lower levels of institutional quality (Sachs and Warner, 1997). Ethnically polarized nations reacted more adversely to external terms of trade shocks (Rodrik, 1999).

Any impact of cultural diversity on economic growth is influenced by the relative size of ethnic groups in a complicated way. Evidence shows that as the size of a particular ethnic group approaches 50 per cent, political protest tends to become more violent. A possible interpretation is that as the largest ethnic group reaches 50 per cent or more, then other ethnic groups face the possibility of permanent political exclusion in a democracy so switch from participating in democratic processes to protest and violence. Countries with large ethnic minorities include Malaysia, Belgium, Canada, South Africa and Rwanda and here majority voting has been perceived by minorities as having led to such permanent exclusion (Bates, 2000). This is what Collier calls 'dominance' and Engelbert 'suffocation'. There are numerous examples of dominated/suffocated minorities undertaking secession attempts in Africa. These include the Katanga, Kwilu, Kivu, and Haut-Congo provinces of Congo, Ogaden and Eritrea in Ethiopia, Biafra in Nigeria, Ewe of Ghana, Sanwi of Côte d'Ivoire, the coastal peoples and Somalis in Kenya, Tuaregs of Mali, non-Arab populations of the Sudan, Baganda of Uganda and the Casamance region of Senegal. Of these only Eritrea and to some extent Somaliland have ever been successful (Englebert *et al.*, 2002). A famous example of political dominance being associated with poor economic policy and destructive redistribution is post-independence Ghana (see Box 12.1).

Ethnicity as cultural determinant: a critique

There are three problems with these general arguments: first, that culture is the central argument; second, the problem of distinguishing cultural from competitive political mobilization; and third, that they ignore the issue of causation. Finally, institutions can provide a possible solution to problems of social divisions and conflict.

Is culture the key driving force?
The first criticism suggests that economic change, not culture, was the key to understanding divisions based on ethnicity or other factors. For many developing countries political evolution after 1945 was characterized by conflict based on ethnicity and class, such as rioting, frequent coups, loss of authority by legislatures and courts, and disintegration of broadly based political parties. Huntingdon explains that this conflict was due to 'rapid social change and mobilisation of new groups into politics and slow development of political institutions' (1968:4). Conflict was the result not of pre-existing culturally determined divisions but of economic change leading to new fissures in society. Social and economic changes such as urbanization, industrialization, increased literacy and expansion of the mass media had extended political consciousness, multiplied political demands and increased political participation. The new elites such as civil servants and teachers competed with the traditional sources of political authority – the secular and religious leaders of the villages, and social networks based around family, class and caste. The primary problem was the slower development of political institutions relative to this social and economic change: 'Economic development and political stability are two independent goals and progress toward one has no necessary connection with progress toward the other' (Huntingdon, 1968:6). A specific

Box 12.1 The 'vampire state' in Ghana

Ghana the world's largest producer of cocoa, had strong initial conditions at the time of independence. Ghanaians had gradual experience of internal self-government in stages between 1951 and final independence in 1957, and the country had ample foreign exchange reserves. The new President Nkrumah was committed to promote industrialization, welfare and economic independence and was widely praised among donors and political commentators. Nkrumah was overthrown in 1966 and a series of governments in the late 1960s and 1970s presided over economic collapse that lasted until the 1980s. GDP per capita declined by 40 per cent between 1974 and 1984 and several million people migrated. Gareth Austin (1996) termed the Ghanaian state a 'vampire state', one that sucked out so much wealth and gave so little in return that it destroyed the economy.

In post-independence Ghana there was a dominant coalition among urban groups (largely the Akan tribe) that included the bureaucracy, the military, police, trade unions and students. The formation of this coalition dated to Nkrumah's defeat of the federalist National Liberation Movement (NLM) in 1955–56 led by the minority wealthy rural cocoa producers (mainly the smaller Ashanti tribe). This was followed by an end to the tradition of independent cocoa farmers' associations. Two particular sets of government intervention have been identified by many as the principal instruments of the vampire state. The Cocoa Marketing Board was a statutory export monopoly whose main purpose was made clear by Nkrumah in 1954 when the government responded to a sharp rise in the world price of cocoa by freezing the price paid to producers to raise revenue to fund urban-industrial expenditure. The second mechanism was the Ghanaian currency which became progressively overvalued after 1961, and especially after 1975. This made imported inputs and equipment cheaper for urban industry and consumer goods cheaper for urban consumers at the cost of less competitive export prices for cocoa growers. The brutal extraction of resources through these two means destroyed the productive base of the rural Ashanti and created an inefficient urban-industrial economy that functioned only as long as subsidies were flowing; as they dried up urban declined followed quickly.

example is the 'crisis of governance' in India after the mid-1960s. Atul Kohli (1990) defined this crisis as a failure of political coalitions to endure, policy ineffectiveness and the incapacity to accommodate political conflict without violence. The competitive politics of distribution, he suggested, had politicized existing divisions in society such as class, ethnicity, language, religion, region and caste. The spread of democratic values had hastened the decline of traditional sources of authority such as the 'big men', often of high caste, who had previously controlled lower-caste voters. This was exacerbated by the decline of party organization and the rise of low-quality leaders with demagogic rather than programmatic appeal. This mobilization had been focused on the state, which by the mid-1960s was responsible for half of all investment in India and a key source of livelihoods in a poor developing country.

Culture or cash?

What appears to be a demand for ethnic justice or liberation based on identity (conflict caused by cultural divisions) may be better interpreted as, at root, an attempt to control lucrative resources. In Zaire copper and diamonds are concentrated in the South-east; the secessionist Katanga movement was formed in this region shortly after independence. In Nigeria oil discoveries were concentrated in the South-east; the secessionist Biafra movement was formed in this region in 1967. In Ethiopia the richest area was the coastal belt which later gained independence as Eritrea. Here it could easily be argued that ethnicity is secondary to geography (Collier *et al.*, 2001).

Cultural divisions: cause or effect?

The third criticism sees these empirical studies as having forgotten to consider the big question of cause and effect. Finding that ethnic or any other form of diversity is related to poor economic outcomes says nothing about the direction of causation. In both the historical and contemporary world the poorest countries tend to be the most diverse. Self-sufficient subsistence agriculture and the poor infrastructure and communications typical of those poorest countries imply the separation and isolation of small communities and consequent linguistic and cultural diversity. Modern economic growth, migration, urbanization, mixing in schools and the labour market, and exchange being increasingly based through the market rather than kinship groups leads to mixing and the emergence of a national culture. Chapter 9 gave the example of nineteenth-century France where the expansion of the central state, spread of education, a national language and symbols such as the national anthem led to the creation of *France*. Returning to Easterly and Levine (1997) we can then argue that poor policy choices led to slow economic growth which in turn perpetuated cultural and linguistic diversity.

Institutions as a solution?

Institutions that give protection to legal minorities, guarantee freedom from expropriation, grant freedom from repudiation of contracts, and facilitate cooperation for public services would constrain the amount of damage that one ethnic group could do to another and prevent one ethnic group from expropriating the incomes and wealth of another. Such institutions could make a given degree of ethnic fractionalization less damaging for development. There is empirical evidence to show that in countries with very highly developed institutions ethnic diversity does not significantly undermine the quality of economic policy (Easterly, 2001a). The big problem is that the measure of institutions is negatively correlated with ethnic division. So the dilemma is: where can such diverse countries acquire those strong institutions?

In every society affected by social change new groups arise to participate in politics. These groups can gain entry into politics without being part of established political organizations; in a more institutionalized political system, political socialization impels changes in the attitudes and behaviour of politically mobilized new groups. In such a system the most important positions of leadership can normally only be attained by those who have served an apprenticeship in less important positions. Such institutions impose political socialization as the price of participation (Huntingdon, 1968). The distinctive organization in a developing society is the political party.

The Congress Party in India, founded in 1885, is one of the most successful political parties of any developing country (see Box 12.2). Another example is the PRI in Mexico (see Box 12.3) which ruled the country for much of the twentieth century, bringing political order out of political chaos.

Box 12.2 The Congress Party in India

Between independence in 1947 and the mid-1960s the Congress Party functioned through an elaborate network of factions at every level of political and governmental activity (Menon, 2003:24, 48). The party provided a system of coordination between layers of government, different social groups and across the geographical spread of India. This coordination was typically done through vertical faction chains that 'provided a subtle and resilient mechanism for conflict management and transactional negotiations among the proprietary classes' (Bardhan, 1984:77). In power Congress monopolized patronage resources right down to village government (*panchayats*), sugar co-operatives, banking corporations, and state-allocated resources such as licenses, fertilizers, seeds and road construction. This meant that even those losing out in the struggle for resources had the incentive to remain within the party system and resume the argument at a later stage. The central leadership provided a system of mediation, arbitration and inter-level co-ordination in the party. Congress acted to neutralize some of the more important cleavages within society, incorporating for example the labour movement and the leaders of various regionally based language/nationalist movements.

Box 12.3 The National Revolutionary Party (PRI) in Mexico

The PRI was created by various military leaders at the end of the 1920s after the Mexican Revolution. The PRI was an autonomous, coherent and flexible political system that combined a reasonably high centralization of power with its own expansion of power; by the 1940s organized social forces such as the military, labour and farmers had been successfully incorporated into the party. Once inside they were subject to the institutionalized bargaining and compromises of the party structure. A limit of six years on presidential terms gave candidates an incentive to remain in the party and attain office at a later attempt. After repeated military interventions in politics before the 1930s Mexico acquired a striking degree of political stability (Huntingdon, 1968).

Networks

Much economic activity takes place with some sort of reference to the future, such as goods and services or labour being provided now in exchange for future payment. An employment contract often specifies the responsibility to carry out current tasks in exchange for promise of a monthly salary. Investment decisions by private corporations rely on assurances by governments that they will not expropriate those assets through higher taxes should the investment prove profitable. Such future-orientated activities are accomplished at lower cost in an environment of higher trust. When individuals can rely on trust they do not need lawyers to write expensive contracts, nor does the government need so many resources to provide the apparatus of contract enforcement and the judicial system (Knack and Keefer, 1997). While economists have proved quite adept at measuring the stock of trust at a given point in time they have found it harder to ascribe trust to particular cultures. Trust could be an inherited cultural variable or a characteristic acquired through repeated interaction; or people may simply behave as if they were trustworthy because they fear some sort of legal or personal retaliation.

Recent surveys have helped solve this longstanding problem. The World Values Survey now contains data from more than 100 countries. The question on trust asks 'generally speaking, would you say that most people can be trusted, or that you can't be too careful in dealing with people?' Data from the US show a gradual decline in trust from the late 1950s to the 1990s. Among other countries trust tends to be more stable over time. Government performance tends to be better and economic growth higher in high-trust societies as measured by this variable. Trust (even more so than education or per capita income) is strongly related to the faith people have in various government institutions such as the security of property rights (Knack and Keefer, 1997).

Data from the World Values Survey, reports from the International Social Survey and the Gallup Millennium Survey for various dates in the 1980s and 1990s show that various religious beliefs also have an impact on economic variables. In particular they find that belief in hell or heaven has a significantly positive and monthly attendance at a religious service a significantly negative relation with economic growth. The important finding is that it is strength of belief not just belonging to a religion that encourages economic growth (McCleary and Barro, 2006). Different religions also have different effects on people's attitudes. Attendance at religious service increases trust only among Christians, and is stronger for Protestants than Catholics, but the effect is zero or negative for other denominations (Guiso *et al.*, 2003). Being raised religiously has a small positive impact on trust. Among Catholics and Protestants regular attendance at religious services has a more significant positive effect, but being Muslim, Hindu or Buddhist has no clear impact (Guiso *et al.*, 2006).

Nevertheless, it is still not possible to gauge if this trust is inspired by religion or is simply a product of continued interaction with people through membership and participation in a (religious) group. Is it religion that is crucial or would repeated interaction in any group, such as a bowling club, be sufficient? The impact of group membership and participation has been widely discussed, in particular since Robert Putnam famously argued in a 1992 book that civic engagement gives rise to social capital – the networks, norms and trust that can then facilitate coordination and cooperation for wider economic benefit. Putnam showed that the intensity of civil society or social capital (measured by him as the vibrancy of associational life, newspaper reading and other indicators of political participation) in different parts of Italy has been the principal determinant of government performance.

Trying to explain the general causes of trust is more difficult than generalizing from a single case study. Group membership may build trust by facilitating repeated interaction and familiarity between individuals independently of the nature of that group, whether sporting or religious. One may be less likely to cheat someone in business if one is going to be meeting them at the bowling club next week. But, it may be that more trusting and cooperative individuals are more inclined to join clubs. Greater social and income inequality may reduce feelings of social cohesion and reduce trust by increasing the perceived distance between ourselves and other groups of people (Wilkinson and Pickett, 2010). Strong legal institutions may reassure people that individuals will behave (even if they secretly want to take the money and run) in a trustworthy manner for fear of the legal consequences. Knack and Keefer (1997) test these hypotheses and find that income, secondary education and checks on the operation of executive power have a positive impact on trust; income inequality and the degree of ethnic and linguistic divisions a negative effect on trust. Urbanization, population density and government size, they found, had no impact on trust. Protestantism was associated with significantly greater trust and Catholicism and Islam had negative but only weak relations to trust. There is a strong effect of ethnic origin. Relative to an American of British ancestry, there are higher levels of trust among those from Japan, Norway, Finland and Sweden, and much lower levels among African Americans, Indians or Africans. There is also evidence that trust is closely and positively related to levels of trust within a person's country of origin. This result is consistent with the idea that trust is based on a prior cultural endowment which is transported during migration and continues to operate in a different country among different people (Guiso *et al.*, 2006).

There is a debate about whether these positive effects benefit just the members and in what way they impact on outsiders. Social capital for some necessarily implies social exclusion for others (Harriss and Renzio, 1997). Caste in India, for example, can act in ways that benefit members by solving problems of information and contract enforcement in a traditional economy. Individuals are born into a particular caste and (traditionally) into a hereditary occupation. Interacting with fellow caste members, through dining, kinship networks and in the workplace can stimulate relations of trust and facilitate the acquisition of skills. Being able to observe the behaviour of individuals combined with the gossip of relatives ensures the group is well informed about anti-social behaviour such as cheating on contracts. Caste groups can enforce bilateral contracts among members, and provide group-level insurance or defence based on a network of reciprocal obligations. The dark side of this is that caste membership can hinder relations of trust between caste groups. Caste membership can facilitate exploitation as individuals may be deprived of the option to leave the caste and its hereditary occupation for a more lucrative occupation; this can also be prevented by higher-caste groups using their own caste membership.

Other types of horizontal associations (such as professional associations or trade unions) can hurt growth by acting as special-interest groups that seek to capture private benefits, prevent outsiders entering and so protect their monopoly benefits (Olson, 1982). Trade unions in Britain, for example, were often criticized for insisting on very long apprenticeships in various professions, not just because it facilitated more learning by new members but also because it slowed entry to the occupation and preserved the wages of insiders. There is little sign of a general relation between membership of associational groups and economic growth (Knack and Keefer, 1997). A particular problem with any such statistical testing is that it is difficult to account for the intensity of participation in such groups which would be obviously important.

A related example is that of the family business. Some of the biggest and most successful corporations in the world have been of this type, including the Murdochs at News Corporation and the Waltons at Walmart. Nearly three-quarters of firms in Hong Kong have at least a 20 per cent stake that is family owned. We can ask whether family firms evolve as an efficient response to market failures or are an outcome of cultural norms that might hinder corporate success. Family ties may, like caste or trust, substitute for either weak legal systems or the need to negotiate expensive contracts in countries without strong legal systems. A business may be able to trade over long distances through well-placed family members. As with the example of caste above, a family business may facilitate the exchange of skills and sharing of contacts among members. An important advantage of a family farm (and the often-cited reason why their productivity tends to be higher) is that fewer resources need to be spent on monitoring the effort of labour, though it makes it more difficult to dismiss a family member should they fail to perform efficiently.

An alternative cultural explanation for the existence of family in business is that the structure may be the result of norms of behaviour rather than a response to market incentives. Profit, for example, may be sacrificed to preserve other values such as nepotism through appointing a relative rather than the best-qualified manager. The growth of a family firm may be restricted to enable the existing pool of family members to cope with the managerial functions and avoid appointing any outsiders. Non-managerial employees may find that their aspirations for promotion are blocked so will be either less likely to exert effort or the most productive among them will seek promotion elsewhere. Evidence from the World Values Surveys from 1980 to 2000, which contain specific questions about the importance of family life, respect for parents, and duty to or independence from parents shows that countries where family is regarded as more important have smaller firms and lower levels of per capita GDP. There is also a strong negative correlation across countries between the strength of families and the level of trust a citizen places in other people (Bertrand *et al.*, 2006).

Key points

- There is a problem defining culture, which has led many economists to either ignore the concept or treat it as a residual in their analysis – ascribing to culture anything not explained by economics.
- The Weber hypothesis argues that Protestantism both discourages the luxurious and idle enjoyment of wealth and at the same time celebrates labour. Weber called the mix of hard work and the moral imperative to save 'worldly asceticism' and argued it is good for promoting economic growth.
- There is fairly consistent evidence in support of Weber, that Protestantism (and Catholicism a little less so) is good for economic growth.
- Among Protestants trust, belief in private ownership, anti-redistribution attitudes and literacy are stronger than in other religions. There are no consistent results for any other religions.
- There are particular problems with distinguishing the effects of belonging to a religion and participating in regular attendance/worship from the effects of group membership more generally.
- Various influential works argue that cultural diversity has been bad for economic growth. While many have argued that public policies impact on growth, some scholars have argued that ethnic differences help explain policy choice, so culture is the deep determinant of economic growth.
- There are three problems with the cultural diversity arguments: that culture is the central argument; distinguishing cultural from competitive political mobilization; and that they ignore the issue of causation.
- Institutions, in particular modern political parties, are a possible solution to problems of social divisions and conflict.
- Networks can have positive (and negative) impacts on economic outcomes and though religion can operate as a network like any other there is evidence of religion having an independent impact.
- Networks can benefit their members in part at the expense of individuals and groups who are not members.
- There is a debate about the merits or otherwise of the family firm for promoting economic growth.

Chapter 13

International Trade, Openness and Integration

Openness provokes widely different responses, depending on what aspects of openness are under discussion. While trade openness has long received much support from economists, it has frequently been viewed with suspicion by industry groups and trade unions threatened by foreign competition. Openness in terms of easier migration is generally supported by business keen to access cheap and educated labour from the global economy but strongly opposed by many who fear the greater competition for jobs and pressure on social services. FDI has been both opposed by nationalist governments anxious to avoid any sign of dependence on big foreign business (such as India's in the 1970s) and welcomed by nationalist governments keen to promote economic growth, modernization and national glory through accessing new technology (such as India's in the 1990s and 2000s). Much of this debate has been difficult for economists to engage with, particularly when openness is considered in terms of 'ideas from other countries' and so has been left to the more narrative-historical approaches of historians. Good examples of such debates discussed here include the closure of China to the rest of the world after the fifteenth century and the impact of the Spanish Inquisition in Europe from the late fifteenth century.

Openness and economic growth

Should 'openness' be considered as a deep determinant of growth? The most commonly debated aspect of openness is whether policy (tariffs and taxes) permits the free movement of goods and capital across international boundaries, so perhaps openness should be better considered as a policy-related proximate determinant. Other aspects of openness, such as to ideas or whether a country is landlocked and cannot participate competitively in international markets, have been considered to be aspects of culture and geography respectively.

Openness as a deep determinant influences economic growth through its impact on the proximate determinants: on the supply of labour via net immigration or migration; by changing the supply of capital through inward (or outward) foreign direct investment (FDI) or the drain of surplus (for example capital flight to safe investments in developed countries); by changing the incentives to invest (expanding domestic productive capacity to export onto a

Figure 13.1 *Openness as a deeper determinant of economic growth*

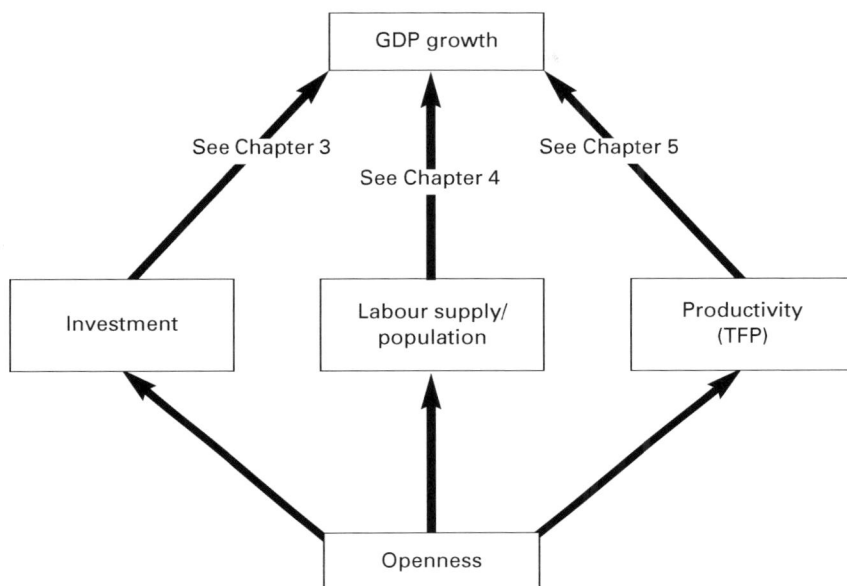

larger world market); and influencing productivity (through competition from the world market, exposure to new ideas and ability to import technology from the rest of the world). These links are illustrated in Figure 13.1.

This chapter shows how technological change is frequently an important driver of openness and has often been neglected in models of foreign trade (such as comparative advantage). Being able to export manufactured goods (and import agricultural goods) can be a driver of the structural change commonly associated with economic growth and development (see Chapter 8).

The basic trade model

The basic trade model forms the centrepiece of textbook treatments of international trade. The key result for the purposes of this chapter is the impact of an import tariff on a small developing country. The tariff will raise the price of imports and so prices of the good for domestic consumers. Higher prices will encourage more domestic production (import substitution) and reduced domestic consumption. The tariff will raise revenue for the government. The first impact is redistribution from consumers (what is known in economic theory as reduced consumer surplus) to producer profits and to government tax revenue. The second impact is a decline in efficiency. Higher domestic prices/profits of the good cause resources (land, labour, capital) to be re-allocated from other sectors of the economy to expand production in the now-protected sector. This re-allocation is caused by the trade intervention that raised the profitability in one sector by creating an artificial shortage. This is the loss in production efficiency due to the tariff. The higher prices faced by consumers cause them to shift consumption to other goods and services that they preferred not to consume before the price rise. This is the consumption cost due to the tariff. These latter two effects represent pure efficiency losses to the economy as a result of the tariff. The benefit from trade liberalization (removing this tariff) would be a one-off re-allocation of resources, removing this source of inefficiency.

Many economists have argued that there are also dynamic effects of trade protection/liberalization that may offset or reinforce these one-off effects (discussed in more detail later in the chapter). The government could use the tax revenue to invest in infrastructure and education which will raise the long-run growth rate of the economy. Trade protection may cut producers off from world competition, making them less inclined to undertake the efforts associated with cutting costs and mastering new technology.

Openness is about more than just trade. Openness also encompasses exposure to ideas and learning from overseas based on access to information and the physical movement of people. Openness can be related to policy, for example, controls on migration; it can be a matter of geography, such as whether a country is physically isolated; or it can be a matter of culture – how receptive is one culture to the innovations or heresies of another culture?

Patterns of openness

Table 13.1 shows that since the late nineteenth century there have been several major changes in patterns of openness. After the 1870s the UK's overwhelming dominance in the export of manufactured goods declined, though rising shares from elsewhere, particularly Germany, ensured Western Europe's share remained above 60 per cent. 'Western offshoots' saw their share increase, led by the US between the 1870s and 1950s, then subsequently decline, first with the emergence of Japan, and then in the 1980s and 1990s with the rise of China. In 2011, China was estimated to account for about 10 per cent of world exports. The growing presence of China in world manufactured exports is nothing new, nor yet on anything like the same scale as that experienced by previously dominant exporters.

Historically trade and other measures of global integration followed a 'U' shape, rising from the nineteenth century, declining between 1913 and 1950 then rising again to new heights in the post-war era. World merchandise exports as a percentage of world GDP increased from 5.1 per cent in 1850 to 11.9 per cent in 1913, fell to 7.1 per cent in 1950, then increased steadily to 17.1 per cent by the early 1990s (Krugman, 1995:331). For many countries only by the 1990s did trade ratios surpass levels achieved in 1910.

After about 1870 there was a surge in global capital market integration. This was led by London as the centre of the world's financial system and was

Table 13.1 *Regional percentage shares of world exports, 1870–1998*

	1870	1913	1950	1998
Western Europe	64.4	60.2	41.1	42.8
Western offshoots	7.5	12.9	21.3	18.4
Eastern Europe and former USSR	4.2	4.1	5.0	4.1
Latin America	5.4	5.1	8.5	9.8
Asia	13.9	10.8	8.5	4.9
Africa	4.6	6.9	10.0	2.7

Source: Data compiled from Maddison (2006:127).

facilitated by free movement of finance within the British Empire and through treaties with other countries. Between 1870 and 1913 the growth of foreign portfolio investment exceeded the growth of trade, FDI and GDP. Gross foreign assets as a ratio of world GDP increased from 6.9 per cent in 1870 to 17.5 per cent in 1913. With the dislocations of World War I and the onset of the world depression, by 1930 the ratio had collapsed to 8.4 per cent and the earlier peak was not reached again until the 1970s (Crafts, 2003:46). There was a looser relation between domestic investment and domestic savings (a measure of capital market integration) between 1890 and 1910 than in all subsequent periods up to 1990 (Wolf, 2004). This lending was funnelled to then-developing countries. As a share of GDP, capital outflow from the UK peaked at 9 per cent of GDP between 1870 and 1913. In late nineteenth-century Argentina the current account deficit was a huge 18.7 per cent of GDP which was largely funded by lending from Britain. These massive flows have no contemporary parallels. In the late nineteenth century half of all global lending went to Asia, Latin America and Oceania-Africa and a further 25 per cent to the US (Bairoch and Kozul-Wright, 1996). This forms an interesting comparison with the contemporary world, highlighted by the dependency theorists (see later in this chapter), with Africa currently a capital exporter to the developed world reversing this earlier pattern. By 1990 nearly 40 per cent of private wealth in Africa was held abroad, including in 1998 an estimated $100 billion held abroad by Nigerians (Collier, 2007).

International migration was important in the pre-World War I era and represented a degree of openness that has never been seen since. Between 1815 and 1915 about 60 million people left Europe for the Americas, 10 million migrated to Russia from Siberia and Central Asia, 1 million from southern Europe to Northern Africa, and 12 million Chinese and 6 million Japanese to East and South-east Asia. The peak of this process occurred in the 1890s when migrants totalled 26 per cent of the population of Argentina and 17 per cent of Australia; and over the decade 5 per cent of the population of the UK, 6 per cent of Spain and 7 per cent of Sweden migrated. By contrast during the 1990s immigration into the US was equal to about 4 per cent of initial population (Wolf 2004).

Influences on openness: policy

The traditional history of international trade explains the rising trade ratios of the nineteenth century as a consequence of trade policy liberalization that created a 'liberal international economic order'. This story has often been focused on Britain. The argument goes that Britain adopted free market and free trade policies in the eighteenth century, which were a key to its subsequent rise to trade and economic supremacy. This link became increasingly evident to other countries that later followed Britain's example leading to that global liberal order by 1870. A key event was the Cobden–Chevalier treaty of 1860 which saw the establishment of free trade between Britain and France. Free trade was achieved in the European colonies by colonial diktat and in independent developing countries (Latin America, China, Thailand and the Ottoman Empire) through the imposition of treaties. The Opium Wars of 1839–42 forced open China to British trade, which was recognized in the Treaty of Nanking in 1842. This traditional history sees this system unravelling after 1913 as import tariffs were increased with the outbreak of World War I and free trade being finally abandoned in the 1930s as Germany and Japan created controlled trade systems around the needs of their military-based economies and the US raised tariffs under the Smoot-Hawley Act in 1930. Between 1929 and 1932, due to a combination of trade protection and the Great Depression world trade fell by 70 per cent in value terms and 25 per cent in real terms. After World War II the world returned gradually to free(er) trade, this time promoted through the General Agreement on Trade and Tariffs (GATT) and World Trade Organization (WTO) under US leadership. After 1982 trade liberalization was given a new boost by the global debt crisis in which developing countries swapped policy reform (including, prominently, trade liberalization) for emergency lending from the IMF and World Bank. The reform movements in communist China (1980s onwards) and Russia (1990s onwards) saw them move away from autarchy and regionally based trade respectively to become more integrated with the global economy.

Other research shows that the real history of globalization is very different (Bairoch, 1993; Wolf, 2004; Chang, 2007). There was only a very brief period between the 1860s and 1870s when there was free trade in Europe. Trade protection returned much earlier than allowed for in the conventional history. Germany increased tariffs in 1879, France in 1892 and Italy, Sweden, and Spain throughout the 1880s and 1890s. The motivation was both to protect farmers from cheap New World agricultural imports and promote newly emerging heavy and chemical industries. Free trade was maintained much longer in Britain and tariffs were reintroduced only in 1932. As treaty obligations lapsed Japan regained its autonomy over tariff policy in the late 1890s and increased tariffs, as did some Latin American countries, including Brazil, after 1870. In both cases the motive was to promote domestic industrialization. The granting by Britain of tariff independence to the self-governing colonies, Canada, Australia and New Zealand, saw them all (especially Canada) raise tariffs though they continued to give some preference to imports from Britain (Bairoch and Kozul-Wright, 1996). In the US the 1816 tariff law imposed an average tariff of 35 per cent on almost all manufactured goods, in particular cotton, woollen and iron goods, which were raised again in 1824 and 1864. US tariffs on manufactured goods averaged about 45 per cent in 1875 and 44 per cent in 1913 which was one of the highest average rates in the world (Bairoch and Kozul-Wright, 1996:8; Chang, 2002, 2003). This alternative view shows that rising trade ratios were related to deliberate policies to promote the production and subsequent export of manufactured goods rather than to opening up to free competition from imports.

In the contemporary global economy it is a longstanding criticism of developed countries that their trade tariffs and subsidies undermine exports from developing countries. The highest tariffs in the US are commonly those on imports of labour-intensive manufactured goods, especially textiles and clothing. The average European cow receives a subsidy of $2 a day while more than half the people in the developing world live on less than that. OECD figures show that total assistance to rich-country farmers was $311 billion in 2001, which was then six times greater than all development assistance and greater than the GDP of Sub-Saharan Africa. Evidence of the impact of developed-country subsidies comes from patterns of trade displacement. Sub-Saharan African market shares of oil seeds, vegetable oils, groundnuts, kernels and palm oil steadily declined after independence. The biggest source of displacement from the 1960s through to the 1990s was not other developing countries but a highly subsidised OECD agriculture (Ng and Yeats, 1997). In the early 2000s the US and EU accounted for around half of all world wheat exports with prices 46 per cent and 34 per cent below costs of production. The EU is the world's largest exporter of skimmed milk powder, provided at half the costs of production, and also the largest exporter of white sugar, provided at quarter of the costs of production (Wolf, 2004). In Benin, Burkina Faso, Chad, Mali and Togo cotton production amounts to a significant proportion of GDP and a large share of agricultural earnings. In Mali cotton production in 2000–01 was 9 per cent of GDP and 38 per cent of merchandise exports and in Benin 5.3 per cent of GDP and 66 per cent of merchandise exports. At the same time in the US, 25,000 cotton farmers shared $3–4 billion in subsidies with a quarter of this total going to 30,000 large farms (Sachs *et al.*, 2004).

Other research casts doubt on the argument that the key reasons for poor African export performance are the policy decisions of developed countries. The pattern of protection cannot explain the failures of African countries relative to other developing countries. UNCTAD statistics on OECD trade barriers between the early 1960s and early 1990s show that Sub-Saharan Africa faced lower tariffs on exports to Japan, US and EU than the average of all developing countries. Tariffs on Zambian exports to the EU were 2.9 per cent lower than the developing-country average, while those for Taiwan were 4.0 per cent and South Korea 4.2 per cent higher than the average. Non-tariff barriers covered an average of 11 per cent of Africa's non-fuel exports compared with an average of 17 per cent for all developing countries. 19 per cent of African textile exports were covered by non-tariff barriers (mainly Mauritius to US) compared with an average of 53 per cent for all developing countries (Ng and Yeats, 1997). Developed countries do not protect many of the key agricultural products exported by the poorest African countries, such as coffee, tea, and cocoa, because they do not have any domestic production to protect. Protection and subsidies are mainly focused on temperate-zone agricultural products like wheat, beef and dairy. Only two developing countries (Brazil and Argentina) are major exporters of these products (Chang, 2007). This implies that the main beneficiaries of the opening up of agricultural markets in developed countries would be those countries with strong agriculture such as the US, Canada, Australia and New Zealand. There is little evidence that liberalization in products produced and exported by developing countries would have much impact. An estimate shows that global cotton liberalization would raise the world price by approximately 13 per cent, giving West African cotton exporters a 1–2 per cent increase in GDP. By comparison their foreign aid needs have been estimated to be over 20 per cent of GNP (Sachs *et al.,* 2004).

Influences on openness: technology

The second explanation/hypothesis focuses on technological change: usually that some form of new or improved infrastructure facilitates the growth of international trade. This is an interesting case study for those landlocked parts of the globe who, many argue, need a 'big push' in investment to enable them to participate in global trading networks.

In the US the construction of the Erie canal between 1817 and 1825 reduced the cost of transport between Buffalo and New York by 85 per cent and cut the journey time from 21 to 8 days. The US transcontinental railways reduced the cost of shipping a bushel of wheat from New York to Liverpool by half between 1830 and 1880, then by half again between 1880 and 1914. The Suez Canal, opened in 1869, reduced the length of a journey from London to Bombay by 41 per cent and from London to Shanghai by 32 per cent. Over the 1850s and 1860s four innovations (the screw propeller, iron hulls, compound engines and surface condensers) significantly lowered the cost of steam-powered ocean transport. Iron-hulled ships were 30–40 per cent lighter and offered 15 per cent more cargo capacity for a given amount of steam power (Clark, 2007:308). Mechanical refrigeration was developed between 1834 and 1861, and by the 1880s South American meat, Australian meat and New Zealand butter were being exported to Europe in large quantities. Before the first transatlantic cable was laid in 1866, it took ten days for information to travel from London to New York and ten days back; this was reduced to one. There was an immediate 69 per cent reduction in average price differentials for the same financial asset in the two cities. Over the twentieth century new improvements have included radio, television, transcontinental telephone links, satellite, computer and internet technology. Between 1930 and 1990 the unit cost of air transport fell more than 80 per cent. The cost of a three-minute phone call from New York to London fell from $250 in 1930 to few cents by the 1990s and with the internet it is now close to zero (O'Rourke and Williamson, 1999; Wolf 2004).

Trade liberalization: the debate

There has been an extensive theoretical and empirical debate about the impact of trade liberalization. The general trend over recent decades has been towards more support from academics and policy-makers for trade liberalization. There are important pre-conditions for trade liberalization to be good for growth: a sufficient time lag for the economy to adjust; sufficient infrastructure; trade liberalization considered credible; liberalization not squeezing out other more beneficial reforms and not leading to a serious squeeze on government finances.

The first step towards the contemporary popularity of trade liberalization was the accumulation in the 1970s of empirical evidence against trade protection and import substitution. In the late 1960s the OECD sponsored a study of seven developing countries which were summarized in an influential volume by Little, Scitovsky and Scott (1970). These studies found that the use of tariffs had raised the relative price of industrial output and so had motivated a shift in investment from agriculture to industry. These newly emerging industrial sectors were discovered to be very inefficient as tariffs had simultaneously removed the pressures to compete against imports by improving quality or price competitiveness. The use of over-valued exchange rates was a common tool to promote import substitution by making the imports of capital equipment and inputs for industry cheaper. This tended to made exports less competitive so made export pessimism self-fulfilling, reduced the incentive to produce such capital equipment domestically and biased domestic production to the use of imported and capital-intensive production methods. This latter feature led to slow employment growth as employers imported machines cheaply to carry out tasks in factories and farms rather than employ people, reduced the progress of poverty reduction and led to continued import dependence. The use of tariffs, quotas and licenses to allocate resources replaced the market with a bureaucratic form of allocation and opened up opportunities for corruption of the political and administrative systems.

The second step was a growing belief that governments, however well-intentioned, would be unable to implement good trade interventions. Theory and evidence offered no guide as to what 'good trade policy' actually constituted. How, for example, were policy-makers in the 1950s and 1960s supposed to distinguish an infant industry? How much protection was necessary to stimulate dynamic externalities? In practice many countries granted trade protection as soon as production became feasible and the policy contained no provision to measure whether learning was occurring or externalities being stimulated or for protection to be reduced after a specified period. Even had the mechanics of trade policy been clear, Friedrich Hayek argued that it was a 'fatal conceit' that the economy can be brought under central direction and control and that the state could plan for infant industries or dynamic external-ities. Planners cannot find out what needs to be done to co-ordinate the production of a modern economy. It is impossible for planners to know what hundreds of millions of different people would choose or desire. The avail-ability of skilled manpower is limited in developing countries and there are real opportunity costs to employing the skilled/educated in the public sector. Focusing policy-making on areas such as manufacturing, foreign exchange markets, regulating credit and investment licensing diverts government resources away from those activities where they might be better advised to intervene, such as the enforcement of contracts, provision of public services like primary school and basic public goods such as roads and communications (Krueger, 1997).

The third step was a closer examination of the assumption that governments are well-intentioned. The early development economists had focused on market failures as an argument against free trade but had not given equivalent consideration to the government. They seem to have suggested the state was some sort of selfless guardian that could costlessly intervene to give a big push to investment or to correct externalities. They assumed a combination of self-interest in the private sector and public interest in the public sector. An impor-tant question they ignored was whether government failure could be worse than market failure. Decisions regarding economic policy are made by politi-cians who respond to political pressures. The creation of a new industrial sector automatically creates an interest group keen for more subsidies and unlikely to want any exposure to the perils of foreign competition. This means there will be a tendency for an increasing proliferation of policy instruments as various groups assert competing and conflicting claims (Krueger, 1990). There is general agreement that the measureable benefits from re-allocating resources as a consequence of trade liberalization are no more than 2–3 per cent of GDP. To the direct costs of government controls or intervention we then need to add all the resources expended in acquiring, protecting and expanding the benefits from government intervention (subsidies and protection against imports). Resources will also have been wasted by individuals who lobbied for but failed to acquire rents (Krueger, 1974).

The fourth step was the development of more positive arguments in favour of trade liberalization. Trade liberalization, according to its proponents, is likely to be good for growth for a variety of reasons. Trade liberalization will divert entrepreneurial energies away from trying to boost profits by securing more trade protection from the government and towards efforts to introduce new products and processes to compete with imports. Competition from foreign imports and for foreign markets will force firms to reduce inefficiency, reduce costs and improve quality. Trade liberalization will give firms access to better-quality imported capital goods which will increase the efficiency and productivity of domestic production. Openness to world markets will give domestic firms access to the ideas, spillovers and learning associated with engaging in a larger world economy.

This argument has certainly been influential. There has been a general shift towards more open trade regimes the world over. In 1960, 22 per cent of all countries (21 per cent of the global population) had open trade policies and by 2000 this had risen to 93 per cent of all countries (and 46 per cent of the world's population) (Wacziarg and Welch, 2008:187).

Trade liberalization and statistical testing

Empirical testing has come a long way since those OECD studies of the early 1970s but very profound problems remain with both the methodology and results.

Dollar (1992) constructed an index that measures the extent to which the real exchange rate is distorted away from its free-trade level by the trade regime through, for example, import tariffs or export subsidies. He found that this index had a significant and negative relation with investment and growth. Between 1976 and 1985 exchange rates in Latin America were 33 per cent and in Africa 86 per cent overvalued relative to Asia. From this he concludes that 'outward oriented countries grow more rapidly'. However, the index does not necessarily achieve Dollar's claims for it. Changes in the nominal exchange rate due to concerns about a country's debt solvency, for example, would be likely to produce large changes in the real exchange rate which would lead to a change in the index for reasons unrelated to trade policy.

Sachs and Warner's influential index (1995) used a binary measure, meaning countries would be classified as either 'open' or 'closed'. Their index labelled countries as open if they fulfilled five criteria: average tariffs were less than 40 per cent; non-tariff barriers covered less than 40 per cent of imports; the country did not have a socialist economic regime; there was no state monopoly of major exports; and the black-market premium on the exchange rate was less than 20 per cent over the 1970s and 1980s. The index accounts for the difficulty otherwise faced in statistical work that there are different ways to close the economy. This study showed that countries passing all five tests had GDP growth 2.5 per cent higher between 1970 and 1989 than those not passing all five. This index has been criticized, as only two of these variables ('state export monopoly' and 'black-market premium') explained most of the growth impact of the index and these variables were in turn correlated with other determinants of growth. State export monopolies are closely related to being a country in Sub-Saharan Africa and the black-market premium for being a country in Latin America. Therefore the statistical tests of the index were actually concluding that Sub-Saharan Africa and Latin America were slow growing in the 1970s and 1980s and so the index was really a proxy for variables uncorrelated to trade policy (Rodriquez and Rodrik, 2000).

Three studies address these specific empirical problems. The first notes that despite the problems with methodology the results of test after test point relentlessly to trade liberalization having a positive effect on growth (Edwards, 1998), the second improves measures of trade policy (Dollar and Kraay, 2004) and the third corrects many of the problems in the 1995 Sachs and Warner paper (Wacziarg and Welch, 2008).

Edwards (1998) uses nine different indices of trade policy for 93 countries and finds a generally positive link between openness and TFP growth. Rodriquez and Rodrik (2000) criticize various aspects of the methodology but less convincingly, given that so many measures of trade policy all point to a positive relation. Dollar and Kraay (2004) make a convincing statistical effort that addresses some of the concerns raised by the critics. A key problem in many studies is that there is no generally accepted measure of trade policy or trade liberalization. Dollar and Kraay use decade-by-decade changes in trade volumes as a proxy for changes in trade policy. Focusing on changes in trade volumes means the results are less likely to be driven by fixed geographical factors such as whether a country is landlocked. They define those countries who cut import tariffs significantly (22 percentage points on average) as 'globalizers' and the rest (11 percentage point reduction in tariffs on average) as 'non-globalizers'. The post-1980s globalizers are well known reformers and include China, India, Mexico, Uganda, Vietnam, Bangladesh and Nepal. Among globalizers GDP growth was 1.7 per cent per annum in the 1970s, 2.6 per cent in the 1980s, and 5.3 per cent during the 1990s. Non-globalizers experienced declining growth 2.8 per cent in the 1970s, 0.2 per cent 1980s, and –0.8 per cent during the 1990s. This measure is better and the results more convincing but it is still not ideal. Changes in trade volume may happen for reasons unrelated to policy such as bad weather reducing output and so exports of agricultural goods.

Wacziarg and Welch (2008) update the data, method and results from Sachs and Warner (1995) to present a comprehensive cross-country database of trade indicators (tariffs, non-tariff barriers and other measures of trade restrictions). This new data set includes more data on non-tariff barriers and thirty new countries. The Export Marketing Board variable that was criticized as applying only to African countries is expanded in the new data to encompass any form of state monopoly over exporters and so no longer applies just to African countries. They also extend the Sachs and Warner results on outward orientation and growth into the 1990s. Finally they identify the changes in growth, investment rates and openness associated with a significant change in trade policy. They define a date of liberalization as being that moment after which all of the Sachs-Warner openness criteria are continuously fulfilled. Over the entire sample period (1950 to 1998) Wacziarg and Welch find growth of per capita GDP in a country with a liberalized trade regime is 2.71 per cent and in a country without a liberalized trade regime 1.18 per cent. The results vary over time. Trade liberalization in the 1970s has a weaker impact than in the 1980s and the impact of trade liberalization is positive but only very weakly so during the 1990s. They also examine how GDP growth and investment rates evolve for 20 years before and after liberalization in a sample of 81 countries that underwent permanent liberalizations. The results show that economic growth increases by about 1.5 per cent (from 1.5 to 3.0 per cent) after reforms and the impact is immediate and persistent. The investment rate takes off during the 10 years after liberalization and remains high thereafter. After separating out other reforms (such as domestic deregulation and privatization) they find that it was trade liberalization that explained the bulk of the positive impact on growth and investment.

The literature discussed above relates to trade policy and economic growth. The evidence linking productivity growth to trade liberalization is probably even more confusing. It is often argued that long-term productivity gains will result from trade liberalization working through the competitive pressures of the world economy. The literature examining this link shows no clear empirical results. Some studies show a negative and weak correlation between import substitution and productivity growth; in others TFP is high in protected sectors; in others there is continued and accelerating TFP pre- and post-protection; and in still others high levels of import penetration are associated with low rates of productivity growth. The common finding that more efficient firms *do* engage in exporting could be because exporting compels improvements in efficiency, but it could also be because more efficient firms are better able to compete in overseas markets (Deraniyagala and Fine, 1999).

Trade liberalization and case-study evidence

A case for case studies in studying economic growth was made in Chapter 2. In-depth case studies of single or several countries can allow scholars to get a general feel for whether trade liberalization is associated with more rapid economic growth.

Contemporary case studies

Detailed case-study data is available for the change in growth, investment rates and openness ratios between pre- and post-liberalization periods for 24 countries. This uses the Sachs and Warner (1995) index for openness further developed by Wacziarg and Welch (2008). The measure defines 'trade liberalization' as being that moment when a country was defined as being continuously 'open' according to the five criteria listed by Sachs and Warner. The data reveal increased economic growth in 13 of the 24 countries, negative in six and no discernible growth impact in 5. Among countries with a positive growth difference, the magnitude of the growth increase ranged from a 0.83 percentage points increase in per capita income growth in Poland to 3.62 percentage points in Mauritius. There are large variations in before-and-after comparisons of investment. Post-liberalization increases in investment rates were striking in South Korea, Taiwan, Indonesia, Jordan and Guinea-Bissau, while about half of the 24 countries exhibited zero or negative changes in investment rates. Examination of the case studies suggests that the packaging and timing of reforms are important factors in explaining difference in post-liberalization growth patterns. Countries that liberalized then continued to deepen trade reforms over time appeared to do the best.

Historical case studies
In Britain trade liberalization after 1846 was accompanied by an acceleration in the growth of foreign trade and in economic growth. Export growth increased from 5 per cent annually between 1830 and 1845 to over 6 per cent until 1860. Economic growth between 1845 and 1860 averaged 2.4 per cent which was the highest that Britain would attain until after 1945. This, the outcome of the world's first free-trade experiment, was positive but was based on a unique starting point. It occurred long after the onset of the industrialization in Britain that had been achieved behind high tariff barriers. Britain in 1846 was the overwhelmingly dominant world manufacturing nation and could rely on exporting manufactured goods from sectors with increasing returns to scale (Bairoch, 1993; Chang, 2002). Britain also possessed an enormous colonial empire to which it had guaranteed access for both exports and imports. The evidence about whether trade liberalization also benefited the contemporary and more backward economies of Europe is more complicated.

At first glance there appears to be a negative relationship between trade openness and economic growth in nineteenth-century Europe. The liberal phase of European trade policies after 1860 reached its height between 1866 and 1877 and occurred with the onset of a generalized economic slowdown. Per capita GDP growth in European countries slowed from an annual rate of 1.6 per cent in the 1850s and 1860s to 0.6 per cent for the next two decades. This can be explained by the flood of imported grain leading to slower growth in agriculture which then still accounted for a large share of GDP across Europe. In France, for example, imports of wheat rose from 0.3 per cent of domestic production in the 1850s to 19 per cent in the late 1880s and in Belgium from 6 per cent in 1850 to 100 per cent in 1890. The problem was that offsetting exports of manufactured goods from Europe which could have sustained growth did not occur. Between the 1870s and 1880s the US as the main supplier of grain to Europe did not increase imports of European manufactures. In 1870 continental Europe's trade deficit with North America represented 5–6 per cent of imports from that region and this reached 32 per cent by 1890 and 59 per cent by 1900. The US was growing and industrializing rapidly behind high levels of import tariffs (Bairoch, 1993). The rise of trade protectionism in Europe from the 1880s onwards coincided with more rapid growth of GDP and trade. Average annual GDP growth increased from 1.3 per cent to 3.1 per cent in Germany during the ten years after trade protection increased in 1885. Similar increases occurred in Sweden, France, Belgium and Denmark. Export growth tended to slow in the ten years immediately after increased trade protection but after the passing of another decade showed significant acceleration across Western Europe (Bairoch and Kozul-Wright, 1996:22).

Examining all of this with a broad statistical test shows that there is a clear positive correlation between tariff rates and economic growth among 17 now-developed countries between 1870 and 1913. The result seems to show openness was bad for economic growth, but note that this historical correlation is driven by several key outliers (US, Canada and Argentina). These three countries were high-tariff/high-growth countries. Without them the correlation disappears. These three were the labour-scarce/land- and resource-abundant New World economies that had the most potential for rapid growth. In Argentina and Canada trade policy was not designed to promote import-substituting industrialization. Growth in both cases was based on an FDI-led infrastructure investment boom that in turn promoted an export boom in staple products. Tariffs in these countries tended to be levied on key commodities such as alcohol, coffee, sugar, tea and tobacco, motivated by the need to raise revenue for the government not to protect and promote the growth of domestic manufacturing. The US did achieve high, industrial-led growth based on high tariff protection but the link was not a general one (Irwin, 2000).

Even more disaggregated industry-level case-study evidence suggests further caution regarding the apparent positive link between trade protection and economic growth. The important question or counterfactual we need to ask is: how would industry have developed in the absence of tariffs? A detailed case study of the US tinplate industry attempts to answer this question. Tin plate is a sub-sector of the iron and steel industry. There was virtually no domestic production of tinplate in the late 1860s and US consumption was largely met through imports from the UK. The McKinley tariff of 1890 raised the duty (from 30 to over 70 per cent) on imported tinplate to encourage the entry and growth of domestic producers. Domestic production expanded after 1891, capturing nearly 90 per cent of the market by 1899. In 1869 the price of basic bar iron in the US was double that in the UK and only by about 1910 did the price of US tinplate fall below UK prices and the US become a net exporter. Douglas Irwin estimates that without the McKinley tariff the US tinplate industry would have established itself about a decade later based on the country's abundance of iron ore and coal. Further, he argues that the initial large loss of consumer welfare/surplus resulting from higher domestic prices was not offset by the stream of profits received by protected domestic producers, so protection had a net cost to the US economy (Irwin, 2000).

Trade liberalization and growth

The empirical and case-study results generally indicate a positive if small but non-robust, varied and seemingly unpredictable link from trade liberalization to economic growth and an even more confusing and ambiguous link from trade liberalization to productivity growth. A good reason is that we are asking the wrong question. Rather than asking *if* trade liberalization is good for growth, we would be better to ask: *under what circumstances* is trade liberalization good for growth?' There is very good reason to believe that the relationship is a heavily contingent one. Trade liberalization is only likely to be good for growth with a sufficient time lag, if there is sufficient infrastructure, if trade liberalization is considered credible, and if trade liberalization does not lead to a serious squeeze on government finances. These contingent factors are discussed here in turn.

Trade liberalization and resource re-allocation

The theory underlying the expectations of a positive link between trade liberalization and higher income (the model outlined very briefly at the outset of this chapter) assumes perfect markets (Stiglitz, 2007:28). Markets must work efficiently to ensure that resources displaced from one sector as a result of trade liberalization are quickly re-allocated to other sectors. Labour, for example, is assumed to migrate easily into other jobs without facing lingering unemployment. The inevitable time delay in such adjustment could account for the failure of empirical studies (which tend to focus on the contemporaneous impact) to reveal a strong link from trade liberalization to higher incomes or higher growth. However, it is not easy to measure the lagged benefits of trade liberalization.

Trade liberalization and geography

Trade liberalization is not enough. Countries need infrastructure to take advantage of trade liberalization; these include the roads, ports and warehouses necessary for producers to send goods overseas at low cost. Chapter 11 shows that being landlocked and hence isolated from international markets has a significant impact on levels and growth of GDP in developing countries.

Trade liberalization and policy credibility

The link from trade policy to growth may be difficult to discern unless the 'credibility' of trade policy reform is properly accounted for. Trade-policy reform will only work to the extent that it motivates entrepreneurs and workers to shift factors of production (land, capital and labour) away from less productive import substitution/non-traded sectors to more productive export oriented/traded sectors. In the process there are various adjustment costs such as re-training workers or the physical loss of machinery that is not suitable for producing in new sectors. The willingness of entrepreneurs and workers to bear these costs depends on their shared expectations as to the likely staying power of reforms (this is discussed in relation to investment in Chapter 3). Trade liberalization may not be considered credible if it is accompanied by an import surge (as import tariffs are reduced), resulting in an unsustainable balance-of-payments deficit; if the cuts in tariffs generate an unsustainable government budget deficit; if liberalization causes redistribution of income in the domestic economy that is not politically sustainable (if those benefiting from import controls are politically influential); or if government is not really committed to the liberalization (because it has been imposed by the IMF/World Bank in return for emergency lending). If individuals don't believe in the credibility of trade reform or even just wait to gauge whether the government will sustain it, investment and labour will not shift to the export sector. Liberalization will then lead to an import surge and no export response and the reform effort will likely collapse in face of an unsustainable balance-of-payments deficit (Rodrik, 1989).

The government can undertake efforts to enhance the credibility of reform by convincing the private sector of its commitment to reform, reducing any possible future incentives to reverse policies, and making it more difficult to change course if such temptation does nonetheless arise. A good example of such efforts is to sign international treaties to join up with a free trade bloc. Such agreements were when Eastern European countries have joined the EU to lock in free trade after the collapse of communism, or in Mexico's decision to join NAFTA. A crisis may make reforms easier to implement. In Poland in the early 1990s a macroeconomic crisis motivated a new leadership to implement reform including trade liberalization and provided an outgoing leadership and ideology (communism) to take the political blame for any problems experienced. The 1980s world debt crisis gave the IMF/World Bank great leverage in pushing for the implementation of sustained trade liberalization, especially in poorer African countries.

Trade liberalization and government revenue
Trade liberalization in a developing country will almost inevitably lead to a loss of government revenue and so force fiscal adjustment elsewhere. The structural features typical of a developing country include the large dispersed, low-income subsistence sector in agriculture and small-scale informal sector in urban areas, the weakness of the tax administration, and the lack of good accounting systems which together make raising tax revenue from income and consumption taxes very difficult. Imports tend to enter a country through a few ports and airports so are usually easier to collect taxes on than millions of income earners or consumers or thousands of (small) businesses. In the 1990s trade taxes (predictably) contributed almost 35 per cent of tax revenue in low-income countries and less than 1 per cent in high-income countries. It is not therefore just a trade-policy choice that developing countries have relied on import tariffs to raise tax revenue. A dataset of 80 countries between 1970 and the late 1980s shows that developing countries, especially the lowest-income countries, suffered declining tax revenues as a result of trade liberalization, which forced reductions in infrastructure and education spending (Khattry and Rao, 2002; Khattry, 2003).

Openness and the bigger picture: power, ideas and consumption

So far this chapter has focused on the narrower question of trade in goods. The influence of openness is potentially far more general: openness can encompass power or ideas and can transform people's living conditions.

Dependency theory

Much theorizing about development, and indeed the very expressions 'developed country' and 'less developed country' suggest that economic development occurs in a succession of stages and today's developing countries are at some earlier stage. The implicit argument is that development is something diffused from developed to developing countries so openness is crucial and beneficial even if it has to be managed. Recent critiques of current international economic relations have focused on arguing for more donor aid or greater access to developed-country agricultural markets. Free-market economists have instead emphasized the need to push developing countries to adopt good (i.e., free-market) policies. Both perspectives accept that openness is inherently a good thing even if they disagree on how to manage the engagement between developed and developing countries. The dependency school of economics and social science takes a very different view. Dependency scholars argue that openness and integration, whether considered in terms of economics, social or political criteria, is a 'bad thing' and has an adverse impact on growth and development (Lall, 1975:800).

The dependency school agrees that openness is the crucial deep determinant of long-run economic growth and development. Dependency writers begin with a global-historical perspective. Andre Gunner Frank argues 'We cannot hope to formulate adequate development theory and policy for the majority of the world's population who suffer from underdevelopment without first learning how their past economic and social history gave rise to their present underdevelopment' (1966:4), and a focus on single country case studies 'fails to explain the structure and development of the capitalist system as a whole and to account for its simultaneous generation of underdevelopment in some of its parts and of economic development in others' (1966:5). Dependency theorists argue that underdevelopment is not an original starting point and that the present of developing countries does not resemble the past of the now-developed countries. Contemporary underdevelopment, they argue, is in large part 'the historical product of past and continuing economic and other relations between the satellite and the now-developed metropolitan countries' (1966:5). Contemporary underdevelopment, according to this argument, is the result of past exploitation. The corollary of these viewpoints is that the underdeveloped parts of the world will do better when isolated from contact with developed countries. This has happened, argues Frank, during the Napoleonic wars, World War I, the Great Depression in the 1930s and World War II, when Latin America (especially Argentina, Brazil and Mexico) lost contact with developed countries and experienced promising spells of industrialization. Frank advocates a deliberate severing of ties with the developed world (called 'delinking') to promote independent growth and industrialization.

While dependency scholars may agree on some fundamental issues there is much less agreement on how exactly this exploitation and underdevelopment actually occurs. The nature of dependency has certainly changed over time.

Early dependency centred on the sixteenth-century Spanish and Portuguese conquest of the Americas, which was based around exploitation through a colonial monopoly of trade, land, mines and labour. Minerals and primary products were forcibly extracted, often through various forms of coerced labour, to yield a substantial surplus which was then 'drained' back to the colonial home base. By the nineteenth century this had shifted to a pattern of exploitation based on foreign investment to extract raw materials and agricultural products (again) at low prices for the home market/industry (Dos Santos, 1970). Other authors have recently emphasized instead the technological dependence of developing countries. Tightened regulations on patents and copyrights on technology (Chapter 10) may hinder the process of technological diffusion to developing countries and strengthen the monopoly power of developed countries who can earn more from royalties and licensing fees and cement their monopoly position in lucrative high-tech sectors. Financial dependency may today be even more important than that based on technology. The ability of the US government to control the issue of dollars which is the international reserve currency and means of international payment has given the US coercive power through its ability to manipulate interest rates and influence capital flows (Vernengo, 2006).

The most commonly discussed economic characteristics of dependence are high levels of foreign investment, the use of advanced, foreign, capital intensive technologies in a relatively small industrial sector, specialization in the exports of primary commodities and (sometimes) labour-intensive manufactures, elite consumption patterns influenced by those of the advanced countries, unequal exchange in various senses and growing inequalities in income distribution and rising unemployment, especially in urban areas. It is, very difficult to define a state of dependence or look for evidence of dependence on this basis. Some countries in the centre such as Denmark, Belgium, and Switzerland have always been economically dependent upon some larger capitalist countries such as Germany or France. Switzerland historically used a close and subordinate relation to Germany to its own advantage. The Swiss chemical and pharmaceutical industries were based on technologies actively stolen and copied from Germany. Concerning consumption, the fact that elite tastes are influenced from abroad and different from the mass of the population is not a new phenomenon nor confined to dependent countries. Ancient Britons in the second century were quick to adopt the dress and consumption habits of their imperial Roman masters. The assumption that dependent economies are *forced* to specialize in the export of primary products or simple manufactured goods is contradicted by the experience of numerous developing countries that have upgraded and diversified the structure of their exports. Increasing inequalities in income and the growing marginalization of large numbers of people in developing countries is not true of all dependent economies and was also typical of the early stages of capitalist growth among the now developed countries. There are also marginalized under-classes in the developed countries typified by growing informal sectors, sweat-shop labour and a population of floating and often illegal migrants (Lall, 1975).

In summary, the concept of dependence as applied to developing countries 'is usually given an arbitrary selective definition which picks certain features of a much broader phenomenon of international capitalist development, and its selectivity only serves to misdirect analysis and research in this area' (Lall, 1975:809).

The strongest evidence against the notion of generalized 'development of underdevelopment' is the rapid and sustained growth performances of many developing countries, which makes the predictive powers of the dependency school very poor. Some developing countries have experienced rapid and sustained growth including, among others, South Korea, Taiwan, Thailand and Malaysia. Chapter 8 showed that diversification away from agriculture to manufacturing and services is now characteristic of the developing world as a whole. Measures of dependence from the mid-1960s relating to foreign aid and international trade show no significant correlation with 23 measures of subsequent economic performance (McGowan, 1976).

There have been two principal responses to these criticisms. The first argues that these empirical problems exist because the nature of dependency has changed over time and this change is difficult to capture in statistical testing. MNCs in the 1960s started investing in the industrial sectors of dominated economies instead of just in agriculture and minerals, and so the old pattern of exchanging raw materials for industrialized goods was no longer true. Increasingly MNCs (dependency theorist Fernando Henrique Cardoso mentions GM, Sears Roebuck and GE) wanted to not just extract resources but to produce for markets in developing countries. This more pragmatic view no longer saw the combination of dependency, MNC investment and economic development as an empirical puzzle; some scholars now argued that growth in developing countries was possible even in a context of dependency – a sort of dependent development as opposed to dependent underdevelopment (Cardoso, 1972). While more accommodating to the facts, this theoretical flexibility started losing the dependency school many adherents. If the theory is flexible enough to fit any facts, has the theory any value? The second approach, and one that became increasingly common, has been to dismiss dependency. This has been done both by mainstream scholars arguing in favour of the theory of comparative advantage and trade liberalization and also, as outlined in Chapter 9, in work most famously by Bill Warren who made a powerful contribution from a Classical Marxist perspective arguing that dependency had declined sharply in the post-1945 era.

Openness to ideas: a case study of China and Europe

Much of this chapter has been concerned with trade liberalization, the problems of defining and measuring trade liberalization and relating it empirically to economic growth. Openness to ideas is a much bigger question and one not so suitable to statistical testing, but one which has had a crucial impact on world history: if 'the gains from trade in commodities are substantial, they are small compared with trade in ideas' (Landes,1998:136).

The Spanish Inquisition from the late fifteenth century was an attempt to assert the dominance of the Catholic Church and its ideas against free-thinking heresy and foreign ideas in the late sixteenth century. Copernicus, Galileo and Newton were banned by the Spanish Jesuits until 1746 and those printing presses that were permitted were monopolized by clerical hands. This attempt at despotism in Europe was mitigated by territorial partition. If ideas were banned in one country they could move and their inventors with them (see Chapter 11 on the importance of geographical fragmentation in Europe). While the Spanish attempted repression, cheaper printing and spreading literacy were elsewhere giving new ideas wider circulation (Roberts, 1985). Thousands of Europeans in the eighteenth century came to feel that they were part of a movement in which educated men (and less often women) could think and reject inherited tradition. This became known as the Enlightenment. The movement was based on a new scientific emphasis and rational scepticism that gradually undermined religious belief. Though modern science had roots in Islamic and Chinese science and Indian mathematics it was fundamentally an 'artefact of post-Renaissance western culture; (Roberts, 1985:158). The new science was found first in observations, then in recording and dissemination of those records. The notion of experimentation and the testing of hypotheses by replicable means was aided by generalized explanations of how the universe worked from Copernicus, Kepler and Galileo. The 'crucial change in the making of the modern mind was the widespread acceptance of the idea that the world is essentially rational and explicable' (Roberts, 1985:161). Their ideas spread rapidly across Protestant Europe but long remained heretical in Spain and other Catholic countries.

China had two chances (Landes, 1998, 2006). The first was to generate a sustained internal process of scientific and technological advance on the basis of its indigenous achievement and the second was to learn from European science and technology once contact was made in the sixteenth century. China failed at both (this is discussed in more detail in Chapter 7). Pre-empting Britain and Europe in industry (textiles, porcelain and iron manufacture), agricultural technology (wheelbarrow, stirrup, rigid horse collar), the means of order and administration (clocks and paper), trade (the compass and shipping) and military (gunpowder), China yet failed to realize the potential of these inventions and go on to have an industrial revolution after the fifteenth century. Many authors have stressed the lack of openness as being crucial in explaining this failure. In 1368, for example, the new Ming Emperor wished to enforce social stability and so ordered that people were to stay put and move only with state permission, whether home or abroad. Migration was made subject to the death penalty. After the early decades of its rule the Ming Dynasty (1368–1644) prohibited all overseas trade. The second, later chance was to learn from foreigners. But China was the self-proclaimed 'celestial empire', in its own view the leading nation in terms of age, experience, cultural achievement, moral and spiritual superiority. Cultural triumphalism made China a bad learner. Chinese scientific enquiry tended to look back at own writings to confirm there was nothing new in the rest of the world. China lacked the insti-tutions and organizations that made for a cumulative process of finding and learning. Schools, academies, learned societies, challenges, competitions and the idea of progress were weak or absent in China. Though the Chinese formally worshipped their intellectual ancestors, they had no tradition of 'standing on the shoulder of giants' (Landes, 2006:17).

The opposite occurred in fifteenth-century Europe which benefited greatly from the 'Colombian exchange' as imports of new goods had a huge impact (unlike in China) on everyday life. This term refers to the exchange of diseases, ideas, food crops and populations between the New World and the Old World after the voyages of Colombus starting in 1492. These included new calorie-rich staple food crops such as potatoes, sweet potatoes, maize and cassava and less calorie-intensive tasty foods such as tomatoes, chilli pepper, cacao, peanuts and pineapples that are now key components of many Old World diets. Equally, the exchange dramatically increased the availability of many Old World crops such as sugar and coffee which were well suited to the soils of the New World. Colonial trade did have a significant impact on welfare if not (as discussed in Chapter 9) profit and production. Welfare gains in England from the import of new (largely colonial) products between 1600 and 1850 (mainly tea, coffee, sugar and treacle) was by 1850 estimated to be equivalent to about 15 per cent of national income. This was a large impact on general welfare (Hesh and Voth 2009).

The introduction of potatoes from the New to the Old World had a signifi-cant impact on the potential for urbanization. From a nutritional standpoint potatoes were superior to pre-existing (before 1700) staple crops as they provided more vitamins and nutrients and a greater supply of calories. Humans can have healthy diets from consuming potatoes, supplemented with only dairy which contain the two vitamins not present in potatoes (vitamin A and D) (Nunn and Qian, 2011:599). Potatoes relative to Old World staples require less land to produce the same amount of calories. In terms of labour per calorie harvested potatoes are comparable to or better than cereals (Nunn and Qian, 2011:600). Potatoes also provided indirect benefits. They are easy to store and provide excellent fodder for livestock (mainly pigs and cattle) especially during the winter so could increase both meat consumption and manure (a valuable input for crop production).

European regions suitable for potato cultivation began to experience systematic increases in population and urbanization after 1700. The strength of the relationship increased between 1750 and 1900 consistent with the gradual European diffusion of potato cultivation. Potatoes increased fertility, life expectancy and urbanization through raising the productivity of agriculture and making nutritious food cheaper. When aggregating the potato impact across all Old World countries, its introduction is estimated to explain 26 per cent of the observed increase in Old World population between 1700 and 1900 and also 34 per cent of the observed increase in Old World urbanization between 1700 and 1900 (Nunn and Qian, 2011).

Key points

- Openness can influence economic growth through its impact on the supply of labour via net immigration or migration; by changing the supply of capital through inward FDI; or the drain of surplus through capital flight; through changing the incentives to invest; or through influencing productivity.
- Patterns of openness have in general shown a 'U' shape, increasing in the late nineteenth century, declining between around1913 and 1950, then increasing again, generally reaching new heights by the 1990s.
- The two most common explanations for changing patterns of openness are policy and technology.
- There has been an extensive theoretical and empirical debate about the impact of trade liberalization. Some of this is rooted in the theory of comparative advantage, but many other ideas are also included.
- The influence of openness is potentially far more general and openness can encompass power and ideas, and can transform people's living conditions.

Conclusion: Eight Principles for Policy-Makers

The introduction to this book posed three big questions:

- When did the massive inequalities in the contemporary world originate?
- How have a relatively small number of countries managed to achieve such high levels of income and welfare?
- Why have so many countries remained at low levels of income and welfare?

If the reader is in future wary of or questions carefully any clear answers given by journalists or scholars to these questions, then the book will have served its purpose. A simplistic proclamation such as 'Education is the key to economic growth and poverty reduction' is not a serious answer; it is a way of avoiding clear thinking. The widely accepted finding that investment has a robust relationship with economic growth still leaves open the questions of the deep causes of investment: is it geography, institutions, colonialism, openness or culture? Growth is a complicated phenomenon and to understand it requires a deep knowledge of a particular country rather than the application of one set of economic theories (whether free-market or any other variety) to all countries.

Despite these complications and emphasis on the importance of case studies we *can* draw a number of general principles to help policy-makers desiring to both promote economic growth and make that growth more development-friendly.

Prioritize reform

Even though we may feel overwhelmed by the number of processes that influence economic growth, we should not draw the conclusion that a long list of policy changes is required in the immediate future. We do need to prioritize reform. This requirement is very often ignored by consultancy organizations and academic scholars whose long lists of economic problems are accompanied by equally long lists of solutions. Given that the author conducts much of his research on Pakistan, here are two such examples from that context.

A report from the Competitiveness Support Fund (2010), financed generously by USAID, notes that in evaluations of its economic competitiveness Pakistan scores poorly on security (terrorism, organized crime, business costs of crime and violence, and the reliability of the police services), infrastructure

290

(especially energy), health and education (primary, higher and training), and the business environment (international distribution networks, supplier quality). The report argues that a 'comprehensive institutional reform program is vital to Pakistan's competitiveness strategy' (Competitiveness Support Fund, 2010: 62). Aspects of this 'comprehensive strategy' include 'working with Pakistan's leading export industries to remove obstacles to competitiveness, lower cost of inputs, enhance efficiency of trade logistics, increase productivity and introduce innovative technology' (2010: 43); also modernizing the financial sector; ending electricity shortages; improving infrastructure; improving education and training; commercializing research in Pakistani universities; and creating an effective security and police system that reduces the costs of doing business. This is no clearly articulated strategy for policy reform but rather is a bewildering and overwhelming list of desirable outcomes.

A further example comes from the government. 'Pakistan: A Framework for Economic Growth' (Government of Pakistan, 2011) contains a familiar litany of aspirations posing as policy advice: to 'strive for institutions that support free and fair markets, create a professional, well trained civil service' (2011: 17–18); 'developing physical and regulatory space for entrepreneurial and innovative investments' (2011: 27); 'governance and institutions reforms are required' (2011: 41); 'a focused effort will be required in areas such as science and technology, attracting talent and investment, venture capital and education policies that promote enterprising talents' (2011: 56). The appendix to the report (2011: 136–44) lists the short-term policies that should be achieved within a year. These include: restructure public enterprises; rationalize subsidies; amend zoning laws and building regulations; establish a regulatory body for the real-estate market; enforce rules and regulations in energy provision; and enhance literacy.

It is important to prioritize reform because policy change is not free but has real costs. Open economies require foreign exchange reserves (usually dollars) as an insurance, to reassure foreign investors they will be able to buy and sell the country's currency and, most importantly, be able to change it back into dollars and exit if necessary. These reserves generate a huge cost in interest or investment income forgone. India's reserves, for example, grew from nearly nothing on the eve of trade liberalization in 1991 to nearly $300 billion in October 2012. This would have been enough to fund India's rural employment guarantee programme for almost forty years. Trade liberalization to promote greater openness is likewise not just about mandating lower tariffs on imports and correcting any overvaluation of the exchange rate. In fact trade liberalization and trade integration actually have highly demanding legal and organizational requirements. WTO obligations including customs valuation, phyto and sanitary measures (food safety and animal and plant health measures), and enforcing intellectual property rights were estimated by Dani Rodrik in the mid-1990s to cost the typical developing country $150 million. The 1997–98 Asian crisis generated a new round of complicated international codes and standards covering banking transparency, banking supervision and accounting standards, further increasing this cost (Rodrik, 2000). That sum would have represented a very sizeable chunk of the annual government budget of many African countries. The demanding complexities of such reforms may overwhelm the limited skilled personnel and capacity of the civil service.

Once we have accepted the idea that we should prioritize reform we face the daunting task of selecting those key policies. One method of doing just this was developed by Hausman *et al.* (2005) and is known as 'growth diagnostics'. This method seeks to derive policy priorities from an understanding of how the binding constraints on economic activity differ from setting to setting, and it asks a series of questions derived from specific country case studies. As we noted using the model of proximate and deeper determinants in the Introduction, growth can be low because of slow productivity growth or the lack of investment, education or land. Starting from this model of economic growth we first need to examine a country case study in detail to ascertain which of these factors are responsible. Low investment of significantly below 20 per cent of GDP (various studies in this book have shown investment rates above 30 per cent of GDP are associated with rapid and sustained growth) can be due to three factors: there are inadequate returns to investment (so little incentive to invest); there could be high returns but these are lost to the original investor (called a problem of appropriability); or investors are unable to access the finance necessary to undertake even profitable investment projects. If returns are low this could be due to lack of investment in complementary factors such as roads to transport goods to market, tariffs hindering the import of necessary technologies or to the lack of skilled labour to engage in production. If returns are high but lost to the original investor the causes could be high taxation, poor property rights and contract enforcement, or labour conflicts. If potential investors lack access to necessary finance this could be due to problems with domestic or external financial markets. If savings were scarce and were constraining investment we would expect to see high foreign debt or a high current account deficit as signals that the country was drawing resources from elsewhere to compensate for low domestic savings; or we would expect to see competition to attract the existing limited pot of savings leading to high interest rates for depositors or government bondholders. If the amount of education/human capital is a constraint we would expect to see evidence of limited schooling such as low average years of schooling and low literacy and also that those with schooling and skills were in high demand so returns (wages) of the most educated would be very high, leading to substantial labour market inequality. Once we have identified key constraints related to the proximate determinants of growth then we can look to the deeper determinants to complete our analysis.

Qayyum *et al.* (2008) use the method to look for constraints on growth in Pakistan in the mid-2000s. Availability of investible resources was not a constraint on growth. In the mid-2000s savings in Pakistan (around 24 per cent of GDP) were similar to those in other developing countries. Other indicators pointed to the same conclusion. Foreign debt was declining and the current account was showing sharp improvement. The real interest rate was low or even negative, showing that borrowers were not chasing scarce savers. Investment remained below savings, indicating that banks had a surplus of funds they could have lent for productive use. Investment, at around 17 per cent of GDP, was significantly less than in other developing countries. A reason for low investment could be the low return to economic activity. Pakistan did by the mid-2000s have most of the symptoms of low economic returns, low interest rates implied that lenders were chasing borrowers and increased remittances from overseas Pakistanis were being invested in real estate rather than industry. There was certainly evidence that Pakistan suffered from low appropriability of returns. In the Global Competitiveness Reports from the mid-2000s Pakistan rated poorly in terms of judicial independence and the existence of well-defined property rights, while launching a small business was a long, expensive and cumbersome procedure. A poorly functioning legal system made banks more reluctant to lend, banks typically faced a significant default risk from borrowers who could continue for years until being declared bankrupt by a corrupt and inefficient court system and be pushed to repay the debt; even then typically once assets were scheduled for auction to repay debtors they would typically disappear. Lending for property in Pakistan was hindered by inefficient, unclear and frequently disputed rights to land and land titling. The proximate constraint on growth was low investment and its deeper causes lay in the lack of protection afforded to potential investors.

Be careful with lessons and history

Too often policy advisers, donors and scholars confine themselves to comparing policies and institutions of poorly performing developing countries with either the successful developing countries (often those East Asian countries like South Korea and Singapore) or now-developed countries. The comparison is typically and not surprisingly unfavourable. Reformers then tend to urge that poorly performing developing countries copy such 'good policies' and 'good institutions'. This type of approach ignores what we can learn from history in two ways: the history of how institutions have changed; and the relation between economic growth and institutional change. First, the possibility of the rapid institutional change urged by many commentators is contradicted by the historical experience of today's developed countries. Now-developed countries experienced, according to Chang (2003), a 'long and winding road' of institutional development which took 'decades'. From the first stirrings of democracy to universal suffrage took France and Switzerland a hundred years after the nineteenth century. The need for a modern professional bureaucracy in Britain was first discussed in the eighteenth century and became a reality only in the early nineteenth century. Such slow change was often because of the widespread realization that many changes were expensive (labour laws and social security) or because of the resistance of those who would lose out (democracy, income tax), lacking supporting changes (the tax revenue needed to pay for professional bureaucracies) or prejudice (female suffrage) (Chang 2003).

Second, in historical terms 'good institutions' have tended to follow rather than being a pre-condition for rapid economic growth, industrialization or technological upgrading. Khan notes that measures of the quality of bureaucracy, rule of law, expropriation risk and contract repudiation by government were little different between successful East Asian countries and poorly performing developing countries in the mid-1980s. Fast-growing Indonesia scored the same as Burma or Ghana, and South Korea, Malaysia, and Thailand the same as Côte d'Ivoire. The corruption index of 54 countries created by Transparency International shows that between 1980 and 1990 rapidly growing East Asian countries had corruption scores little different from other developing countries (Khan, 2002). There is much broader evidence to show that now-developed countries also had poor institutions during their initial transitions to rapid growth (Chang, 2002). The UK in 1820 had a broadly similar per capita income to India today but did not have many institutions and organizations found in contemporary India, including universal suffrage, a central bank, income tax, generalized limited liability, a modern bankruptcy law, a professional bureaucracy and securities legislation (Chang, 2003). An interesting comparison which allows for a historical dimension is that from Johnson *et al.* (2007) who compare current institutional quality in African countries with those countries in East Asia in 1960 that subsequently experienced rapid economic growth. They support the findings of Chang and Khan and find that the average institutional quality for East Asian countries experiencing sustained growth after 1960 was about the average for all developing countries. They find that constraints on the executive, economic risk and trade openness are today better in Africa, while the control of corruption, primary education, infrastructure (quality of roads and telephone access) and costs of doing business are similar in Africa to those East Asian countries in 1960. Only the extent of currency overvaluation and health conditions are significantly worse in Africa. Africa today has less inter-state conflict but more internal conflict; measures of enthno-linguistic fractionalization (an indicator of the potential for conflict) are significantly worse in African countries than in East Asia in 1960. This historical comparison allows us more optimism than is often the case for Africa as it shows that breaking away from a poor institutional legacy is possible and has been achieved by many others.

Distinguish policy goals and policy means

We may have decided upon our policy priority, perhaps to improve the supply of skilled and educated labour, or perhaps to boost the profitability of investment. Desiring an outcome, however, does not give us any information on how to achieve that goal. As we noted in Chapter 3, many scholars have made the link between investment and economic growth. But this finding offers no guidance to policy-makers on how to increase investment. Private or public investment? Foreign or domestic investment? Investing in roads or electricity supply? Reducing interest rates to make it cheaper for firms to borrow for investment projects of their own choices or offering government subsidies for specific investment projects according to some view of national needs?

Reform must be compatible with Political Economy

There are three types of economic analysis. Positive Economics purports to show what will happen in the advent of a change in any economic policy: what, for example, will be the effects on investment of raising interest rates? Normative Economics adds to this a value judgement: what policies or goals of economic change should be pursued? For example, faster economic growth is desirable therefore the government should reduce interest rates to stimulate investment. The third type is Political Economy which seeks to answer the questions: 'Who owns what? Who does what? Who gets what? What do they do with it?' (Bernstein, 2010:22). In contemporary Britain, for example, many have argued that big MNCs should pay more taxes to protect government spending on health and education, but the political influence of such large firms expressed through lobbying and donations to political parties may make this difficult to achieve. Any efforts or reform programmes to increase the rate of economic growth or perhaps make a given rate of economic growth more pro-poor or less environmentally damaging must consider these sorts of political economy issues, of which there have been many examples in this book.

Economic growth and technological change are in general accompanied by what the scholar Joseph Schumpeter called 'creative destruction'. Even if overall incomes rise (economic growth) there will be both winners and losers and the fear of the destruction may be enough to prevent the creation. Chapter 4 noted that technological change is likely to create losers whose skills become obsolete or who lose employment as a task becomes mechanized. The organization and political influence of the losers is likely to be important in determining the feasible pace of technological change. In 1753 John Kay the inventor of the Flying Shuttle (an important technological innovation in the English textile industry) had his house burned down by those fearing for their employment as skilled craftsmen. In eighteenth-century Britain the Luddite movement started in Nottingham, spreading rapidly after 1811. The participants (allegedly led by a Captain Ludd) smashed wool and cotton mills, believing that mechanization had deprived them of employment and left people destitute. The rising was brutally suppressed by the government. Between 1750 and 1850 the British political system continued to give consistent support to innovators and those winning out from technological change (Mokyr, 1990: 256). Across Europe resistance to new technology came from guilds of skilled artisans fearful of unemployment. The ribbon loom was resisted Europe-wide in contrast to its more rapid adoption in Lancashire, England after 1816. In France and elsewhere printing and cotton textiles were among the industries in which new techniques were successfully resisted by pressure groups (Mokyr, 1990: 258).

One solution could be for the government to allow the innovation and then tax the beneficiaries to compensate those losing out. There are parallels here with the conflicts in contemporary India surrounding compensation for agricultural land acquired for conversion to industrial use (Chapter 10). In India the huge number of those potentially losing out (thousands of small farmers and landless labourers) and the weak capacity of the state make this a very difficult task. In some historical cases landlords allowed industrialization; some grew rich from coal mining or building factories on their large aristocratic estates. In other cases they opposed industrialization for fear this would create a new class of politically influential industrialists. Remember Chapter 7. The Chinese undertook seven major naval expeditions in the early fifteenth century to explore the Indian Ocean. The expeditions comprised hundreds of vessels and tens of thousands of men but came to an abrupt halt in the 1430s, and further maritime adventure was banned. The rise of merchant-traders was feared by traditional groups in the court as a threat to their powers (Landes, 1998).

Chapter 6 discussed an effort to improve the quality of basic village-level health care in rural Rajasthan, India. Here there was no obvious shortage of primary health care facilities or qualified staff. The NGO Seva Mandir monitored the attendance of nurses with time-clocks, using the data to fine staff for excessive absence. Over the first six months staff attendance doubled and after sixteen months attendance dropped back to its original low levels. Over time the political influence of nurses proved more potent than any pressures from the poor who actually used the health system. This, according to Acemoglu and Robinson (2006) demonstrates the difficulty of implementing meaningful changes when institutions are the cause of the problems in the first place. The problem was that institutions were controlled by an elite and used to distribute resources to that same small elite, which here included government-employed health care professionals. Banerjee and Duflo (2013) have a less pessimistic view of this case study. The underlying problem, they argue, was not deep political economy but the fact that the 'official job requirement was crazy'. Nurses were expected to come to work six days a week, sign in, walk up to three miles a day to reach a distant hamlet in baking temperatures and go from house to house to check the health status of women and children. After five or six hours of this, then to walk back to the health centre, sign out and take a two-hour bus home. The more mundane problems were those job requirements that were developed without any regard to local conditions and lazy thinking at the stage of policy design. Banerjee and Duflo argue that promoting good policies can in turn promote good politics; or in the language of this book, good policy can promote good institutions. Big changes can result from sustained efforts to invite more people to village meetings to discuss local service provision, by monitoring government workers and holding them accountable for failures in performing their duties, and monitoring politicians at all levels and sharing this information with voters. Expectations about what people should expect from government often end up turning into self-fulfilling prophecies. Nurses who are expected to be in work are more likely to be present and when present villagers are more likely to attend the health centre, thus further encouraging norms of attendance.

Chapter 10 explored the long history of institutions that were successful in developed countries but withered away once transplanted to developing countries. The most egregious example is that of democracy quickly becoming dictatorship in so many newly independent countries in the 1950s and 1960s. A good principle here is that to be successful, institutional reform needs to be carefully mapped onto the existing underlying informal institutional and organizational constraints. Chapter 10 examined the paradox of thirty years of rapid growth in China since the mid-1970s with its massive levels of (private) investment in the absence of well-protected property rights. In this case China's institutions seem to have made reform compatible with the interests of the powerful (Qian, 2003). The Township and Village Enterprises (TVEs) were not private but collectively owned by local communities and managed by local government. The latter provided protection against anti-private property campaigns by the Communist Party. The absence of other revenue sources gave the local government the incentive to ensure the TVEs successfully generated the profits necessary to fund local government spending. Local officials in turn had an incentive to promote the local economy in the hope this would be noticed and contribute to promotion through the ranks of the Communist Party.

Don't forget government capacity

Chapter 3 noted that some policy changes are very demanding of government capacity. Recall the 'state business model' whereby the state ensures high rates of profit, investment and technological upgrading. To implement this policy package requires that the state be 'developmental'. This required that the state fulfil six criteria: that leaders have a politically driven desire to promote growth; that state institutions be autonomous; that the bureaucracy be competent and insulated from politics; that civil society be weak or crushed; that the state has acquired its power and autonomy before national or MNC capital became consolidated; and finally, that the state enjoy widespread legitimacy, whether of the democratic variety or not.

State capacity is not a variable that can easily be 'constructed' and such capacity has its own deep causes. Chapter 9 showed how the nature of the contemporary state has often been a legacy of colonialism. Chapter 12 showed how state capacity can be weakened by cultural diversity. Chapter 11 showed how geography could influence the nature of the state.

The deep determinants can be modified

The deep determinants may be deep but they are not destiny; they can be modified to promote long-run sustainable economic growth.

Chapter 11 noted that geographical constraints can be overcome. Landlocked countries can reduce transport costs through improving port facilities, giving duty-free access to imported inputs and capital goods, and ensuring efficient customs administration. What looks like geographical isolation can in truth be a product of poor policy. Policies that restrict competition in cargo transport and give monopolies to official national carriers (often airlines) have been adopted by many African governments and have increased freight costs. There is a market failure in the construction of many transport links, including railways and roads. For any landlocked country there are external benefits to them from any country lying between them and the coast investing in transport infrastructure. Why would any country help a landlocked country become a more viable competitor in world export markets?

Chapter 12 noted that good institutions can potentially resolve the ethnic conflicts that may result from diverse social structures – a cultural explanation. Institutions that give protection to legal minorities, and guarantee freedom from expropriation and from repudiation of contracts would constrain the amount of damage that one ethnic group could do to another. The example in this book was that of one tribe getting into power and plundering the resources of another less powerful tribe, specifically the case of Ghana and the Ashanti cocoa producers being plundered. Such institutions could make a given degree of ethnic fractionalization less damaging for development. The big problem is that the measure of institutions is negatively correlated with ethnic division so there is an original dilemma of wondering where such diverse countries can acquire those strong institutions.

An optimistic chapter 10 in Banerjee and Duflo (2013) argued that a 'view from below' allows us to see it is not always necessary fundamentally to change institutions to improve accountability and reduce corruption. As they point out, limited democracy can even be introduced into an authoritarian regime at the local level. Local elections were introduced in Vietnam in 1998, Saudi Arabia 2005, and Yemen 2001. Since the early 1980s village-level elections have been gradually introduced into rural China and research shows an increase in accountability and public expenditures being re-allocated to reflect the needs of local inhabitants. In Indonesia engineers sampled material to build roads in 600 villages and compared those samples with construction norms. The threat of audit reduced the theft of wages and materials by one-third compared with villages where audits were not conducted. The introduction of electronic voting in Brazil reduced the number of invalid votes by 11 per cent; these votes were especially likely to be among the poorer and less well educated. Again in Brazil, since 2003, sixty municipalities have been drawn at random every month in a televised lottery and their accounts are audited. These audits are made public through the internet and the local media.

Being audited hurts corrupt incumbents. In the 2004 election corrupt incumbents were 12 percentage points less likely and honest incumbents were 13 percentage points more likely to be elected if their audit was revealed before the election. Minor interventions at the margin here made a significant difference and there was scope for improving the functioning of institutions even in relatively hostile environments.

Think about demand as well as supply

Many of the factors we have identified in this book as being important drivers of economic growth, such as education, health, family planning services, investment and technology, can be considered (and reformed) from both the demand and supply sides. We need to ask whether education is better promoted by increasing the supply of teachers and schools, or by stimulating the demand of parents for better education by offering incentives to encourage them to send girls to school, or by raising the salaries of employees with education?

William Easterly has argued in a string of influential publications that the poor should be viewed not as helpless recipients of aid but as experts at surviving in poverty. He argues that governments should stop pushing services onto the poor but rather empower the poor to demand health and education through their own actions. Other supply-side solutions have included incentives to increase savings or opening up an economy to international financial markets to increase the supply of resources available for firms to borrow and invest. Supply-side solutions may fail because policy-makers do not consider demand. Family planning services, Easterly (2001) argues, have often failed because they fail to address the reasons people want children, such as high rates of child mortality or the need for children to work in subsistence agriculture. Fertility is high because people want lots of children and offering them a cheap means to reduce fertility will have no impact. Improving the supply of investible resources with more savings and FDI, as noted in the first principle above, will have no impact on investment if there are no incentives for firms or households to invest. Empowering citizens' groups to hold service providers accountable has been a key policy recommendation based on these arguments. An example would be empowering local communities to hire and fire teachers previously accountable to distant central government bureaucracies. The local beneficiaries are those most likely to be hurt by bad services; the local inhabitants are also likely to have much better information than distant bureaucracies as to the underlying cause of poor services.

The diagnostic results of these kinds of empowerment effort remain generally disappointing. Chapter 6 illustrated the results of an effort to generate some of that countervailing pressure by giving greater control over public- service recruitment and pay to poor beneficiaries. The assumption was that the poor need public services so have an incentive to monitor service providers and by living in the local community would be better able to monitor the services and so punish absence. In Udaipur, India a member of the community was paid to check to attendance of health care professionals; they found low rates of attendance but nothing was done by the local community with this information.

Just because the majority of the population of a typical developing country are poor and the poor would benefit from good public services, we cannot jump to the conclusion that an empowered and democratic local community will lead to better public services. Chapter 6 noted that incentives faced by politicians mean that there will be an inherent problem in delivering 'good services'. It is generally much harder for politicians to take credit for 'health status' or 'teaching quality' than for clearly observable inputs like cutting the ribbon when opening a new building. Hospitals, for example, tend to be prioritized because, first, large facilities are prominent so politicians get more plaudits for opening a big hospital than a small rural health centre, and second, it is much easier to take the credit for the construction of facilities than for their successful functioning. The former is visible and can be accompanied by a single visit from a ribbon-cutting politician; the latter depends on the sustained efforts of many different actors. The resulting misallocation of resources means that too little is spent on traditional public health measures like vector control, sanitation and hygiene education, or improving the functioning of public-service facilities, and too much on building facilities and employing health care workers.

Such empowerment may have little impact if it runs up against powerful countervailing forces. Teachers may be well connected. In India, for example, they are unionized; many are politically influential and can resist such local pressures. Educated and literate teachers may be intimidating opponents for poor and illiterate village people who want to improve their children's education. This is the big lesson from Acemoglu and Robinson's (2006) book *Why Nations Fail*. Bad (or what they term extractive) institutions, they suggest, are likely to persist. At the expense of the rest of society, extractive institutions will strengthen an elite minority who will then acquire the incentives and resources to organize, mobilize and control political power to ensure the perpetuation of their elite status. This takes the form of a vicious circle. Prosperity, they argue, requires that institutions be transformed from extractive to inclusive and it is not easy to do so. Nations cannot then rely on economic growth automatically leading to better institutions as suggested perhaps by the historical studies of Chang and modernization theory.

Don't get too hung up on democracy

It is self-evident to many that democracy is a good thing and so promoting it should take priority over efforts to influence other deep determinants of growth. Typical is Amartya Sen who argues democracy itself is a good thing in that it enhances freedoms but is also a vital means to promote wider growth and development. Famously Sen (1982) pointed out that no substantial famine has ever occurred in an independent country with a democratic form of government and a free press. A democratic government exposed to the glare of a viable opposition and a free press will have the incentives to ensure adequate and timely interventions to ward off any threat of famine. Rodrik (1999) shows detailed empirical evidence that democracy also generates more predictable long-run growth rates and greater economic stability, handles adverse shocks better and reduces income inequality. But there is no reason to suppose that democracy automatically produces desirable growth and developmental outcomes and this is particularly true in the poorest developing countries. Collier (2010) finds that in low-income countries (GDP per capita less than $2,700) democracy increases political violence. Elections in poor ethnically divided societies are often brutal winner-takes-all processes, the loser(s) facing bankruptcy and persecution and the winner(s) the opportunity to enrich themselves and their ethnically determined followers. This dichotomy motivates the use of any means including inflaming ethnic tensions and actual violence to secure victory. Elections in such situations do not confer the legitimacy that allows the incumbent government to take tough, unpopular decisions. In fact in poor ethnically divided societies democracy is likely to weaken any discipline on governments to perform well. Political loyalty is organized on the basis of ethnicity, which at the extreme means that votes are 'frozen in blocs of rival identities' and fixed independently of government performance. What wins votes is benefiting a narrowly and usually ethnically defined group of supporters at the expense of the rest of the population – remember the 'vampire state' example of Ghana (see Chapter 12). Democracy equalizes the right to influence the allocation of resources so may exacerbate the threat to property from landless peasants and organized labour in particular.

The question of whether democracy is good for promoting growth and development misses the more crucial relationship, which is that historically democracy has been an outcome (not a cause) of development. The typical franchise during industrialization in today's developed countries was tiny, in France between 1830 and 1848 only 0.6 per cent of the population, and the 1832 Reform Act in England extended voting rights from 14 to 18 per cent of men. Economic development promotes the pre-requisites for democracy such as literacy, urbanization, the breakdown of traditional hierarchical communities, and social mobility (Lipset, 1959; Rueschemeyer *et al.* 1992; Huber *et al.*, 1993; Barro, 1999). But of course, as noted above, the relationship is not automatic. Growth will not automatically bring about Western-style democracy, as the citizens of Singapore will no doubt have noticed.

Bibliography

Ablo, E. and R. Reinikka (1998), *Do Budgets Really Matter? Evidence from Public Spending on Education and Health in Uganda*, World Bank Policy Research Working Paper No. 1926, Washington.

Abramovitz, A. (1986), 'Catching Up, Forging Ahead and Falling Behind', *Journal of Economic History*, 46:2, pp. 384–406.

Acemoglu, D. (2009), *Introduction to Modern Economic Growth*, Oxford, Princeton University Press.

Acemoglu, D., S. Johnson and J.A. Robinson (2001), 'The Colonial Origins of Comparative Development: An Empirical Investigation', *American Economic Review*, 91, pp. 1369–1401.

Acemoglu, D., S. Johnson and J.A. Robinson (2002a), *Reversal of Fortune: Geography and Institutions in the Making of the Modern World Income Distribution*, mimeo, University of California at Berkeley.

Acemoglu, D., S. Johnson, J. Robinson, and Y. Thaicharoen (2002b), *Institutional Causes, Macroeconomic Symptoms: Volatility, Crises and Growth*. Mimeo, University of California at Berkeley.

Acemoglu, D., S. Johnson and J. Robinson (2005), 'The Rise of Europe: Atlantic Trade, Institutional Change, and Economic Growth', *American Economic Review*, 95:3, pp. 546–79.

Aghion, P. and P. Howitt (1992), 'A Model of Growth through Creative Destruction', *Econometrica*, 60:2, pp. 323–51.

Aghion, P. and P. Howitt (1998), *Endogenous Growth Theory*, London, MIT Press.

Agnihotri, S. (2000), *Sex Ratio Patterns in the Indian Population: A Fresh Exploration*, New Delhi, Sage Publications.

Ahuja, M. and A.P. Singh (2006), 'Evaluation of Computerisation of Land Records in Karnataka: A Study from Gulbarga District', *Economic and Political Weekly*, 7 January, pp. 69–77.

Aitken, B.J. and A.E. Harrison (1999), 'Do Domestic Firms Benefit from FDI? Evidence from Venezuela', *American Economic Review*, 89:3, pp. 605–18.

Alderman, H. and P. Gertler (1997), 'Family Resources and Gender Differences in Human Capital Investments: The Demand for Children's Medical Care', in Haddad, L., J. Hoddinott and H. Alderman (eds), *Intrahousehold Resource Allocation in Developing Countries: Models, Methods and Policy*, London, Johns Hopkins University Press.

Alesina, A. and D. Rodrik (1994), 'Distributive Politics and Economic Growth', *Quarterly Journal of Economics*, 106:2, pp. 465–90.

Alesina, A., R. Baqir and W. Easterly (1999), 'Public Goods and Ethnic Divisions', *Quarterly Journal of Economics*, 114:4, pp. 1243–84.

Ali, I. (2003), *The Punjab Under Imperialism, 1885–1947*, Karachi, Oxford University Press.

Allen, R.C. (2008), 'A Review of Gregory Clark's A Farewell to Alms: A Brief Economic History of the World', *Journal of Economic Literature*, 46:4, pp. 946–73.

Allen, R.C., J.-P. Bassino, M.A. Debin, C. Moll-Murata and J.L. van Zanden (2007), *Wages, Prices, and Living Standards in China, 1738–1925: In Comparison with Europe, Japan, and India*, Department of Economics Discussion Paper Series No, 316, Oxford.

Alkire, S. (2005), 'Why the Capability Approach?', *Journal of Human Development*, 6:1, pp. 115–33.

Amjadi, A. and A.J. Yeats (1995), *Have Transport Costs Contributed to the Relative Decline of Sub-Saharan African Exports?*, World Bank Policy Research Working Paper, No 1559, Washington.

Amsden, A.H. (1989), *Asia's Next Giant: South Korea and Late Industrialisation*, Oxford, Oxford University Press.

Anand, S. and M. Ravallion (1993), 'Human Development in Poor Countries: On the Role of Private Incomes and Public Services', *Journal of Economic Perspectives*, 7:1, pp. 133–50.

Arbache, J.S. and J. Page (2008), *Hunting for Leopards: Long Run Country Income Dynamics in Africa*, World Bank Policy Research Working Paper No 4715, Washington.

Arbache, J.S. and J. Page (2009), 'How Fragile is Africa's Recent Growth?', *Journal of African Economies*, 19:1, pp. 1–24.

Arnold, F., A. Choe, and T. Roy (1998) 'Son Preference, the Family-building Process and Child Mortality in India', *Population Studies*, 52: pp. 301–15.

Arokiasamy, P. (2009), 'Fertility Decline in India: Contribution by Uneducated Women Using Contraception', *Economic and Political Weekly*, 25 July, pp. 55–64.

Arokiasamy, P., K. McNay and R.H. Cassen (2004), 'Female Education and Fertility Decline: Recent Developments in the Relationship', *Economic and Political Weekly*, 9 October, pp. 4491–5.

Arora, D. (1996), 'The Victimising Discourse: Sex-Determination Technologies and Policy', *Economic and Political Weekly*, 17 February pp. 420–4.

Arrighi, G. (2010), *The Long Twentieth Century: Money, Power and the Origins of Our Times*, London, Verso.

Aschauer, D. (1989), 'Is Public Expenditure Productive?', *Journal of Monetary Economics*, 23:2, pp. 177–200.

Austin, G. (1996), 'National Poverty and the 'Vampire State' in Ghana: A Review Article', *Journal of International Development*, 8:4, pp. 553–83.

Austin, G. (2008), 'The "Reversal of Fortune" Thesis and the Compression of History: Perspectives from African and Comparative Economic History', *Journal of International Development*, 20, pp. 996–1027.

Bagchi, A.K. (1976), 'De-Industrialisation in India in the Nineteenth Century: Some Theoretical Implications', *Journal of Development Studies*, 12:2, pp. 135–64.

Bagchi, A.K. (1982), *The Political Economy of Underdevelopment*, Cambridge, Cambridge University Press.

Bairoch, P. (1993), *Economics and World History: Myths and Paradoxes*, Chicago, University of Chicago Press.

Bairoch, P. and R. Kozul-Wright (1996), *Globalization Myths: Some Historical Reflections on Integration, Industrialisation and Growth in the World Economy*, UNCTAD Discussion Paper, UNCTAD/OSG/DP/113, Geneva.

Balasubramanyam, V.N., M. Salisu and D. Sapsford (1996), 'Foreign Direct Investment and Growth in EP and IS Countries', *Economic Journal*, 106, pp. 92–105.

Banerjee, A.V. and E. Duflo (2013), *Poor Economics: Rethinking Poverty and the Ways to End it*, London, Random House.

Banerjee, A., A. Deaton and E. Duflo (2004), 'Health Care Delivery in Rural Rajasthan', *Economic and Political Weekly*, 28 February, pp. 944–9.

Banga, R. (2005), *Critical Issues in India's Service-Led Growth*, ICRIER Working Paper No 171, October.

Banga, R. and B. Goldar (2004), *Contribution of Services to Output Growth and Productivity in Indian Manufacturing: Pre and Post Reforms*, ICRIER Working Paper, No 139, New Delhi.

Baran, P. (1957), *The Political Economy of Growth*, London, Penguin Books.

Baran, P. and P.M. Sweezy (1966), *Monopoly Capitalism: An Essay on the American Economic and Social Order*, London, Penguin.

Bardhan, P. (1984), *The Political Economy of Development in India,* New Delhi, Oxford University Press.

Bardhan, P. and S. Klasen (1999), 'UNDP's Gender-Related Indices: A Critical Review', *World Development*, 27:6, pp. 985–1010.

Bar-Ilan, A. and W.C. Strange (1996), 'Investment Lags', *American Economic Review*, 86:3, pp. 610–22.

Barro, R.J. (1991), 'Economic Growth in a Gross Section of Countries' *Quarterly Journal of Economics*, 106:2, pp. 407–43.

Barro, R.J. (1999), 'Determinants of Democracy', *Journal of Political Economy*, 107:6, pp. 158–183.

Baru, R., A. Acharya, S. Acharya, A.K.S. Kumar and K. Nagaraj (2010), 'Inequities in Access to Health Services in India: Caste, Class and Region', *Economic and Political Weekly*, 18 September, pp. 49–58.

Basu, A. (1995), 'Women's Role and the Gender Gap in Health and Survival', in Das Gupta, M., Chen, L. and Krishnan, T. (1995) *Women's Health in India: Risk and Vulnerability*, New Delhi, Open University Press.

Basu, A. (1999), 'Fertility Decline and Increasing Gender Imbalance in India, Including a Possible South Indian Turnaround', *Development and Change*, 30, pp. 237–63.

Bates, R.H (2000), 'Ethnicity and Development in Africa: A Reappraisal', *American Economic Review*, 90:2, pp. 131–4.

Becker, S.O. and L. Woessmann (2009), 'Was Weber Wrong? A Human Capital Theory of Protestant Economic History', *Quarterly Journal of Economics*, 124:2, pp. 531–94.

Beenstock, M. and P. Sturdy (1990) 'The Determinants of Infant Mortality in Regional India', *World Development*, 18:3, pp. 443–53.

Behrman, J.R. and A.B. Deolalikar (1987), 'Will Developing Country Nutrition Improve with Income? A Case Study from Rural South India', *Journal of Political Economy*, 95:3, pp. 492–507.

Benhabib, J. and M.M. Spiegel (1994), 'The role of human capital in economic development evidence from aggregate cross-country data', *Journal of Monetary Economics*, 34:2, pp. 143–73.

Berg, M. and P. Hudson (1992), 'Rehabilitating the Industrial Revolution', *Economic History Review*, 45:1, pp. 24–50.

Bernstein, H. (2010), *Class Dynamics of Agrarian Change: Agrarian Change and Peasant Studies*, Nova Scotia, Fernwood Publishing.

Bertrand, M. and A. Schoar (2006), 'The Role of the Family in Family Firms', *Journal of Economic Perspectives*, 20:2, pp. 73–96.

Besley, T. (1995), 'Property Rights and Investment Incentives: Theory and Evidence from Ghana', *Journal of Political Economy*, 103:5, pp. 903–37.

Bhagwati, J. (1958), 'Immiserising Growth: A Geometrical Note', *Review of Economic Studies*, 25:3, pp. 201–5.

Bhagwati, J. (1978), *Foreign Trade Regimes and Economic Development: Anatomy and Consequences of Exchange Control Regimes*, Chicago, University of Chicago Press.

Bhagwati, J. (1984), 'Splintering and the Disembodiment of Services and Developing Countries', *The World Economy*, 7:2, pp. 133–44.

Bhagwati, J. (2007), 'Why Multinationals Help Reduce Poverty', *The World Economy*, pp. 211–28.

Bhalotra, S.R. (1998), 'The Puzzle of Jobless Growth in Indian Manufacturing', *Oxford Bulletin of Economics and Statistics*, 60:1, pp. 5–32.

Bhat, P.N.M. (2002), 'Returning a Favour: Reciprocity Between Female Education and Fertility in India', *World Development*, 30:10, pp. 1791–1803.

Bhat, P.N.M. (2006), 'Sex Ratio in India', *The Lancet*, 367:9524, pp. 1725–6.

Bhattacharya, B.B. and A. Mitra (1991), 'Excess Growth of Tertiary Sector', *Economic and Political Weekly*, 1 June, pp. 1423–4.

Biao, X. (2005), 'Gender, Dowry and the Migration System of Indian Technology Professionals', *Indian Journal of Gender Studies*, 12:2–3, pp. 357–80.

Bigsten, A., P. Collier, S. Dercon, M. Fafchamps, B. Gauthier, J.W. Gunning, J. Habarurema, A, Isaksson, A. Oduro, R. Oostendorp, C. Pattillo, M. Sonderbom, F. Teal and A . Zeufack, (1999), 'Exports of African Manufactures: Macro Policy and Firm Behaviour', *Journal of International Trade and Economic Development*, 8:1, pp. 53–71

Bils, M. and P.J. Klenow (2000), 'Does Schooling Cause Growth?', *American Economic Review*, 90:5, pp. 1160–83.

Blanchard, O.J. (2009), *Macroeconomics*, Fifth Edition, London, Pearson Education.

Blanchard, O.J. and S. Fischer (1989), *Lectures on Macroeconomics*, Cambridge, The MIT Press.

Blaut, J.M. (1993), *The Colonisers Model of the World: Geographical Diffusionism and Eurocentric History*, New York, the Guilford Press.

Bleaney, M.F. (1996), 'Macroeconomic Stability, Investment and Growth in Developing Countries', *Journal of Development Economics*, 48, pp. 461–77.

Blejer, M.I. and M.S. Khan (1984), 'Government Policy and Private Investment in Developing Countries', *IMF Staff Papers*, 31, pp. 379–403.

Block, S.A. (2001), 'Does Africa Grow Differently?', *Journal of Development Economics*, 65, pp. 443–67.

Blomstrom, M., R.E. Lipsey and M. Zejan (1996), 'Is Fixed Investment the Key to Economic Growth', *Quarterly Journal of Economics*, 111: pp. 269–76.

Bloom, D.E. and J.G. Williamson (1998), 'Demographic Transitions and Economic Miracles in Emerging Asia', *World Bank Economic Review*, 12:3, pp. 419–55.

Bloom, D.E., D. Canning and D.T. Jamison (2004), 'Health, Wealth, and Welfare', *Finance and Development*, March, pp. 10–15.

Bloom, D.E., D. Canning and M. Weston (2005), 'The Value of Vaccination', *World Economics*, 6:3, pp. 15–39.

Boserup, E. (1965), *The Conditions of Agricultural Growth: The Economics of Agrarian Change under Population Pressure*, London, Earthscan Publications.

Bosworth, B. and S.M. Collins (2008), 'Accounting for Growth: Comparing China and India', *Journal of Economic Perspectives*, 22:1, pp. 45–66.

Bozzoli, C., A. Deaton and C. Quintana-Domeque (2009), 'Adult Height and Childhood Disease', *Demography*, 46:4, pp. 647–69.

Brammall, C. (1993), 'The Role of Decollectivisation in China's Agricultural Miracle, 1978–90', *The Journal of Peasant Studies*, 20:2, pp. 271–95.

Brammall, C. (2009), *Chinese Economic Development*, London, Routledge.

Braudel, F. (1984), *Civilisation and Capitalism, 15th–18th Century, III: The Perspective of the World*, New York, Harper and Row.

Braudel, F. (1993), *A History of Civilisations*, London, Penguin Books.

Brecher, R.A. and C.F. Diaz-Alejandro (1977), 'Tariffs, Foreign Capital and Immiserizing Growth', *Journal of International Economics*, 7, pp. 317–22.

Brenner, R. and C. Isett (2002), 'England's Divergence from China's Yangzi Delta: Property Relations, Microeconomics, and Patterns of Development', *Journal of Asian Studies*, 61:2, pp. 609–22.

Brock, W.A. and S.N. Durlauf (2001), 'Growth Empirics and Reality: What Have We Learned from a Decade of Empirical Research on Growth?', *World Bank Economic Review*, 15:2, pp. 229–72.

Brunetti, A, G. Kisunko and B. Weder (1998), 'Credibility of Rules and Economic Growth: Evidence from a Worldwide Survey of the Private Sector', *World Bank Economic Review*, 12:3, pp. 353–84.

Bruton, H.J. (1992) *The Political Economy of Poverty, Equity and Growth: Sri Lanka and Malaysia*, New York, Oxford University Press.

Burda, M. and C. Wyplosz (1993), *Macroeconomics a European Text*, Oxford, Oxford University Press.

Caldwell, J.C. and P. Caldwell (1987), 'The Cultural Context of High Fertility in sub-Saharan Africa', *Population and Development Review*, 13:3, pp. 409–37.

Caldwell, J.C., O. Orubuloye and P. Caldwell (1992), 'Fertility Decline in Africa: A New Type of Transition?', *Population and Development Review*, 18:2, pp. 211–42.

Callinicos, A. (2010), *The Revolutionary Ideas of Karl Marx*, London, Bloomsbury Publications.

Cantoni, D. (2010), *The Economic Effects of the Protest Reformation: Testing the Weber Hypothesis in the German Lands*, mimeo, Departament d'Economia i Empresa, Universitat Pompeu Fabra, Barcelona.

Cardoso, F.H. (1972), 'Dependency and Development in Latin America', *New Left Review*, 74, pp. 83–95.

Carlin, W. and D. Soskice (1990), *Macroeconomics and the Wage Bargain: A Modern Approach to Employment, Inflation, and the Exchange Rate*, Oxford, Oxford University Press.

Carmody, P. (2009), 'An Asian-Driven Economic Recovery in Africa? The Zambian Case', *World Development*, 37:7, pp. 1197–207.

Chandra, N.K. (1982), 'Long-term Stagnation in the Indian Economy, 1900–75', *Economic and Political Weekly*, Annual Number, April, pp. 517–60.

Chandrasekhar, C.P., J. Ghosh and A. Roychowdhury (2006), 'The "Demographic Dividend" and Young India's Economic Future', *Economic and Political Weekly*, 9 December, pp. 5055–64.

Chang, H.-J. (1993), 'The Political Economy of Industrial Policy in Korea', *Cambridge Journal of Economics*, 17, pp. 131–57.

Chang, H.-J. (1999), 'The Economic Theory of the Developmental State', in Woo-Cumings, M. (1999) (ed.), *The Developmental State in Historical Perspective*, Ithaca: Cornell University Press.

Chang, H.-J. (2002), *Kicking Away the Ladder: Development Strategy in Historical Perspective*, London, Anthem Press, London.

Chang, H.-J. (2003), 'Kicking the Ladder Away: Infant Industry Promotion in Historical Perspective', *Oxford Development Studies*, 31:1, pp. 21–32.

Chang, H.-J. (2007), *Bad Samaritans: Rich Nations, Poor Policies and the Threat to the Developing World*, London, Random House.

Chataway, J. and J. Smith (2006), 'The International AIDs Vaccine Initiative (IAVI): Is it getting new science and technology to the world's neglected majority?', *World Development*, 34:1, pp. 21–37.

Chaudhury, N., J. Hammer, M. Kremer, K. Muralidharan and F. Halsey-Rogers (2006), 'Missing in Action: Teacher and Health Workers in Developing Countries', *Journal of Economic Perspectives*, 20:1, pp. 91–116.

Chen, L., E. Huq and S. Souza (1981), 'Sex Bias in the Family Allocation of Food and Health Care in Rural Bangladesh', *Population and Development Review*, 7:1, pp. 55–70.

Chenery, H.B. (1960), 'Patterns of Industrial Growth', *American Economic Review*, 50:4, pp. 624–54.

Chenery, H.B. and L. Taylor (1968), 'Development Patterns: Among Countries and Over Time', *Review of Economics and Statistics*, 50:4, pp. 391–416.

Chaudhury, N. and J.S. Hammer (2004), 'Ghost Doctors: Absenteeism in Rural Bangladeshi Health Facilities', *The World Bank Economic Review*, 18:3, pp. 423–41.

Chima, R.I., C.A. Goodwin and A. Mills (2003), 'The Economic Impact of Malaria in Africa: A Critical Review of the Evidence', *Health Policy*, 63, pp. 17–36.

Chuang, Y. and C. Lin (1999), 'Foreign Direct Investment, R&D and Spillover Efficiency: Evidence from Taiwan's Manufacturing Firms', *Journal of Development Studies*, 35:4, pp. 117–37.

Chunkath, S. and Athreya, V. (1997) 'Female Infanticide in Tamil Nadu: Some Evidence', *Economic and Political Weekly*, 26 April, pp. S21–8.

Clark, C. (2007), *A Farewell to Alms: A Brief Economic History of the World*, Princeton, Princeton University Press.

Clark, G., M. Huberman and P.H. Lindert (1995), 'A British Food Puzzle, 1770–1850', *The Economic History Review*, 48:2, pp. 215–37.

Clark, G. and D. Jacks (2007), 'Coal and the Industrial Revolution, 1700–1869', *European Review of Economic History*, 11, pp. 39–72.

Clark, G. and S. Wolcott (2001), *One Polity, Many Countries: Economic Growth in India, 1873–2000*, Mimeo.

Cline, W.R. (1982), 'Can the East Asian Model of Development Be Generalised?', *World Development*, 10:2, pp. 81–90.

CMH (2001), *Macroeconomics and Health: Investing in Health for Economic Development*, World Health Organization, Geneva.

Cohen, B. (1998), 'The Emerging Fertility Transition in Sub-Saharan Africa', *World Development*, 26:8, pp. 1431–61.

Collier, P. (2007), *The Bottom Billion: Why the Poorest Countries Are Failing and What Can Be Done About It*, Oxford, Oxford University Press.

Collier, P. (2010), *Wars, Guns, and Votes: Democracy in Dangerous Places*, London, Vintage.

Collier, P., P. Honohan and K.O. Moene (2001), 'Implications of Ethnic Diversity', *Economic Policy*, 16:32, pp. 129–66.

Competitiveness Support Fund (2010), *The State of Pakistan's Competitiveness: Report 2010–11*, Islamabad.

Coulibaly, S. and L. Fontagne (2005), 'South–South Trade: Geography Matters', *Journal of African Economies*, 15:2, pp. 313–41.

Crafts, N.F.R. (1983), 'British Economic Growth, 1700–1831: A Review of the Evidence', *Economic History Review*, 36:2, pp. 177–99.

Crafts, N.F.R. (1987), 'British Economic Growth, 1700–1850: Some Difficulties of Interpretation', *Explorations in Economic History*, 24, pp. 245–68

Crafts, N.F.R. (1995), 'Exogenous or Endogenous Growth? The Industrial Revolution Reconsidered', *Journal of Economic History*, 55:4, pp. 745–772.

Crafts, N.F.R. (1999), 'Economic Growth in the Twentieth Century', *Oxford Review of Economic Policy*, 15:4, p. 18–34.

Crafts, N.F.R. (2002), 'The Human Development Index, 1870–1999: Some Revised Estimates', *European Review of Economic History*, 6, pp. 395–405.

Crafts, N.F.R. (2004), 'Globalisation and Economic Growth: A Historical Perspective', *World Economy*, 27:1, pp. 45–58.

Crafts, N.F.R. and C.K. Harley (1992), 'Output growth and the British industrial revolution: a restatement of the Crafts–Harley view', *Economic History Review*, 45:4, pp. 703–30.

Cuberes, D. and M. Jerzmanowski (2009), 'Democracy, Diversification and Growth Reversals', *Economic Journal*, 119, pp. 1270–302.

Cutler, D. M. (2004), *Your Money or Your Life,* Oxford, Oxford University Press.

Cutler, D and G. Miller (2005), 'The Role of Public Health Improvements in Health Advances: The Twentieth-Century United States', *Demography,* 42:1, pp. 1–22.

Cutler, D., A. Deaton and A.L Leras-Muney (2006), 'The Determinants of Mortality', *Journal of Economic Perspectives*, 20:3, pp. 97–120.

Cutler, D., W. Fung, M. Kremer, M. Singhal and T. Vogl (2010), 'Early-life Malaria Exposure and Adult Outcomes: Evidence from Malaria Eradication in India', *American Economic Journal: Applied Economics*, 2, pp. 72–94.

Cypher, J.M. and J.L Dietz (2004), *The Process of Economic Development*, Third Edition, London, Routledge.

Darity, W. (1992), 'A Model of 'Original Sin': Rise of the West and Lag of the Rest', *American Economic Review*, 82:2, pp. 162–67.

Das, J. and J. Hammer (2007), 'Money for nothing: the dire straits of medical practise in Delhi, India', *Journal of Development Economics*, 83, pp. 1–36.

Das, J. and T. Zajonc (2010), 'India shining and Bharat drowning: Comparing two Indian states to the worldwide distribution in mathematics achievement', *Journal of Development Economics*, 92, pp. 175–87.

Das Gupta, M. (1987), 'Selective Discrimination against Female Children in Rural Punjab, India', *Population and Development Review*, 13:1, pp. 77–100.

Das Gupta, M. and P.N.M. Bhat (1998), 'Intensified Gender Bias in India: A Consequence of Fertility Decline', in Krishnaraj, M., R. Subarshan and A. Shariff (eds), *Gender, Population and Development*, New Delhi, Oxford University Press.

Dasgupta, P. and M. Weale (1992), 'On Measuring the Quality of Life', *World Development*, 20:1, pp. 119–31.

Deane, P. and W. Cole (1962), *British Economic Growth, 1688–1959*, Cambridge, Cambridge University Press.

Deaton, A (2007), 'Height, Health, and Development', *Proceedings of the National Academy of Sciences*, 104:33, pp. 13232–7.

Deaton, A. (2008), 'Height, Health and Inequality: The Distribution of Adult Heights in India', *American Economic Review*, 98:2, pp. 468–74.

Deaton, A. and J. Drèze (2009), 'Food and Nutrition in India: Facts and Interpretations', *Economic and Political Weekly*, 14 February, pp. 42–65.

Deaton, A. and J. Drèze (2010), 'Nutrition, Poverty and Calorie Fundamentalism: Response to Utsa Patnaik', *Economic and Political Weekly*, 3 April pp. 78–80.

Deininger, K. and Jin, S. (2003), 'Land Sales and Rental Markets in Transition: Evidence from Rural Vietnam', *Oxford Bulletin of Economics and Statistics*, 70:1, pp. 67–101.

Delderbos, R., G. Capannelli and K. Fukao (2001), 'Backward Vertical Linkages of Foreign Manufacturing Affiliates: Evidence from Japanese Multinationals', *World Development*, 29:1, pp. 189–208.

De Long, J.B. and L.H. Summers (1991), 'Equipment Investment and Economic Growth', *Quarterly Journal of Economics*, 106, pp. 445–502.

De Long, J.B. and L.H. Summers (1992), *Equipment Investment and Economic Growth: How Strong is the Nexus*, Brookings Papers on Economic Activity 2, pp. 157–211.

De Long, J.B. and L.H. Summers (1993), 'How Strongly do Developing Economies Benefit from Equipment Investment?', *Journal of Monetary Economics*, 32, pp. 395–415.

Deolalikar, A. and V. Rao (1998), 'The Demand for Dowries and Bride Characteristics in Marriage: Empirical Estimates for Rural South-Central India', in Krishnaraj, M., R. Subarshan and A. Shariff (eds), *Gender, Population and Development*, New Delhi, Oxford University Press.

Deraniyagala, S. and B. Fine (1999), 'New Trade Theory versus Old Trade Policy: A Continuing Enigma', *Cambridge Journal of Economics*, 25:6, pp. 809–25.

Deshpande, S. and L. Deshpande (1998), 'Impact of Liberalisation on Labour Market in India: What do Facts from NSSO's 50th Round Show?', *Economic and Political Weekly*, 30 May, pp. L-31–39.

De Soto, H. (2001), *The Mystery of Capital: Why Capitalism Triumphs in the West and Fails Everywhere Else*, London, Black Swan Books.

Devarajan, S., W.R. Easterly and H. Pack (2003), 'Low Investment is Not the Constraint on African Development', *Economic Development and Cultural Change*, pp. 547–71.

Diamond, J. (1998), *Guns, Germs and Steel: A Short History of Everybody for the Last 13,000 Years*, London, Vintage.

Dixit, A.K. and R.S. Pindyck (1994), *Investment Under Uncertainty*, Princeton, Princeton University Press.

Dollar, D. (1992), 'Outward Orientated Economies Really Do Grow More Rapidly: Evidence from 95 LDC's, 1976–1985', *Economic Development and Cultural Change*, 40:4, pp. 523–44.

Dollar, D. and A. Kraay (2002), 'Growth is Good for the Poor', *Journal of Economic Growth*, 7:3, pp. 195–225.

Dollar, D. and A. Kraay (2004), 'Trade, Growth and Poverty', *Economic Journal*, 114, pp. 22–49.

Dornbusch, R. and S. Fischer (1994), *Macroeconomics*, Fifth Edition, London, McGraw-Hill.

Dos Santos, T. (1970), 'The Structure of Dependence', *American Economic Review*, 60:2, pp. 231–6.

Drèze, J. and M. Murthi (2001), 'Fertility, Education and Development: Evidence from India', *Population and Development Review*, 27:1, pp. 33–63.

Drèze, J. and A. Sen (1995), *India: Economic Development and Social Opportunity*, New Delhi, Oxford University Press.

Drèze, J. and A. Sen (2002), *India: Development and Participation*, New Delhi, Oxford University Press.

Dyson, T. (2001), 'The Preliminary Demography of the 2001 Census', *Population and Development Review*, 27:2, pp. 341–56.

Dyson, T. (2005), 'India's Population – The Past', in Dyson, T., R. Cassen and L. Visaria (eds), *Twenty-First Century India: Population, Economy, Human Development, and the Environment*, Oxford, Oxford University Press.

Easterly, W. (2001a), 'Can Institutions Resolve Ethnic Conflict', *Economic Development and Cultural Change*, 49:4, pp. 687–706.

Easterly, W. (2001b), *The Elusive Quest for Growth: Economists' Adventures and Misadventures in the Tropics*, Cambridge, Mass, MIT Press, Cambridge.

Easterly, W. (2005), *Reliving the '50s: the Big Push, Poverty Traps, and Takeoffs in Economic Development*, Centre for Global Development Working Paper No. 65, Washington.

Easterly, W. (2008), 'Institutions: Top down or Bottom up?', *American Economic Review*, 98:2, pp. 95–9.

Easterly, W. and R. Levine (1997), 'Africa's Growth Tragedy: Policies and Ethnic Divisions', *Quarterly Journal of Economics*, 112:4, pp. 1203–50.

Easterly, W. and R. Levine (2001), 'It's Not Factor Accumulation: Stylised Facts and Growth Models', *World Bank Economic Review*, 15:2, pp. 177–219.

Easterly, W. and S. Rebelo (1993), 'Fiscal Policy and Economic Growth an Empirical Investigation', *Journal of Monetary Economics*, 32, pp. 417–58.

Edwards, S. (1998), 'Openness, Productivity and Growth: What Do We Really Know?', *Economic Journal*, 108, pp. 383–98.

Ehrlich, P. (1968), *The Population Bomb*, New York, Ballantine Books.

Emmanual, A. (1972), *Unequal Exchange: A Study of the Imperialism of Trade*, London, Monthly Review Press.

Englebert, P., S. Tarango and M. Carter (2002), 'Dismemberment and Suffocation: A Contribution to the Debate on African Boundaries', *Comparative Political Studies*, 35:10, pp. 1093–118.

Ermisch, J.F. and W.G. Huff (1999), 'Hypergrowth in an East Asian NIC: Public Policy and Capital Accumulation in Singapore', *World Development*, 27:1, pp. 21–38.

Fahnbulleh, M. (2006), 'In Search of Economic Development in Kenya: Colonial Legacies and Post-Independence Realities', *Review of African Political Economy*, 107, pp. 33–47.

Fanon, F. (2001), *The Wretched of the Earth*, London, Penguin Classics.

Feinstein, C.H. (1978), 'Capital Formation in Great Britain' in P. Mathias and M.M. Postan (eds), *Cambridge Economic History of Europe*, Vol 7, Part 1, Cambridge, Cambridge University Press.

Felipe, J. (1999), 'Total Factor Productivity Growth in East Asia: Critical Survey', *Journal of Development Studies*, 35:4, pp. 1–41.

Ferguson, N (2012), *Civilization: The Six Killer Aps of Western Power*, London, Penguin.

Fernandes, A.M. (2009), 'Comparing Property Rights, Institutions, Contracting Institutions and Growth in South Asia and East Asia', in E. Ghani and S. Ahmed (eds), *Accelerating Growth and Job Creation in South Asia*, New Delhi, Oxford University Press.

Filmer, D., E. King and L. Pritchett (1998), *Gender Disparity in South Asia: Comparison between and within Countries,* World Bank Development Research Group, Poverty and Human Resources, Policy Research Working Paper No.1867, Washington.

Filmer, D., J.S. Hammer and L.H. Pritchett (2000), 'Weak Link in the Chain: A Diagnosis of Health Policy in Poor Countries', *World Bank Research Observer*, 15:2, pp. 199–224.

Findlay, R. (1980), 'On W. Arthur Lewis' Contributions to Economics', *Scandinavian Journal of Economics*, 82:1, pp. 62–79.

Fogel, I.R.W. (1997), 'The Global Struggle to Escape from Chronic Malnutrition since 1700', CPE Working Papers 0006, University of Chicago, Centre for Population Economics.

Frank, A.G. (1966), 'The Development of Underdevelopment', *Monthly Review*, 18 September, pp. 4–17.

Frank, A.G. (1998), *ReOrient: Global Economy in the Asian Age*, Berkeley, University of California Press.

Frey, B.S. and A. Slutzer (2002), 'What can Economists Learn from Happiness Research?', *Journal of Economic Literature*, 40:2, pp. 402–35.

Fukuda-Parr, S. and A.K.S. Kumar (2003), 'Introduction', in S. Fukuda-Parr and A.K.S. Kumar (eds), *Readings in Human Development: Concepts, Measures and Policies for a Development Paradigm*, New Delhi, Oxford University Press.

Gadgil, S. and S. Gadgil (2006), 'The Indian Monsoon, GDP and Agriculture', *Economic and Political Weekly*, 25 November, pp. 4887–95.

Galeano, E. (2009), *The Open Veins of Latin America: Five Centuries of the Pillage of a Continent*, London, Serpents Tail.

Gallup, J.L. and S.D. Sachs (1999), *Geography and Economic Development*, Centre for International Development, Working Paper No 1, Harvard University.

Gallup, J.L. and J.D. Sachs (2000), *The Economic Burden of Malaria*, Centre for International Development Working Paper No. 52, Harvard University.

Gardner, D. (2003) Where have all the girls gone? http://www.freeindiamedia. com/women/17_feb_women.htm (accessed 12 April 2006).

Garenne, M. and V. Joseph (2002), 'The Timing of the Fertility Transition in Sub-Saharan Africa', *World Development*, 30:10, pp. 1835–43.

Gauri, V. and P. Khaleghian (2002), 'Immunisation in Developing Countries: Its Political and Organisational Determinants', *World Development*, 30:12, pp. 2109–32.

George, A.L. and A. Bennett (2005), *Case Studies and Theory Development in the Social Sciences*, Cambridge, MA, MIT Press.

Gerring, J. (2007), *Case Study Research: Principles and Practises*, Cambridge, MA, Cambridge University Press.

Gerschenkron, A. (1962), *Economic Backwardness in Historical Perspective*, Cambridge, Harvard University Press.

Ghani, E. and M-Ud. Din (2006), 'The Impact of Public Investment on Economic Growth in Pakistan', *Pakistan Development Review*, 45:1, pp. 87–98.

Gibbon, E (1996), *The History of the Decline and Fall of the Roman Empire*, Volume 1, London, Penguin Classics.

Gordon, J. and P. Gupta (2004), *Understanding India's Service Revolution*, IMF Working Paper WP/04/171, Washington.

Gorg, H. and D. Greenaway (2004), 'Much Ado About Nothing? Do Domestic Firms Really Benefit from Foreign Direct Investment?', *World Bank Research Observer*, 19:2, pp. 171–97.

Goulet, S.D. (1992), 'Development: Creator and Destroyer of Values', *World Development*, 20:3, pp. 467–75.

Government of Pakistan (2011), *Pakistan: Framework for Economic Growth*, Planning Commission, Islamabad.

Gray, R.H (1974), 'An Estimate of the Demographic Effects of Malaria Control: A Case Study of Sri Lanka', *World Development*, 2:2, pp. 19–21.

Greif, A. (1994) 'Cultural Belief and the Organisation of Society: A Historical and Theoretical Reflection on Collectivist and Individualist Societies', *Journal of Political Economy*, 102:5, pp. 912–50.

Greene, J. and D. Villanueva (1991), 'Private Investment in Developing Countries: An Empirical Analysis', *IMF Staff Papers*, 38:1, pp. 33–58.

Grossman, G.M. and E. Helpman (1991), 'Quality Ladders in the Theory of Economic Growth', *Review of Economic Studies*, 58:1, pp. 43–61.

Guiso, L., P. Sapienza and L. Zingales (2003), 'Peoples Opium? Religion and Economic Attitudes', *Journal of Monetary Economics*, 50, pp. 225–82.

Guiso, L., P. Sapienza and L. Zingales (2006), 'Does Culture Affect Economic Outcomes?', *Journal of Economic Perspectives*, 20:2, pp. 23–48.

Habib, I. (2006), *Indian Economy, 1858–1914*, New Delhi, Tulika Books.

Haddad, L., H. Alderman, S. Appleton, L. Song and Y. Yohannes (2003), 'Reducing Child Malnutrition: How Far Does Income Growth Take Us?', *World Bank Economic Review*, 17:1, pp. 107–31.

Haggard, S., D. Kang and C. Moon (1997), '*Japanese Colonialism and Korean Development: A Critique*', World Development, 25:6, pp. 867–81.

Hall, J.A. (2007), 'Book Review of Hobson (2004) The Eastern Origins of Western Civilization', *English Historical Review*, 122:495, pp. 149–51.

Hall, R.E. and C.I. Jones (1999), 'Why do Some Countries Produce so Much More Output per Worker than Others?', *Quarterly Journal of Economics*, 114, pp. 83–116.

Hammer, J., Y. Aiyar and S. Samji (2007), 'Understanding Government Failure in Public Health Services', *Economic and Political Weekly*, 6 October, pp. 4049–57.

Hanley, S.B. (1983), 'A High Standard of Living in Nineteenth-Century Japan: Fact or Fantasy?', *The Journal of Economic History*, 43:1, pp. 183–92.

Hanley, S.B. and K. Yamamura (1977), *Economic and Demographic Change in Preindustrial Japan*, Princeton, Princeton University Press.

Hanushek, E.A. and L. Woessmann (2009), *Do Better Schools Lead to More Growth? Cognitive Skills, Economic Outcomes, and Causation*, NBER Working Paper No 14633, Cambridge, Massachusetts.

Hanushek, E.A. and D.D. Kimko (2000), 'Schooling, Labor-Force Quality, and the Growth of Nations', *American Economic Review*, 90:5, pp. 1184–1208.

Hurd, J. (1975), 'Railways and the Expansion of Markets in India, 1861–1921', *Explorations in Economic History*, 12, pp. 263–88.

Harkness, S. (2004), *Social and Political Indicators of Human Well-being*, Helsinki, WIDER Research Paper No. 2004/33, May.

Harriss-White, B. (1996), 'Liberalisation and Corruption: Resolving the Paradox (A Discussion Based on South Indian Material)', *IDS Bulletin*, 27:2, pp. 1–5.

Harriss-White, B. (2001), *Development and Productive Deprivation: Male Patriarchal Relations in Business Families and their Implications for Women in South India*, QEH Working Paper No 65, Oxford University.

Harriss, J. and P.D.E. Renzio (1997), 'Missing Link or Analytically Missing?: The Concept of Social Capital (An Introductory Bibliographical Essay)', *Journal of International Development*, 9:7, pp. 919–37.

Hausmann, R., L. Pritchett and D. Rodrik (2004), *Growth Accelerations*, JFK School of Government, Harvard University.

Hazarika, G. (2000), 'Gender Differences in Children's Nutrition and Access to Health Care in Pakistan', *Journal of Development Studies*, 37:1, pp. 3–92

Hesh, J. and H.-J. Voth (2009), 'Sweet Diversity and the Rise of European Living Standards after 1492', Mimeo.

Heyer, J. (1992), 'The Roles of Dowries and Daughters' Marriages in the Accumulation and Distribution of Capital in a South Indian Community', *Journal of International Development*, 4:4, pp. 419–36.

Hirschman, A.O. (1958), *The Strategy of Economic Development*, New Haven, Yale University Press.

Ho, S.P.S. (1995), 'Rural Non-agricultural Development in Post-Reform China: Growth, Development Patterns, and Issues', *Pacific Affairs*, pp. 360–91.

Hobday, M. (1995), 'East Asian Latecomer Firms: Learning the Technology of Electronics', *World Development*, 23:7, pp. 1171–93.

Hobsbawm, E. (1995), *The Age of Revolution: Europe 1789–1848*, London, Weidenfeld & Nicolson.

Hobson, J.A. (2004), *The Eastern Origins of Western Civilisation*, Cambridge, Cambridge University Press.

Hochschild, A. (1999), *King Leopold's Ghost: A Story of Greed, Terror and Heroism*, London, Pan.

Hoekman, B.R., K.E. Maskus and K. Saggi (2005), 'Transfer of Technology to Developing Countries: Unilateral and Multilateral Policy Options', *World Development*, 33:10, pp. 1587–602.

Huber, E., D. Rueschemeyer and J.D. Stephens (1993), 'The Impact of Economic Development on Democracy', *Journal of Economic Perspectives*, 7:3, pp. 71–85.

Huff, W.G. (1999), 'Turning the Corner in Singapore's Developmental State?', *The Asian Survey*, 39:2, pp. 214–42.

Hunt, D. (1989), *Economic Theories of Development: An Analysis of Competing Paradigms*, London, Harvester Wheatsheaf.

Huntingdon, S.P. (1968), *Political Order in Changing Societies*, New Haven, Yale University Press.

Hussain, A. (2002), 'Demographic Transition in China and its Implications', *World Development*, 30:10, pp. 1823–34.

Ibarra, L.A. (1995), 'Credibility of Trade Policy Reform and Investment: The Mexican Case', *Journal of Development Economics*, 47, pp. 39–60.

Ingham, B. (1993), 'The Meaning of Development: Interactions Between Old and New Ideas', *World Development*, 21:11, pp. 1803–21.

Inikori, J.E. (1989), 'Slavery and the Revolution in Cotton Textile Production in England', *Social Science History*, 13:4, pp. 343–79.

Iqbal, Z. and G.M. Zahid (1998), 'Macroeconomic Determinants of Economic Growth in Pakistan', *Pakistan Development Review*, 37:2, pp. 125–48.

Irwin, D.A. (2000), 'Did Late-Nineteenth-Century US Tariffs Promote Infant Industries? Evidence from the Tinplate Industry', *Journal of Economic History*, 60:2, pp. 335–60.

Isham, J., M. Woolcock, L. Pritchett and G. Busby (2005), 'The Varieties of Resource Experience: Natural Resource Export Structures and the Political Economy of Economic Growth', *World Bank Economic Review,* 19:2, pp. 141–74.

Jacoby, H.G and B. Minten (2007), 'Is Land Titling in Sub-Saharan Africa Cost-Effective? Evidence from Madagascar', *World Bank Economic Review*, 21:3, pp. 461–85.

Jeffrey, P. and R. Jeffrey (2002), 'A Population out of Control? Myths about Muslim Fertility in Contemporary India', *World Development*, 30:10, pp. 1805–22.

James, O. (2007), *Affluenza: How to be Successful and Stay Sane*, London, Vermilion.

James, K.S. and S.N. Nair (2005), 'Accelerated Decline in Fertility in India since the 1980s: Trends among Hindus and Muslims', *Economic and Political Weekly*, 29 January, pp. 375–83.

Jejeebhoy, S. and Z. Sathar (2001) 'Women's Autonomy in India and Pakistan: The Influence of Religion and Region', *Population and Development Review*, 27:4, pp. 687–712.

Jha, P., R. Kumar, P. Vasa, N. Dhingra, D. Thiruchelvam and R. Moineddin (2006), 'Low Male-to-Female Sex Ratio of Children Born in India: National Survey of 1.1 Million Households', *The Lancet*, 367:9506, pp. 185–6.

Jha, R. (2000), *Reducing Poverty and Inequality in India: Has Liberalisation Helped?*, WIDER, Working Paper No 204, Geneva.

Joe, W., U.S. Mishra and K. Navaneetham (2008), 'Health Inequality in India: Evidence from NFHS 3', *Economic and Political Weekly*, 2 August pp. 41–7.

John, M.E. (2011), 'Census 2011: Governing Populations and the Girl Child', *Economic and Political Weekly*, 16 April, pp. 10–12.

Johnson, S., J.D. Ostry and A. Subramanian (2007), *The Prospects for Sustained Growth in Africa: Benchmarking the Constraints*, IMF Working Paper WP/07/52, Washington.

Jones, B.F. and B.A. Olken (2008), 'The Anatomy of Start–Stop Growth', *Review of Economics and Statistics*, 90:3, pp. 582–7.

Jones, C.I. (1994), 'Economic Growth and the Relative Price of Capital', *Journal of Monetary Economics*, 34, pp. 359–82.

Jong-a-Pin, R. and J. De Haan (2011), 'Political regime change, economic liberalization and growth accelerations', *Public Choice*, 146, pp. 93–115.

Jutting, J.P. (2004), 'Do Community-based Health Insurance Schemes Improve Poor People's Access to Health Care? Evidence from Rural Senegal', *World Development*, 32:2, pp. 273–88.

Kabeer, N. and S. Mahmud (2004), 'Globalisation, Gender and Poverty: Bangladesh Women Workers in Export and Local Markets', *Journal of International Development*, 16, pp. 93–109.

Kahneman, D. and A.B. Krueger (2006), 'Developments in the Measurement of Subjective Well-Being', *Journal of Economic Perspectives*, 20:1, pp. 3–24.

Kaplinsky, R (2005), 'Revisiting the Revisited Terms of Trade: Will China Make a Difference?', IDS, Sussex, Mimeo.

Kaplinsky, R., D. McCormick and M. Morris (2007), *The Impact of China on Sub-Saharan Africa*, IDS Working Paper, No. 291, University of Sussex, Brighton.

Kapur, S. and S. Kim (2006), *British Colonial Institutions and Economic Development in India*, NBER Working Paper No. 12613, Cambridge, Massachusetts.

Kenny, C. (2005), 'Why Are We Worried About Income? Nearly Everything that Matters is Converging', *World Development*, 33:1, pp. 1–19.

Khan, M.A., A. Qayyum and S.A. Sheikh (2005), 'Financial Development and Economic Growth', *Pakistan Development Review*, 44:4, pp. 819–37.

Khan, M.H (2002), *State Failure in Developing Countries and Strategies of Institutional Reform*, Paper for ABCDE Conference, Oslo, 24–26 June.

Khan, M.H. (2010), *Governance Capabilities and the Property Rights Transition in Developing Countries*, Department of Economics, SOAS, London.

Khan, M.S. (2005), 'Human Capital and Economic Growth in Pakistan', *Pakistan Development Review*, 44:4, pp. 455–78.

Khattry, B. (2003), 'Trade Liberalisation and the Fiscal Squeeze: Implications for Public Investment', *Development and Change*, 34:3, pp. 401–24.

Khattry, B. and J.M. Rao (2002), 'Fiscal Faux Pas?: An Analysis of the Revenue Implications of Trade Liberalisation', *World Development*, 30:8, pp. 1431–44.

Kim, J.-L. and L.J. Lau (1994), 'Sources of Economic Growth of the East Asian Newly Industrialized Countries', *Journal of the Japanese and International Economies*, pp. 235–71.

King, R.G. and R. Levine (1993), 'Finance and Growth: Schumpeter May be Right', *Quarterly Journal of Economics*, 108, pp. 717–37.

Kingdon, G.G. (2007), 'The Progress of School Education in India', *Oxford Review of Economic Policy*, 23:2, pp. 168–95.

Kishor, S. (1993), '"May God Give Sons to All" Gender and Child Mortality in India', *American Sociological Review*, 58: pp. 247–65.

Klasen, S. and C. Wink (2002), 'A Turning Point in Gender Bias in Mortality: An Update on the Number of Missing Women', *Population and Development Review*, 28:2, pp. 285–312

Klasen, S. and Wink, C. (2003), '"Missing Women": Revisiting the Debate', *Feminist Economics*, 9:2–3: pp. 263–99.

Klenow, P.J. and Rodriguez-Clare, A. (1997), 'Economic Growth: A Review Essay', *Journal of Monetary Economics*, Elsevier, 40 (3), pp. 597–617, December.

Knack, S. and P. Keefer (1997), 'Does Social Capital Have an Economic Payoff: A Cross-Country Investigation', *Quarterly Journal of Economics*, 112, pp. 1251–88.

Kochhar, K., U. Kkumar, R. Rajan, A. Subramanian and I. Tokatlidis (2006), *India's Pattern of Development: What Happened, What Follows?*, IMF Working Paper, WP/06/22, Washington DC.

Koenig, M.A., V. Fauveau and B. Wojtyniak (1991), 'Mortality Reductions from Health Interventions: The Case of Immunisation in Bangladesh', *Population and Development Review*, 17:1, pp. 87–104.

Kohli, A. (1994), 'Where Do High Growth Political Economies Come From? The Japanese Lineage of Korea's "Developmental State"', *World Development*, 22:9, pp. 1269–93.

Kohli, A. (1997), 'Japanese Colonialism and Korean Development: A Reply', *World Development*, 25:6, pp. 883–8.

Kohli, A. (2004), *State-Directed Development: Political Power and Industrialisation in the Global Periphery*, Cambridge, Cambridge University Press.

Kohli, A. (2006), 'Politics of Economic Growth in India, Part I: The 1980s', *Economic and Political Weekly*, 1 April, pp. 1251–9.

Kok-Fay, C. and K.S. Jomo (2000), 'Financial Rents in Malaysia', in Khan, M.H and K.S.Jomo (eds), *Rents, Rent-Seeking and Economic Development: Theory and Evidence in Asia*, Cambridge, Cambridge University Press.

Kokko, A. (1994), 'Technology, Market Characteristics and Spillovers', *Journal of Development Economics*, 34, pp. 279–93.

Kokko, A. and M. Blomstrom (1995), 'Policies to Encourage Inflows of Technology through Foreign Multinationals', *World Development*, 23:3, pp. 459–68.

Kollor, M. (1990), 'Female Infanticide: A Psychological Analysis', *Grass Roots Action*, Special Issue on Girl Child, 3 April.

Komlos, J. (1998), 'Shrinking in a Growing Economy? The Mystery of Physical Stature during the Industrial Revolution', *Journal of Economic History*, 58:3, pp. 779–803.

Koolwal, G.B. (2007), 'Son Preference and Child Labour in Nepal: The Household Impact of Sending Girls to Work', *World Development*, 35:5, pp. 881–903.

Kravdal, O. (2004), 'Child Mortality in India: The Community-level Effect of Education', *Population Studies*, 58:2, pp. 177–92.

Kremer, M. (1993), 'Population Growth and Technological Change: One Million B.C. to 1990', *Economic Journal*, 108, pp. 681–716.

Kremer, M. (2002), 'Pharmaceuticals and the Developing World', *Journal of Economic Perspectives*, 16:4, pp. 67–90.

Kremer, M., K. Muradlidaharan, N. Chaudhury, F.H. Rogers, and J. Hammer (2005), 'Teacher Absence in India: A Snapshot', *Journal of the European Economic Association*, 3:2–3, pp. 658–7.

Kremer, M. and A.P. Zwane (2005), 'Encouraging Private Sector Research for Tropical Agriculture', *World Development*, 33:1, pp. 87–105.

Kriekhaus, J. (2002), 'Reconceptualising the Developmental State: Public Savings and Economic Growth', *World Development*, 30:10, pp. 1697–712.

Krishnaji, N. (1987), 'Poverty and Sex Ratio: Some Data and Speculations', *Economic and Political Weekly*, 6 June, pp. 892–97.

Krueger, A.O. (1974), 'The Political Economy of the Rent-Seeking Society', *American Economic Review*, 64:3, pp. 291–303.

Krueger, A.O. (1978), *Liberalization Attempts and Consequences*, Cambridge, National Bureau of Economic Research.

Krueger, A.O. (1990), 'Government Failures in Development', *Journal of Economic Perspectives*, 4:3, pp. 9–23.

Krueger, A.O. (1997), 'Trade Policy and Economic Development: How We Learn', *American Economic Review*, 87:1, pp. 1–22.

Krugman, P. (1987), 'Is Free Trade Passé?', *Journal of Economic Perspectives*, 1:2, pp. 131–44.

Krugman, P. (1994), 'The Myth of Asia's Miracle', *Foreign Affairs*, 73:4, pp. 62–78.

Krugman, P. (1995), 'Growing World Trade: Causes and Consequences', *Brookings Papers on Economic Activity*, I, pp. 327–77.

Kumar, A. (1999), *The Black Economy in India*, New Delhi, Penguin.

Kumar, N. and A. Agarwal (2000), *Liberalisation, Outward Orientation and In-house R+D Activity of Multinational and Local Firms: A Quantitative Exploration for Indian Manufacturing*, RIS Discussion Paper, No 07/2002, New Delhi.

Kumar, N. (1998), 'Liberalisation and Changing Patterns of Foreign Direct Investments: Has India's Relative Attractiveness as a Host of FDI Improved?', *Economic and Political Weekly*, 30 May, pp. 1321–29.

Kumar, N. (2005), 'Liberalisation, Foreign Direct Investment Flows and Development: Indian Experience in the 1990s', *Economic and Political Weekly*, 2 April, pp. 1459–69.

Kunio, Y. (1988), *The Rise of Ersatz Capitalism in South-East Asia*, Manila, Ateneo de Manila University Press.

Kurian, N. (2000), 'Widening Regional Disparities in India: Some Indicators', *Economic and Political Weekly*, 12 February, pp. 539–50.

Kwarteng, K. (2011), *Ghosts of Empire: Britain's Legacy in the Modern World*, London, Bloomsbury.

Laderchi, C.R., R. Saith and F. Stewart (2003), 'Does it Matter that we do not Agree on the Definition of Poverty? A Comparison of Four Approaches', *Oxford Development Studies*, 31:3, pp. 243–74.

Lai, E.L.C. (1998), 'International Intellectual Property Rights Protection and the Rate of Product Innovation', *Journal of Development Economics*, 55, pp. 133–53.

Lal, D. (1998), *Unintended Consequences: The Impact of Factor Endowments, Culture, and Politics on Long-Run Economic Performance*, Cambridge, MIT Press.

Lal, D. (1997), *The Poverty of Development Economics*, London, The Institute of Economic Affairs.

Lal, D. (2004), *In Praise of Empires: Globalization and Order*, New York, Palgrave Macmillan.

Lall, S. (1975), 'Is 'Dependence' a Useful Concept in Analysing Underdevelopment?', *World Development*, 3:11–12, pp. 799–810.

Lall, S. (1992), 'Technological Capabilities and Industrialisation', *World Development*, 20:2, pp. 165–86.

Lall, S. (1994), 'The East Asian Miracle: Does the Bell Toll for Industrial Strategy', *World Development*, 22:4, pp. 645–54.

Lall, S, (1995a), 'Structural Adjustment and African Industry', *World Development*, 23:12, pp. 2019–31.

Lall, S (1995b), 'Malaysia: Industrial Success and the Role of Government', *Journal of International Development*, 7:5, pp. 759–73.

Lall, S. (2000), 'The Technological Structure and Performance of Developing Country Manufactured Exports, 1985–98', *Oxford Development Studies*, 28:3, pp. 337–69.

Lampton, D.M. (1978), 'Development and Health Care: Is China's Medical Programme Exportable?', *World Development*, 6, pp. 621–30.

Landes, D. (1998), *The Wealth and Poverty of Nations: Why Some Are So Rich and Some So Poor?*, London, Abacus.

Landes, D.S. (2006), 'Why Europe and the West? Why Not China?', *Journal of Economic Perspectives*, 20:2, pp. 3–22.

Lange, M.K. (2004), 'British Colonial Legacies and Political Development', *World Development*, 32:6, pp. 905–22.

Lanjouw, J. and I. Cockburn (2001), 'New Pills for Poor People? Empirical Evidence After GATT', *World Development*, 29:2, pp. 265–89

Lee, J.W. (1995), 'Capital Goods Imports and Long-run Growth', *Journal of Development Economics* 48:1, pp. 91–110.

Lee, J (1997), 'The Maturation and Growth of Infant Industries: The Case of Korea', *World Development*, 25:8, pp. 1271–81.

Levien, M. (2011), 'Special Economic Zones and Accumulation by Dispossession in India', *Journal of Agrarian Change*, 11:4, pp. 454–83.

Levine, R. (1997), 'Financial Development and Economic Growth', *Journal of Economic Literature*, 35:2, pp. 688–726.

Levine, R. and D. Renelt (1992), 'A Sensitivity of Cross-Country Growth Regressions', *American Economic Review*, 82:4, pp. 942–63.

Lewis, W.A. (1954), 'Economic Development with Unlimited Supplies of Labour', *The Manchester School,* 22 (2), pp. 139–91.

Li, X. and X. Liu (2005), 'Foreign Direct Investment and Economic Growth: An Increasingly Endogenous Relationship', *World Development*, 33:3, pp. 393–407.

Lieven, A. (2011), *Pakistan: A Hard Country*, London, Allen Lane.

Limao, N. and A. Venables (2001), 'Infrastructure, Geographic Disadvantage, Transport Costs and Trade', *World Bank Research Observer*, 22:1, pp. 22–51.

Lipset, M. (1959), 'Some Social Prerequisites of Democracy: Economic Development and Political Legitimacy', *American Political Science Review*, 52:1, pp. 69–105.

Little, I.M.D., T. Scitovsky and M. Scott (1970), *Industry and Trade in Some Developing Countries: A Comparative Study*, Oxford, Oxford University Press.

Maddison, A. (1971), *Class Structure and Economic Growth: India and Pakistan Since the Moghuls*, New York, W.W. Norton.

Maddison, A. (2006), *The World Economy*, Paris, OECD Publishing.

Maddison, A. (2007), *Contours of the World Economy: Essays in Macro-Economic History*, Oxford, Oxford University Press.

Maddison Project (http://ggdc.net/maddison/maddison–project/home.htm)

Manhoff, A.W. (2005), 'Banned and Enforced: The Immediate Answer to a Problem Without an Immediate Solution – How India Can Prevent another Generation of Missing Girls', *Vanderbilt Journal of Transnational Law*, 38, pp. 889–920.

Mankiw, N.G., D. Romer and D.N. Weil (1992), 'A Contribution to the Empirics of Economic Growth', *Quarterly Journal of Economics*, 107:2, pp. 407–27.

Maundeni, Z. (2001), 'State culture and development in Botswana and Zimbabwe', *Journal of Modern African Studies*, 40:1, pp. 105–32.

Mauro, P (1995), 'Corruption and Economic Growth', *Quarterly Journal of Economics*, 110:3, pp. 681–712.

Mayer, J. (2002), 'The Fallacy of Composition: A Review of the Literature', *World Economy*, 25:6, pp. 875–94.

McCartney, M. (2011), *Pakistan – the Political Economy of Growth, Stagnation and the State – 1951 to 2009*, London, Routledge.

McCleary, R.M. and R.J.Barro (2006), 'Religion and the Economy', *Journal of Economic Perspectives*, 20:2, pp. 49–72.

McGowan, P.J. (1976), 'Economic Dependence and Economic Performance in Black Africa', *The Journal of Modern African Studies*, 14:1, pp. 25–40.

Mendelsohn, O. (2005), 'The Indian legal profession, the courts and globalisation', *South Asia: Journal of South Asian Studies*, 28:2, pp. 301–20.

Meng, X., X. Gong and Y. Wang (2009), 'Impact of Income Growth and Economic Reform on Nutrition Availability in Urban China: 1986–2000', *Economic Development and Cultural Change*, 57:2, pp. 261–95.

Menon, V. (2003), *From Movement to Government: The Congress in the United Provinces, 1937–42*, New Delhi, Sage.

Meredith, M. (2005), *The State of Africa: A History of Fifty Years of Independence*, London, Free Press.

Miller, B. (1999), 'Wife Beating in India: Variations on a Theme', in D. Counts, J. Brown and J. Campbell (eds), *To Have and to Hit: Cultural Perspectives on Wife Beating*, Urbana, University of Illinois Press.

Milner, C., O. Morrissey and N. Rudaheranwas (2000), 'Policy and Non-Policy Barriers to Trade and Implicit Taxation of Exports in Uganda', *Journal of Development Studies*, 37:2, pp. 67–90.

Mishra, V., T. Roy and R. Retherford (2004), 'Sex Differentials in Childhood Feeding, Health Care and Nutritional Status in India', *Population and Development Review*, 30:2, pp. 269–95.

Mkandawire, T. (2001), 'Thinking about Developmental States in Africa', *Cambridge Journal of Economics*, 25, pp. 2989–3013.

Mohanty, M. (2007), 'Political Economy of Agrarian Transformation: Another View of Singur', *Economic and Political Weekly*, 3 March, pp. 737–41.

Mokyr, J. (1990), *The Lever of Riches: Technological Creativity and Economic Progress*, New York, Oxford University Press.

Moradi, A. (2008), 'Confronting Colonial Legacies – Lessons from Human Development in Ghana and Kenya, 1880–2000', *Journal of International Development*, 20, pp. 1107–21.

Morisset, J. (1998), 'Unfair Trade? The Increasing Gap between World and Domestic Prices in Commodity markets during the Past 25 Years', *World Bank Economic Review*, 12:3, pp. 503–26.

Morrissey, O. and I. Filatotchev (2000), 'Globalisation and Trade: The Implications for Exports from Marginalised Economies', *Journal of Development Studies*, 37:2, pp. 1–12.

Mosley, P. (2000), 'Globalisation, Economic Policy and Convergence', *World Economy*, 23:5, pp. 613–34.

Mukherjee, A. (2007), *The Return of the Colonial in Indian Economic History: The Last Phase of Colonialism in India*, Presidential Address to the Indian History Congress, December, New Delhi.

Mukherjee, A. and X. Zhang (2007), 'Rural Industrialisation in China and India: Role of Policies and Institutions', *World Development*, 35:10, pp. 1621–34.

Mukhopadhyay, S. (2012), 'Agriculture-Nutrition Pathways: Recognising the Obstacles', *Economic and Political Weekly*, 21 April, pp. 79–80.

Murphy, K.M., A. Shleifer and R.W. Vishny (1991), 'The Allocation of Talent: Implications for Growth', *Quarterly Journal of Economics*, 106:2, pp. 503–30.

Murthi, M., A.-C. Guio and J. Drèze (1996), 'Mortality, Fertility and Gender Bias in India: A District Level Analysis', in Drèze, J and A. Sen (eds), *Indian Development: Selected Regional Perspective*, New Delhi, Oxford University Press.

Murthi, M. (2002), 'Fertility Change in Asia and Africa', *World Development*, 30:10, pp. 1769–78.

Naude, W. (2007), *Geography and Development in Africa: Overview and Implications for Regional Cooperation*, WIDER Discussion Paper No 2007/03, Helsinki.

Naude, W. and M. Matthee (2007), 'The Significance of Transport Costs in Africa', *United Nations University Policy Brief*, No 6, Tokyo.

Naughton, B. (2007), *The Chinese Economy: Transitions and Growth*, Cambridge, MIT Press.

Nayab, D. (2006), *Demographic Dividend or Demographic Threat in Pakistan*, PIDE Working Papers No 10, Islamabad.

Ndikumaru, L. (2000), 'Financial Determinants of Domestic Investment in Sub-Saharan Africa: Evidence from Panel Data', *World Development*, 28:2, pp. 381–400.

Nef, J.U. (1934), 'The Progress of Technology and the Growth of Large-Scale industry in Great Britain, 1540–1640', *Economic History Review*, 5:1, pp. 3–24.

Nehru, J. (1946), *The Discovery of India*, New Delhi, Oxford University Press.

Ng, F. and A. Yeats (1997), 'Open Economies Work Better! Did Africa's Protectionist Policies Cause its Marginalisation in World Trade?', *World Development*, 25:6, pp. 889–904.

Nolan, P. (1995), *China's Rise, Russia's Decline: Politics, Economics and Planning in the Transition from Stalinism*, London, Macmillan.

Nordhaus, W.D. (2006), 'Geography and Macroeconomics: New Data and New Findings', *Proceedings of the National Academy of Sciences*, 103:10, pp. 3510–17.

Nicholson, W. (1995), *Microeconomic Theory: Basic Principles and Extensions*, 6th Edition, Fort Worth, The Dryden Press.

Nolan, P. (1995), *China's Rise, Russia's Decline: Politics, Economics and Planning in the Transition from Stalinism*, London, Macmillan.

Nolan, P. (2001), *China and the Global Economy: National Champions, Industrial Policy and the Big Business Revolution*, Basingstoke, Palgrave Macmillan.

North, D.C. (1990), *Institutions, Institutional Change and Economic Performance*, Cambridge, Cambridge University Press.

North, D.C. (1994), 'Economic Performance through Time', *American Economic Review*, 84:3, pp. 359–368.

North, D.C and N.P. Thomas (1973), *The Rise of the Western World: A New Economic History*, Cambridge, Cambridge University Press.

Nunn, N. (2007), *Slavery, Inequality, and Economic Development in the Americas: An Examination of the Engerman–Sokoloff Hypothesis*, MPRA Paper No. 5869, Munich.

Nunn, N. (2008), 'The Long-Term Effects of Africa's Slave Trade', *Quarterly Journal of Economics*, 123:1, pp. 139–76.

Nunn, N. and N. Qian (2010), 'The Colombian Exchange: A History of Disease, Food and Ideas', *Journal of Economic Perspectives*, 24:2, pp. 163–88.

Nunn, N. and N. Qian (2011), 'The Potato's Contribution to Population and Urbanisation: Evidence from a Historical Experiment', *Quarterly Journal of Economics*, 126, pp. 593–650.

Nurkse, R. (1953), 'Problems of capital formation in underdeveloped countries', reprinted in A.N. Agarwala and S.P. Singh (eds) (1958), *The Economics of Underdevelopment*, Oxford. Oxford University Press.

O'Brien, P. (1982), 'European Economic Development: The Contribution of the Periphery', *Economic History Review*, 35:1, pp. 1–18.

Ocampo, J.A. (2004), 'Latin America's Growth and Equity Frustrations during Structural Reforms', *Journal of Economic Perspectives*, 18:2, pp. 67–88.

Olson, M. (1982), *The Rise and Decline of Nations*, Yale, Yale University Press.

Olson, M. (1993), 'Dictatorship, Democracy and Development', *American Political Science Review*, 87:3, pp. 567–76.

Olson, M (2000), *Power and Prosperity: Outgrowing Communist and Capitalist Dictatorships*, New York, Basic Books.

Ojo, O. and T. Oshikoya (1995), 'Determinants of Long-term Growth: Some African Results', *Journal of African Economies*, 4:2, pp. 163–91.

O'Rourke, K.H. and J.G. Williamson (1999), *The Heckscher-Ohlin Model between 1400 and 2000: When it Explained Factor Price Convergence, When it did not and why?*, National Bureau of Economic Research, Working Paper No. 7411, Cambridge.

Oshikoya, T.W. (1994), 'Macroeconomic Determinants of Domestic Private Investment in Africa: An Empirical Analysis', *Economic Development and Cultural Change*, 42 (4), pp. 573–96.

Oster, E. (2005), 'Hepatitis B and the Case of the Missing Women', mimeo, Harvard University, 12 March.

Oswald, A.J. (1997), 'Happiness and Economic Performance', *Economic Journal*, 107, pp. 1815–31.

Owens, T. and A. Wood (1997), 'Export Orientated Industrialisation through Primary Processing?', *World Development*, 25:9, pp. 1453–70.

Palma, G. (1978), 'Dependency: A Formal Theory of Underdevelopment or a Methodology for the Analysis of Concrete Situations of Underdevelopment', *World Development*, 6, pp. 881–924.

Park, C. and N. Cho (1995), 'Consequences of Son Preference in a Low-fertility Society: Imbalance of the Sex Ratio at Birth in Korea', *Population and Development Review*, 21:1, pp. 59–84.

Parthasarathi, P. (1998), 'Rethinking Wages and Competitiveness in the Eighteenth Century: Britain and South India', *Past and Present*, 158:1, pp. 79–109.

Pantibala, M. and B. Pedersen (2002), 'Role of transactional Corporations in the Revolution of a High-Tech Industry: The Case of India's Software Industry', *World Development*, 30:9, pp. 1561–77.

Patnaik, U. (2007), Neoliberalim and Rural Poverty in India', *Economic and Political Weekly*, 28 July pp. 3132–50.

Patnaik, U. (2010), 'A Critical Look at Some Propositions on Consumption and Poverty', *Economic and Political Weekly*, 6 February pp. 74–80.

Pebley, A. and A. Amin (1991), 'The Impact of a Public-health Intervention on Sex Differentials in Childhood Mortality in Rural Punjab, India', *Health Transition Review*, 1: 2, pp. 143–67.

Perkins, D.H., S. Radelet and D.L. Lindauer (2006), *Economics of Development*, Sixth Edition, London, W.W. Norton & Company.

Pollard, S. (1964), 'Fixed Capital in the Industrial Revolution in Britain', *The Journal of Economic History*, 24:3, pp. 299–314.

Pomeranz, K. (2000), *The Great Divergence: China, Europe and the Making of the Modern World Economy*, Princeton, Princeton University Press.

Popkin, B.M. (2003), 'The Nutrition Transition in the Developing World', *Development Policy Review*, 21:5–6, pp. 581–97.

Preston, S.H. (1975) reprinted in (2007), 'The changing relation between mortality and level of economic development', *International Journal of Epidemiology*, 36, pp. 484–90.

Pritchett, L. (1997), 'Divergence, Big Time', *Journal of Economic Perspectives*, 11:3, pp. 3–17.

Pritchett, L. (2000), 'Understanding Patterns of Economic Growth: Searching for Hills among Plateaus, Mountains, and Plains', *World Bank Economic Review*, 14:2, pp. 221–50.

Pritchett, L. (2001), 'Where has All the Education Gone?', *World Bank Economic Review*, 15:3, pp. 367–91.

Pritchett, L. and L.H. Summers (1996), 'Wealthier is Healthier', *Journal of Human Resources*, 31:4, pp. 841–68.

PROBE Team (1999), *Public Report on Basic Education in India*, New Delhi, Oxford University Press.

Przeworski, A., M.E. Alvarez, J.A. Cheibub and F. Limongi (2000), *Democracy and Development: Political Institutions and Well-Being in the World, 1950–1990*, Cambridge, Cambridge University Press.

Putnam, R. (1992), *Making Democracy Work: Civic Traditions in Modern Italy*, Princeton, Princeton University Press.

Qayyum, A., I. Khawaja and A. Hyder (2008), 'Growth Diagnostics in Pakistan', *PIDE Working Papers* No 47, Islamabad.

Qian, Y. (2003), 'How Reform Worked in China', in Rodrik, D. (ed.), *In Search of Prosperity: Analytic Narratives on Economic Growth*, Princeton, Princeton University Press.

Rahman, L. and Rao, V. (2004), 'The Determinants of Gender Equity in India: Examining Dyson and Moore's Thesis with New Data', *Population and Development Review*, 30:2, pp. 239–68.

Rajan, S., Sudha, S. and Mohanachandran, P. (2000), 'Fertility Decline and Worsening Gender Biasin India: Is Kerala no Longer an Exception?', *Development and Change*, 31: 1085–92.

Randolph, S.M. and W.F. Lott (1993), 'Can the Kuznets Effect Be Relied on to Induce Equalizing Growth?', *World Development*, 21:5, pp. 829–40.

Ranis, G., F. Stewart and A. Ramirez (2000), 'Economic Growth and Human Development', *World Development*, 28:2, pp. 197–219.

Rao, V. (1993) 'Dowry "Inflation" in Rural India: A Statistical Investigation', *Population Studies*, 47, pp. 283–93.

Ravallion, M. (1997), 'Good and Bad Growth: The Human Development Reports', *World Development*, 25:5, pp. 631–8.

Ravallion, M. and D. van de Walle (2006), 'Land Reallocation in an Agrarian Transition', *The Economic Journal*, 116:514, pp. 924–42.

Ravindran, T. (1995), 'Women's Health in a Rural Poor Population in Tamil Nadu', in Das Gupta, M., L. Chen and T. Krishnan (eds), *Women's Health in India: Risk and Vulnerability*, New Delhi, Open University Press.

Rebelo, S. (1991), 'Long-Run Policy Analysis and Long-Run Growth', *Journal of Political Economy*, 99:3, pp. 500–21.

Reinikka, R. and J. Svensson (2004), 'Local Capture: Evidence from a Central Government Transfer Program in Uganda', *Quarterly Journal of Economics*, 119:2, pp. 679–705.

Rhee, Y.W. (1990), 'The Catalyst Model of Development: Lessons from Bangladesh's Success with Garment Exports', *World Development*, 18:2, pp. 333–46.

Ringmar, E. (2006), 'Audience for a Giraffe: European Exceptionalism and the Quest for the Exotic', *Journal of World History*, 17:4, pp. 375–97.

Riskin, C. (1991), *China's Political Economy: The Quest for Development Since 1949*, Oxford, Oxford University Press.

Roberts, J.M. (1985), *The Triumph of the West: The Origin, Rise and Legacy of Western Civilisation*, London, Phoenix Press.

Robinson, J.A. (2009), 'Botswana as a Role Model for Country Success', *UNU–WIDER Research Paper* No 2009/40, Helsinki.

Rodney, W. (1972), *How Europe Underdeveloped Africa*, Washington, Howard University Press.

Rodrik, D. (1989), 'Credibility of Trade Reform – a Policy Maker's Guide', *World Economy*, 12:1, pp. 1–16.

Rodrik, D. (1990), 'How Should Structural Adjustment Programs be Designed?', *World Development*, 18:7, pp. 933–47.

Rodrik, D. (1997), 'Trade Strategy, Investment and Exports: Another Look at East Asia', *Pacific Economic Review*, 2:1, pp. 1–24.

Rodrik, D. (1998a), *Democracy and Economic Performance*, Conference prepared on democratisation and economic reform in South Africa, Cape Town, 16–19 Jan.

Rodrik, D. (1998b), *Democracies Pay Higher Wages*, Harvard University, mimeo.

Rodrik, D. (1999), 'Where Did All the Growth Go? External Shocks, Social Conflict, and Growth Collapses, *Journal of Economic Growth*, 4:4, pp. 385–412.

Rodrik, D. (2000), *Can Integration into the World Economy Substitute for a Development Strategy*, World Bank EBGDE European Conference, pp. 26–28 June.

Rodrik, D. (ed) (2003), *In Search of Prosperity: Analytic Narratives on Economic Growth*, Woodstock, Princeton University Press.

Rodrik, D. and A. Subramanian (2003), 'The Primacy of Institutions (and what this does and does not mean)', *Finance and Development*, June, pp. 31–4.

Rodrik, D., A. Subramanian and R. Trebbi (2002), 'Institutions Rule: The Primacy of Institutions over Geography and Integration in Economic Development', *Centre for International Development Working Paper* No.97, Harvard University.

Rodriquez, F. and D. Rodrik (2000), 'Trade Policy and Economic Growth: A Skeptic's Guide to Cross-National Evidence', *NBER Working Paper* No,7081, Cambridge.

Roll Back Malaria Partnership (2011), 'A Decade of Partnership and Results', *Progress and Impact Series*, Number 7, WHO, Geneva.

Romer, D. (1994), *Advanced Macroeconomics*, London, McGraw-Hill.

Rosenstein-Rodan, P. (1943), 'Problems of Industrialisation of Eastern and South-Eastern Europe', reprinted in A.N. Agarwala and S.P. Singh (eds) (1958), *The Economics of Underdevelopment*, Oxford, Oxford University Press.

Ross, M. (2001), 'Does Oil Hinder Democracy', *World Politics*, 53:3, pp. 297–322

Rostow, W.W. (1956), 'The Take-Off Into Self-Sustained Growth', *Economic Journal*, 66:261, pp. 25–48.

Rostow, W.W. (1960), *The Stages of Economic Growth: A Non-Communist Manifesto*, Cambridge, Cambridge University Press.

Rosenzweig, M. and Scultz, T. (1982), 'Market Opportunities, Genetic Endowments, and Intrafamily Resource Distribution: Child Survival in Rural India', *American Economic Review*, 72:4: pp. 803–15.

Rothermund, D. (1993), *An Economic History of India: From Pre-Colonial Times to 1991*, 2nd edn, London, Routledge.

Roy, T. (2002), 'Economic History and Modern India: Redefining the Link', *Journal of Economic Perspectives*, 16:3, pp. 109–30.

Rueschemeyer, D., E.H. Stephens and J.D.Stephens (1992), *Capitalist Development and Democracy*, Chicago, University of Chicago Press.

Sachs, J.D. (2005), *The End of Poverty: How We Can Make it Happen in Our Lifetime*, London, Penguin Books.

Sachs, J.D., J.W. McArthus, G. Schmidt-Traub, M. Kruk, C. Bahadur, M. Faye and G. McCord (2004), 'Ending Africa's Poverty Trap', *Brookings Papers on Economic Activity*, 1, pp. 117–240.

Sachs, J.D and A. Warner (1995), 'Economic Reform and the Process of Global Integration', *Brookings Papers on Economic Activity*, 1, pp. 1–95.

Saggi, K. (2002), 'Trade, Foreign Direct Investment, and International Technology Transfer: A Survey', *World Bank Research Observer*, 17:2, pp. 171–235.

Sahn, D.E. and D.C. Stifel (2003), 'Progress Towards the Millenium Development Goals in Africa', *World Development*, 31:1, pp. 23–50.

Sakthivel, S. (2005), 'Access to Essential Drugs and Medicines: Financing and Delivery of Health Care Services in India', National Commission on Macroeconomics and Health Background Papers, Ministry of Health and Family Welfare, New Delhi, Government of India.

Sambanis, N. (2003), 'Using Case Studies to Expand the Theory of Civil War', *CPR Working Paper* No. 5.

Sampat, P. (2008), 'Special Economic Zones in India', *Economic and Political Weekly*, 12 July, pp. 25–30.

Samuelson, P.A. and W.D.Nordhaus (1989), *Economics*, 13th edn, London, McGraw Hill.

Sapsford, D. and V.N. Balasubramanyam (1999), 'Trend and Volatility in the Net Barter Terms of Trade, 1900–92: New Results from the Application of a (Not So) New Method', *Journal of International Development*, 11:6, pp. 851–7.

Sarkar, A. (2007), 'Development and Displacement: Land Acquisition in West Bengal', *Economic and Political Weekly*, 21 April, pp. 1435–42.

Sastry, D.V.S., B. Singh, K. Bhattacharya and N.K. Unnikrishnan (2003), 'Sectoral Linkages and Growth Prospects: Reflections on the Indian Economy', *Economic and Political Weekly*, 14 June, pp. 2390–7.

Saxena, N.C. (2005), 'Updating Land Records: Is Computerisation Sufficient?', *Economic and Political Weekly*, 22 January, pp. 313–21.

Scitovsky, T. (1954), 'Two Concepts of External Economies', reprinted in Agarwala, A.N and S.P. Singh (eds) (1958), *The Economics of Underdevelopment*, Oxford, Oxford University Press.

Sen, A. (1982), 'How Is India Doing?', *New York Review of Books*, 29:20.

Sen, A. (1997), 'Editorial: Human Capital and Human Capability', *World Development*, 25:12, pp. 1959–61.

Sen, A. (1998), 'Mortality as an Indicator of Economic Success and Failure', *Economic Journal*, 108, pp. 1–25.

Sen, A. (1999), *Development as Freedom*, Oxford, Oxford University Press.

Sen, A. (2003), 'Human Capital and Human Capability', in S. Fukuda-Parr and A.K.S. Kumar (eds), *Readings in Human Development: Concepts, Measures and Policies for a Development Paradigm*, New Delhi, Oxford University Press.

Sen, A. and Sengupta, S. (1983), 'Malnutrition of Rural Children and the Sex Bias', *Economic and Political Weekly*, Annual Number, May: pp. 855–64.

Serven, L. (1997), 'Irreversibilty, Uncertainty and Private Investment: Analytical Issues and Some Lessons for Africa', *Journal of African Economies*, 6:3, pp. 229–68.

Sharma, U. (1994), 'Dowry in North India: Its Consequences for Women', in Uberoi, P. (ed.), *Family, Kinship and Marriage in India*, New Delhi, Oxford University Press.

Shergill, H.S. and G. Singh (1995), 'Poverty in Rural Punjab: Trend over Green Revolution Decades', *Economic and Political Weekly*, 24 June .

Sieff, D., L. Betzig, L. Cronk, A.G. Fix, M. Flinn, L. Sattenspiel, K. Gibson, A. Herring, N. Howell, S.R. Johansson, Z. Pavlik, J.W. Sheets, E.A. Smith, E. Voland and E. Siegelkow (1990), 'Explaining Biased Sex Ratios in Human Populations: A Critique of Recent Studies', *Current Anthropology*, 31:1, pp. 25–48.

Singh, N. (2006), *Services-Led Industrialisation in India: Assessment and Lessons*, Department of Economics, University of Santa Cruz.

Sivasubramonian, A. (2004), *The Sources of Economic Growth in India, 1950/51 to 1999/00*, New Delhi, Oxford University Press.

Skarstein, R. (2007), 'Free Trade: A Dead End for Underdeveloped Economies', *Review of Political Economy*, 19:3, pp. 347–67.

Smith, A. (1981), *An Inquiry into the Causes of the Wealth and Poverty of Nations*, Volume 1, Indianapolis, Liberty Press.

Smith, J.P. (1999), 'Healthy Bodies and Thick Wallets: The Dual Relation Between Health and Economic Status', *Journal of Economic Perspectives*, 13:2, pp. 145–66.

Snowdon, B. and H.R. Vane (2005), *Modern Macroeconomics: Its Origins, Development and Current State*, Cheltenham, Edward Elgar.

Sokoloff, K.L. and S.L. Engerman (2000), 'History Lessons: Institutions, Factor Endowments, and Paths of Development in the New World', *Journal of Economic Perspectives*, 14:3, pp. 217–32.

Sonderbom, M. and F. Teal (2000), 'Skills, Investment and Exports from Manufacturing Firms in Africa', *Journal of Development Studies*, 37:2, pp. 13–43.

Southgate, D. (2002), 'Forest Conservation and Development: The Role of Institutions', in J. Morriss (ed), *Sustainable Development: Promoting Progress or Perpetuating Poverty?*, London, Profile Books.

Srinivas, S. (2006), 'Industrial Development and Innovation: Some Lessons from Vaccine Procurement', *World Development*, 34:10, pp. 1742–64.

Srinivasan, T.N. (1994), 'Human Development: A New Paradigm or Reinvention of the Wheel', *American Economic Review*, 84:2, pp. 238–43.

Srinivasan, S. (2005), 'Daughters or Dowries? The Changing Nature of Dowry Practices in South India', *World Development*, 33:4, pp. 593–615.

Srinivasan, S. and A.S. Bedi (2007), 'Domestic Violence and Dowry: Evidence from a South Asian Village', *World Development*, 35:5, pp. 857–80.

Srinivasan, P. and G.R. Lee (2004), 'The Dowry System in Northern India: Women's Attitudes and Social Change', *Journal of Marriage and Family*, 66, pp. 1108–17.

Steckel, R.H. (1995), 'Stature and the Standard of Living', *Journal of Economic Literature*, 33:4, pp. 1903–40.

Strauss, J. and D. Thomas (1998), 'Health, Nutrition and Economic Development', *Journal of Economic Literature*, 36:2, pp. 766–817.

Streeten, P. (1984), 'Basic needs: Some unsettled questions', *World Development*, 12:9, pp. 973–8.

Streeten, P. (1994), 'Human Development: Means and Ends', *American Economic Review*, 84:2, pp. 232–7.

Stiglitz, J.E. (2007), *Making Globalisation Work*, London, Penguin.

Sudha, S. and Rajan, S. (1999) 'Female Demographic Disadvantage in India 1981–1991: Sex Selective Abortions and Female Infanticide', *Development and Change*, 30, pp. 585–618.

Tahir, R. (1995), 'Defence Spending and Economic Growth: Re-examining the Issue of Causality for Pakistan and India', *Pakistan Development Review*, 34:4, pp. 1109–17.

Tawney, R.H. (1926), *Religion and the Rise of Capitalism*, London, Pelican Books.

Taylor, K., A. Nguyen and J. Stephenne (2009), 'The Need for New Vaccines', *Vaccine*, 275, PG3–G8.

Teal, F. (1999), 'Why Can Mauritius Export Manufactures and Ghana Not?', *World Economy*, 22:7, pp. 981–3.

Temple, J. (1999), 'The New Growth Evidence', *Journal of Economic Literature*, 38, pp. 112–56.

Tendler, J. and S. Freedheim (1994), 'Trust in a Rent-Seeking World: Health and Government Transformed in Northeast Brazil', *World Development*, 22:12, pp. 1771–91.

Thirlwall, A.P. (2006), *Growth and Development: With Special Reference to Developing Economies*, 8th edn, Basingstoke, Palgrave Macmillan.

Thirlwall, A.P. and J. Bergevin (1985), 'Trends, Cycles and Asymmetries in the Terms of Trade of Primary Commodities from Developed and Less Developed Countries', *World Development*, 13:7, pp. 805–17.

Tisdell, C., K. Roy and A. Ghose (2001), 'A Critical Note on UNDP's Gender Inequality Indices', *Journal of Contemporary Asia*, 31:3, pp. 385–99.

Todaro, M.P. and S.C. Smith (2011), *Economic Development*, 11th edn, London, Addison-Wesley.

Tripathi, D. and J. Jumani (2007), *The Concise Oxford History of Indian Business*, New Delhi, Oxford University Press.

Tsui, A.O. (2001), 'Population Policies, Family Planning Programmes, and Fertility: The Record', *Population and Development Review*, 27 (Supplement), pp. 184–204.

Ul Haq, M. (2003), 'The Human Development Paradigm', in S.Fukuda-Parr and A.K.S. Kumar (eds), *Readings in Human Development: Concepts, Measures and Policies for a Development Paradigm*, New Delhi, Oxford University Press.

Ulrich, Y. (1989), 'Cross-cultural Perspective on Violence against Women', *Response Nursing Network on Violence against Women*, 12, pp. 21–3.

Unisa, S., S. Pujari and R. Usha (2007), 'Sex Selective Abortion in Haryana: Evidence from Pregnancy and Antenatal Care', *Economic and Political Weekly*, 6 January pp. 60–6.

Unni, J. (1998), 'Gender Differentials in Schooling in Gender, Population and Development', in Krishnaraj, M., R. Subarshan and A. Shariff (eds), *Gender, Population and Development*, New Delhi, Oxford University Press.

Unni, J. (2007), 'Earnings and Education among Social Groups', in A. Shariff (ed.), *State, Markets and Inequalities: Human Development in Rural India*, New Delhi, Orient Longman.

Varma, P.V. (1998), *The Great Indian Middle Class*, New Delhi, Viking.

Vaz, L. and S. Kanekar (1990), 'Predicted and Recommended Behaviour of a Woman as a Function of her Inferred Helplessness in the Dowry and Wife-beating Predicaments', *Journal of Applied Social Psychology*, 20, pp. 751–70.

Vernengo, M. (2006), 'Technology, Finance, and Dependency: Latin American Radical Political Economy in Retrospect', *Review of Radical Political Economics*, 38:4, pp. 551–68.

Vindhya, U. (2000), '"Dowry Deaths" in Andhra Pradesh, India: Response of the criminal justice system', *Violence against Women*, 6, pp. 1085–108.

Visaria, L. (2005), 'Mortality Trends and the Health Transition', in Dyson, T., R.Cassen and L.Visaria (eds), *Twenty-First Century India: Population, Economy, Human Development, and the Environment*, Oxford, Oxford University Press.

Vision 2020, *Malaysia: The Way Forward*, Government of Malaysia, Kuala Lumpur.

Vlassoff, C. (1991) 'Progress and Stagnation: Changes in Fertility and Women's Position in an Indian Village', *Population Studies*, 46, pp. 195–212.

Wacziarg, R. and K.H. Welch (2008), 'Trade Liberalization and Growth: New Evidence', *World Bank Economic Review*, 22:2, pp. 187–231.

Wade, R. (1990), *Governing the Market: Economic Theory and the Role of Government in East Asian Industrialisation*, Princeton, Princeton University Press.

Wade, R. (2001), 'Is Globalisation Making World Income Distribution More Equal?', *DESTIN Working Paper* No 01, LSE, London.

Wade, R. (2002), 'Globalization, Poverty and Income Distribution: Does the Liberal Argument Hold?', *DESTIN Working Paper* No. 02–33, LSE, London.

Wallerstein, I. (1974), *Capitalist Agriculture and the Origins of the European World-Economy in the Sixteenth Century*, London, University of California Press.

Wallerstein, I. (1980), *Mercantilism and the Consolidation of the European World-Economy, 1600–1750*, London, University of California Press.

Wallerstein, I. (2011), *Centrist Liberalism Triumphant, 1789–1914*, London, University of California Press.

Warner, A. (2002), 'Institutions, Geography, Regions, Countries and the Mobility Bias', *CID Working Paper* No.91, Harvard University.

Warren, B. (1973), 'Imperialism and Capitalist Industrializaton', *New Left Review*, 81, pp. 3–46.

Warren, B. (1980), *Imperialism: Pioneer of Capitalism*, London, Verso.

Weber, M. (1992), *The Protestant Ethic and the Spirit of Capitalism*, Routledge, London.

Wechsler, J. (2010), 'Manufacturers Look to Vaccines for Growth and Innovation', *Pharmaceutical Technology,* 34: 2, pp. 30–7

Wedgwood, R. (2007), 'Education and poverty reduction in Tanzania', *International Journal of Educational Development*, 27, pp. 383–96.

Weil, D.N. (2005), *Economic Growth*, London, Addison-Wesley.

Weyland, K. (1998), 'From Leviathan to Gulliver? The Decline of the Developmental State in Brazil', *Governance*, 11:1, pp. 51–75.

Whittington, D., D. Sur, J. Cook, S. Chatterjee, B. Maskery, M. Lahiri, C. Poulos, S. Boral, A. Nyamete, J. Deen, L. Ochiai and S.K. Bhattacharya (2009), 'Rethinking Cholera and Typhoid Vaccination Policies for the Poor: Private Demand in Kolkata, India', *World Development*, 37:2, pp. 399–409.

Wilkinson, R. and K. Pickett (2010), *The Spirit Level: Why Equality is Better for Everyone*, London, Penguin.

Wisniewski, S.L.W. (2010), 'Child Nutrition, Health Problems and School Achievement in Sri Lanka', *World Development*, 38:3, pp. 315–32.

Wolcott, S. and G. Clark (1999), 'Why Nations Fail: Managerial Decisions and Performance in Indian Cotton Textiles, 1890–1938', *Journal of Economic History*, 59:2, pp. 397–423.

Wolf, M. (2004), *Why Globalisation Works: The Case for the Global Market Economy*, London, Yale University Press.

Wolmar, C. (2009), *Blood, Iron and Gold: How Railways Transformed the World*, London, Atlantic Books.

Wood, A. and K. Bege (1997), 'Exporting Manufactures: Human Resources, Natural Resources and Trade Policy', *Journal of Development Studies*, 34:1, pp. 35–59.

Wood, A. and M. Calandrino (2000), 'When the Other Giant Awakes: Trade and Human Resources in India', *Economic and Political Weekly*, 30 December, pp. 4677–94.

Wood, A. and K. Jordan (2000), 'Why Does Zimbabwe Export Manufactures and Uganda Not? Econometrics Meets History', *Journal of Development Studies*, 37:2, pp. 91–116.

Wood, A. and J. Meyer (2001), 'Africa's Export Structure in a Comparative Perspective', *Cambridge Journal of Economics*, 25:3, pp. 369–94.

Woods, D. (2004), 'Latitude or Rectitude: geographical or institutional determinants of development', *Third World Quarterly*, 25:8, pp. 1401–14.

World Bank (2007), *India: Land Policies for Growth and Poverty Reduction*, Washington.

World Development Indicators (2013), World Bank, Washington.

World Development Indicators (2014), World Bank, Washington.

Wrigley, E.A. and R. Schofield (1981), *The Population History of England, 1541–1871*, London, Arnold.

Wu, X. (2000), 'Foreign Direct Investment, Intellectual Property Rights, and Wage Inequality in China', *China Economic Review*, 11, pp. 361–84.

Yin, R.K. (2003), *Case Study Research: Design and Methods*, London, Sage.

Yasuba, Y. (1986), 'Standard of Living in Japan Before Industrialisation: From what Level did Japan Begin?: A Comment', *Journal of Economic History*, 46:1, pp. 217–24.

Yong, T.T. (2005), *The Garrison State: The Military, Government and Society in Colonial Punjab*, Lahore, Vanguard Books.

Young, A. (1995), 'The Tyranny of Numbers: Confronting the Statistical Realities of the East Asian Growth Experience', *Quarterly Journal of Economics*, 114, pp. 641–80.

Zeufack, A. (2001), 'Export Performance in Africa and Asia's Manufacturing: Evidence from Firm-level Data', *Journal of African Economies*, 10:3, pp. 258–81.

Index

14933455R00204

Printed in Germany
by Amazon Distribution
GmbH, Leipzig